# Powers of Congress

## SECOND EDITION

# Congressional Quarterly Inc.

Congressional Quarterly Inc., an editorial research service and publishing company, serves clients in the fields of news, education, business and government. It combines specific coverage of Congress, government and politics by Congressional Quarterly, founded in 1946, with the more general subject range of an affiliated service, Editorial Research Reports, founded in 1923 and merged with Congressional Quarterly in 1956.

Congressional Quarterly publishes the CQ *Weekly Report* and a variety of books, including college political science textbooks under the CQ Press imprint. CQ also publishes information directories and reference books on the federal government and elections, including *The Guide to Congress* from which *Powers of Congress* is taken. In addition, CQ publishes paperback books that are designed as timely reports to keep journalists, scholars and the public abreast of developing issues, events and trends.

CQ publishes *The Congressional Monitor,* a daily report on present and future activities of congressional committees. CQ Direct Research is a consulting service that performs contract research and maintains a reference library and query desk for clients.

*Editor:* Nancy Lammers

*Contributors:* Prentice Bowsher, Mary Cohn, Barbara R. de Boinville, Martha V. Gottron, Patricia Ann O'Connor, Park Teter, Margaret C. Thompson, Elder Witt, Michael D. Wormser, Esther D. Wyss

*Designer:* Mary McNeil

*Indexer:* Janet Hoffman

*Cover:* Richard A. Pottern

*Photo Credits:* Library of Congress, pp. 70, 126, 154, 228, 276, 296.



Printed in the United States of America

**Library of Congress Cataloging in Publication Data**

Main entry under title:

Powers of Congress.

Bibliography p.
Includes index.
1. United States. Congress — Powers and duties. I. Congressional Quarterly, inc.
JK1061.P68 1982 328.73'074 82-14331
ISBN 0-87187-242-0

# Table of Contents

# PREFACE

The authors of the U. S. Constitution recognized that the new government needed an executive to carry out the laws and a judiciary to resolve disputes arising from them. But the Founding Fathers intended for Congress to be the heart of the new Republic. The House of Representatives was the only part of the federal government originally elected by the people; consequently, Congress was the branch of government expected to respond directly to their needs.

It was thus to the national legislature that the framers entrusted most of the power necessary to govern the new nation. The Constitution enumerates the powers given to Congress. Yet, while presidential power has been enhanced by precedent and by law since 1789, Congress has not always chosen to exercise the powers it originally was given. The result has been that congressional strength, particularly in the area of foreign policy, has been less than the drafters of the Constitution envisioned.

Long considered the comparatively passive branch of government, Congress in the last two decades has taken significant actions to challenge presidential and executive branch supremacy. The first edition of the *Powers of Congress*, published in 1976, outlined modifications in the relationship between the presidency and the Congress that had developed up to that point. Watergate and the Vietnam War complicated what already was an inherently uneasy relationship. The 1973 War Powers Act, enacted over President Richard Nixon's veto, set limits on the authority of the chief executive to commit American forces to combat abroad without congressional approval. And in an effort to enhance its power of the purse, Congress in 1974 devised a new method of dealing with the federal budget. The 1973 Watergate investigation and the 1974 impeachment proceedings proved to be successful challenges to an abuse of presidential power. During this period the presidency was weakened and the balance of power tipped toward Congress.

This 1982 edition of the *Powers of Congress* looks at the long-lasting effects of that traumatic era. In the years following the Johnson and Nixon administrations, Congress further gnawed away at executive authority by injecting itself into areas that formerly were the exclusive preserves of the president, such as the everyday administration of the executive branch, the issuance of federal rules and regulations and the conduct of foreign policy. The debates on the Panama Canal and SALT II treaties during the Carter administration and the controversy over the proposed sale of Airborne Warning and Control System (AWACS) surveillance planes to Saudi Arabia during the Reagan administration provide examples of moves by the Senate to expand its power in the foreign policy field. Yet in an ironic twist the reconciliation procedures of the 1974 budget act, designed to force committees to comply with congressionally approved spending ceilings, were used by President Ronald Reagan to impose his economic policies upon the country.

The developments of the past few years make it appropriate to take a fresh look at congressional power. Included in this second edition are detailed examinations of the constitutional origins, the evolution and current status of major powers of Congress. The pace of congressional change — institutional, procedural and attitudinal — and the enduring qualities of the Constitution's basic provisions are the first observations one is likely to make about Congress in comparing this edition of the *Powers of Congress* with the first.

The introduction presents an overall survey. Parts I through VIII examine Congress' powers to declare war and approve treaties, confirm nominations of public officials, investigate issues concerning Congress, seat and discipline its own members, impeach federal officers, regulate foreign and interstate commerce, amend the Constitution, and elect the president in the case of an electoral college deadlock. The complete text of the Constitution is included after the last chapter, for easy reference to its many citations in the book. The footnotes have been moved from the back of the book to the end of each chapter, and the bibliography and index have been expanded and updated. The improvements in the second edition — the new design and revised content — make it a more comprehensive and readable survey of the powers of Congress.

Nancy Lammers
August 1982

# INTRODUCTION

The delegates to the Constitutional Convention in 1787 gave their broadest grant of authority to Congress. Article I, Section 1, of the U. S. Constitution gives to Congress "all legislative Powers." Set forth in detail in the remaining nine sections of Article I, these included the powers to tax, regulate commerce, declare war, consent to ratification of treaties, and raise and maintain armies.

The framers also granted Congress certain authority over the other two branches of government. It has the power to confirm nominations of public officials and to investigate, impeach and convict the president, federal judges and other federal officers for treason, bribery or other high crimes and misdemeanors. Congress also has two responsibilities relating to the election of the president and vice president. First, it is directed to receive and in joint session count the electoral votes certified by the states. Second, if no candidate has a majority of the electoral vote, the House must elect the president and the Senate, the vice president.

## Fiscal Powers

Perhaps the most important of Congress' constitutional prerogatives are its powers to tax, to spend and — since the 1930s when Congress no longer seriously attempted to balance receipts and outlays — to borrow. The congressional "power of the purse" includes raising revenues, through taxes or borrowing, and directing the spending of those revenues, through the appropriations process. Congress may use its power to tax both to raise revenue to run the country and as a regulatory device. The power to spend allows Congress to determine policy on almost every matter that affects daily life in the United States.

Taxes on the income and profits of individuals and corporations have become the federal government's basic sources of revenue since the Sixteenth Amendment (income tax) was ratified in 1913. In addition, Congress has imposed an excess profits tax on corporations during wartime, has levied a variety of excise, estate and gift taxes and has imposed payroll taxes to underpin the old-age insurance and unemployment compensation systems.

Under Article I, Section 7, of the Constitution, tax legislation must originate in the House of Representatives. Tax bills are handled there by the Ways and Means Committee. After the House acts, tax bills go to the Senate Finance Committee where further amendments may be proposed. Amendments adopted by the Senate may be far-reaching. Thus the Senate also can exercise important control over tax legislation.

Generally, the initiative on raising, lowering or enacting new taxes in the post-war period has been taken by the executive branch, which has prepared the basic proposals on which Congress has acted. A major part of President Ronald Reagan's economic recovery program was his tax bill, which Congress passed in August 1981. Yet there is no requirement that the White House take the lead in tax matters. Indeed, in 1969 Congress itself initiated a major tax reform bill.

Revenue raised through taxation cannot be spent by the executive branch simply as agency officials deem proper. The Constitution gives to Congress the basic authority to determine how monies collected shall be expended and requires a regular statement of expenditures.

The appropriations procedure works in two steps after the president presents his annual budget requests to Congress. First, the various congressional committees consider the parts of the request that fall under their jurisdictions and report out bills authorizing programs and setting a ceiling on the amount of funds that can be spent for them. Second, in separate legislation after the authorization is law, Congress actually provides (appropriates) the money. The amount of money appropriated often is less than the maximum amount specified in the authorization for the program.

Appropriation of the money is considered initially by the relevant subcommittee of the House Appropriations Committee. The Subcommittee on Defense, for example, considers Defense Department appropriations; the Subcommittee on Energy and Water Development considers appropriations under its jurisdiction. Then a bill is sent to the House floor by the full committee. The general structure of any appropriations bill is derived from House consideration of the measure. What the Senate does, in effect, is to review the House action and hear appeals from agencies seeking changes in the allotments accorded them by the House.

The powers to tax and spend were exercised separately until 1974, when the Congressional Budget and Impoundment Control Act established a mechanism to help Congress coordinate all federal spending and taxing. The law, fully implemented for the first time in 1976, set up House and Senate Budget Committees to formulate overall spending and tax goals and a Congressional Budget Office to provide Congress with technical information about the economy and the budget.

The law also created a complicated series of deadlines for congressional action on the budget. The key dates each year are May 15, when Congress is supposed to have completed action on a resolution setting targets for spending and revenues to guide committees as they process fiscal legislation during the summer months, and Sept. 15, when Congress is to replace the targets with a ceiling on spending and a floor on revenues for the fiscal year beginning Oct. 1.

If the amounts adopted in the fall differ from those adopted during the summer in actual spending and tax bills, Congress must reconcile the differences. Once this reconciliation process is completed, the limits become binding unless Congress itself revises them. In 1981, President Ronald Reagan skillfully used reconciliation as a budget-cutting tool. The final reconciliation measure passed by Congress slashed nearly $35.2 billion from a projected fiscal 1982 spending level of approximately $740 billion.

In addition to forcing Congress to compare total spending with total receipts, the 1974 budget act required members for the first time to vote on a budget deficit. The act also curtailed the president's power to refuse to spend appropriated funds, a traditional practice that grew into a heated dispute when President Richard Nixon impounded billions of dollars Congress had appropriated for programs that the executive branch wanted to curb. *(Powers of the Purse, Part I, pp. 11-69)*

## Foreign Affairs

While initiative in foreign relations generally is taken by the president, Congress has several constitutionally granted powers that are indispensable to the success of those initiatives. These include the powers to raise taxes (to finance wars), create and maintain an armed force, regulate foreign commerce and consent to the ratification of treaties. With the exception of a few votes during the Vietnam War in the early 1970s, Congress in the 20th century has chosen to use its powers to support the president in his conduct of war rather than to challenge him.

And so, while the Constitution gives Congress the power to declare war and "provide for the common Defence," both the initiation and conduct of war have come to be directed almost entirely by the president.

In November 1973 Congress sought to restore some of its control over war efforts when it enacted, over President Nixon's veto, a war powers resolution. That measure restricted the president's authority to commit U.S. troops in the case of an "attack upon the United States, its territories or possessions or its armed forces," and limited his power to wage undeclared war.

Legislative authority over other aspects of foreign policy has increased greatly in recent years. The massive, post-World War II foreign aid and military assistance programs provide a case in point. The programs have required specific congressional authorizations and repeated congressional appropriations. Frequently, especially since the Vietnam War, Congress has disagreed with the president over the amounts and allocations for these programs. Included in the 1976 foreign military aid bill was language giving Congress authority to review commercial sales above $7 million for major military equipment and $25 million for other military items. But sentiment began to shift by the end of the 1970s. In response to both the Carter and Reagan administrations' requests for greater flexibility in administering the military aid program, a more conservative Congress relaxed some of the Vietnam-era aid restrictions and prohibitions.

The Constitution gives the president the power to make treaties if two-thirds of the Senate concurs and for years this clause served as a cornerstone of American foreign policy. Treaties forged peace agreements with other nations, supported American territorial expansion, established national boundaries, protected U.S. commerce and regulated government affairs with Indian tribes. Membership in the United Nations was accomplished by Senate consent to ratification of the U.N. Charter.

In recent years treaties have been replaced, in part, by executive agreements with foreign countries; such agreements do not require Senate approval. Except for rejection of the Versailles Treaty, Senate action on treaties has not been a major factor in foreign policy; only 19 treaties have been rejected since 1789. However, the heated debates on the Panama Canal and SALT II treaties were seen as moves by the Senate to expand its power in the foreign policy field. *(Foreign Affairs, Part II, pp. 71-125)*

## Commerce Power

Congress' power to regulate interstate and foreign commerce has become nearly as important as its fiscal powers. The virtually exclusive authority of Congress in these areas has produced extensive government regulation not only of the actual transport of goods but also of their manufacture, sale and, in many cases, their purity and safety.

The Constitution gave Congress a broad and positive grant of power to regulate interstate and foreign commerce but left interpretation of the extent of the power to precedent and judicial determination. Although the Supreme Court initially gave Congress almost complete control over interstate commerce, the legislative branch seldom exercised its power. But with the passage of the Interstate Commerce Act of 1887, Congress moved decisively into the area of domestic regulation. The act, prompted by the individual states' inability to curb increasing abuses by railroads, ultimately was broadened to include regulation of trucking companies, bus lines, freight forwarders, water carriers, oil pipelines, transportation brokers and express agencies. The act, which established the Interstate Commerce Commission as the first regulatory agency, also led to creation of several other agencies that regulate various aspects of commercial transactions in the United States, as well as entire industries, such as communications.

In 1890 Congress moved into federal regulation of commercial enterprise with enactment of the Sherman Antitrust Act "to protect commerce against unlawful restraints and monopolies." With the turn of the century, Congress began to exercise its power to regulate interstate commerce as a tool to protect the health and morals of the general populace. To this end, it banned the interstate shipment of lottery tickets, impure food and drugs and prostitutes.

Although the Supreme Court sanctioned most of these new uses of the Congress' commerce power, it balked at Congress' attempt in 1916 to outlaw child labor by barring the shipment of goods made by children. It was this narrower view of the commerce power that prevailed when the Supreme Court reviewed and declared unconstitutional many of the early New Deal economic recovery programs that were based on the commerce power. The court's actions precipitated a confrontation among the president, Congress and the court, which resulted in the court's recognition of Congress' authority to regulate virtually all aspects of business and manufacture that affected interstate commerce.

Since 1937 Congress has sanctioned broadened uses of the commerce power. In the 1960s the scope of this authority was expanded to include civil rights. In the Civil Rights Act of 1964, Congress found justification in the commerce clause and the "equal protection" clause of the 14th Amendment for a ban on racial discrimination in most public accommodations.

Congressional power to regulate foreign commerce is tied to its powers over foreign relations and fiscal affairs. The earliest actions in this field were efforts to replace markets lost when the nation won its independence from England. Modern laws have ranged from antitrust exemptions for exporters, to use of tariff reductions to stimulate trade. While the Constitution gives Congress the power to set all tariffs, since 1934 general tariff agreements have been negotiated with foreign countries by the executive. *(Commerce Power, Part III, pp. 127-153)*

## Impeachment

Impeachment is perhaps the most awesome, although the least used, power of Congress. It is specifically granted by the Constitution, which provides that the House should consider an impeachment resolution (usually reported by the House Judiciary Committee). If the resolution is adopted by the House, a trial is held by the Senate with the House acting as prosecutor. Conviction requires approval of two-thirds of the senators present. The Constitution provides for removal from office and possible disqualification from further federal office. There is no appeal.

The two most famous impeachment cases ended in acquittal after sensational Senate trials. They involved President Andrew Johnson — accused of violating the Tenure of Office Act — and Supreme Court Justice Samuel Chase — accused of partisan conduct on the bench. Prior to 1982, 13 officers had been impeached by the House. Of the 12 cases that reached the Senate, two were dismissed, six resulted in acquittal and four ended in conviction. President Nixon's resignation in 1974 terminated House action on three articles of impeachment approved by the Judiciary Committee. *(Impeachment, Part IV, pp. 155-179)*

## Investigations

The much publicized power of Congress to mount investigations is not specified in the Constitution. The first congressional investigation, justified by the tradition of investigative actions in the House of

Commons, was held in 1792. One-hundred and thirty-five years later, in 1927, a landmark Supreme Court decision upheld the constitutionality of investigations, contending that they often were indispensable to the effective exercise of "all legislative powers" granted to Congress by Article I, Section 1, of the Constitution.

No period of American history has been without congressional investigations. They have gathered information on the need for possible future legislation, tested the effectiveness of past legislative action, questioned executive branch proceedings and laid the groundwork for impeachment proceedings. Investigations have elevated comparatively minor political figures to national fame, broken the careers of important public men and captured the attention of millions of newspaper readers and television viewers.

The congressional investigative power has been given wide berth by the judiciary. In May 1975 the Supreme Court barred lower courts from interfering with a subpoena that is issued within the "sphere of legislative activity" of a congressional committee or member. Furthermore, the court said, courts may not question the motives behind a congressional subpoena.

Congress' investigative power goes hand in hand with its power to punish for contempt. Such power also is not specifically granted by the Constitution, but an 1821 Supreme Court decision confirmed Congress' power to punish a person for contempt of its authority. Congress since then has voted contempt citations in cases where a witness refused to appear before a committee, refused to answer questions before a committee or refused to produce documents for a committee. *(Investigations, Part V, pp. 181-227)*

## Confirmations

The Constitution provides for Senate approval of presidential nominations of federal officers. Most nominations involve promotions of military officers in various specialized services, and Senate action is only a formality. But each year the Senate scrutinizes several hundred nominations to major federal posts. These include nominations to Cabinet and sub-Cabinet positions, independent boards and agencies, major diplomatic and military posts and the federal judiciary.

The Senate role in Supreme Court appointments is particularly important. The Senate may not be able to dictate Supreme Court appointments, but historically it has not been afraid to reject them.

Roughly one in five nominations to the Supreme Court is rejected by the Senate.

Appointments to lower federal courts are another matter. Historically, the president has used these judgeships, especially for the district courts, to please members of Congress. In general, a district court judge is nominated by the president at the request of a member of Congress from that district. Thus lower court appointments provide presidential patronage — an opportunity for the president to win a members' goodwill — and sometimes a crucial vote.

Nominations of Cabinet officers are considered carefully by the Senate, but such officers usually are confirmed with little difficulty, on the theory that the president should have great leeway in selecting the members of his official "family." Since 1789, the Senate has rejected only eight Cabinet nominations. For many of the same reasons, major diplomatic nominations normally encounter little difficulty.

Most independent boards and commissions are viewed as an arm of Congress rather than of the executive because they are usually created by an act of Congress and are not subordinate to any executive department. Therefore, members of Congress expect to play a large role in the selection process. Contests over these nominations have been frequent, although few nominees actually have been rejected. *(Confirmations, Part VI, pp. 229-275)*

## Amending Power

Congress shares with the state legislatures the power of proposing amendments to the Constitution. The Constitution provides that amendments may be proposed either by two-thirds vote of both houses of Congress or by a convention called by the legislatures of two-thirds of the states. Amendments must be ratified by the legislatures or conventions of three-fourths of the states as directed by Congress.

Although the constitution's authors envisioned a substantial role for the states in the amendment process, Congress has dominated the rewriting of the Constitution. Not once have the states been successful in calling for a convention to propose an amendment to the Constitution. The states have approved 26 of the amendments proposed by Congress, failing to ratify only six. The Equal Rights Amendment was turned down in 1982, failing by three states to win ratification.

Restrained use of the constitutional amendment procedure has enabled the Constitution to remain the fundamental law of the land even though the United States has been transformed beyond recognition since it was drafted in 1787. Major amendments include: Extending the vote to blacks (Fifteenth) and women (Nineteenth) and levying the income tax (Sixteenth). The Fourteenth Amendment, which became the most fundamental formal revision of the Constitution, altered the relationship between national and state governments. Its consequences still are unfolding in Supreme Court decisions. *(Amending Power, Part VII, pp. 277-295)*

## Electing the President

Congress under the Constitution has two key responsibilities relating to the election of the president and vice president. First, it is directed to receive and in joint session count the electoral votes certified by the states. Second, if no candidate has a majority of the electoral vote, the House must elect the president and the Senate the vice president.

In modern times the formal counting of electoral votes has been largely a ceremonial function. The House actually has chosen a president only twice, in 1801 and 1825. However, in the course of the nation's history a number of campaigns have been deliberately designed to throw elections into the House. Apprehension over this has nurtured many electoral reform efforts. The most recent attempt occurred in 1977 when President Jimmy Carter recommended the adoption of a constitutional amendment abolishing the electoral college and replacing it with direct, popular election of the president. However, the Senate in 1979 refused to approve Carter's proposed constitutional amendment.

In addition to its role in electing the president, Congress, under the Twentieth and Twenty-fifth Amendments, has authority to settle problems arising from the death of the president-elect and disputes over presidential disability. The Twenty-fifth Amendment, ratified in 1967 to cover what its authors considered would be rare contingencies, was applied twice in 12 months and gave rise to executive branch leadership unique in the nation's history. The amendment provides that whenever the office of vice president becomes vacant, the president shall appoint a replacement, subject to confirmation by both houses. *(Electing the President, Part VIII, pp. 297-321)*

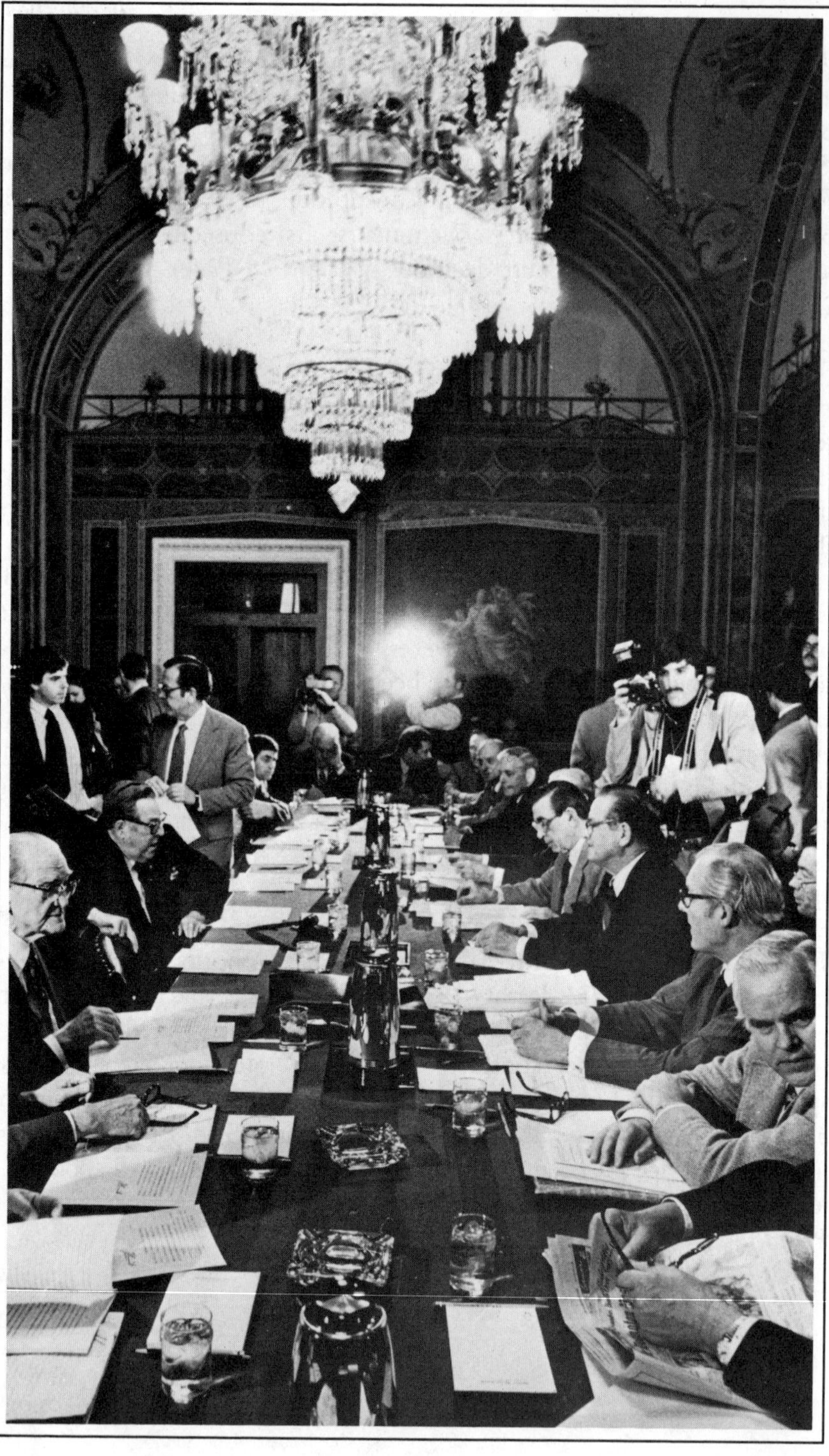

*Part I*

# Powers of the Purse

A House-Senate conference committee discusses a 1980 appropriations bill.

*Chapter 1*

# THE POWER TO TAX, SPEND AND BORROW

Of the numerous powers of Congress, the "power of the purse" is perhaps the most important. For nearly 200 years, the constitutional grant of the powers to tax, spend and borrow has given the legislative branch paramount authority to command national resources and direct them to federal purposes. No other congressional prerogative confers so much control over the policies and goals of government or has such an impact on the nation's well-being.

Since the 1930s Congress has made especially broad use of its taxing, spending and borrowing powers to vastly enlarge the government and expand its influence over the U.S. economy. Federal spending mounted to $657.2 billion in fiscal 1981, accounting for more than one-fifth of the gross national product. And the way the government spends its money — and raises it through taxes or borrowing — carries enormous consequences for the nation's economic performance and its political and social balance.

Through the years the House and Senate have jealously guarded their congressional powers to finance the machinery of government. But Congress has had trouble using its tax and spending powers to shape a coherent federal budget policy. The result has been runaway budget deficits, expected to exceed $100 billion in fiscal 1982, as well as constant battling between Congress and successive presidents for final authority to set federal fiscal policy. Except for the Vietnam War and the Watergate scandal, no other issue since World War II has so divided Congress and at times paralyzed government decision-making. *(Details on the growth of the federal debt, pp. 30-31)*

Congressional historian George B. Galloway noted in a 1955 book that directly or indirectly "perhaps nine-tenths of the work of Congress is concerned ... with the spending of public money." [1] The preoccupation with budget decisions was compounded during the following years as federal deficits mounted, inflation ran rampant and Congress and presidents fought for control of government outlays.

Much as it wanted to control the purse strings, Congress rarely bothered until the mid-1970s to tie its separate funding bills to an overall budget plan encompassing all tax and spending decisions. Since 1921 it had left to the executive branch the task of drawing up a yearly federal budget proposing fiscal policy and setting forth revenue, outlay and deficit or surplus targets. But in the early 1970s a heavily Democratic Congress fiercely resisted when Republican President Richard Nixon refused to spend billions of dollars already appropriated to federal agencies.

Congress responded in 1974 by limiting the president's power to impound funds and setting up its own elaborate budget-making procedures. That process compels Congress to set overall revenue and spending targets before considering individual tax and appropriations measures. That in turn forces the House and Senate to make budget choices and go on record with regard to its decisions on taxes, spending and deficits. But it also allows Congress to choose between sticking to those overall budget targets or bending them to encompass other objectives.

Between 1975, when Congress first tried its new budget-making procedures, and 1980 the House and Senate backed away from politically tough decisions to bring the budget closer to balance by cutting spending or raising taxes. It took a determined Republican President Ronald Reagan — and a conservative swing in the 1980 elections that gave Republicans control of the Senate — to ram large cutbacks through Congress using shortcut procedures that bypassed the normal spending process. The precedent dismayed some legislators, who feared that Congress was once again abdicating its constitutional powers over fiscal matters. And it raised new — and unanswered — questions about the viability of the fledgling budget process and its effect on the traditional exercise of Congress' taxing, spending and borrowing powers.

## Constitutional Roots

The congressional power of the purse is firmly rooted in the U.S. Constitution. That document's first article granted Congress authority to raise revenues through taxes, tariffs and other levies; to direct the spending of the funds raised; and to borrow money on the nation's credit. Those powers are spelled out in three clauses:

— **Article I, Section 8, Clause 1,** gives Congress the power "to lay and collect taxes, duties, imposts and excises, to pay the debts and provide for the common defense and general welfare of the United States. . . ."

— **Article I, Section 8, Clause 2,** gives Congress the power "to borrow money on the credit of the United States."

— **Article I, Section 9, Clause 7,** declares that "no money shall be drawn from the Treasury, but in consequence of appropriations made by law. . . ."

The taxing power is specific, and it was vastly enlarged in 1913 by the 16th Amendment authorizing a federal tax on incomes. Over the years, Congress has devised a tax system that was expected to raise more than $625 billion in fiscal 1982, mostly from individual income taxes.[2]

The spending power, which Galloway described as "the constitutional birthright of Congress," is more vague.[3] But it has been enlarged by expansive interpretation of the other authorities that the Constitution grants to Congress. Outlays in fiscal 1982 were expected to reach or exceed $725 billion.

The borrowing power carries no constitutional restrictions at all, allowing Congress to borrow funds in any amounts for any purposes. With the budget in deficit for 43 out of the 50 fiscal years from 1931 through 1981, the national debt topped $1 trillion in late 1981.

Those enormous sums may be beyond the comprehension of most Americans, including members of Congress. But they suggest the power that the congressional tax, spending and borrowing authorities provide — and indicate the economic and social stakes involved in federal budget battles.

## The Power to Tax

Without sufficient revenues, no government could function effectively. The Constitution, along with the 16th Amendment, therefore granted Congress the right to enact virtually any taxes, except for duties on exports. In Article I, Section 8, the framers of the Constitution granted authority broad enough to encompass nearly all known forms of taxation, including tariffs on imported goods and excise taxes on the manufacture, sale, use or transfer of property within the United States. And, in general, both Congress and the courts have construed the taxing power liberally to generate additional sources of revenue for the federal government.

The constitutional historian C. H. Pritchett, in his book *The American Constitution*, noted that adequate sources of funds and broad authority to use them are "essential conditions for carrying on an effective government." As a result, he observed,

> the first rule for judicial review of tax statutes is that a heavy burden of proof lies on anyone who would challenge any congressional exercise of fiscal power. In almost every decision touching the constitutionality of federal taxation, the Supreme Court has stressed the breadth of congressional power and the limits of its own reviewing powers. [4]

The Constitution did set some limits. Article I, Section 9, Clause 5, forbade export duties. Section 9, Clause 4, prohibited direct taxes unless each state paid a share in proportion to its population. And Section 8, Clause 1, directed that "all duties, imposts and excises" be imposed uniformly throughout the nation. Implied limitations, as interpreted by the Supreme Court in *McCulloch v. Maryland* (1819), exempted state and local governments — and income from state and local bonds — from federal taxes.

**Early Reliance on Tariffs.** The first congressional measure to raise revenue was a tariff act approved on July 4, 1789. Until the Civil War, customs duties produced sufficient revenue to meet most of the government's needs, accounting for more than 90 percent of total federal receipts. Tariffs, in addition to supplying funds for government operations, protected the nation's fledgling industries against competition from foreign imports. Through most of the nation's history, until the early years of the Great Depression in the 1930s, regions and economic interests often fought over tariff policy.

During the first half of the 19th century, the tariff laws offered protection mainly to manufactured goods. Western and northern farmers supported a protectionist policy for manufacturers on the assumption that industrial development, aided by high tariffs, would create a profitable home market for their products.

The Republican Party, founded in the West in 1854, lined up behind the protectionist principle on the eve of the Civil War, thereby availing itself of a policy that was to ensure it the enduring adherence of northern and eastern industrialists after the slavery issue was settled. The Democratic Party, on the other hand, generally favored a moderate- or low-tariff policy that helped it to retain the solid support of the agricultural South for years.

After the Civil War, tariff policy was the major issue in many presidential and congressional elections. Before World War I, a change in administrations often led to passage of new tariff laws. Congress devoted an inordinate amount of time to tariff-making, not only because the customs duties were made and remade so frequently but also because tariffs potentially affected the interests of many segments of American commercial life.

Congress finally delegated virtually all of its tariff-making power to the president, beginning with the Fordney-McCumber Act of 1922 and the Reciprocal Trade Agreements Act of 1934. By then, individual and corporate income taxes had begun replacing customs receipts as the main source of government revenue. In 1910 customs duties still brought in more than 49 percent of federal revenues; by fiscal 1981 they contributed slightly more than 1 percent, even though customs receipts had passed the $8 billion level.[5]

**Shift to the Income Tax.** Since the adoption of the 16th Amendment, federal taxes on individual incomes and corporate profits have become the principal revenue sources. That amendment, ratified in 1913, removed an obstacle to income taxes posed by the constitutional prohibition on direct taxes unless apportioned among the states according to population.

Congress in 1862 levied a tax on individual incomes to help finance the Civil War. That tax brought in a total of $376 million, and at its peak in 1866 it accounted for 25 percent of the year's internal revenue collections. It expired in 1872. The levy was challenged as violative of the constitutional requirement that direct taxes be apportioned among the states, but the Supreme Court ruled that it was not a direct tax.[6]

During the 1870s and 1880s, little interest was shown in enactment of a new income tax law. But the country's growth and the accumulation of large fortunes began in the 1890s to generate pressure for a return to income taxation. After the depression of 1893 had reduced federal revenues, Congress yielded and in 1894 levied a tax of 2 percent on personal incomes in excess of $3,000. Before the new tax law became operative, however, it was challenged, and this time the Supreme Court held that an income tax was a direct tax and therefore unconstitutional without apportionment (*Pollock v. Farmers' Loan & Trust Co.*, 1895).[7]

Although the court had blocked the road to this attempted expansion of the tax system, a solution was afforded by the power of Congress and the states to revise the Constitution. A campaign to do so was begun immediately, and on Feb. 23, 1913, the 16th Amendment was officially declared ratified. The one-sentence amendment stated tersely: "The Congress shall have power to lay and collect taxes on incomes from whatever source derived, without apportionment among the several states, and without regard to any census or enumeration."

Thus the problem of apportioning income taxes was swept away, and Congress was left free to do what it had tried to do two decades earlier. The new grant of power came at a providential time; the great expansion of federal revenues, made necessary by America's entry in World War I, would have been difficult if not impossible to achieve by any other means.

Congress imposed a federal income tax the same year the amendment was ratified, applying the tax to wages, salaries, interest, dividends, rents, entrepreneurial income and capital gains from the sale of assets. It set the initial rate at 1 percent, plus a surtax of 1 to 6 percent on larger incomes. The 1913 law exempted income up to $3,000 ($4,000 for a married couple). It allowed deductions for personal interest, tax payments and business expenses.

In the years following passage of the 1913 law, Congress complicated the federal income tax code with numerous changes that granted tax advantages to encourage specific types of activities. It also frequently changed tax rates and the level of exempted income. Maximum marginal rates — the tax rate imposed on the last dollar of income — reached as high as 94 percent during World War II. In 1981 Congress cut the maximum rate on investment income from 70 percent to 50 percent.[8]

**Corporate Taxes.** Congress did not have the constitutional difficulty with a corporate income tax that it had experienced with the tax on individual income. A corporate income tax was levied in 1909 in the guise of "a special excise tax" at a rate of 1 percent of net income in excess of $5,000. That tax, like the 1894 individual income tax, was challenged in the courts, but the Supreme Court let it stand as an excise on the privilege of doing business as a corporation.[9]

After ratification of the 16th Amendment, an outright corporate income tax at the same rate was made a part of the Revenue Act of 1913 alongside the individual income tax. The two taxes together, broadened and modified through the years as circumstances required, became the basic elements of the nation's revenue system.

In most years, corporate taxes have produced less revenue than individual income taxes. But during World War I, World War II and the Korean War, Congress raised additional revenues by imposing an excess profits tax to supplement corporate income taxes. And in 1980 Congress approved President Carter's request to levy a so-called "windfall profits tax" that was expected to raise $20 billion in fiscal 1982 by taxing the rising value of domestically produced crude oil as federal price controls were lifted.

**Excise and Other Taxes.** Excise taxes always have been a part of the federal tax system. They were mentioned specifically in Article I, Section 8, of the Constitution among the various levies that Congress was authorized to impose. The excises levied upon ratification of the Constitution included taxes on carriages, liquor, snuff, sugar and auction sales. These and similar taxes have been controversial throughout the Republic's history, in part because they were considered unfair and burdensome to the poor. Over the years, excises have been imposed and repealed or lowered. During every major war, the perennial liquor and tobacco taxes were supplemented by taxes on manufactured goods, licenses, financial transactions, services, luxury articles and dozens of other items that lent themselves to this form of taxation.

The power of Congress to tax in other areas has become well established. One of the most important areas has been payroll taxes, which underpin financially the Social Security, Medicare and unemployment compensation systems. Estate taxes date from the Civil War period and have been part of the national tax structure since 1916. The gift tax, levied to check avoidance of the estate tax, has been permanent since 1932.

**Regulation Through Taxation.** Congress has the power, confirmed by use over the years, to impose taxes for regulatory as well as revenue purposes. The leading example is the imposition of tariffs primarily to protect domestic industries against competition from imports rather than to raise revenue.

Regulation through taxation has been employed in other situations even to the extent of destroying a business enterprise. In 1863 Congress enacted a law providing for the incorporation of national banks with authority to issue currency notes. In 1866 it imposed a 10 percent tax on new state bank notes with the avowed purpose of driving such notes out of existence — which it did. Congress enacted numerous laws of this kind in the ensuing years.

## The Power to Spend

In the five decades since the beginning of the Great Depression, the growth of federal revenues provided the funds for an even more explosive increase in government spending. Since President Franklin D. Roosevelt launched the New Deal, Congress has made extensive and imaginative use of its constitutional powers to finance an expanding array of federal programs that benefit many Americans.

The Constitution gives Congress the basic authority to decide how the government should spend the money it collects. That power is protected by Article I, Section 9, Clause 7, which stipulates that the federal government may spend its revenues only in such amounts and for such purposes as Congress specifically has approved.

**Limits on Spending Power.** The Constitution sets few other limits on the spending power. Section 9, Clause 7, requires that "a regular statement and account of the receipts and expenditures of all public money shall be published from time to time." Elsewhere, Article I, Section 8, Clause 12, prohibits appropriating money "to raise and support armies" for longer than two years.

The Constitution explicitly directs the government to perform various functions — establish post offices, roads, armed forces and courts, pay debts and take a decennial census — that can be accomplished only by spending money. But by authorizing Congress to "provide for the common defense and general welfare of the United States," the Constitution by implication grants broad authority to spend. This implied spending power opened the way for expansive interpretation.

**The "General Welfare" Clause.** When the Republic was founded, political leaders differed over what spending for the general welfare meant. One strict interpretation, voiced by James Madison in *The Federalist*, No. 41, insisted that such outlays were limited to the purposes connected with the powers specifically mentioned by the Constitution.[10] A looser construction, advocated by Alexander Hamilton, contended that the general welfare clause conferred upon the government powers separate and different from those specifically enumerated in the Constitution. Under the latter interpretation, the federal government was potentially far more powerful than the strict constructionists intended.

Deep disagreement about the extent of congressional spending powers continued well into the 20th century. The broad interpretation came to be the generally accepted view, but it was not until 1936 that the Supreme Court found it necessary to give its opinion on the meaning of the controversial wording. In a decision that year *(United States v. Butler)*, the court invalidated the Agricultural Adjustment Act of 1933, which had provided federal payments to farmers who participated in a program of production control for the purposes of price stabilization. Although this law was held unconstitutional, the court construed the general welfare clause to mean that the congressional power to spend was not limited by the direct grants of legislative power found in the Constitution. Rather, an expenditure was constitutional "so long as the welfare at which it is aimed can be plausibly represented as national rather than local." The 1933 law was overturned on other grounds but was later re-enacted on a different constitutional basis and was upheld by the court.[11] Decisions in the following years upheld the tax provisions of the Social Security Act, thus confirming the broad authority of Congress to use its taxing and spending powers to provide for the general welfare.[12]

## The Power to Borrow

Debt is incurred by the federal government when it spends more than the Treasury collects in taxes and other forms of revenue. When expenditures outstrip revenues, the deficit must be made up by borrowing. Through much of the nation's history, a surplus resulting from an excess of revenues over expenditures has been used, at least in part, to reduce outstanding debt. Since the long string of federal budget deficits began in fiscal 1931, there have been budget surpluses in only seven years.

It was during this period that the bulk of the national debt (estimated to reach $1.0798 trillion by the end of fiscal 1982) was incurred. In the process, Congress stepped up its use of the power to borrow money on the nation's credit.

The borrowing power is extensive. In their *Introduction to American Government*, Frederic A. Ogg and P. Orman Ray noted that the "power to borrow not only is expressly conferred in the Constitution, but is one of the very few federal powers entirely unencumbered by restrictions — with the result that Congress may borrow from any lenders, for any purposes,

## Politics of the Federal Debt: . . .

Although it holds the power to borrow, Congress generally has sidestepped responsibility for the mounting federal debt. By permanently appropriating funds for interest owed by the government, Congress has spared members the pain of voting each year to set funds aside for that purpose. Only since 1975 have the House and Senate gone on record on the level of the deficit projected by the annual budget resolutions.

The federal government, unlike some states, does not have a constitutional restriction on budget deficits. Since World War I, Congress has set statutory limits through legislation. But as the federal debt rose — because Congress continued to approve spending without adequately increasing revenues — the House and Senate have had no choice but to raise the ceiling, while members lamented deficit spending.

### Debt Ceiling

Congress established the first overall debt ceiling in 1917, when the Second Liberty Bond Act fixed the limit at $11.5 billion. By 1945 Congress had amended that act 16 times, lifting the ceiling to $300 billion to accommodate World War II borrowing. In 1946 Congress reduced the limit to a "permanent" $275 billion level. In 1972 the permanent level rose to $400 billion, where — legally — it has remained. Since then, however, Congress repeatedly has approved a "temporary" debt limit, which in 1981 surpassed the $1 trillion mark.

Although Congress actually had little choice but to increase the statutory debt limit, the heated debates — primarily in the House — suggested that the events were milestones in public financial affairs. The controversy over increasing the debt ceiling flowed essentially from the broader issue of government spending. The proponents of a statutory debt ceiling saw the ceiling as a form of expenditure control, but officials in the executive branch responsible for paying the government's bills were convinced that a debt ceiling could not control expenditures. Throughout the postwar period, secretaries of the Treasury expressed their opposition to using the debt ceiling for that purpose.

Practice proved them right. When it came down to the final vote, Congress always has raised the debt limit enough to allow the govern-

## . . . Hiding Deficit Spending Decisions

ment to keep borrowing funds to finance daily operations. But congressional conservatives used the debate to throw a spotlight on the federal debt and take symbolic stances against rising spending.

### House Experiment

As a result of this politicization of the issue, the government on several occasions nearly ran out of money as Congress rushed to keep the "temporary" debt ceiling from falling to its permanent level. In 1980, the House finally began experimenting with new short-cut procedures to make debt battles unnecessary.

Under that plan, adopted in 1979, the House agreed simply to set the debt limit at whatever level was projected by the most recently enacted congressional budget resolution. After the House gave final approval to the budget resolution, the debt limit would be incorporated in a joint resolution that would be deemed approved by the House and sent — without a separate House vote — to the Senate for consideration.

That strategy presumed that budget resolutions would be enacted on time. In fact, in 1980, action on the first budget resolution fell behind schedule, forcing Congress to consider a stopgap resolution increasing the debt ceiling. Seizing the opportunity, Congress added to that measure a provision overturning President Carter's highly unpopular oil import fee. Carter vetoed the debt limit resolution, but Congress promptly overrode the veto.

The House plan also did not apply to the Senate and thus did not prevent that chamber from turning debt limit extensions into political footballs. For example, during consideration of a 1981 measure to raise the debt ceiling above a trillion dollars for the first time in the nation's history, Democrats offered a series of amendments, several of which involved repealing parts of President Reagan's recently passed tax cut.

The amendments were defeated, but the measure faced yet another hurdle — an all-night filibuster. Sen. William Proxmire, D-Wis., spoke from early in the evening of Sept. 28 to mid-morning Sept. 29, urging his colleagues to keep the debt limit at $995 billion as a means of holding down federal spending. Proxmire's filibuster was unsuccessful.

in any amounts, on any terms, and with or without provision for the repayment of loans, with or without interest." [13]

Ogg and Ray noted also that the United States has no constitutional debt limit, whereas many state constitutions and state charters for counties and local governments impose debt ceilings. The United States has had a statutory debt ceiling for many decades, but the ceiling is raised repeatedly by Congress — usually at least once a year — although seldom without an intense political fight in Congress.

## Notes

1. George B. Galloway, *The Legislative Process in Congress* (New York: Thomas Y. Crowell Co., 1955), p. 91.
2. Executive Office of the President, Office of Management and Budget, *Budget of the United States Government, Fiscal Year 1983* (Washington, D.C.: U.S. Government Printing Office, 1982), p. 4-2.
3. Galloway, *Legislative Process*, p. 91.
4. C. Herman Pritchett, *The American Constitution*, 3rd ed. (New York: McGraw-Hill Book Co., 1977), p. 167.
5. OMB, *Fiscal 1983 Budget*, pp. 9-48—9-49. For background on tariffs, see Daniel T. Selko, *The Federal Financial System* (Washington, D.C.: The Brookings Institution, 1940), pp. 60, 557-572; Frederic A. Ogg and P. Orman Ray, *Introduction to American Government*, 10th ed. (New York: Appleton-Century-Crofts, 1951), p. 518; Paul Webbink, "Deadlocks in Tariff Legislation," *Editorial Research Reports*, Nov. 1, 1929.
6. *Springer v. United States*, 102 U.S. 586 (1881).
7. *Pollock v. Farmers' Loan and Trust Co.*, 158 U.S. 601 (1895).
8. See Joseph A. Pechman, *Federal Tax Policy*, 3rd ed. (Washington, D.C.: The Brookings Institution, 1977) pp. 56-200.
9. *Flint v. Stone Tracy Co.*, 220 U.S. 107 (1911).
10. *The Federalist Papers*, with an introduction by Clinton Rossiter (New York: Mentor, 1961), No. 41, p. 263.
11. *United States v. Butler*, 297 U.S. 1 (1936).
12. *Steward Machine Co. v. Davis*, 301 U.S. 548 (1937); *Helvering v. Davis*, 301 U.S. 619 (1937).
13. Ogg and Ray, *American Government*, p. 527.

## *Chapter 2*

# CONGRESS SHAPES THE ECONOMY

Significant changes have occurred in the way Congress exercises its taxing, spending and borrowing powers. In the 1960s Congress began to use its power to tax not only to raise revenue but as a tool to shape the nation's economy. But it is the way Congress has exercised its spending and borrowing powers since the 1930s that has so profoundly affected individual Americans, the nation's economy and the established institutions of government.

### Growth of Federal Revenues

Since its inception in 1913 the federal tax system has steadily produced huge increases in government revenues. Even though Congress periodically cut taxes, individual and corporate income tax revenues rose almost without interruption as a growing population and an expanding economy enlarged the base on which they were levied. By fiscal 1981 individual income taxes mounted to $285.9 billion. Corporate taxes were $61.1 billion. Together, they accounted for nearly 58 percent of the $599.3 billion in federal revenues for that fiscal year.[1]

Initially, low rates kept revenues from federal income taxes at modest levels until the United States entered World War I. Then Congress sharply increased the tax rates, raising the revenue yield to $2.3 billion in fiscal 1918 from $360 million in fiscal 1917. Since then, federal income taxes have produced more revenue annually than all excise and other internal revenue taxes combined—except for the nine fiscal years from 1933 through 1941 when the government levied numerous excise taxes to replace revenues as incomes sagged during the Depression.

During World War II high rates and a broadened tax base doubled and redoubled receipts from income and profits taxes. Those revenues fell off after the war, rose again during the Korean conflict and fell once more after hostilities ended and wartime tax rates were reduced. In the following three decades, federal income tax revenues climbed year after year even as Congress reduced rates and introduced new benefits.

In the 1960s Congress and the president began to use the federal tax power as a means to promote certain economic policies. The theory for using the tax power in this way is based on the writings of British economist John Maynard Keynes. Very simply put, Keynesian economics holds that a slow economy can be stimulated by cutting taxes or increasing spending while an inflation-ridden economy can be defused by raising taxes or cutting spending.

By the 1980 presidential election, it was clear that the economy was not responding to tax stimulation in the manner predicted. Inflation remained extraordinarily high at the same time that productivity decreased and joblessness was on the rise. President Reagan campaigned successfully on a new "supply-side" theory which held that high taxes were a disincentive to work, save and invest. This theory advocated broad tax cuts, particularly at the high end of the rate scale, to encourage more productivity and greater investment.

Congress in 1981 went along with Reagan's request for massive tax reductions that slashed individual tax rates 25 percent over 33 months and then, for the first time ever, indexed the tax system to keep inflation from forcing taxpayers into higher brackets as their incomes kept pace with prices. By fiscal 1986 these reductions were expected to shave federal revenues by $267.7 billion. [2]

## Expansion of Federal Spending

Before the Great Depression of the 1930s, government spending was limited by a consensus that outlays should not exceed revenues except in times of war. In their study, *Democracy in Deficit*, James M. Buchanan and Richard E. Wagner maintained that the unwritten "fiscal constitution" constrained the federal government's impulse to launch new spending programs. "Barring extraordinary circumstances," they wrote, "public expenditures were supposed to be financed by taxation, just as private spending was supposed to be financed from income." [3] As Donald G. Ogilvie, associate dean of the Yale University School of Organization and Management, has noted, "The original role of the federal government was limited both by the precise language of the Constitution and by the prevailing social consensus that powerful central governments should be avoided." [4]

Annual federal outlays reached the $1 billion level only in 1865, the last year of the Civil War, then subsided below that mark until the nation entered World War I. The government spent $18.4 billion in fiscal 1919, but, as in the decades after the Civil War, outlays again fell off in peacetime, holding steady between $2 billion and $3 billion a year during the 1920s.

The nation's federal system reached a turning point in the 1930s during the Great Depression. Under President Franklin D. Roosevelt's direction, Congress launched massive federal programs to pull the economy out of the worst downturn in U.S. history. Spending for domestic assistance programs jumped to $7 billion by 1939 as outlays for civilian needs surpassed spending on the military, veterans and war-incurred debt. During the Depression, strict adherence to balanced budgets was impossible to follow. At the same time, economists advising the government gave theoretical support to deficit spending during peacetime years to stimulate production. The old link between taxes and spending gradually gave way.

Roosevelt's New Deal programs marked a fundamental shift away from the limited role that the federal government previously had filled in the nation's economic and social life. During the 1930s, the government first took on responsibility for managing an economy that previous *laissez-faire* policy assumed to be self-regulating. The New Deal also produced a host of programs that redistributed the nation's wealth from one group to another and from some regions to others. Most New Deal initiatives were implemented as countercyclical programs to be phased out as economic conditions improved. Some were terminated within a few years. Others—such as the Social Security system and federal credit assistance for housing, small business and farmers—remain major functions of the government in 1982. More significantly, the New Deal set precedents for federal efforts to provide for the poor and ensure economic security for all Americans when times were hard.

After the Depression ended when the country began to mobilize for war, the federal government continued to expand income transfer programs and take over more and more functions that states, local governments and individuals previously had performed. Those programs grew gradually from the late 1930s to the mid-1960s. Then, starting in 1965, with a forceful Lyndon Johnson as president prodding a heavily Democratic 89th Congress, the government launched a stream of Great Society programs extending its role in providing medical care, education assistance, urban renewal, job-training and other services for people and localities. During the 1970s, Congress kept enlarging most of these programs—and adding a few new ones—despite the opposition of Republican presidents.

These new programs translated into increased federal spending. A government that spent 3.7 percent of America's gross national product in calendar 1930 was spending more than 23 percent by 1980. During the 1930s, outlays rose from $3.5 billion in fiscal 1931 to $9.5 billion in fiscal 1940. In fiscal 1981 federal outlays reached $657 billion. In every year since fiscal 1955, with the exception of fiscal 1965, the budget has increased. In Ogilvie's words: "It took 186 years for the federal budget to exceed $100 billion; it took only nine more years to reach $200 billion; four more to exceed $300 billion; two more to reach $400 billion; and an additional two years to go to $500 billion." [5]

**Changing Budget Priorities.** Shifting national priorities resulted not only in increased spending but also in changed spending patterns. Federal outlays grew rapidly for tasks, notably national defense, that the federal government traditionally had performed. But as new social programs came on line they absorbed more and more of the government's resources. The share that the government poured into defense declined as a proportion of the budget.

Annual U.S. military spending peaked at $85 billion during World War II and again at $50 billion during the Korean War. Defense outlays fell off in the mid-1950s but climbed back above $50 billion in fiscal 1963. Since then, defense spending climbed steadily to a Vietnam War peak of $79 billion. After declining slightly, defense outlays accelerated as the country sought to upgrade its military capabilities, reaching an estimated $187.5 billion for fiscal 1982.

Except for three years during the Vietnam buildup, however, military-related purchases of goods and services accounted for a declining share of federal spending as measured by the Commerce Department's national income and product account (NIA). By fiscal 1981 defense outlays were 5.1 percent of gross national product, down from the 8.9 percent average 20 years before.

At the same time, federal government payments to individuals—the poor, the sick, the elderly, retired government workers—jumped. From $76 billion in the fiscal 1967 budget, such payments rose to an estimated $306 billion in fiscal 1982, accounting for nearly half of total estimated outlays. And federal grants to state and local governments—for purposes such as highway construction, mass transit, sewage treatment plants, job-training, revenue sharing, community development, education and welfare services—escalated from $2 billion in 1950 to more than $90 billion 30 years later.

Although most of the post-Depression social programs were intended to assist the poor and to improve public services in parts of the nation with hard-pressed regional or local economies, many of them also benefited middle-income Americans, and even the wealthy. Moreover, state and local governments had grown dependent on federal grants for operating funds. "We have, in effect, created a special interest group that includes a majority of the population," Ogilvie contended.[6]

Congress, being a political institution, obviously is attuned to the broad appeal that its benefit programs carry. Beneficiaries of federal programs—particularly state and local officials, teachers and students, social workers and welfare recipients, and entrepreneurs who win government contracts—have become adept at lobbying for ever-higher funding. Such lobbying organizations often work with the agency officials who run the programs and with congressional committees that authorize them in so-called "iron triangles" to preserve and increase funding.

**Backdoor Spending.** In political reality, such broad-based and determined support makes any program tough to cut. Congress in some cases has made budget cutting even harder by insulating programs against budget restraint. Through various legislative routes, Congress has exempted from the annual appropriations process about three-quarters of the money it spends each year.

Congress deliberately authorized some so-called uncontrollable, or "backdoor," spending simply because the government must shield certain obligations from political controversy. An example of that kind of spending is the permanent appropriation, passed in 1847, to pay interest as it comes due on the national debt. The government must meet that obligation to retain its borrowing credibility. For many other programs, particularly social programs providing benefits primarily to urban areas, Congress set up backdoor financing arrangements to shield their budget from annual scrutiny from the Appropriations committees.[7]

Backdoor spending obligations take several forms. For some programs, Congress authorizes agencies to enter contracts, borrow money or guarantee loans that eventually obligate the government to make payments. And Congress excludes some quasi-government agencies

—such as the Post Office—from the annual federal budget, effectively exempting them from overall fiscal controls. But by far the largest backdoor outlays result from the tremendous growth of federal entitlement programs—so-called because Congress by law entitles their recipients to the benefits the government programs provide. *(Forms of backdoor spending, box, pp. 60-61)*

By the late 1970s, between 16 percent and 17 percent of the funds the government spent annually fulfilled contracts and obligations that agencies committed themselves to in previous years. And a growing proportion of outlays—58 percent to 59 percent—was set aside to meet open-ended commitments the government had made through provisions Congress previously wrote into law.

## The Federal Debt

The explosive growth in federal spending since the 1930s has affected significantly the nation's perception of the borrowing power and the national debt. Throughout most of the nation's history, the principal concern of government budget policy was to ensure that revenues were sufficient to meet expenditures. That philosophy, which in application meant an approximate balance between receipts and outlays, was generally accepted during most of the nation's history.

Writing in *Federal Budget and Fiscal Policy, 1789-1958,* Lewis H. Kimmel pointed out that three key ideas generally were accepted by federal officials and economists alike in the period leading up to the Civil War: a low level of public expenditures was desirable; the federal budget should be balanced in peacetime; and the federal debt should be reduced and eventually extinguished. "These ideas," he observed, "were a reflection of views that were deeply rooted in the social fabric." [8]

The Civil War, like the major wars of modern times, resulted in a much enlarged national debt. However, after the Civil War there was less concern about eliminating the outstanding debt. Increasingly, the emphasis was on servicing the debt in an orderly manner. Proposals to liquidate it became fewer and fewer. The entrance of the United States into World War I in 1971 again escalated the federal debt. Then in the 1930s the government turned away from its former insistence on balancing revenues and outlays, gradually adopting in its place Keynes' economic philosophy that justified peacetime deficits when needed to ensure stable economic growth. Discussing the early years of the Depression, Kimmel noted:

> A concerted effort was made by the president and the leadership of both parties in Congress to adhere to the balanced-budget philosophy. Yet a balanced federal budget was almost impossible to attain—the annually balanced-budget dogma in effect gave way to necessity. Alternatives soon were suggested, and within a few years what came to be known as compensatory fiscal theory gained numerous adherents. [9]

The practice of using the federal budget to help solve national economic problems became acceptable. Budget deficits and a rapidly increasing national debt were the result. The debt rose to nearly $50 billion—almost twice the World War I peak—at the end of fiscal 1941. Then came Pearl Harbor. The debt passed the $100 billion mark in fiscal 1943 and there was no steady reduction after World War II. The debt total fluctuated for a few years but then began a new rise that took it past the World War II peak in fiscal 1954, past $300 billion in fiscal 1963 and all the way to $475 billion at the end of fiscal 1974. The debt more than doubled—surpassing the $1 trillion level—as the government ran unprecedented peacetime deficits in fiscal 1975-82.

## Notes

1. Executive Office of the President, Office of Management and Budget, *Budget of the United States Government, Fiscal Year 1983* (Washington, D.C.: U.S. Government Printing Office, 1982), p. 4-2.
2. For background on tax policy, see Joseph A. Pechman, *Federal Tax Policy*, 3rd ed. (Washington, D.C.: The Brookings Institution, 1977); Allen Schick, *Congress and Money: Budgeting, Spending and Taxing* (Washington, D.C.: The Urban Institute, 1980), pp. 483-505.
3. James M. Buchanan and Richard E. Wagner, *Democracy in Deficit: The Political Legacy of Lord Keynes* (New York: Academic Press, 1977), p. 21.
4. Donald G. Ogilvie, "Constitutional Limits and the Federal Budget," in *The Congressional Budget Process After Five Years,* ed. Ralph Penner (Washington, D.C.: American Enterprise Institute for Public Policy Research, 1981), pp. 103-104.
5. Ibid., p. 106.
6. Ibid., p. 115.
7. Harrison Donnelly, "Uncontrollable U.S. Spending Limits Hill Power of the Purse," *Congressional Quarterly Weekly Report*, Jan. 19, 1980, pp. 117-124.
8. Lewis H. Kimmel, *Federal Budget and Fiscal Policy, 1789-1958* (Washington, D.C.: The Brookings Institution, 1959), p. 55.
9. Ibid., p. 306.

*Chapter 3*

# TAX AND APPROPRIATIONS COMMITTEES

Until 1975, when the congressional budget act went into effect, four committees wielded the bulk of Congress' fiscal powers. The House Ways and Means and Senate Finance committees have jurisdiction over all tax and other revenue legislation. And while all legislative committees have some authority over spending by establishing the maximum that may be spent on specific programs, it is the House and Senate Appropriations committees that recommend what actually will be spent.

Article I, Section 7, Clause 1, of the Constitution requires that the House of Representatives originate tax legislation: "All Bills for raising Revenue shall originate in the House of Representatives." By tradition, the House has assumed the privilege of initiating appropriations measures as well, although the Constitution does not mention such a requirement for spending legislation.

Under normal procedures, House panels write tax and appropriations legislation that the chamber in the past usually accepted without major change. Senate committees then review the House-passed measures, in the case of appropriations bills often listening to appeals by agencies and special interest groups who do not agree with House-approved funding levels. The full Senate, with a tradition of unlimited debate, generally has been more likely than the House to revise committee recommendations during floor consideration.

At the end of the 1970s, newly formed House and Senate Budget committees began asserting an important role in congressional tax and spending deliberations. In 1980 and 1981, the Budget committees enforced spending cutbacks by winning House and Senate support to direct other panels to approve budget reconciliation legislation. But the Congressional Budget and Impoundment Control Act of 1974 did not provide the Budget committees with automatic authority to force Congress to adhere to tax and spending limits. And the long-established

House and Senate tax and Appropriations committees continue to exercise impressive clout over congressional budget decisions. *(Budget reconciliation process, pp. 63-65)*

## Writing Tax Legislation

In both the House and Senate, powerful and prestigious committees control the complicated process of putting tax legislation together. The collection of federal revenues affects virtually all Americans, and a growing band of labor, industry and public interest organizations has sought to win special treatment for particular interests. Furthermore, the Internal Revenue Code over the years has evolved into an elaborate, often-convoluted body of laws that even few members of Congress fully understand.

Traditionally, senators and representatives have been reluctant to go on record on complex and controversial tax-law changes. Most members preferred to let tax-writing committees handle the task of deciding not only how to raise revenue but also which taxpayers should bear what proportion of the tax burden. Those committees—Ways and Means in the House and Finance in the Senate—as a result accumulated vast power to shape the federal tax system and to influence the varied economic interests at stake in the tax laws.

In the decades after World War II, the tax committees worked closely with the executive branch in drawing up tax legislation. Before the 1970s, Treasury officials usually offered tax proposals and Congress acted on their recommendations. Congress itself initiated major tax-revision measures in 1969 and again in 1975. But committee members, congressional staffs and Treasury officials continued to consult throughout the process to ensure agreement on tax-code changes.

Because revenue measures must originate in the House, the Ways and Means Committee writes the first draft of virtually all tax measures. The House most often passes Ways and Means measures with few, if any, changes, and then sends them to the Senate. The Finance Committee may rework the House provisions—and often tacks on additional tax changes. The full Senate as a rule approves even more far-reaching amendments before passing the measure. As with all legislation, the House and Senate must resolve their differences on the bill before sending the bill to the White House for the president's signature. Both committees are assisted by the Joint Committee on Taxation, which exists largely to provide the staff expertise needed in dealing with complex tax bills.

In both the House and Senate, the influential tax committee chairmen have dominated congressional revenue deliberations. Carefully balancing competing interests during committee action, the chairmen usually receive strong backing from their panel's members in fending off floor amendments that would change the basic shape of the legislation.

Two members of Congress—Ways and Means Chairman Wilbur D. Mills, D-Ark. (1939-77), and Finance Chairman Russell B. Long, D-La. — were especially adept during the 1960s and 1970s at guiding tax measures through committee and floor action and through the hard bargaining at House-Senate conference sessions.

**Ways and Means Role.** During Mills' tenure as chairman from 1958 through 1974, the Ways and Means Committee held virtually unchallenged authority over legislation in its jurisdiction. The House created Ways and Means in 1802 and gave it responsibility for spending as well as taxes. In subsequent years, the House gradually reduced the panel's control over spending legislation, and in 1865 it set up a separate Appropriations Committee.

By 1982 Ways and Means had jurisdiction over revenue, debt, customs, trade and Social Security legislation. The committee traditionally had been composed of senior House members with close ties to party leaders. Between 1911 and 1975, Ways and Means Democrats acted as their party's Committee on Committees, assigning other Democrats to vacancies on House panels, a role which gave it great political influence within the House.[1]

Seven members, including five Democrats and two Republicans, led Ways and Means between 1947 and 1982. But none of the other chairmen matched the extraordinary authority over tax legislation that Mills exercised during the 16 years he led the committee. Mills' long tenure and command of complex tax laws won wide respect from House members. Mills also kept control over all tax measures by bringing them before the whole committee and refusing to establish permanent subcommittees to consider different issues. Mills solidified his power by accurately sensing what the House would support and drafting legislation accordingly.

Through the years, Ways and Means members took pride in careful, professional work on tax legislation. The committee's conservative leanings and cautious approach to tax-law changes reflected majority House sentiment on such issues. House leaders sent Ways and Means measures to the floor under so-called "closed rules"—which barred amendments—and the full House regularly passed the panel's bills by large margins.

By the 1970s, however, the House was changing. Democratic supporters of sweeping tax-law "reforms" grew restless with the power that Mills held over revenue legislation. In 1974 Mills' self-confessed alcoholism and erratic personal behavior forced him to resign as chairman. House Democrats took the opportunity in October and December of that year to make the committee more liberal and break the chairman's grip over tax deliberations. The committee was enlarged from 25 to 37 members, and subcommittees were established. The authority to make Democratic committee assignments was transferred to the Democratic Steering and Policy Committee.

Al Ullman, D-Ore. (1957-81), succeeded Mills, chairing Ways and Means from 1975 through 1980. But Ullman was a weaker leader than Mills, and the expanded committee proved too fragmented and contentious for him to forge the consensus that Mills had constructed on behalf of the panel's tax bills. As a result, Ways and Means suffered some embarrassing defeats during House debate on its measures. And unlike Mills, Ullman was unable to match Finance Committee Chairman Long's experience and expertise in House-Senate negotiations on tax legislation. When Ullman was defeated for re-election in 1980, House Democrats named Dan Rostenkowski, D-Ill., to chair Ways and Means.

In 1975 Ways and Means set up six subcommittees to handle welfare, trade, Social Security, unemployment compensation, health and special revenue legislation. But the full committee still considers basic tax law proposals, conducting lengthy hearings with testimony from the secretary of the Treasury and other expert witnesses.

After hearings, the committee normally begins markup sessions to draft the bill. The Treasury Department may have submitted its own proposals, but preparation of legal language often is left to congressional and Treasury experts. Until 1973 markups generally were held in executive (closed) session, but following House adoption of new rules on committee secrecy in March of that year, most of the markup sessions have been open to the public.

**The Closed Rule Tradition.** Changing House procedures have loosened Ways and Means' control over the bills it writes and reports to the House. Before 1973 the House took up tax measures under special procedures that had become traditional for Ways and Means legislation and all but guaranteed acceptance of the committee's work without change. Technically, under House rules in effect until 1975, revenue legislation was "privileged" business, which meant that it could be brought up for consideration on the floor ahead of other measures and without a special rule from the Rules Committee. In practice, Ways and Means usually obtained a closed rule before sending its bills to the floor. Under that procedure, the bill was not open to amendment in the course of House debate; essentially, the House had to accept or reject the bill as a whole. Opponents of the bills had one opportunity, at the end of the debate, to try to make changes in the legislation, but significant revisions seldom resulted.

There was one exception to the prohibition against floor amendments. Any amendments that were approved by the Ways and Means Committee (after the committee had reported the bill to the House) could be offered by a committee member and voted on. This gave the committee an opportunity to backtrack on any provision that appeared to be in danger of drawing unusual House opposition.

Use of a closed rule was justified on the ground that tax, trade and other Ways and Means bills were too complicated to be revised on the floor. Floor amendments, it was argued, might upset the carefully balanced legislation considered and approved by the committee. Nonetheless, the closed rule tradition came under attack as members of the House began to challenge the power of the Ways and Means Committee.

**Rules Reforms.** Finally, in 1973, Democrats modified the closed rule by adopting a proposal that allowed 50 or more Democrats to bring up proposed amendments to Ways and Means bills at the party caucus. If the caucus voted to approve them, the Rules Committee was instructed to write a special rule permitting the amendments to be offered on the floor. In 1975 the House went a step further by changing its rules to require that all Ways and Means revenue bills receive a rule before they are brought to the floor; their "privileged" status was eliminated.

Almost immediately, the impact of these reforms was vividly demonstrated. The House on Feb. 27, 1975, passed a Ways and Means Committee tax-cut bill, but tacked on a provision repealing the oil depletion allowance despite Chairman Ullman's objections. The issue was forced upon the House by the Democratic Caucus, which had voted to allow a floor vote on amendments repealing the depletion allowance that had been drafted by dissident Ways and Means members. In a long-sought victory for tax revision advocates, the House accepted the amendment by a 248-163 vote.

But the full effect of the House reforms was not fully evident until 1981 when the Democratic-controlled Ways and Means Committee brought a tax-cut bill to the House floor that differed significantly from the large, three-year tax reduction proposal offered by President Ronald Reagan. Even though committee Democrats had added "sweeteners" to the committee bill in an effort to win votes, enough Democrats voted with Republicans to defeat the committee bill wholesale and replace it with a Reagan-endorsed version. The vote was 238-195. To add insult to injury, the prevailing substitute was sponsored by two Republican members of Ways and Means, including the ranking minority member, Barber B. Conable, N.Y.

**Senate Finance Committee**. Created in 1816, the Senate Finance Committee shares the same jurisdiction as Ways and Means. But its power and influence on revenue matters in the past have been more limited. Because of the constitutional directive that tax legislation originate in the House, the Finance panel usually has taken on a review or appellate role for interests trying to change House-approved provisions.

Despite the constitutional stricture, the Senate on occasion has all but originated tax legislation. This is usually done either in the Finance Committee or in the Senate by attaching a major revenue-affecting amendment to a minor House-passed tax bill awaiting Senate action.

In 1981 the Senate went a step further. The Finance Committee drafted its own tax-cut bill, which was reported by the committee and considered by the Senate. After amendments were added on the floor, the Senate waited for the House to complete action on its version of the legislation. Two days after the House passed the bill, the Senate gave final approval to its own version and sent it to conference with the House.[2]

Through the years, the Finance Committee acquired a reputation for being receptive to special-interest tax schemes. That impression may trace to the second clause in Article I, Section 7: "All bills for raising Revenue shall originate in the House of Representatives; *but the Senate may propose or concur with amendments as on other bills.*" [Emphasis added] At times, the Finance panel has had little to do except tinker with the House-passed bills and add provisions in which individual senators have a special interest.

In its markup sessions the committee proposes amendments to the House-passed bills, sometimes making changes in the House-passed language but more often adding new provisions. The committee, like Ways and Means, is assisted by congressional and Treasury Department experts.

**Floor Action.** Senate floor action on tax legislation often radically departs from the careful consideration that the House and the Finance Committee give revenue proposals. The Senate has no procedures or rules to ward off amendments to tax bills. And at times senators have used their prerogative to offer amendments to rewrite House bills or load them with unrelated provisions.

Senate tax-bill debates often have evolved into legislative logrolling and mutual accommodation, particularly late in congressional sessions when members try to push through favorite proposals before adjournment. Senate amendments, germane to tax legislation only because they would amend some Internal Revenue Code provision, have turned many tax measures into "Christmas-tree bills" bestowing benefits on varied economic interests.

The Senate sometimes approves popular amendments in full knowledge that House conferees will insist that they be dropped. Finance Committee leaders sometimes accept amendments out of courtesy to a sponsoring senator. As Finance chairman, Long frequently agreed to take amendments to conference with the House as bargaining chips that could be discarded in trade-offs for other provisions that senators considered essential. Senate floor maneuvering on tax bills often lasts several weeks.

**Conference Negotiations.** Like other acts of Congress, most tax legislation is put in final form by a House-Senate conference committee. But because the economic stakes are high, tax-bill conferences have produced intense and dramatic bargaining. The conference sessions usually have been held in a small room on the House side of the Capitol maintained by the Ways and Means Committee. The conference is presided over by the Ways and Means chairman. As a rule, the conferees are three members from the majority party and two from the minority on the Ways and Means and Finance committees. The number may be enlarged for major bills, but a larger number of one side or the other makes no difference in resolving disputes because each side votes as a unit, with the majority view determining the position of each side on every issue.

The conference may last from a day or two to several weeks on controversial bills. Congressional and Treasury tax experts are present to assist the conferees. Once all differences are resolved, the bill is sent back to each chamber for approval of the conference agreement. The House files a conference report (usually for both chambers, although the Senate may file an identical report) listing the differences and how they were resolved. It is a rather technical document and of most use to an expert; simpler explanations of conference decisions are given by senior committee members during floor discussion of the bill in both houses. If the conference agreement is approved by both, the bill is sent to the president.

House and Senate action on tax legislation often is not completed until late in a congressional session, when conferees must negotiate their differences under tight deadlines to finish by adjournment. Astute conference leaders such as Rep. Mills and Sen. Long have used the pressures of time to strengthen the case for their positions. The final products, sometimes negotiated in all-night sessions, usually represent careful compromises that take account of House and Senate politics. The legislation that conferees fashion also may determine how much money the government collects for years to come.

During conference negotiations, Treasury officials and Joint Taxation Committee staff aides help members keep track of the impact of their decisions on revenue. But in many cases, conferees have given revenue gains or losses only secondary consideration. By the end of the 1970s, however, congressional budget control procedures had begun to force House and Senate tax negotiators to trim tax-cut legislation to keep revenue losses within the annual budget resolution targets. *(Budget process, pp. 57-69)*

## The Appropriations Process

The Constitution gives the House power to originate tax bills, but it contains no specific provision to that effect concerning appropriations bills (or legislation setting tariff policy). However, the House traditionally has assumed the responsibility for initiating all appropriations as well as tariff bills and has jealously guarded this self-assumed prerogative whenever the Senate has attempted to encroach upon it. The practical result, as far as appropriations are concerned, is that the House Appropriations Committee is more powerful than its counterpart on the Senate side because the bulk of basic appropriations decisions are made in the House committee.

The general shape of any appropriations bill is derived from House consideration of the measure. What the Senate does in effect is to review the House action and hear appeals from agencies and special interests seeking changes in the allotments accorded their programs by the House. The Senate is free to make alterations as it deems appropriate. Senate changes usually are limited to revisions in the financing for a relatively small number of politically significant or controversial government programs; the Senate seldom recommends entirely different appropriations than the House for any department or agency.[3]

**Early Funding Procedures.** Before World War I, neither the expenditures nor the revenues of the federal government exceeded $800 million a year. No comprehensive system of budgeting had been developed, although the method of handling funds had undergone various changes in Congress. During the pre-Civil War period, both taxing and spending bills were handled in the House by the Ways and Means Committee. But this eventually proved too difficult a task for a single committee, and in 1865 the House established an Appropriations Committee. The Senate Appropriations Committee was created in 1867.

In subsequent years, both the House and Senate dispersed appropriations functions to other committees as well. Between 1877 and 1885 the House removed jurisdiction over eight of 14 annual appropriations bills from the Appropriations Committee and gave it to various authorizing panels. The Senate eventually followed the House lead in reducing the authority of what members considered the excessive independence of the appropriations panels. Such actions gave the committees most familiar with a government agency and its programs the power to control that agency's appropriations. But this division of responsibility also frustrated any attempt to unify control over government budget policy.

After World War I, Congress again consolidated the appropriations function while giving the executive branch stronger budgeting capabilities. The House in 1920 restored to the Appropriations Committee exclusive appropriations authority, and the Senate in 1922 similarly concentrated power over spending measures in its Appropriations panel. What evolved from those steps was a two-stage process by which legislative committees draft legislation authorizing federal programs and setting ceilings on expenditures for such programs, while the Appropriations panels recommend the specific level of funding up to the maximum authorized.

**Mandatory Authorizations.** By its own rules, Congress cannot consider appropriations for a federal program until the president has signed legislation authorizing its functions during a fiscal year. The House has had a rule since 1837 which provides that "No appropriation shall be reported in any general appropriations bill, or be in order as an amendment thereto, for any expenditure not previously authorized by law. . . ." The Senate has a similar rule but, because appropriations bills originate in the House, the House rule is governing in any case. There are some exceptions. For example, a portion of the annual appropriations for the military is authorized by the Constitution, and occasionally Congress turns a blind eye to its rule. Generally, however, appropriations must await congressional action on the authorizations.

This requirement has led to conflict in Congress on numerous occasions. Since the 1950s Congress has required annual authorizations of more and more programs that previously had permanent or multi-year authorizations. The trend to annual authorizations represented a victory for the legislative committees—such as the Education and Labor Committee in the House—which felt that they had lost effective control over their programs to the Appropriations committees. The Appropriations committees, particularly in the House, took a dim view of annual authorizations, in part because they felt the procedure tended to diminish their power.

Annual authorizations also have slowed the process. The House and Senate seldom have all appropriation bills in place before the fiscal year begins. With government programs growing in number and becoming more complex, congressional committees needed more time to review agency operations and financing needs. Beginning in the late 1950s, Congress rarely finished work on more than a few of the 13 annual appropriation bills before the start of the fiscal year on July 1.

In its 1974 budget law, Congress pushed the fiscal year back three months to Oct. 1. The budget measure also set a deadline of May 15 for legislative committees to report authorization bills and mid-September for Congress to complete action on appropriation bills. Even with more time, however, Congress has continued to slip badly behind schedule in considering the required legislation. *(Budget timetable, box, p. 64)*

**Continuing Resolutions.** As a result, the government frequently has begun the fiscal year without many funding measures having been enacted. Congress has gotten around the problem by adopting emergency funding bills—called continuing appropriations resolutions—that allow agencies to keep spending money for a specified period, usually at the level Congress approved for the previous fiscal year. Use of continuing resolutions has grown in recent years. Controversy over spending levels for several government departments, such as Labor, Health and Human Services and Education, has been so great at times that those agencies have had to operate for entire fiscal years under continuing resolutions. Foreign aid programs were funded under the emergency measures for all of fiscal 1980 and 1981.

Continuing resolutions, like debt limit bills, have become politicized in recent years. On the assumption that the president will have to sign a continuing resolution or face the political consequences of closing down entire federal departments, Congress frequently has attached controversial legislative riders to these measures. Such riders, or nongermane amendments, have included pay raises for members and prohibitions on federal funding of abortions.

In 1981, however, President Reagan called that bluff. By late November of that year Congress had enacted only one of the regular appropriations bills for fiscal 1982. It therefore had to approve a continuing resolution to fund virtually the entire federal government. But the spending levels were higher than Reagan wanted, and he vetoed the "budget-busting" bill in November. The veto left government agencies without legal authority to operate, except for essential activities such as defense and law enforcement. Thousands of government workers left their jobs for part of the day; the rest were ordered to prepare to close down their offices. Congress quickly passed a new continuing resolution acceptable to the president, and most government workers returned to work the following day.

The 1974 budget law gave Congress a procedure for debating the president's budget as a whole. But the House and Senate still act on budget details in piecemeal fashion, through the 13 annual appropriations bills and often one or two supplemental appropriations measures. And power to shape actual government appropriations remains fragmented among 26 House and Senate subcommittees.

**House Handling of Appropriations.** In the House, the Appropriations Committee rivals Ways and Means in power and prestige. Traditionally composed of senior members elected from safe congressional districts, the Appropriations Committee for the most part has been a fiscally conservative body that customarily recommends cuts in the amounts requested in the president's budget.

Its 13 subcommittees have functioned largely as independent kingdoms. The subcommittees, organized along functional lines, divide up the president's budget requests soon after Congress receives them. Generally, members of the subcommittees become expert in their assigned areas. The subcommittees, and particularly their chairmen, consequently wield substantial power over spending.

Until the 1970s, most House Appropriations subcommittee hearings were closed, with testimony almost always restricted to that given by agency officials. A voluminous record of the hearings, along with the parent committee's report, usually was not made public until shortly before House floor action on the appropriation bill. As a result, few if any members not on the subcommittee were prepared to challenge the bill.

The Legislative Reorganization Act of 1970 opened all House committee and subcommittee hearings unless a majority of the committee determined otherwise. In 1974 the Appropriations Committee opened 90 percent of its hearings although almost half of its markup sessions remained closed. Nine of the panel's 13 subcommittees opened all of their markups in 1974 compared with only two in 1973.

House Democrats in the 1970s also took steps to weaken the hold on the committee by conservative Chairman George H. Mahon, D-Texas (1935-79), and other senior Democrats who chaired most of the subcommittees. In 1971 the House Democratic Caucus permitted the selection of all committee chairmen to be based on factors other than seniority. In 1975 the caucus went even further, requiring a secret vote on nominations for committee chairmen and all Appropriations subcommittee chairmen.

The Democratic Caucus in 1975 also voted to limit senior Democrats to serving on only two subcommittees of the same committee. Aimed mainly at the Appropriations Committee, that rule was intended to keep senior members from continuing to dominate the key subcommittees that handle defense, agriculture, and health, education and labor funding. Those changes gave committee liberals a stronger voice on the subcommittees. Liberal influence on the Appropriations Committee was enhanced in the mid-1970s by a caucus decision to maintain the ratio of Democrats to Republicans on the committee at two-to-one and to appoint more liberals when vacancies occurred.

As budget specialist Allen Schick has noted, in 1967 there were 30 Democrats and 21 Republicans on the Appropriations Committee, and conservative Democrats, with Republican support, controlled the committee. In 1977 the ratio was 37 Democrats to 18 Republicans. That meant that liberal and moderate Democrats often could overcome an alliance of conservative Democrats and Republicans in both committee and subcommittee deliberations on appropriations bills.[4]

The House procedure used for appropriations bills permits amendments from the floor. However, the prestige of the Appropriations Committee is such that relatively few major changes are made. Although the 1970s witnessed the offering of more amendments, by and large the amounts endorsed by the Appropriations Committee in the post-World War II period have been accepted by the House. Efforts to increase funding for various programs have concentrated on the Senate.

**Senate Handling of Appropriations.** Once an appropriation bill has been passed by the House, it is sent to the Senate and referred to the Appropriations Committee, where a parallel system of subcommittees exists. The Senate subcommittees review the work of the House at hearings that are open to the public. Because the House already has gone over a bill thoroughly, the Senate usually does not attempt to do the same amount of work on it; the time required and the heavy workload of most senators precludes the same detailed consideration that is given in the House.

Senate subcommittees normally restore some of the House-denied funds, although they may make cuts in other places. The Senate itself may add or restore more funds when the bill reaches the floor. Until the mid-1970s most Senate-passed appropriation bills were larger than the House-approved versions. Since the congressional budget process has been in use, the House-passed figures are frequently higher than the Senate appropriations. House-Senate disputes over funding are resolved in conference, generally by splitting the differences.

## Notes

1. For additional background on the House Ways and Means and Senate Finance committees, see John F. Manley, *The Politics of Finance, The House Committee on Ways and Means* (Boston: Little, Brown & Co., 1970); Allen Schick, *Congress and Money: Budgeting, Spending and Taxing* (Washington, D.C.: The Urban Institute, 1980), pp. 483-562.
2. *Congressional Quarterly Almanac 1981* (Washington, D.C.: Congressional Quarterly, 1982), pp. 91-104.
3. For additional background on the Appropriations committees, see Richard F. Fenno Jr., *The Power of the Purse: Appropriations Politics in Congress* (Boston: Little, Brown & Co., 1966); Schick, *Congress and Money*, pp. 415-481; Stephen Horn, *Unused Power: The Work of the Senate Committee on Appropriations* (Washington, D.C.: The Brookings Institution, 1970).
4. Allen Schick, "The Three-Ring Budget Process: The Appropriations, Tax and Budget Committees in Congress," in *The New Congress*, ed. Thomas E. Mann and Norman J. Ornstein (Washington, D.C.: American Enterprise Institute for Public Policy Research, 1981), p. 302.

# *Chapter 4*

## THE SEARCH FOR BUDGET CONTROL

The formulation of a comprehensive federal budget is a relatively recent development in the nation's history. The federal government has operated under a budget only since 1921. Perhaps ironically, Congress at that time granted the president power to shape the federal budget by giving the executive branch the tools to view federal fiscal policy as a whole and by requiring the chief executive to recommend to Congress how federal funds should be raised and spent.

Congress exercised its powers to tax, spend and borrow, but until 1975 it never successfully integrated those individual decisions into a comprehensive review of the budget. The diffusion of fiscal power among congressional committees may have been a political necessity for a smoothly running Congress, but it did not permit the centralization of decision-making needed for a coherent budget system. That institutional dispersion of power, combined with economic forces, made it more and more difficult for Congress to take responsibility for a federal budget that by the late 1970s appeared to be racing out of control.

### Budget Policy Before 1921

The federal government did not operate under a federal budget for its first 130 years, but, as Lewis Kimmel has noted, "The budget idea . . . was clearly in the minds of leading political and financial leaders as early as the Revolutionary and formative periods. The absence of logical or systematic budget methods during the early years and throughout the nineteenth century should not be construed as a lack of appreciation of the role of public finance." [1]

Ratification of the Constitution cleared the way for establishment of a government financial system. In September 1789 Congress enacted a law establishing the Treasury Department and requiring the secretary of the Treasury "to prepare and report estimates of the public revenues, and the public expenditures." However, according to Kimmel, "Alexander Hamilton's efforts in the direction of an executive budget were unsuccessful, mainly because of congressional jealousy and existing party divisions." [2]

Because the federal government relied on customs duties for the bulk of its revenues throughout the 19th century — and there was an abundance of such revenues — there was no need to weigh expenditures against revenues. Consequently, the budget-making process underwent a progressive deterioration. According to Kimmel, the first important step toward establishing a federal executive budget was taken in 1910, when President William Howard Taft appointed a Commission on Economy and Efficiency to study the need for a federal budget. The commission concluded that a restructuring of the system for determining and providing for the financial needs of the government was of paramount importance. But Congress resented the commission's proposed system, and the report was not even considered by the House Appropriations Committee, to which it was referred.[3]

## The 1921 Budget Act

After World War I, the diffuse appropriations system that had grown up in place of a budget procedure could no longer meet the needs of an increasingly complex government. Congress decided it must reorganize its financial machinery, both to retrench on expenditures and to tighten control over the administration of fiscal policy. The reorganization was accomplished through enactment of the Budget and Accounting Act of 1921. First, however, the House on June 1, 1920, restored exclusive spending powers to its Appropriations Committee and enlarged the committee to 35 members, from 21 (in 1982 the membership was 55). The Senate on March 6, 1922, similarly concentrated spending powers in its Appropriations Committee but left the membership at 16 (in 1982 it was 29).

In the Budget and Accounting Act, Congress sought to reform the financial machinery of the executive branch. The 1921 act established two important offices — the Bureau of the Budget and the General Accounting Office (GAO). The former was created to centralize fiscal management of the executive branch directly under the president; the latter was designed to strengthen congressional oversight of spending.

## Bureau of the Budget

With passage of the 1921 act, Congress ended the right of federal agencies to decide for themselves what appropriations levels to request from Congress. The Budget Bureau, serving under the president's direction, was to act as a central clearinghouse for budget requests.

Budget Circular 49, approved by President Warren G. Harding on Dec. 19, 1921, required all agency proposals for appropriations to be submitted to the president before they were presented to Congress. Agency proposals were to be studied for their relationship to "the president's financial program" and were to be sent to Capitol Hill only if approved by the president. The bureau, though placed in the Treasury, was kept under the supervision of the president.[4]

In 1935 President Franklin D. Roosevelt broadened the clearance function to include legislative as well as appropriation requests. According to political scientist Richard E. Neustadt, Roosevelt's new clearance system was not a mere extension of the budget process: "On the contrary . . . this was Roosevelt's creation, intended to protect not just his budget, but his prerogatives, his freedom of action, and his choice of policies in an era of fast-growing government and of determined presidential leadership." [5]

Roosevelt in 1939 issued, and Congress approved, Reorganization Plan No. 1, creating the Executive Office of the President and transferring the Budget Bureau from the Treasury to the new office. The bureau's legislative clearance procedures were further strengthened by Roosevelt and later presidents.

In 1970 President Richard Nixon streamlined the budget process by restructuring the Bureau of the Budget. The new office, called the Office of Management and Budget (OMB), was given sweeping authority to coordinate the execution of government programs as well as the Budget Bureau's old role of advising the president on agency funding requests. In 1974 Congress approved legislation making future OMB directors and deputy directors subject to Senate confirmation.

## General Accounting Office

Congress, in setting up the General Accounting Office (GAO), attempted to strengthen its surveillance of government spending. The GAO is headed by the comptroller general and an assistant comptroller general, appointed by the president with the àdvice and consent of the Senate, for a period of 15 years. They can be removed only by joint resolution of Congress, thus making the agency responsible to Congress rather than the administration. The comptroller general was granted wide powers to investigate all matters relating to the use of public funds and was required to report annually to Congress and to include in his report recommendations for greater economy and efficiency.

Many of the auditing powers and duties of the comptroller general already had been established by the Dockery Act of 1894, which assigned them to the then new office of the comptroller of the Treasury. But under that act the comptroller and his staff remained executive branch officers, and Congress lacked its own agency for independent review of executive expenditures.

In their book *Federal Budget Policy*, David J. Ott and Attiat F. Ott described the three major types of audits made by the GAO:

> Recently, the comprehensive audit has become the most important. This audit concentrates on the accounting and reporting system used by a particular agency and checks transactions selectively. The general audit examines the accounts of agency disbursing and certifying officers to determine the legality of each transaction. If illegal or improper handling of receipts or expenditures is discovered, recovery procedures are instituted against the responsible officer. The commercial audit is applied to government corporations and enterprises. No recovery is possible in this case, but Congress is informed of questionable or improper practices. [6]

The results of GAO audits are transmitted to Congress by the comptroller general. The results of special investigations of particular agencies and the annual report are referred to the House and Senate Government Operations committees.

## Early Budget Experiments

Although Congress saw the need to centralize budget making in the executive branch, it left authority for its own fiscal decisions dispersed among its committees. As a deliberative body representing different regions and economic interests, Congress always has been ambivalent about budget control.

In the few instances that the House and Senate had voted for overall budget restraints, they were unable or unwilling to cut enough from individual programs to meet those goals. Throughout the 30 years following World War II the momentum of those separate spending decisions sooner or later overwhelmed whatever devices Congress used to try to keep the budget in check.

Immediately after World War II, Congress attempted to draw up its own budget priorities to relate appropriations to overall fiscal objectives. In three years of trying, the House and Senate never fully implemented a legislative budget process created by the Legislative Reorganization Act of 1946. After unsuccessful attempts in 1947, 1948 and 1949, Congress abandoned the experiment as an unqualified failure.

Similar in some respects to the reform procedures later adopted by Congress in 1974, the 1946 act required Congress to approve a concurrent resolution setting a ceiling on the amount to be appropriated in each fiscal year. The ceiling was to be part of a budget drawn up by Congress based on revenue and spending estimates prepared by a massive Joint Budget Committee composed of all members of the House and Senate Appropriations committees and of the tax-writing House Ways and Means and Senate Finance committees.

One of the principal reasons the legislative budget failed was the inability of the Joint Budget Committee to make accurate estimates of spending early in the congressional session, before individual agency requests had been considered in detail. In addition, the committee was said to be inadequately staffed and, with more than 100 members, much too unwieldy for effective operation.[7]

Failure of the legislative budget prompted a serious effort in Congress in 1950 to combine the numerous separate appropriations bills into one omnibus measure. The traditional practice of acting on the separate bills one by one made it difficult to hold total outlays in check. Although the omnibus approach adopted by the House Appropriations Committee in 1950 was well received by those seeking reductions in federal spending, the committee voted the following year to go back to the traditional method of handling appropriations bills separately. The omnibus bill required more time and effort than separate bills, opponents argued. Equally important was the opposition of the House Appropriations subcommittee chairmen, who feared that their power would be eroded under the omnibus approach.[8]

With the failure of those efforts, Congress' only means of budget restraint was to write into appropriations bills specific restrictions on how funds could be spent. Those provisions provided little overall control on spending, and for the remainder of the 1950s and 1960s Congress discussed several other plans for restraining outlays, but no steps were taken.

## Spending Ceilings

The situation came to a head in the late 1960s and early 1970s, when spending for Great Society programs and military outlays for the Vietnam War accelerated the budget deficit. Distressed by ever-increasing levels of federal spending growth, House Republicans launched an economy drive in 1966. Their first efforts — to cut several annual appropriations bills by 5 percent — were unsuccessful.[9]

Fiscal conservatives were more successful in the next four years. Four times between 1967 and 1970 Congress wrote federal spending limits into law. But those limits proved ineffective. Congress simply raised or ignored the limits when they proved too low to accommodate spending required by existing programs. No spending ceiling was enacted in 1971, but Nixon's request for a fiscal 1973 spending ceiling provoked a dispute with Congress that was thrashed out amid the 1972 presidential election campaign.

In what Democrats conceded was a masterful political stroke, Nixon in July 1972 asked Congress for authority to trim federal spending as he saw fit to meet a $250 billion ceiling on fiscal 1973 outlays. If such power were denied, Nixon warned, Congress would be responsible for tax increases in 1973. The House complied by writing the ceiling into a debt limit extension bill, but the Senate balked at giving the president unlimited discretion to cut federal outlays, and the ceiling was eventually dropped altogether.

Controversy in 1973 and 1974 also killed enactment of any spending ceiling. President Gerald R. Ford tried to regain the initiative on spending restraint in 1975 by proposing that continuation of tax cuts approved earlier in the year be offset by spending reductions. But congressional Democrats, just starting to use the new House and Senate budget procedures for the first time, were unwilling to bind themselves to steep cutbacks before considering the administration's 1976 budget proposal.

## Nixon, Ford Vetoes

With Congress unwilling to observe spending limitations, both Nixon and Ford resorted to the president's veto power to hold down outlays. In some cases, the threat of a veto prompted Congress to tailor appropriations measures to accommodate the president's budget plans. Nixon vetoed five bills in 1970, three in 1971, 16 in 1972 and five more in 1973, primarily on budgetary grounds. Congress overrode two 1970 vetoes, but the others were sustained. Of the seven measures Ford vetoed on budgetary grounds in 1975, Congress overrode four. The battle of wills continued in 1976 as Congress continued to pass legislation designed to stimulate the severely recessed economy through increased spending.

In addition, Congress steadfastly resisted proposals by both Nixon and Ford to trim government costs by terminating some programs, curtailing others and turning some categorical grants to state and local governments into block grants with fewer administrative requirements. In 1973, after his landslide re-election in 1972, Nixon had proposed a fiscal 1974 budget that outlined plans to curtail or eliminate more than 100 federal programs through administrative actions. Concerned about potential erosion of congressional powers and Nixon's sweeping interpretation of presidential authority, House and Senate leaders protested Nixon's claim to a re-election mandate for spending cutbacks. They also pushed ahead with plans to curb the president's power to impound appropriated funds and to set up procedures for Congress to legislate its own budget each year.

## Conflict Over Impoundments

Nixon's campaign to curb federal spending brought to a head long-simmering differences over whether the government must spend all the money that Congress appropriates. Continuing a practice that many presidents had followed, Nixon in the early 1970s impounded billions of dollars Congress had provided for certain government programs. The Constitution does not spell out whether the president is required to promptly spend funds appropriated by Congress or whether he can make independent judgments on the timing and even the necessity of putting appropriated funds to use. Despite that constitutional ambiguity, presidents have impounded funds almost from the beginning of the Republic.

In the post-World War II period, presidents more and more began to use impoundment as a fiscal policy tool. Presidents Harry S Truman, Dwight D. Eisenhower and John F. Kennedy all got into scrapes with Congress by withholding appropriated funds for defense projects. In 1966 President Lyndon B. Johnson cut back federal spending by $5.3 billion to curb the inflationary impact of the Vietnam War; major impoundments included $1.1 billion in highway funds, $760 million for housing and urban development and large amounts for education, agriculture, health and welfare.

**Nixon Impoundments.** Nixon's extensive use of the power to withhold funds intensified the conflict between a Republican administration pledged to hold domestic spending down and a Democratic Congress determined to preserve the health, welfare, environment, public works and other programs it had put in place during the preceding decade. According to Louis Fisher, a Congressional Research Service specialist, "[T]he Nixon administration treated the president's budget as a ceiling on Congress. Any funds that Congress added to the president's budget could be set aside and left unobligated." [10]

Nixon argued that he was withholding funds only as a financial management technique, primarily to slow inflation through temporary reductions in federal spending. House and Senate Democratic leaders contended that Nixon used impoundments to impose his own priorities in defiance of laws passed by Congress. The dispute embittered Nixon's relations with Congress and probably contributed to congressional support for 1974 impeachment proceedings that forced the president to resign in the wake of the Watergate scandal.

A 1975 Supreme Court decision subsequently backed the congressional position. Congress in the meantime had restricted the use of impoundments as part of its landmark 1974 budget law. *(The 1974 Budget Act, pp. 57-65)* In the following years, Congress monitored more closely executive branch agencies and policies to make sure that legislative mandates were observed.

**New Impoundment Procedures.** The 1974 budget law set up two procedures whereby presidents could delay or cancel the expenditure of congressionally appropriated funds: deferrals and rescissions. The act's impoundment provisions were tacked on as Title X of the 1974 law.

To simply delay spending temporarily, the president under the law can defer outlays. The deferral stands unless either the House or Senate passes a resolution directing that the money be spent. Congress may act on a deferral at any time. If the president feels the money should not be spent at all, he must propose that Congress rescind the appropriation making the funds available. In that case, both the House and Senate must approve the rescission within 45 days. If the two houses do not act, the president must release the funds at the end of the 45-day period.

Title X requires the president to keep Congress informed of impoundments by sending deferrals and rescission requests to Capitol Hill. The General Accounting Office may review deferral and rescission messages for accuracy, and the comptroller general has authority to report to Congress any executive branch action that impounds funds without proper notification of Congress. Such a report triggers rescission or deferral proceedings as though the president had made a request to Congress. The comptroller general also may reclassify deferrals as rescissions, or vice versa, and may go to federal court to enforce the law's impoundment requirements.

There is disagreement, even within Congress, about exactly what Title X was intended to accomplish and did accomplish. Congressional and executive branch employees who must deal with Title X generally agree that its language is vague in many respects and is without sufficient legislative history to explain Congress' intent. Congressional critics of the procedure find fault with the rescission provisions because the president, by asking that appropriations be canceled, can block spending for nearly seven weeks. Even if Congress refuses to approve a rescission measure, the law provides no opportunity for the House and Senate to force the administration to spend the funds before the 45-day period is up.

On the other hand, some claim that Title X erodes the president's basic budgetary powers by exposing to congressional scrutiny previously hidden budget-juggling maneuvers of the executive branch. That exposure, coupled with Congress' power to block presidential impoundments, worried some observers — generally, officials in the executive branch. They feared that Title X, along with other new congressional budget authority, might tip the spending powers toward Congress by destroying presidential control over the federal budget. Probably the complaint most often heard about Title X initially was that the requirements of the law generated a mountain of paperwork by requiring formal action on administrative matters and other minutiae that were never brought through the system in the past.

**Ford and Carter Impoundments.** Criticisms aside, the congressional authors of the 1974 law predicted that impoundment proposals for policy reasons would amount to only a few dozen each year. But once the law went into effect, their estimates proved low. President Ford requested 330 deferrals and 150 rescissions in less than three years. Fisher classified 120 deferrals and 133 rescissions that Ford sought as policy impoundments rather than routine cost-saving steps. "The large number of policy rescission proposals shows that Ford attempted to continue the presidential custom of reshaping budget priorities enacted by Congress," Fisher contended. ". . . Ford used the rescission-deferral mechanism to frustrate congressional adjustments to his budget." [11]

President Jimmy Carter proposed far fewer policy deferrals, and Congress took exception to fewer impoundment actions. But defense-minded members protested in 1977 when Carter took steps to terminate contracts for the B-1 bomber and Minuteman III missile programs and then requested rescissions two weeks later.

**Reagan Impoundments.** In 1981 and 1982 President Ronald Reagan used deferrals to hold fiscal 1982 spending to the austere levels in his economic recovery program, and impoundment again began to earn the bad name it had during the Nixon administration. In 1981, according to Rep. Norman Y. Mineta, D-Calif., chairman of the House Budget Committee's Task Force on Enforcement, Credit and Multi-year Budgeting, Reagan proposed $16.2 billion in rescissions and $7.5 billion in deferrals. Congress supported the president on 90 percent of the rescissions and 95 percent of the deferrals. By the end of March 1982, Reagan had submitted rescissions totaling $10.8 billion and deferrals totaling $7.8 billion.[12]

The main source of consternation, however, was not the number of rescissions and deferrals requested but the belief among some members of Congress that the administration was circumventing the process and impounding funds without telling Congress what it had done. "Through a series of mechanisms, such as failing to report impoundments, reprogramming funds without congressional actions, and misclassifying impoundments, the administration has been able to pursue its own objectives," Mineta said at a hearing of his panel in March 1982.[13]

By April 1982 two groups had filed suit against the administration. One charged the administration with illegally impounding $21.8 million appropriated for the Solar Energy and Energy Conservation Bank. The second sought the release of nearly $20 million in federal library service funds, with the result that the Department of Education later that same month released the library funds.

## Notes

1. Lewis H. Kimmel, *Federal Budget and Fiscal Policy, 1789-1958* (Washington, D.C.: The Brookings Institution, 1959), p. 2.

2. Ibid., p. 3.
3. Ibid., p. 4; see also Frederic A. Ogg and P. Orman Ray, *Introduction to American Government*, 10th ed. (New York: Appleton-Century-Crofts, 1951), pp. 505-512; and Daniel T. Selko, *The Federal Financial System* (Washington, D.C.: The Brookings Institution, 1940), pp. 101-131.
4. Louis Fisher, *Presidential Spending Power* (Princeton, N.J.: Princeton University Press, 1975), p. 39.
5. Richard E. Neustadt, "Presidency and Legislation: The Growth of Central Clearance," *American Political Science Review,* 48 (1954): 641.
6. David J. Ott and Attiat F. Ott, *Federal Budget Policy,* rev. ed. (Washington, D.C.: The Brookings Institution, 1969), p. 41.
7. *Congress and the Nation*, 5 vols., *Congress and the Nation: 1945-1964,* vol. 1 (Washington, D.C: Congressional Quarterly, 1965), I: 349, 352, 354.
8. George B. Galloway, *The Legislative Process in Congress* (New York: Thomas Y. Crowell Co., 1955), pp. 123-124; Robert Ash Wallace, *Congressional Control of Federal Spending* (Detroit: Wayne State University Press, 1960), pp. 131-136.
9. For additional information on spending ceiling legislation, see *Congress and the Nation: 1965-1968,* vol. 2 (Washington, D.C.: Congressional Quarterly, 1969), II: 135-136, 140; *Congress and the Nation: 1969-1972,* vol. 3 (Washington, D. C.: Congressional Quarterly, 1973), III: 64, 67, 72-75; and *Congress and the Nation: 1973-1976,* vol. 4 (Washington, D. C.: Congressional Quarterly, 1977), IV: 62, 63, 65.
10. Louis Fisher, "Effect of the Budget Act of 1974 on Agency Operations," in *The Congressional Budget Process After Five Years,* ed. Ralph Penner (Washington, D.C.: American Enterprise Institute for Public Policy Research, 1981), p. 150; for additional background on impoundments, see *Congressional Quarterly Almanac 1973* (Washington, D.C.: Congressional Quarterly, 1974), pp. 252-262.
11. Fisher, "Effect of the Budget Act," pp. 152-153.
12. Dale Tate, "Impoundment, An Old Dispute Resurfaces," *Congressional Quarterly Weekly Report,* April 17, 1982, pp. 853-854.
13. Ibid, p. 853.

## *Chapter 5*

# 1974 BUDGET ACT

Frustrated by the impoundment battle and acknowledging that it had forfeited control of the budget through its haphazard treatment of presidential spending requests, Congress in 1974 set up a new process, significantly changing the way it handled the federal budget. Under the Congressional Budget and Impoundment Control Act of 1974, Congress votes each year to set specific spending, tax and deficit limits.

For the first time since the legislative budget experiments of the post-World War II years, lawmakers are forced to consider thoroughly the president's fiscal policy goals as they act on the annual appropriations measures. And by requiring Congress to set initial budget targets — and subsequently to adhere to them or make adjustments — the budget law compels the House and Senate to go on record for each fiscal year on how much the government should spend, how much revenue it should raise and how much money it should borrow to make up for any deficit.

The budget law steered a careful course through the cross-currents of congressional politics. It left the jurisdictions of the existing tax and Appropriations committees intact and it left legislative committees free to push new and additional spending proposals. The 1974 measure did not require a balanced budget or impose specific spending ceilings. Instead it superimposed an annual budget review process on top of the yearly procedure of appropriating funds for government agencies.

### Genesis of the Process

In revising its budgetary procedures, Congress undertook a task that had been tried and abandoned in the budget experiments nearly 25 years earlier. But in the early 1970s, in the midst of angry spending fights with Nixon, congressional leaders finally concluded that the House and Senate had to put their fiscal procedures in order to hold their own in future budget policy battles.

After a lively political sparring match completed a month before the 1972 presidential election, Congress denied Nixon's request to set a $250 billion ceiling on fiscal 1973 spending and the authority necessary to enforce it. But it did enact a little-noticed provision setting up a joint House-Senate study committee to review the way Congress acted on the budget. The 32-member panel, composed almost entirely of members from the House and Senate tax-writing and Appropriations committees, proposed major changes in congressional procedures in April 1973. Their recommendations included establishment of House and Senate Budget committees. The panel urged enactment of a first concurrent resolution early in each session to set limits on spending and appropriations for the coming fiscal year, followed by a second resolution later in the session to adjust ceilings and subceilings as necessary to meet unanticipated budget requirements.

The joint committee plan called for instituting procedures requiring that amendments to budget resolutions raising outlays for one program category be accompanied by equivalent cuts from another category or by tax increases to provide the additional funding. It also proposed that all future backdoor spending programs, including entitlements, be subject to spending ceilings set through the annual appropriation process. Other proposals included binding limits on outlays written into appropriations measures and a general appropriation bill to reconcile spending totals at the end of each congressional session.

What followed during the rest of 1973 and first six months of 1974 turned into a complex exercise in congressional power brokering. Powerful committee chairmen jockeyed behind the scenes to preserve their panels' existing authority to shape tax and spending decisions. Conservative members sought budget procedures that would restrict congressional spending habits as much as possible, while liberals resisted proposals that they felt would squeeze funding for domestic programs.

After considerable debate, the House passed its version of the bill in December 1973. The Senate's compromise version was passed without dissent in March 1974. Conferees negotiated further refinements, particularly on impoundment controls, and the conference report won easy approval in both houses in June. President Nixon signed the final measure into law on July 12, 1974, less than a month before the threat of impeachment forced him to resign.

## Provisions of the Act

The new budget act set up a permissive, and in many ways ambiguous, process for Congress to act on the budget. That process and the major features of the act are described in this section.

**Budget Committees.** To give Congress a more expert perspective on budget totals and on fiscal policy requirements, the budget act established House and Senate Budget committees, which study and recommend changes in the president's budget. To the 23-member House Budget Committee, the act assigned five seats to Ways and Means Committee members and five to Appropriations Committee members. The remaining seats are occupied by one member from each of the 11 legislative committees, one member from the majority leadership and one from the minority leadership. The act rotated House Budget Committee membership by prohibiting any member from serving for more than four years out of a 10-year period. Members on the committee must serve for a full Congress.

The 15-member Senate Budget Committee is picked by normal Senate committee selection procedures. No rotation is required.

**Congressional Budget Office.** The act established an office within Congress to provide the experts and the computer support services needed to absorb and analyze information that accompanies the president's budget. The act requires the Congressional Budget Office to make its staff and resources available to all congressional committees and members, but with priority given to work for the House and Senate Budget committees. The office is run by a director appointed for a four-year term by the Speaker of the House and the president pro tempore of the Senate.

**Budget Submission.** To give Congress more time to consider the budget during its annual sessions, which start in January, the law pushed back the start of the fiscal year, formerly July 1, to Oct. 1, effective with fiscal 1977.

To give Congress a quicker start in shaping the budget, the act required the executive branch to submit a "current services" budget by Nov. 10 for the fiscal year beginning the following Oct. 1. Building on the programs and funding levels in effect for the fiscal year that had started the month before, the November current services budget projects the spending required to maintain those programs at existing commit-

## Congress Cloaks Backdoor Spending . . .

Following is a description of the various ways that Congress can shield federal spending from the annual appropriations process.

### Entitlement Programs

Federal entitlement programs range from the massive ones, such as Social Security, Medicare and interest on the national debt, to relatively small, local programs, such as an indemnity for dairy farmers whose milk is contaminated by chemicals or other toxic substances. Federal programs are entitlements if they provide benefits to which the recipients — individuals or, in some cases, government agencies — have a legally enforceable right. Entitlements today have become the major obligation of federal taxpayers. In fiscal 1980, 36 major entitlement programs were on the books, committing the government to pay out $342.9 billion.

Each entitlement is a benefit that some past Congress deemed so important that it bound the federal government to pay it, with the threat of judicial action if necessary to force Uncle Sam to write the check. Entitlements are not totally uncontrollable; Congress can change the basic laws that set them up, but such changes are seldom successful. A notable exception occurred in 1981 when Congress, in making major cuts in federal spending, cut back several entitlement programs.

### Contract Authority

Before passage of the Budget and Impoundment Control Act of 1974, a favorite form of backdoor spending was the use of contract authority, which allows government agencies to enter into contracts without immediately providing money to pay the debts thereby incurred. When the bills do come due, the Appropriations committees have no choice but to provide the money. The budget act required that new contract authority be subject to the appropriations process. But it did not affect existing authority, which agencies can continue to use to enter into contracts. According to a 1976 study, more than $200 billion in existing contract authority could be used in the future.

### Borrowing Authority

A similar type of backdoor spending is in the form of borrowing authority granted by Congress to federal agencies. Agencies can borrow

## ... In Various Resourceful Disguises

from either the Treasury or the public; appropriations are required to pay off the debts incurred. Like contract authority, new borrowing authority was controlled by the budget act. But a large volume remains for future use. Federal agencies have about $90 billion in specific unused borrowing authority; this can be used without further congressional action.

### Guaranteed Loans

Federal guarantees for private loans is another type of uncontrollable spending. Under this arrangement, the federal government does not put up any money to begin with, but only promises to repay a loan if the borrower is unable to do so. Federal Housing Administration and Veterans Administration loan programs account for two-thirds of federal loan guarantees. Loan guarantees are particularly uncontrollable because spending is dependent on the financial health of millions of borrowers, large and small. Each default on a loan creates an unavoidable obligation on the government.

### Off-budget Agencies

A different kind of uncontrollable spending involves the so-called off-budget agencies. The budgets for these agencies, which include the Postal Service and the Federal Financing Bank, are not included in the spending limits established under the 1974 budget act. No clear rule explains why some agencies are on the budget and some are not. In many cases, activities that are carried out off the budget are very similar to activities that are included in the budget. Historically, a number of agencies have been converted to off-budget status to avoid presidential impoundments.

### Tax Expenditures

Critics of tax expenditures also claim that they are a form of backdoor spending. Tax expenditures are exemptions or advantages granted through the tax laws to achieve a specific purpose. They are not expenditures in the sense of funds actually spent, but they do represent revenue deliberately foregone by the government. A popular tax expenditure, which was enacted to encourage home ownership, is the deduction permitted for interest paid on home mortgages.

ment levels, without policy changes, through the following fiscal year. The Joint Economic Committee is directed to review the current services budget outlook and report its evaluation to Congress by Dec. 31.

The president submits his annual budget to Congress about Jan. 20. In addition to the customary budget totals and breakdowns, the act requires the budget document to include a list of existing and proposed tax expenditures — revenues lost to the Treasury through preferential tax treatment of certain activities and income.

The act also requires the president's budget to include estimates of costs for programs whose funds must be appropriated one full year before they are obligated. Other provisions require that the budget figures be presented in terms of national needs, agency missions and basic programs. The budget also must include five-year projections of expected spending under federal programs.

**Budget Resolution**. After reviewing the president's budget proposals, and considering the advice of the Congressional Budget Office and other committees, the House and Senate Budget committees draw up a concurrent resolution outlining a tentative alternative federal budget. Under the law's timetable, congressional committees have until March 15 to report their budget recommendations to the Budget committees. The budget office report is due on April 1. By April 15 the Budget committees must report concurrent resolutions to the House and Senate. By May 15 Congress must clear the initial budget resolution. *(Budget timetable, box, p. 64)*

The initial resolution sets budget target totals for appropriations, outlays, taxes, the surplus or deficit and the federal debt. Within those overall targets, the resolution breaks down appropriations and spending among the functional categories — defense, health and income security, for example — used in the president's budget document. The resolution also includes any recommended changes in tax revenues and in the level of the federal debt ceiling.

Once enacted, the first budget resolution guides but does not bind Congress as it acts on the separate appropriations bills and other measures providing budget authority for spending on federal programs. No measure appropriating funds, changing taxes or the public debt level, or creating a new entitlement program may be considered by either house before adoption of the first budget resolution. In the Senate, however, that prohibition may be waived by majority vote. To clear the way for prompt action on appropriation bills before the fiscal year begins, the law requires that all bills authorizing appropriations be reported by May 15, the deadline for enactment of the budget resolution. That requirement may be waived, however, by majority vote in either house.

Exempted from the May 15 reporting deadline are Social Security legislation, dealing with a variety of trust funds and welfare programs, and other entitlement legislation that may not be considered on the floor until the budget resolution is cleared.

After enactment of the budget resolution, Congress begins processing the 13 regular appropriations bills for the upcoming fiscal year. The law directs the House Appropriations Committee to try to complete action on all appropriation measures and submit a report summarizing its decisions before sending the first bill to the floor.

All appropriations bills have to be cleared by the middle of September — no later than the seventh day after Labor Day. That deadline may be waived, however, for any appropriation bill that was delayed because Congress had not acted promptly on the required authorizing legislation.

If Congress so provides in its initial budget resolution, appropriations and entitlement bills may be held up after they are cleared. Under that procedure, no appropriation bill is sent to the president until Congress has completed a reconciliation of its initial budget targets with the 13-separate spending measures.

**Reconciliation**. After finishing action on all appropriation and other spending bills in mid-September, Congress takes another overall look at its work on the budget. By Sept. 15 Congress must adopt a second budget resolution that either affirms or revises the budget targets set by the initial resolution. If the congressional decisions made in the separate appropriation bills do not fit the final budget resolution totals, the second resolution may dictate changes in appropriations (both for the upcoming fiscal year or in those carried over from previous fiscal years), entitlements, revenues and the debt limit.

The second budget resolution would direct the committees that had jurisdiction over those matters to draft legislation making the required changes. If all the required changes fall within the jurisdiction of a single committee in each house — for example, appropriations changes that the Appropriations committees would consider — those committees then would send a reconciliation bill to the floor.

## Budget Timetable

**Late January:** President submits budget (15 days after Congress convenes).

**March 15:** All legislative committees submit program estimates and reviews to Budget committees.

**April 15:** Budget committees report first resolution.

**May 15:** Committees must report authorization bills by this date.

**May 15:** Congress completes action on first resolution. Before its adoption, neither house may consider new budget authority or spending authority bills, revenue changes or debt limit changes.

**May 15 through the 7th day after Labor Day:** Congress completes action on all budget and spending authority bills.

**Sept. 15:** Congress completes action on second resolution. Thereafter, neither house may consider any bill, amendment or conference report that results in an increase over outlay or budget authority figures, or a reduction in revenues, beyond the amounts in the second resolution.

**Sept. 25:** Congress completes action on reconciliation bill or another resolution. Congress may not adjourn until it completes action on the second resolution and reconciliation measure, if any.

**Oct. 1:** Fiscal year begins.

If the changes involve two committees — for example, appropriations changes by the Appropriations committees and tax changes by the House Ways and Means and Senate Finance committees — those committees would submit recommendations to the Budget committees. The Budget committees then would combine the recommendations without substantial change and send them to the floor as a reconciliation bill.

If Congress withholds all appropriation and entitlement bills from the president, reconciliation may be accomplished by passage of a resolution directing the House clerk and secretary of the Senate to make necessary changes in the bills previously cleared. A reconciliation bill still could be needed, however, to change tax levels or other provisions already enacted into law. *(Reagan and 1981 Reconciliation, pp. 68-69)*

### Backdoor Spending

The 1974 law attempted to bring most forms of new backdoor spending programs under the appropriations process, but existing backdoor programs remained outside that process. The bill required annual appropriation of funds for new contract authority or borrowing authority programs. The bill also established special procedures for entitlement programs. No entitlements could be enacted until Congress had adopted the first budget resolution and set forth guidelines on how much spending on new programs would be permissible.

If an authorizing committee subsequently reported a new entitlement program that exceeded the committee's allocation, as established by the first budget resolution, the bill would be referred to the Appropriations Committee. That committee then would have 15 days to report an amendment setting a limit on appropriations for the program. If the Appropriations Committee did not act within 15 days, the measure would be presumed reported by the authorization committee.

Exempted from the act's backdoor spending procedures were all Social Security trust funds, all trust funds that received 90 percent or more of their financing from designated taxes rather than from general revenues, general revenue sharing funds, insured and guaranteed loans, the federal government and independent government corporations, and gifts to the government.

## *Chapter 6*

# THE BUDGET PROCESS AT WORK

Ever since the budget process was approved in 1974, Congress has argued over how it should be used. Conservatives, at times allied with Republican presidents, have viewed the process as a tool for enforcing wholesale spending cutbacks. Liberals, joined by interest groups lobbying for certain federal programs, have tried to use the procedures to shift resources from defense to the government's domestic functions. Within Congress itself, House and Senate committee rivalry fragmented budget debates as the authorization panels fought to protect the programs they had helped create.

Through the last half of the 1970s, Congress in its annual budget resolutions generally accommodated political pressures within the House and Senate to leave room for new programs and additional spending. Throughout that period the nation's economy was in a slow and halting recovery from the steep recession of 1974-75. Federal fiscal policy, while calling for an eventual balance, gave Congress latitude to add new spending even while budget deficits persisted.

But by the end of the decade the inflation rate was running at an annual rate of more than 20 percent, and federal outlays were far outpacing revenues. Voters turned out President Jimmy Carter in favor of Republican Ronald Reagan, who promised to curb inflation and bring the federal budget into balance through a combination of spending and tax cuts. The 1980 elections also gave Republicans control of the Senate and weakened the Democratic majority in the House.

Reagan's election — and its obvious political message — forced Congress to start disciplining the budget to fiscal scarcity. But faced with the uncomfortable task of drawing the line on federal spending, Congress once again seemingly abdicated to the president. Congress in 1981 cut fiscal 1982 spending by $35.2 billion, but those cutbacks generally imposed Reagan's spending priorities and endorsed the president's fiscal policy. The success of the budget reconciliation process in 1981 demonstrated that Congress could use the process to make politically difficult decisions so long as it had the determined backing and constant prodding of a committed president.

But a backlash also was building in Congress — particularly among members of the authorization committees — who felt that reconciliation had abused normal congressional procedures. Sen. William Proxmire, D-Wis., warned that "unless we stop short, take stock and revise some of the procedures, the budget reform act itself may die or, worse, may destroy the Senate as a distributive body." [1] And by 1982 it appeared that continuation of the process might depend on Congress' ability to choose from among several politically unpalatable options — enormous deficits, tax increases or further spending cuts.

## Testing the New Procedure: 1975-80

Through the first five years the new budget process was used, the House and Senate moved uncertainly. At times, conflicting political pressures raised doubts that the beleaguered system could continue to work. Yet, even though the House and Senate often slipped badly behind the timetable that the budget law established, the process functioned more or less intact.

At first, congressional use of the budget mechanism was largely a matter of accommodation. House and Senate leaders, anxious to keep the process going, steered away from proposing budget resolutions that would force legislative and Appropriations committees to compete openly for budget resources. The Budget committees considered the spending needs for each of 19 budget categories before setting an overall total, rather than first establishing the size of the overall budget. As budget specialist Allen Schick pointed out, "At no time during the first five years of budgeting did either committee vote explicitly to take from one function in order to give more to another. . . . " [2]

As long as Congress remained in an expansive mood, the House and Senate were able to construct budgets in a piecemeal fashion that satisfied the particular interests of various committees and groups. But when Congress tried to shift toward fiscal austerity in mid-1979, it encountered much rougher going.

In both 1979 and 1980 Congress slipped badly behind the budget act's timetable. Congress' budget-making problems were compounded by often inaccurate economic projections. Congressional Budget Office economic forecasts often were less optimistic than the administration's. Both White House and congressional experts misread economic trends, and Congress in midstream found itself forced to make large changes in budget estimates that dramatically altered the expected deficits.

## The Reagan Reconciliation

By the end of 1980 the congressional budget process was being dismissed by some members as irrelevant to fiscal discipline. Many charged that the process had declined into a meaningless exercise having a negligible impact on federal spending. Still, by putting the reconciliation mechanism to use — at the end of a year in which budget balancing efforts had collapsed — Congress salvaged some hope for the process. By following through on reconciliation, Congress in fact set a precedent for a sweeping 1981 budget-cutting feat that gave the budget process unexpected, and to some observers unintended, power to change the whole course of government.

President Reagan, after taking office in 1981, asked Congress to cut Carter's proposed fiscal 1982 budget by $41.4 billion through spending reductions in more than 80 federal programs. With Reagan's Office of Management and Budget (OMB) director, former Rep. David A. Stockman, R-Mich. (1977-81), masterminding the campaign, Republican leaders who had just taken control of the Senate agreed early in the 1981 session to consolidate the budget reductions in one reconciliation measure. By packaging the budget cuts and forcing the House and Senate to vote on a single measure, Republicans hoped to prevent congressional committees and interest groups from chipping away at the president's budget plan through piecemeal changes.

The strategy worked — far better than many dismayed Democrats could have imagined. On Aug. 13 Reagan signed into law the deepest and farthest-reaching package of budget cuts ever approved by Congress. The final reconciliation measure was expected to reduce fiscal 1982 spending by nearly $35.2 billion. In all, the package trimmed estimated outlays in fiscal years 1981-84 by $130.6 billion.[3]

Senate Budget Committee Chairman Pete V. Domenici, R-N.M., proclaimed during the final 1981 debate: "... the entire reconciliation process has done two crucial things: It has strengthened the legislative process, and it has restored confidence in Congress among the American people." [4] But other members were not convinced. Reagan's success startled longtime congressional observers who fully expected Congress to pick the administration's budget cuts apart. The Senate, with its Republican majority, moved smoothly to rubber-stamp the president's requests. The House, in contrast, went along only after momentous floor battles that overturned alternative Democratic budget strategies.

## Future of Budget Process

Congress set up the budget process in part to defend its tax and spending authority from aggressive presidential claims. But after the 1981 reconciliation fight, some members worried that the procedure in fact gave the White House an opening to once more usurp control over budget legislation. The Reagan reconciliation onslaught brought reminders of the "imperial presidency" and fears that Congress was paving the way for abdicating its powers to the executive.

Reconciliation "has strengthened the president in that I can't envision him succeeding in making such large budget cuts without it," said Schick in an assessment of Reagan's budget successes in 1981. But the success was in large part a show of the president's "political skill and popularity — that positively made it work." Schick added:

> While a disadvantaged majority might be subdued for a period of time, it will not endlessly accept its subordinate status. If reconciliation on this year's scale is attempted too often, the process will face strong challenges in the future. [5]

Indeed, by the fall of Reagan's first year, the House and Senate clearly had little appetite for tackling the second round of budget cuts Reagan requested for fiscal 1982. Congress was unable to do more than pass a *pro forma* second budget resolution for fiscal 1982. And by mid-1982 Congress had met none of the early deadlines imposed by the budget act even though congressional leaders had met regularly with White House officials to work out a fiscal 1983 budget that would be acceptable to the president and Congress.

## Notes

1. Dale Tate, "Reconciliation's Long-Term Consequences," *Congressional Quarterly Weekly Report*, Aug. 15, 1981, p. 1464.
2. Allen Schick, *Congress and Money: Budgeting, Spending and Taxing* (Washington, D.C.: The Urban Institute, 1980), p. 333.
3. *Congressional Quarterly Almanac 1981* (Washington, D.C.: Congressional Quarterly, 1982), pp. 247-270.
4. Tate, "Reconciliation's Long-Term Consequences," p. 1464.
5. Ibid., p. 1465.

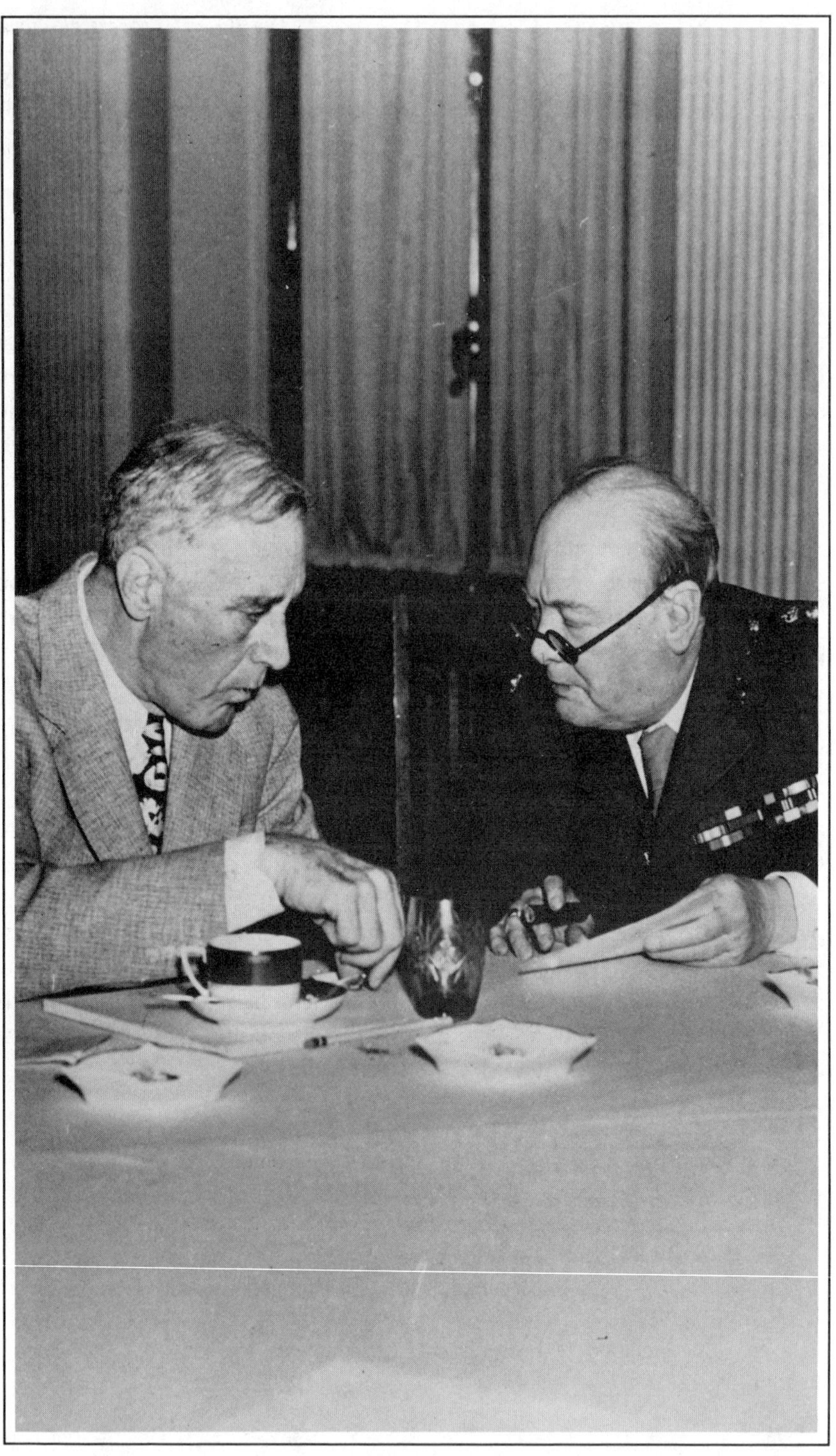

*Part II*

# Foreign Affairs

American President Franklin D. Roosevelt and British Prime Minister Winston Churchill deliberate at the 1945 Yalta Conference after World War II.

*Chapter 7*

# LEGISLATIVE-EXECUTIVE ANTAGONISM

An intense struggle between the executive and legislative branches over foreign policy prerogatives erupted in the 1970s in the wake of U.S. military involvement in Southeast Asia. A resurgent Congress hurled challenge upon challenge at a presidency weakened by the Vietnam ordeal and the Watergate scandal. So extensive were the attempts by Congress to reassert itself in foreign affairs that some observers feared the legislative branch would go too far. In the 1960s and early 1970s the catch phrase had been the "imperial presidency." But less than a decade later there was concern it was becoming an "imperiled presidency." [1]

The White House strongly protested the new limits Congress placed on its foreign policy-making powers. But in other quarters the congressional initiatives were applauded as healthy signs of new vigor on Capitol Hill rather than viewed as debilitating encroachments on presidential prerogatives. And some observers thought Congress had not gone far enough in righting the balance of power.[2]

While the intensity of this conflict between the two branches over foreign policy was seen as unprecedented,[3] the antagonism in this area was not new. As historian Edward S. Corwin has written: "The Constitution . . . is an invitation to struggle for the privilege of directing American foreign policy." [4]

## Constitutional Division of Powers

Article I, Section 8, of the Constitution assigned to Congress these powers which affect the United States' relations with other countries:

> The Congress shall have power To . . . provide for the common Defence and general Welfare of the United States; . . . To regulate Commerce with foreign Nations, and among the several States, and with the Indian Tribes;. . . To define and punish Piracies and Felonies committed on the high Seas, and Offences against the Law of

> Nations; To declare War, grant Letters Of Marque and Reprisal, and make Rules concerning Captures on Land and Water; To raise and support Armies. . . ; To provide and maintain a Navy; . . . And To make all Laws which shall be necessary and proper for carrying into Execution the foregoing Powers, and all other Powers vested by this Constitution in the Government of the United States, or in any Department or Officer thereof.

The Constitution also states in Article II, Section 2:

> The President shall be Commander in Chief of the Army and Navy. . . . He shall have Power, by and with the Advice and Consent of the Senate, to make Treaties, provided two-thirds of the Senators present concur; and he shall nominate, and by and with the Advice and Consent of the Senate, shall appoint Ambassadors, other public Ministers, and Consuls. . . . He shall receive Ambassadors and other public Ministers; he shall take Care that the Laws be faithfully executed. . . .

Throughout American history, constitutional scholars have analyzed and debated this division of foreign policy powers. But, whatever the Founding Fathers' intent, two outstanding facts have emerged from the resulting picture of alternate tension and cooperation: first, the overwhelming importance of presidential initiative in this area; second, the ever-increasing dependence of American foreign policies on congressional cooperation and support.

Issuance of a Proclamation of Neutrality by President George Washington in 1793, upon the outbreak of war between France and Great Britain, marked the start of the continuing struggle between the president and Congress for control of the nation's foreign policy. The pro-French Jeffersonian Democratic-Republicans attacked the proclamation as a usurpation by the president of authority granted to Congress. Washington's actions were defended by Alexander Hamilton in a series of articles published in a Philadelphia newspaper under the pseudonym "Pacificus." Hamilton argued that the conduct of foreign relations was by nature an executive function and therefore, except where the Constitution provided otherwise, belonged to the president upon whom was bestowed "the executive power." Possession by Congress of the power to declare war, as well as other powers affecting foreign relations, did not diminish the discretion of the president in the exercise of the powers constitutionally belonging to him, Hamilton said.[5]

James Madison, writing as "Helvidius," disputed this view. Emphasizing that the vital power to declare war was vested in Congress, Madison took the position that the powers of the executive in foreign relations were to be strictly construed. Doubt concerning the intent of the Constitution in the division of these powers was to be resolved in favor of the legislature. Madison attempted to bolster his argument by pointing to the confusion likely to ensue if concurrent discretionary powers were exercised by different branches of the new government. "A concurrent authority in two independent departments, to perform the same function with respect to the same thing," he declared, "would be as awkward in practice as it is unnatural in theory." Over time, however, Hamilton's view has prevailed.

## Scope of Congress' Authority

Despite the widely recognized prerogatives of the president in foreign relations, Congress has enormous powers that are indispensable to the support of any administration's foreign policy. Its specific foreign policy powers include the power to declare war and the Senate's power to give advice and consent to treaties and to the appointment of ambassadors, public ministers and other diplomatic officers.

Beyond these, Congress has general powers it can use to influence foreign policy. As Louis Henkin has pointed out: "Congress has general powers that, taken together, enable it to reach virtually where it will in foreign as in domestic affairs, subject only to constitutional prohibitions protecting human rights." [6] The most drastic, but least used, of these is the so-called power of the purse — the power to raise revenues and authorize and appropriate funds for national defense, war and the general execution of foreign policy.

Henkin also cites "other, specialized powers" that have international uses:

> Congress has authorized a network of international agreements under its postal power,. . . and there are international elements in the regulation of patents and copyrights. The express power to govern territory . . . may imply authority to acquire territory, and Congress determines whether territory acquired shall be incorporated into the United States. Congress can exercise 'exclusive legislation' in the nation's capital, its diplomatic headquarters. . . . The power to acquire and dispose of property has supported [World War II] lend-lease and other arms programs, and sales or gifts of nuclear reactors

> or fissionable materials.... By implication in the Constitution's grant of maritime jurisdiction to the federal judiciary ... Congress can legislate maritime law.[7]

## Presidential Dominance

The early presidents — Washington, Adams, Jefferson, Madison and Monroe — exercised commanding influence in determining the country's relations with other nations. Washington's Neutrality Proclamation and his Farewell Address, and Monroe's warning against foreign intervention in the Western Hemisphere, laid the basis for American foreign policy.[8]

National attention shifted away from foreign affairs during most of the 19th century, which was dominated by the twin domestic issues of slavery and the development of the American West. A major turn in foreign policy, strongly supported by Congress, was taken in 1898: The country dropped its traditional policy of non-intervention, went to war to rid Cuba of Spanish rule and emerged from the conflict with overseas outposts as far distant as the Philippines in the western Pacific.

In the 20th century, two world wars and other foreign threats to the nation's security made the chief executive, of necessity, the commanding figure in American foreign policy. And during this period, legislation enacted by Congress tended to enhance presidential power much more frequently than it operated to curtail it. One important exception was the 15-year period of congressional dominance following the Senate's rejection of the Treaty of Versailles after World War I. But on the eve of the next great conflict, the country's overseas interests as interpreted by the president once again became the controlling factor in U.S. foreign policy.

## Changing Congressional Role

During and after World War II, the role of Congress in foreign affairs shifted. The Senate, which once had exerted the greater influence of the two houses because of its role in treaty making, could play no part in presidential use of executive agreements, which had increased dramatically during Franklin D. Roosevelt's presidency (1933-45). Executive agreements with other countries do not require Senate approval. *(Types of international agreements, box, next page)*

Congressional influence over other aspects of foreign affairs greatly expanded at this time, however. The postwar development and expansion of foreign aid as an aspect of U.S. foreign policy gave the legislative

## Types of International Agreements

American constitutional law recognizes three basic types of international agreements and leaves it up to the executive branch to determine which type to use in particular international situations, the Senate Judiciary Subcommittee on Separation of Powers concluded in a 1973 report on executive agreements.

— First in importance is the *treaty,* which the report defined as an international — bilateral or multilateral — compact that requires consent by a two-thirds vote of the Senate to take effect.

— Second is the *congressional-executive international agreement,* which is entered into under a statute or an existing treaty. Examples of this type include presidential agreements with foreign countries on the distribution of U.S. assistance, based upon the foreign aid laws, and the 1946 executive agreement providing for the establishment of the United Nations Headquarters District in New York, after Congress gave its approval to the arrangement.

— Third is what the subcommittee called the "pure" or "true" *executive agreement,* negotiated by the president entirely on his constitutional authority as 1) commander in chief, 2) chief executive, a function that the courts have interpreted to include foreign relations, and 3) his other roles as delineated in Article II of the Constitution. According to the report, the State Department estimated that this kind of agreement may constitute no more than 3 percent of all U.S. international agreements.

Source: U.S., Congress, Senate, Committee on the Judiciary, *Congressional Oversight of Executive Agreements,* committee print, 93rd Cong., 1st sess., 1973, p. 4.

branch an unprecedented role in international relations. For the first time, the House — with its constitutional power to originate revenue bills (Article I, Section 7) — had an equal impact on the shape of U.S. foreign policies. Massive military and economic assistance programs for Greece and Turkey and Western Europe (the Truman Doctrine and the Marshall Plan) required specific congressional authorizations and annual funding.

Foreign aid has been the focus of well over 100 laws since 1945. Requiring in almost every instance specific congressional authorizations and the annual passage of appropriations, foreign aid proposals afford senators and representatives their most frequent opportunity to support or oppose the conduct of foreign relations by the executive branch. Inevitably, foreign aid programs and policies are modified in the process through lower-than-requested appropriations and the use of policy provisions to express — and sometimes impose — congressional restraints and directives on how aid to certain countries is to be used.

Legislative considerations also affected many other areas of foreign policy, such as Food for Peace, regulation of immigration, shipping subsidies, space exploration, new foreign alliances and import quotas.

## Postwar Bipartisanship

The postwar period spanning the late 1940s and early 1950s was characterized by Francis O. Wilcox, chief of staff of the Senate Foreign Relations Committee from 1947 to 1955 and then assistant secretary of state for international organization affairs until 1961, as one of "extraordinary executive-legislative cooperation." In this period, he said, "the bipartisan approach to foreign policy reached its zenith." [9] The Senate overwhelmingly approved the United Nations Charter, the peace treaty with Italy and the whole network of regional security treaties — the Rio Treaty, NATO, SEATO, and other collective and mutual security arrangements. Congress approved the Marshall Plan, aid to Greece and Turkey and U.S. participation in a wide variety of U.N. specialized agencies.

After this period of bipartisanship came another period of presidential ascendancy in foreign affairs. Rep. Lee H. Hamilton, D-Ind., a senior member of the House Foreign Affairs Committee, and Michael H. Van Dusen observed:

> For nearly 20 years, from 1950 to the mid-1960s, there was a national consensus on the main lines of foreign policy associated with the cold war; with strong executive leadership there developed a mystique of the president and State Department being absolutely in control, and of Congress, with rare exceptions, going along. [10]

## Congressional Disillusionment

By the late 1960s, however, Congress had become increasingly restive with what many members considered the aggrandizement of presidential power over foreign policy. Critics usually cited as examples the waging of costly undeclared wars in Korea and Vietnam, sending troops to other parts of the world without first securing congressional consent and negotiating an array of international commitments through executive agreements not subject to congressional approval.

Congressional discontent had occurred as early as 1951. During the "great debate" on Truman's authority to send troops to Europe, two resolutions were introduced to require congressional authorization for sending military forces abroad. Neither measure was approved by Congress, however. In 1953 Sen. John W. Bricker, R-Ohio (1947-59), introduced a constitutional amendment intended to restrain the president's power to make executive agreements. The amendment was rejected in 1954 by one vote in the Senate. *(Details on the Bricker amendment, pp. 99-100)*

Disillusionment with the Vietnam War in the 1960s prompted Congress to make new efforts to regain influence in foreign affairs. In June 1969, by a 70-16 vote, the Senate adopted a "national commitments" resolution that declared the sense of the Senate that a national commitment by the United States results "only from affirmative action taken by the executive and legislative branches of the United States government by means of a treaty, statute, or concurrent resolution of both houses of Congress specifically providing for such commitment."

In 1969 and for the next few years there were repeated, albeit unsuccessful, attempts in Congress to terminate funds to continue U.S. military action in Indochina. Although Congress remained sharply divided on the question of U.S. participation in the war, it was becoming, as political scientist Frans R. Bax pointed out, "increasingly united . . . in opposition to the executive around what came to be seen as a crucial issue of institutional integrity — congressional access to information." [11] During this period, an investigation by a Senate Foreign Relations subcommittee chaired by Stuart Symington, D-Mo. (1953-76), revealed for the first time the full extent of major U.S. commitments to other nations. Congress also learned that the White House had not been candid about the extensive U.S. bombing of Laos and Cambodia.

## A Resurgent Congress

In 1972 legislation to require that executive agreements be submitted to Congress was enacted. In June 1973, six months after the signing of a cease-fire in Vietnam, Congress voted to cut off funding of future U.S. combat activities in or over Cambodia and Laos after Aug. 15, 1973. And in July of that year Congress passed over President Nixon's veto a

## Congress Uses Its 'Power of the Purse' . . .

The "power of the purse" — the power to raise revenue and to approve expenditures — has enabled Congress to directly affect U.S. commitments abroad. Political scientist Cecil V. Crabb Jr. has called the "power of the purse" one of Congress' "most potent prerogatives," but notes that "it has seldom been utilized to its fullest potential to affect foreign relations. In the preponderance of cases, Congress relies upon this power *to limit executive activities* in external affairs; the House and Senate tell the president what he *cannot do*, rather than what he can or must do abroad." Nevertheless, Crabb says, "Congress has relied heavily in recent years upon its control over appropriations to achieve specific foreign policy goals enjoying high priority on Capitol Hill." [1]

### Foreign Aid

Foreign economic and military aid programs necessarily are undertaken at the initiative of the executive branch. In the early postwar period, Congress for the most part supported expensive assistance programs, particularly to aid Europe's recovery and to contain Soviet expansionism. In the late 1960s and 1970s, however, disenchantment had set in. Congress repeatedly slashed administration requests for foreign assistance and, in response to the way the executive branch had prosecuted the Vietnam War and made other foreign commitments, began to load the annual foreign aid authorization and appropriation bills with restrictions on the president's use of aid to set foreign policy. Despite administration protests, Congress banned military aid and arms sales to Turkey in 1974 (modified in 1975, lifted in 1978), Angola and Chile in 1976 and Argentina in 1977.

But sentiment began to shift by the end of the decade. In response to both the Carter and Reagan administrations' request for greater flexibility in administering the military aid program, a more conservative Congress relaxed some of the Vietnam-era aid restrictions and prohibitions. In the fiscal 1982-83 foreign aid bill, it lifted the ban on aid to Chile and Argentina, although it retained some conditions on further aid to those countries. And Congress turned down the Reagan administration's request to repeal a 1975 ban on aid to any of the political factions fighting in Angola.

## ...To Influence U.S. Foreign Policy

### Defense Spending

In the area of defense spending, Congress, also tends to use its power negatively — to block presidential decisions rather than to force the White House to take a specified action. In the early 1970s, Congress could not bring itself to cut off funds for U.S. military operations in Indochina or force a reduction in the number of American troops in Western Europe, although there was considerable support in the nation for both steps.[2] Opponents of the war tried to attach riders to various military and foreign policy legislation, but until 1973 they were unable to gain approval for any legislative measures cutting off funds for the war or setting a date for a U.S. military withdrawal from Southeast Asia. The legislation finally passed by Congress in 1973 prohibited all U.S. combat activities in Indochina as of Aug. 15, 1973.

Congress attempted to limit American involvement in another way: by setting ceilings on military aid to countries in the area. Use of this strategy was not effective until 1975, when Congress refused to approve President Ford's request for $522 million in additional military aid for Cambodia and South Vietnam. With the U.S. decision not to become further involved, the communists overran the two countries in April 1975, thus ending 25 years of American economic and military involvement in Indochina.

Reflecting on Congress' failure to use its powers to check America's increasing involvement in Vietnam in the late 1960s, Louis Fisher, specialist in American government with the Congressional Research Service, writes, "...the long prevailing faith in executive 'expertise' in the field of national security, combined with the postwar tradition of 'bipartisan' foreign policy, had accustomed the legislature to accept rather uncritically most presidential definitions of military need." [3]

---

1. Cecil V. Crabb Jr. and Pat M. Holt, *Invitation to Struggle: Congress, the President and Foreign Policy* (Washington, D.C.: CQ Press, 1980), p. 43.
2. *Congress and the Nation*, 5 vols., *Congress and the Nation: 1969-1972*, vol. 3 (Washington, D.C.: Congressional Quarterly, 1973), III: 214-215.
3. Louis Fisher, *President and Congress* (New York: The Free Press, 1972), p. 229.

tough war powers measure setting a 60-day limit on any presidential commitment of U.S. troops abroad where there was fighting, or where hostilities might be imminent, without specific congressional approval.

Procedural and substantive disputes between the two branches continued to mount as Congress attempted to fashion for itself a more influential role in foreign affairs. In 1974 Congress passed a major trade bill only after approving an amendment linking trade concessions for communist countries to Soviet bloc emigration policies. The Soviet Union refused to accept such terms for trade and repudiated a U.S.-Soviet trade agreement. And in reaction to the Turkish invasion of Cyprus, Congress imposed a ban on military aid and arms shipments to Turkey. (The ban, which took effect in February 1975, was partially lifted in October 1975 and completely repealed in 1978.)

In 1975 committees in both chambers conducted a major probe of the American intelligence community — the first such investigation since establishment of the Central Intelligence Agency in 1947. The following year, Congress, fearing U.S. involvement in Angola could draw the United States into another foreign policy failure similar to that of Vietnam, banned aid to anti-Marxist guerrillas in that African country. Fear of a Vietnam-type commitment also prompted Congress in 1981 to impose rigid conditions on U.S. arms aid to El Salvador.

By the mid-1970s, Congress had granted itself new authority to control sales of major U.S. military weapons abroad, and in 1977 it used its new muscle to force the Carter administration to modify a proposed arms sale package to Iran. Subsequently, it delayed for almost two years the sale of sophisticated military equipment to Saudi Arabia. In addition, congressional involvement in the treaty process reached an unprecedented level in the late 1970s during negotiation of the U.S.-Soviet strategic arms limitation treaty (SALT II) and during Senate consideration of the Panama Canal treaties.

The effect of these actions by Congress, and of many others that did not make the headlines, became the subject of much debate. In a 1980 article on the resurgence of Congress, political scientist Thomas E. Cronin observed:

> How long will Congress remain an activist influence in policymaking? How long will the American public support the Congress in its more assertive activities? Much will depend, understandably, on how Congress exercises its regained and new influence. [12]

## Notes

1. Arthur M. Schlesinger Jr., *The Imperial Presidency* (Boston: Houghton-Mifflin Co., 1973); John Spanier and Joseph Nogee, eds., *Congress, the Presidency and American Foreign Policy* (Elmsford, N.Y.: Pergamon Press, 1981), p. xxviii.
2. Thomas E. Cronin, "A Resurgent Congress and the Imperial Presidency," *Political Science Quarterly* (Summer 1980): 209-237.
3. Cecil V. Crabb Jr. and Pat M. Holt, *Invitation to Struggle: Congress, the President and Foreign Policy* (Washington, D.C.: CQ Press, 1980), p. ix.
4. Edward S. Corwin, *The President: Office and Powers, 1787-1957* (Washington Square, N.Y.: New York University Press, 1957), p. 171.
5. On the views of Madison and Hamilton, see Schlesinger, *The Imperial Presidency,* pp. 18-20; Louis Fisher, *President and Congress* (New York: The Free Press, 1972), pp. 32-33; Raoul Berger, *Executive Privilege* (Cambridge: Harvard University Press, 1974), pp. 135-138; and Corwin, *The President: Office and Powers,* pp. 178-184.
6. Louis Henkin, *Foreign Affairs and the Constitution* (New York: W. W. Norton & Co., 1972), pp. 76-80.
7. Ibid.
8. For an account of the historical development, see Schlesinger, *The Imperial Presidency;* Rexford G. Tugwell, *The Enlargement of the Presidency* (Garden City, N.Y.: Doubleday & Co., 1960); and Corwin, *The President: Office and Powers.*
9. Francis O. Wilcox, *Congress, the Executive and Foreign Policy* (New York: Harper & Row, 1971), p. 8.
10. Lee H. Hamilton and Michael H. Van Dusen, "Making the Separation of Powers Work," *Foreign Affairs* (Fall 1978): 17.
11. Frans R. Bax, "The Legislative-Executive Relationship in Foreign Policy: New Partnership or New Competition?" *Orbis* (Winter 1977): 890.
12. Cronin, "A Resurgent Congress," p. 235.

## *Chapter 8*

# THE TREATY POWER

The whole of the treaty-making power is contained in a single clause of the Constitution. Spelling out presidential authority, Article II, Section 2, Clause 2, declares: "He shall have Power, by and with the Advice and Consent of the Senate, to make Treaties, provided two-thirds of the Senators present concur. . . ." For years this clause served as a major tool of American foreign policy. It brought peace with other nations, supported American territorial expansion, established national boundaries, protected U.S. commerce and regulated government affairs with Indian tribes.[1]

In performing its constitutional treaty-making functions, the Senate merely consents to the ratification of a treaty; it does not ratify it. Ratification itself is subject to executive action. Normally, the Senate considers a resolution of advice and consent to ratification of a pending treaty. For example, in the case of the nuclear test-ban treaty, approved by the Senate on Sept. 24, 1963, the resolution of ratification read as follows:

> Be it resolved (two-thirds of the senators present concurring therein), that the Senate advise and consent to the ratification of the treaty banning nuclear weapons tests in the atmosphere, in outer space, and under water, which was signed at Moscow on Aug. 5, 1963, on behalf of the United States of America, the United Kingdom of Great Britain and Northern Ireland and the Union of Soviet Socialist Republics.

Despite its importance, the treaty clause is ambiguous on some points. Neither the Senate procedure for advising the president nor the stage in the treaty-making process at which the Senate should act in an advisory capacity is spelled out. Moreover, the Constitution ignores the role of the House in treaty making, even in cases where legislation or appropriations are needed to make a treaty effective. This issue surfaced in the House when legislation was needed to implement the 1978 Panama Canal treaties.

It is generally agreed that the main purpose of the advice and consent formula is to provide for democratic control of foreign policy. In the early years of the nation, the executive branch sought to incorporate Senate advice into the process of treaty negotiations by such means as presidential meetings with senators, Senate confirmation of negotiators and special presidential messages. But as international relations became more complicated, presidents abandoned, one after the other, the various devices by which the Senate's advice had been obtained.

Feeling deprived of adequate opportunities to make its influence felt in treaty negotiations, the Senate resorted to "advising" the president by tacking on drastic amendments to treaties and rejecting some outright. The classic display of senatorial dissatisfaction came in 1919 and 1920 with the prolonged debate on, and ultimate rejection of, the Treaty of Versailles that embodied not only the World War I treaty of peace with Germany but also U.S. membership in the League of Nations.

Despite the shock caused by rejection of the Versailles pact, and reinforcement of the Senate's popular reputation as a graveyard of treaties, its overall voting record has been overwhelmingly favorable. Between 1789 and mid-1982, only 19 treaties were rejected outright by the Senate. The last treaty rejected, as of 1982, was an optional protocol to the law-of-the-sea conventions, concerning compulsory settlement of disputes. The May 26, 1960, vote was 49 to 30 for the protocol, four votes short of the two-thirds required for consent to ratification.

The Senate, however, has other methods of thwarting treaties besides outright rejection. It can delay a treaty to death, or it can attach amendments that either the president or other signatories may refuse to accept. In some cases, treaties have been blocked in the Foreign Relations Committee. One study found that between 1789 and 1929 about 900 treaties were approved by the Senate but another 200 were either rejected or amended to the point that they were unacceptable to the president or the other parties to the treaty.[2]

After World War II, the treaty-making power took on added importance, temporarily at least. Membership in the United Nations was accomplished by Senate consent to the ratification of the U.N. Charter, while membership in an expanding number of international organizations was brought about either by treaty or by both House and Senate approval of appropriate implementing legislation. Treaties were used to conclude the widening circle of U.S. mutual security agreements designed to provide collective defense against communist aggression. Other agreements were intended to restrict the military use of atomic energy or curtail the spread and production of nuclear armaments. And as new frontiers in space and under the oceans opened up, additional treaties were concluded or proposed to govern their use.

Old conflicts over treaty making were renewed. It was a time of strong executive branch leadership, producing congressional reaction that came to a head in 1953 and 1954 with the introduction of the Bricker amendment, a proposal to limit presidential treaty power. *(Details on the Bricker amendment, pp. 99-100)*

## Conflicts Over Treaty Power

At the root of the recurring conflict between the president and Congress over the treaty-making power has been the basic doctrine of separation of powers. At the Constitutional Convention, it was assumed that the existing power of the Continental Congress to approve treaties by a two-thirds majority vote would be transferred intact to the legislative branch of the new government. Continued legislative control of treaty making was taken for granted even though it was the exclusive prerogative of the executive in all other governments at that time.

The first suggestion that the treaty power should be divided between the legislative and executive branches seems to have been made on June 18, 1787. Hamilton proposed an executive elected for life, who, along with many other powers, would have, "with the advice and approbation of the Senate, the power of making all treaties." [3] There was no discussion of Hamilton's suggestion, and it appeared to be dead when the Aug. 6 report of the five-member Committee of Detail proposed that "the Senate shall have power to make treaties." Debate on the committee's report failed to resolve the issue of who was to exercise the treaty power. The section was referred back to the committee.

On Sept. 4 another committee, the 11-member Committee on Postponed Matters, issued a report recommending that "the president, by and with the advice and consent of the Senate," should have the power to make treaties, and that no treaty could be approved "without the consent of two-thirds of the members present." Several attempts were made to alter the proportion of the Senate whose consent would be required and to add House participation in treaty making, but on Sept. 8 the provision as proposed in the report was accepted in tact.[4]

There was nearly unanimous support in the convention for some means of enabling the new government to require the states to honor treaty provisions. Although the Articles of Confederation entrusted the treaty-making power to Congress, fulfillment of Congress' promises to other nations was dependent on each state legislature. Inaction, or adverse action, by certain states had led to violation of some articles of the Peace Treaty of 1783 with Great Britain. A solution was provided in Article VI, Clause 2, of the Constitution, which states: "all Treaties made, or which shall be made, under the Authority of the United States shall be the supreme Law of the Land; and the judges thereof shall be bound thereby. . . ."

Chief Justice John Marshall elaborated on the meaning of this provision in 1829 (*Foster v. Neilson,* 2 Pet. 253):

> Our Constitution declares a treaty to be the supreme law of the land. It is, consequently, to be regarded in courts of justice as equivalent to an act of the legislature, whenever it operates of itself, without the aid of any legislative provision. But when the terms of the stipulation import a contract — when neither of the parties engages to perform a particular act, the treaty addresses itself to the political, not the judicial department; and the legislature must execute the contract, before it can become a rule for the Court. [5]

Hence, although Congress may have to enact legislation to carry out acts stipulated by a treaty, any self-executing treaty or part of a treaty automatically attains the status of a statute, enforceable by the courts. Provisions of various treaties periodically have been the target of legal challenges, but the Supreme Court never has ruled unconstitutional a treaty of the United States or any provision of a treaty.[6]

Exclusion of the House from the treaty-making process was defended by Hamilton and Jay in *The Federalist.* They contended that the legislative role in treaty making should be limited to the Senate where it would be in the hands of persons chosen by the "select assemblies" of the states instead of by the rank and file. The longer and overlapping Senate terms would provide greater continuity, they said, while the smaller size of the Senate would aid "secrecy and dispatch." On the other hand, reaching agreement among the president, the Senate and the House would be much more difficult to obtain.[7]

## Consideration of First Treaties

On May 25, 1789, a pair of treaties with Indian tribes negotiated and signed under the authority of the Continental Congress was submitted to the Senate. It was not until June 12, 1789, that these two treaties were referred to committee for study. In the meantime, the president had submitted another treaty, a consular convention with France, concluded under the Articles of Confederation. After a series of meetings with John Jay, secretary of foreign affairs (an office held over from the Confederation), the Senate on July 29 unanimously consented to ratification of the consular treaty. This was the first time the Senate had given its advice and consent to ratification of a treaty.[8]

On Aug. 12 the committee studying the two Indian treaties, instead of recommending that the Senate advise and consent to ratification (as had been done with the consular treaty with France), proposed that the president "be advised to execute and enjoin an observance" of the agreements. The Senate on Sept. 8 approved the committee recommendation for one of the treaties (that with the Wyandot, Delaware, Ottawa, Chippewa, Pattawattima and Sacs nations) but took no action on the other (that with the Six Nations, except the Mohawks).

The Senate action confused President Washington. He was not certain whether the Senate meant that he should merely see that the approved treaty went into operation or that he should proceed with a formal ratification. In a message to the Senate, Sept. 17, the president asked for a clarification. His own opinion, he said, was that treaties with Indian tribes should be ratified in the same way as treaties with European nations. The Senate disagreed. A committee that studied the president's message reported Sept. 18 that since past Indian treaties never had been solemnly ratified, it was not "expedient or necessary" to ratify the present treaties. The committee proposed a resolution to advise the president "to enjoin a due observance" of the Wyandot treaty, passing over the treaty with the Six Nations. But on Sept. 22 the Senate substituted a resolution of advice and consent to the Wyandot treaty. No action was taken on the other agreement.

Senate consent to ratification of the Wyandot treaty set a precedent that endured until 1871, when a rider to the Indian Appropriations Act that year provided that, in the future, no American Indian nation or tribe was to be considered an independent nation with which the United

States could conclude a treaty. Indian affairs were handled subsequently by statute.[9]

## Advice of the Senate

The first treaties considered by the Senate had been negotiated under instructions from the Continental Congress because there was no executive in the confederation government. Although the new Constitution established an executive and authorized him to make treaties (with advice from the Senate), it failed to explain what kind of advice was appropriate or how and when it was to be offered. To be effective, the advice would have to be given before negotiations ended.

In practice, procedures developed by Washington and the first Senate established precedents that exerted varying degrees of influence. Washington's usual practice, until the Jay treaty negotiations with Great Britain in 1794, was to ask the Senate for advice about opening negotiations; transmit the full instructions to be given to the negotiators; submit their names for confirmation; and keep the Senate fully informed of the progress of negotiations. If matters came up that were not covered in the original instructions, Washington again would call for the Senate's advice.[10] When treaties required appropriations, he reported the proceedings to the House as well as to the Senate. Additional procedures adopted by early administrations included requests for advance appropriations to cover the cost of the negotiations, appointing senators and representatives to the negotiating team and consulting personally with key members of the Senate, and, after its establishment in 1816, with the Foreign Relations Committee. At times Congress took the initiative by considering resolutions proposing or opposing negotiations.

**Consultation with the President.** When the Senate considered its first treaties, it named a committee of three senators to meet with President Washington to establish ground rules for consultation on drafting the treaties. Washington favored oral communications rather than written exchanges. Following a committee recommendation, the Senate on Aug. 21, 1789, adopted a rule providing for meetings with the president either in the Senate chamber or elsewhere. Later the same day, the Senate received a message announcing that Washington was coming to the Senate chamber the next day "at half past 11 o'clock" to discuss proposed terms for a treaty with the southern Indians. This proved to be an inauspicious visit, as Sen. William Maclay's account of the meeting in his *Journal* reveals.

A paper containing the president's proposals was hurriedly read to the Senate by the vice president, but members were not able to hear because of the noise of carriages in the street. The windows were closed and the proposals read again. Unfamiliar with the proposed treaty terms, the Senate sought to refer the paper to a committee for study. At this suggestion the president "started up in a violent fret," exclaiming: "This defeats every purpose of my coming here." After he had "cooled down, by degrees," Washington consented to a two-day postponement, then withdrew from the chamber. Although the second meeting went more smoothly (the Senate agreed to vote its advice on each of the points raised by the president), Washington never again went before the Senate to consult on treaty terms or discuss foreign policy, nor did any other president until Woodrow Wilson appeared on Jan. 22, 1917, to call for "peace without victory" and propose a League for Peace.[11]

Although Washington's general position was that he considered it advisable to postpone negotiations until he had received the advice of the Senate on the terms to be offered, he did not follow this course in the case of the Jay treaty. He named Jay as the negotiator of the treaty and submitted his name to the Senate for confirmation, but he withheld the instructions to be given him.[12] The same procedure was adopted by Washington's immediate successors, Adams and Madison, and by some other presidents.

Polk returned to the earlier practice in 1846 when he asked for the Senate's advice on whether negotiations should be undertaken with Great Britain on proposals submitted by London for the settlement of the Oregon boundary question.[13] Similar requests for preliminary advice were sent to the Senate by Buchanan, Lincoln, Johnson, Grant and Cleveland. Harding, in 1922, asked the Senate's advice on reinstating a patents treaty with Germany.

**Treaty Initiatives.** The right of the Senate to initiate treaty making by proposing negotiations has been vigorously debated by the Senate. Proponents have defended such initiatives as the right and duty of the Senate under the Constitution and as a demonstration of national unity. Opponents have contended that for the Senate to make the first move was "officious and disrespectful," and that it tended to "shelter" the president from responsibility in treaty making. In 1902 a report by the Foreign Relations Committee stated: "The initiative lies with the president. . . . Whether he will negotiate a treaty, and when, and what its terms shall be are matters committed by the Constitution to the discretion of the president." [14]

Today the right of either house of Congress to offer advice about negotiations is not questioned, but the advice of the legislative branch is merely persuasive, not compelling. In its landmark decision in the Curtiss-Wright case in 1936 (*U.S. v. Curtiss-Wright Export Corp.*, 299 U.S. 304), the Supreme Court ruled: "The President . . . alone negotiates. Into the field of negotiation the Senate cannot intrude; and Congress is powerless to invade it." [15]

Presidents' reactions to Senate attempts to advise them in treaty negotiations has varied. President Jackson acted on a Senate resolution in opening negotiations with Central American governments for an inter-oceanic canal. Cleveland replied with some asperity to a Senate suggestion for negotiations on a treaty to limit the importation of Chinese labor. Harding refused to recognize that a Senate resolution calling for an agreement with Great Britain and Japan on reduction of naval expenditures was responsible for the calling of the Washington Conference on the Limitation of Armament. Sponsored by Sen. William E. Borah, R-Idaho (1907-40), the resolution was adopted by the Senate May 26, 1921, and by the House on June 29. Formal invitations to the conference were issued Aug. 11, 1921.[16]

**Confirmation of Negotiators.** Up to the end of the Madison administration, the names of treaty negotiators were referred to the Senate for confirmation. Subsequent neglect of the practice was repeatedly protested in the Senate. In 1883 the Senate attempted to revive the earlier practice by adopting a resolution stipulating that, in approving a treaty with Korea, the consent given to ratification did not "admit or acquiesce in any right or constitutional power in the president to employ any person to negotiate treaties . . . unless such person shall have been appointed . . . with the advice and consent of the Senate." [17] Cleveland's appointment of a special commissioner with "paramount authority" to negotiate with Hawaii was declared by the Republican members of the Foreign Relations Committee to be "an unconstitutional act in that such appointee was never nominated to the Senate." [18]

Confirmation of negotiators gave the Senate an important power, which was recognized early by both the Senate and the executive branch. Commenting on the situation when one of Adams' nominations was under attack, Jefferson wrote that, if there were a large vote cast against the nominee, even if confirmation resulted, "it is supposed the president would perhaps not act under it, on the probability that more than a third would be against ratification." [19]

Abandonment of the practice of Senate confirmation of negotiators appears to have been due largely to the need for secrecy. This had led to the use of special agents whose appointment was recognized as the right of the executive in carrying out his constitutional duties. It also reflected acceptance of the principle — in Jefferson's words to Citizen Genet, envoy to the United States from the first French Republic — that the president is "the only channel of communication between this country and foreign nations." [20]

In later years, the executive occasionally sought Senate confirmation of treaty negotiators. Polk submitted the names of his appointees to negotiate a treaty with Mexico. Grant submitted the names of the commissioners who were to negotiate the Treaty of Washington with Great Britain. Harding submitted the names of his appointees to the World War Foreign Debt Commission in 1922, but in this case the submission was required by a provision of the act creating the commission. The act stipulated that its members be appointed by the president, "by and with the advice and consent of the Senate." [21]

The United Nations Participation Act of 1945 provided for Senate confirmation of the United States representatives to the United Nations, of members of the U.S. delegation to the General Assembly and of delegates to various U.N. agencies.

**Instruction of Negotiators.** While Washington was president, submission of the negotiators' instructions gave the Senate an opportunity to advise on treaty proposals. Ensuing administrations did not provide the Senate with the opportunity to consider the terms of treaties not yet agreed upon until President James K. Polk in 1846 submitted the skeleton of a treaty ending the war with Mexico.

Drafts of treaties were sent to the Senate by four other presidents — Buchanan, Lincoln, Johnson and Grant. In 1919 the Senate requested a copy of the Treaty of Versailles as presented to the representatives of Germany. The secretary of state replied: "The president feels it would not be in the public interest to communicate to the Senate a text that is provisional and not definite, and finds no precedent for such a procedure." [22]

In at least two instances, the Senate (with the concurrence of the House) "advised" the executive by specifying the limits within which negotiators of international agreements were to operate. In legislation creating the Foreign Debt Commission, enacted Feb. 9, 1922, it was provided that "nothing contained in this act shall be construed to authorize ... the commission to extend the time of maturity of ... obligations due the United States ... beyond June 15, 1947, or to fix the rate of interest at less than 4¼ per centum per annum." [23] In a joint resolution making funds available to send a delegation to the Opium Conference of 1924, Congress specified certain results it wanted the negotiators to obtain.

**Legislators as Negotiators.** The first members of Congress selected to negotiate a treaty were Sen. James A. Bayard of Delaware and House Speaker Henry Clay. Madison named them to help negotiate a treaty of peace with Great Britain in 1814.[24] Both resigned their places in Congress on the ground that the two offices were not compatible.

On at least three occasions resolutions were introduced in the Senate to prohibit members of that body from serving as treaty negotiators.[25] The first resolution, introduced in 1870, was defeated after a heated all-night debate when it was turned into a question of confidence in President Ulysses S. Grant. The second was occasioned by President William McKinley's appointment of three members of the Foreign Relations Committee on a commission to negotiate the Treaty of Paris in 1898. The Senate committee, to which a resolution of protest was referred, hesitated to make a report that might have appeared to censure some of its own members, but it directed its chairman to visit the president and express the Senate's strong disapproval.[26] Theodore Roosevelt's selection of Sen. Henry Cabot Lodge, R-Mass. (1893-1924), to the Alaskan boundary tribunal led to the third attempt of the Senate to prohibit such service by senators. But a resolution opposing the selection was never acted upon.

Senate resentment of Wilson's failure to include any senators on the 1919 peace commission was in sharp contrast to its previous position. To compensate for lack of representation on the commission, a resolution was introduced calling for the appointment of a bipartisan committee of eight senators to visit Paris during the sessions of the Peace Conference to "make itself familiar with all facts" and report to the Senate "as often as it deemed desirable." The resolution, however, was never acted upon.[27] Senate attempts to offer advice on the negotiations through debate on the floor and through a round-robin warning against inclusion of provisions for a League of Nations in the peace treaty proved to be ineffective.

As a result of Wilson's experience, senators frequently have been appointed to important international conferences. President Warren G. Harding in 1921 chose the chairman of the Foreign Relations Committee, Henry Cabot Lodge, and the minority leader, Oscar W. Underwood, D-Ala. (1915-27), as delegates to the Conference on the Limitation of Armament, and members of both houses were appointed by President Herbert Hoover to the American delegation to the London Naval Conference in 1930. President Franklin D. Roosevelt recognized Congress in his selection of commissioners to the World Monetary and Economic Conference in 1933 and to the International Refugee Conference in 1943.

In 1945 the eight-member U.S. delegation to the San Francisco conference that established the United Nations included four members of Congress: Foreign Relations Committee Chairman Tom Connally, D-Texas (1929-53), and committee member Arthur H. Vandenberg, R-Mich. (1928-51), as well as Sol Bloom, D-N.Y. (1923-49), and Charles A. Eaton, R-N.J. (1925-53), chairman and ranking minority member, respectively, of the House Foreign Affairs Committee. Ever since the founding of the United Nations, two senators and two representatives have alternated as members of the U.S. delegation.

During the postwar period, successive administrations have followed the practice of including members of Congress on delegations to international conferences. President Carter in 1977 appointed a diverse group of 14 representatives and 30 senators as advisers to the SALT delegation. Francis Wilcox offers this assessment of the practice:

> On balance, congressional participation in international conferences seems to have done very little harm and some good. In a few cases ... congressional cooperation has been of inestimable value, not only in the drafting process but in securing Senate approval of the finished product. Measured quantitatively over the years, it has most often simply been neutral, having no results commensurate with the time, trouble and money required.[28]

## Consent of the Senate

Treaties are transmitted to the Senate for consent to ratification by the president under an injunction of secrecy, which normally is removed shortly after the Senate receives the treaty. Once a treaty is submitted, it remains before the Senate until it is disposed of favorably, or until the president requests its return and the Senate agrees to withdraw it. Senate consideration of a treaty is open to presidential discretion. The president may refuse to submit a treaty; he may withdraw it after it is submitted; or he may refuse to ratify it even after the Senate has given its consent.[29]

The Foreign Relations Committee has jurisdiction over all treaties, even those that involve subjects that usually fall outside its purview. The committee considers a treaty in much the same way it considers proposed legislation: it may hold open or closed hearings, and it may recommend Senate approval or rejection, with or without modifications. Committee decisions require a majority vote of the members present. According to the Legislative Reorganization Act of 1946, a committee majority must be "actually present" to report a treaty.[30]

After treaties are reported by Foreign Relations, they are considered by the full Senate. In the past, senators debated treaties in closed executive session, preserving the cloak of secrecy. By the late 19th century, however, there were increasing demands to open treaty debates to the public. A fisheries treaty with Great Britain was considered in 1888 — and rejected — in the first open executive session. Other public treaty debates followed, and the Senate on June 18, 1929, amended its rules to provide that all Senate business, including action on treaties, was to be conducted in open session unless a majority of the Senate decided to hold a closed session to consider a particularly sensitive matter.[31]

After a brief experiment in 1801 and 1803 with a rule requiring a two-thirds vote on all floor action on treaties, the Senate limited the two-thirds rule to the final vote on whether to give its advice and consent and to a motion for indefinite postponement. All other questions are decided by majority vote.[32] A separate roll-call vote normally is taken on each treaty. Sometimes, however, the Senate considers a large number of similar treaties, or a variety of non-controversial treaties, in a group, taking one vote on several resolutions of consent, or taking a single vote, which by unanimous consent is shown separately in the *Congressional Record* as the vote on each of the treaty resolutions.

Although Senate rules do not require roll-call votes on treaties, that practice became customary after three non-controversial consular conventions were approved on June 13, 1952, when only two senators were present in the chamber. On July 20, 1953, acting Majority Leader William

F. Knowland, R-Calif. (1945-59), announced that "as a matter of standard operating procedure in the future, we intend, in connection with all treaties . . . not only to ask for a quorum call, but to ask for a yea-and-nay [roll-call] vote. . . ." [33]

**Amendments to Treaties.** There are no provisions in the Constitution setting forth procedures for, or restrictions on, amending treaties. But since the time of the Jay treaty with Great Britain, the Senate has claimed authority to modify treaties after the completion of negotiations. The Senate on June 24, 1795, by a 20-10 vote, consented to ratification of the Jay treaty on condition that an additional article be negotiated to suspend portions of the treaty's 12th article relating to trade between the United States and the British West Indies. Scores of treaties since then have been subjected to amendments, reservations, conditions and qualifications, some of which have been added at the request of the president.[34]

The wisdom of amending treaties was questioned as early as 1805 by John Quincy Adams. In a Senate debate, Adams said, "I think amendments to treaties imprudent. By making them you agree to all the treaty except the particular you amend, and at the same time you leave it optional with the other party to reject the whole." A later opinion was voiced by Secretary of State Richard Olney, after the Senate rejected an Anglo-American arbitration treaty in 1897: "[S]enators have exhausted their ingenuity in devising amendments to the treaty. Before the treaty came to a final vote, the Senate brand had been put upon every part of it, and the original instrument had been mutilated and distorted beyond all possibility of recognition." [35]

On two occasions the Supreme Court has sustained the power of the Senate to amend treaties. In 1869, in the case of *Haver v. Yaker* (9 Wall. 32), the court stated:

> In this country, a treaty is something more than a contract, for the Federal Constitution declares it to be the law of the land. If so, before it can become a law, the Senate in whom rests the authority to ratify it, must agree to it. But the Senate are not required to adopt or reject it as a whole, but may modify or amend it. [36]

And in a 1901 opinion (*Fourteen Diamond Rings v. U.S.*, 183 U.S. 176), the court said: "The Senate may refuse its ratification or make it conditional upon adoption of amendments to the treaty." [37]

One of the best known U.S. qualifications to an international agreement is the so-called Connally reservation to the compulsory jurisdiction clause of the statute of the International Court of Justice. In adhering to the U.N. Charter in 1945, the United States accepted membership in the court. President Truman contended that the country should also accept compulsory jurisdiction under terms of the court's statute, which excluded matters deemed to be within the domestic jurisdiction of any nation. On July 31, 1946, the Senate considered a resolution to that effect. But some senators, recalling fears that had led to Senate refusal in 1935 to approve U.S. membership in the World Court, objected to letting the International Court of Justice determine what matters might or might not be within U.S. jurisdiction. To obviate this possibility, Sen. Connally proposed adding to the resolution's clause excluding "Matters which are essentially within the domestic jurisdiction of the United States" the words "as determined by the United States." The Senate, before approving the resolution on Aug. 2, 1946, agreed to the Connally reservation by a 51-12 vote, in effect negating the U.S. commitment in principle. Subsequent attempts to repeal the reservation have been unsuccessful." [38]

**Treaty Reservations and Other Changes.** A Senate amendment to a treaty, if it is accepted by the president and the other parties to the treaty, changes it for all parties. A Senate reservation limits only the treaty obligation of the United States, although the reservation may be so significant that the other treaty parties may file similar reservations or refuse to ratify the treaty.

The Senate Foreign Relations Committee has identified four major forms that changes in treaties may take:

— The Senate may consent to ratification and include its views or interpretations in a *committee report* accompanying the treaty. This does not alter the text of the treaty or the resolution of consent.

— Senate *understandings* or *interpretations* may be included in the resolution of consent. Such language has no legal effect on the treaty if it does not substantially affect the treaty's terms or U.S. obligations. Under normal practice, the executive branch informs the other treaty parties of the interpretations or understandings.

— The Senate may add a *reservation* to the resolution of consent, involving some change in obligations under the treaty. Again, other parties generally are informed of the reservation.

— The Senate may amend the terms of the treaty itself; *amendments* require new negotiations with the other parties.[39]

The distinction among the various categories over the years has become less important. As law professor Theodor Meron has pointed out: "The legal significance of a 'statement' of the Senate — to use a neutral term — depends upon its substance, not upon its designation." [40] According to the State Department, "a statement that modifies, limits or changes the treaty text or meaning is a true reservation; a statement that clarifies or explains or deals with an incidental matter, does not change the treaty and is therefore not a reservation." [41]

The Senate's substitution of reservations for amendments in recent years has not lessened the difficulty faced by the executive branch. From its point of view, Senate alteration of treaties has become an increasingly serious problem because of the growing tendency to adjust U.S. foreign relations through multilateral treaties. Resubmission of an amended treaty to foreign governments — any one of which may wish to alter other provisions of the treaty in view of U.S. changes — presents almost insuperable obstacles to final agreement.

## Efforts to Alter Senate's Treaty Power

Although the Senate has adopted a simple consent to ratification on the vast majority of treaties submitted to it, the few it has rejected have prompted criticism of the Senate's treaty-making power and led to proposals to eliminate the two-thirds constitutional requirement for Senate approval of treaties, or to require consent to ratification by the House as well as the Senate.

Following the war with Spain, two resolutions were introduced in the House proposing a constitutional amendment giving the power of consent to a majority of the whole Senate. In 1920 amendments were offered in both houses stipulating that consent to ratification should be by majority vote of members present in the Senate. Between 1919 and 1928, five resolutions were introduced in the House to let that body participate in giving "advice and consent" on treaties. As Democratic candidate for president in 1924, John W. Davis endorsed the plan to substitute a majority for a two-thirds vote. William Jennings Bryan, in a Jackson Day address in 1920, advocated associating the House with the Senate. An even more fundamental change was proposed in Congress in 1921 whereby certain treaties would have to be approved by popular vote.

Mindful of Senate rejection of the Treaty of Versailles and the League of Nations, Congress considered a number of proposals during

World War II to change the treaty ratification provisions. The intent of this legislation was to reduce the possibility that new postwar arrangements for world peace would be rejected. Josephus Daniels, Navy secretary in the Cabinet of Woodrow Wilson, suggested in a 1942 speech that the Constitution be amended to provide for consent to ratification by majority vote of both chambers. Proposed amendments to carry out his suggestion were introduced the following year in the House. In the Senate, a proposed amendment was introduced in 1943 to allow Senate consent by a simple majority.

In 1945, while the San Francisco conference was debating the charter of the United Nations — destined for consideration by the Senate alone — the House in May took up a resolution by Hatton Sumners, D-Texas (1913-47). He favored amending the Constitution to require that "Treaties shall be made by the president by and with the advice and consent of both houses of Congress." Despite general agreement that the Senate never would agree to share its treaty power, the House adopted the resolution by a 288-88 vote. Not surprisingly, Sumner's resolution was never acted upon by the Senate.[42]

## Efforts to Alter President's Treaty Power

In the early 1950s Congress engaged in an historic debate on an amendment to the Constitution proposed by Sen. John W. Bricker, R-Ohio (1947-59), that would have curbed the executive's treaty powers. The Bricker amendment reflected fears that American adherence to various United Nations covenants and conventions, such as the genocide convention submitted by President Truman in 1949 (which had not been approved by the Senate as of 1982), would greatly expand the powers of the federal government and jeopardize enforcement of state laws by reason of the constitutional provision making treaties the "supreme law of the land." The proposed amendment stemmed also from resentment at the tendency of the White House to substitute executive agreements, not subject to ratification, for treaties. The Bricker amendment had forceful supporters in Congress, and the controversy between the two branches of government turned a highly technical legal question into a wide-ranging debate between "isolationists" and "one-worlders."

On Jan. 7, 1953, Sen. Bricker and 63 cosponsors (45 Republicans and 19 Democrats) introduced a revised version of the proposed constitutional amendment first introduced by Bricker and 58 cosponsors in 1952. As revised, the proposed amendment stated:

1. A provision of a treaty which denies or abridges any right enumerated in this Constitution shall not be of any force or effect.

2. No treaty shall authorize or permit any foreign power or any international organization to supervise, control, or adjudicate rights of citizens of the United States within the United States enumerated in this Constitution or any other matter essentially within the domestic jurisdiction of the United States.

3. A treaty shall become effective as internal law in the United States only through the enactment of appropriate legislation by the Congress.

4. All executive or other agreements between the President and any international organization, foreign power, or official thereof shall be made only in the manner and to the extent to be prescribed by law. Such agreements shall be subject to the limitations imposed on treaties or the making of treaties in this article.

5. The Congress shall have power to enforce this article by appropriate legislation.[43]

On Feb. 16 Arthur V. Watkins, R-Utah (1947-59), introduced a resolution that covered all of Bricker's provisions except the second. This variation of the Bricker amendment had been drafted by the American Bar Association, which claimed that some 200 treaties proposed or in preparation by U.N. agencies contained provisions at variance with federal or state law.

On June 15 the Judiciary Committee reported another version of the Bricker amendment that closely followed Watkins' proposal. Its key provision still declared that "a treaty shall become effective as internal law only through legislation which would be valid in the absence of a treaty." No further action on the measure was taken before Congress adjourned. Then on Feb. 26, 1954, a final tally on the measure fell one vote short (60-31) of the two-thirds majority required for Senate approval of a constitutional amendment. In the next Congress (the 84th) the Senate again considered the question of revising the Constitution's treaty provisions along the lines advocated by Bricker. But in the absence of administration support, Democratic leaders refused to call up Bricker's proposal, and it died before coming to a vote.

## Executive Agreements

The courts repeatedly have upheld the president's authority to enter into agreements with other governments without consulting the Senate.

Most executive agreements have concerned such routine matters as the regulation of fishing rights, private claims against another government and postal agreements. In other cases, however, major U.S. foreign policies have been carried out by executive agreements, sometimes with far-reaching results — for example, the World War II summit conference agreements reached at Cairo, Tehran, Yalta and Potsdam. Still other executive agreements have been concluded under specific delegations of power by Congress, such as tariff agreements that were made under the Reciprocal Trade Agreements Act of 1934.[44]

Executive agreements have been recognized as distinct from treaties since the presidency of George Washington. The Post Office Act of 1792 authorized the postmaster general to "make arrangements with postmasters in any foreign country for the reciprocal receipt and delivery of letters and packets, through the post offices." But it was not until World War II that the executive agreement assumed a major role as a foreign policy tool.

The number of international agreements rose dramatically in the late 1930s and early 1940s during the Roosevelt administration. This growth alarmed many members of Congress, who charged that some of those agreements, reached without consultation with Congress, had resulted in major commitments of American resources or had implemented significant policy decisions. Opposition to extensive use of executive agreements as a substitute for treaties reached a climax during the Vietnam War era. In the early 1970s, legislation to give Congress a veto over executive agreements was introduced in both houses.

Under a law enacted in 1950, the secretary of state was directed to compile and publish annually the contents of all treaties and executive agreements entered into during the previous year. In practice, however, agreements considered sensitive to national security were withheld from Congress as a whole and even from the committees having jurisdiction over the subject of the agreements.

Two years after rejecting the Bricker amendment, the Senate, over Eisenhower's objections, unanimously passed a bill requiring all executive agreements to be submitted to the Senate within 60 days, but the House never acted on the bill. The issue was rekindled in the 1960s and 1970s because, as Thomas E. Cronin observed, "while the Senate was asked to ratify international accords on trivial matters, the White House arranged critically important mutual aid and military-base agreements without even informing Congress."[45]

In 1972 secret agreements were uncovered by the Senate Foreign Relations Subcommittee on Security Agreements and Commitments Abroad, chaired by Stuart Symington, D-Mo. (1953-76). The subcommittee found that commitments and secret conditions had been made throughout the 1960s to Ethiopia, Laos, Thailand, South Korea and Spain. Causing particular controversy was an agreement permitting U.S. use of Spanish bases in return for American grants, loans and other assistance. Sen. J. William Fulbright, D-Ark. (1945-74), objected:

> We get many treaties dealing with postal affairs and so on. Recently, we had an extraordinary treaty dealing with the protection of stolen art objects. These are treaties. But when we put troops and take on commitments in Spain, it is an executive agreement. [46]

Adding to congressional frustrations were agreements made by the Nixon administration in 1971 with Portugal on the use of an airbase in the Azores and with Bahrain for naval base facilities in the Persian Gulf. These important agreements should have been submitted as treaties, argued members of the Foreign Relations Committee. The Senate passed a sense of the Senate resolution to that effect.

In 1972 Congress approved a bill introduced by Sen. Clifford P. Case, R-N.J. (1955-79), requiring the secretary of state within 60 days to submit to Congress the final text of any international agreement made by the executive branch. Those having national security implications were to be submitted on a classified basis to the House and Senate foreign affairs committees. Sen. Case argued that Congress could not adequately perform its foreign policy role without knowledge of commitments made by the executive branch.[47]

Although the 1972 act dealt with the problem of secrecy, it was a first step only and did not provide for any congressional response to executive agreements. The Senate in 1974 passed a bill introduced by Sam J. Ervin Jr., D-N.C. (1954-74), to establish congressional procedures for disapproving executive agreements, but it died in the House.

## Notes

1. For a general discussion of the treaty power, see Arthur M. Schlesinger, Jr. *The Imperial Presidency* (Boston: Houghton-Mifflin Co., 1973), pp. 79-85; Louis Henkin, *Foreign Affairs and the Constitution* (New York: W. W. Norton & Co., 1972), pp. 130-173; and George H. Haynes, *The Senate of the United States: Its History and Practice,* 2 vols. (Boston: Houghton Mifflin Co., 1938), II: Chapter 12.

2. John F. Lehman, *The Executive, Congress and Foreign Policy: Studies of the Nixon Administration* (New York: Praeger Publishers, 1976), p. 80.
3. Haynes, *The Senate,* II: 574.
4. Ibid., II: 573-575; and Charles Warren, *The Making of the Constitution* (Boston: Little, Brown & Co., 1928), pp. 651-658.
5. Buel W. Patch, "Treaties and Domestic Law," *Editorial Research Reports,* March 28, 1952, p. 247.
6. Ibid., p. 241; and Henkin, *Foreign Affairs,* pp. 156-162.
7. Haynes, *The Senate,* II: 575.
8. Ibid., II: 62-66, 583-584.
9. Ibid., II: 692.
10. Joseph P. Harris, *The Advice and Consent of the Senate* (Westport, Conn: Greenwood Press, 1968), p. 282.
11. Haynes, *The Senate,* I: 62, 63, 68; II: 583, 584.
12. Ibid., II: 591; and F. M. Brewer, "Advice and Consent of the Senate," *Editorial Research Reports,* June 1, 1943, p. 348.
13. Haynes, *The Senate,* II: 586-587, 600.
14. Ibid., II: 581.
15. For a discussion of the decision, see *Guide to the U.S. Supreme Court* (Washington, D.C.: Congressional Quarterly, 1979), pp. 201-202; Schlesinger, *The Imperial Presidency,* pp. 100-104; and C. Herman Pritchett, *The American Constitution* (New York: McGraw Hill Book Co., 1959), pp. 356-357.
16. Haynes, *The Senate,* II: 529.
17. Ibid., II: 593.
18. Ibid., II: 595; Harris, *The Advice and Consent of the Senate,* p. 285; and Brewer, "Advice and Consent of the Senate," p. 350.
19. Jefferson to Madison, March 15, 1798; cited in Brewer, "Advice and Consent of the Senate," p. 350.
20. Jefferson to Genet, Nov. 22, 1793; cited in ibid.
21. Ibid.
22. Ibid, p. 352.
23. Ibid.
24. Haynes, *The Senate,* II: 596.
25. Brewer, "Advice and Consent of the Senate," p. 353.
26. Haynes, *The Senate,* II: 597.
27. Brewer, "Advice and Consent of the Senate," p. 354.
28. Francis O. Wilcox, *Congress, the Executive and Foreign Policy* (New York: Harper & Row, 1971), p. 55.
29. Haynes, *The Senate,* II: 666, 636-639.
30. U.S., Congress, Senate, Foreign Relations Committee, *Background Information on the Committee on Foreign Relations* (Washington, D.C.: U.S. Government Printing Office, 1975), p. 24.

31. Haynes, *The Senate,* II: 665-670.
32. Ibid., II: 663-664.
33. Senate Foreign Relations Committee, *Background Information,* pp. 24-25.
34. Haynes, *The Senate,* II: 604-606.
35. Ibid., II: 608, 657.
36. Ibid., II: 609.
37. Ibid.
38. For a discussion of the Connally reservation, see *Congress and the Nation,* 5 vols., *Congress and the Nation: 1945-1964,* vol. 1 (Washington, D.C.: Congressional Quarterly, 1965), I: 98, 126.
39. Senate Foreign Relations Committee, *Background Information,* p. 24.
40. Theodor Meron, "The Treaty Power: The International Legal Effect of Changes in Obligations Initiated by the Congress," in *The Tethered Presidency: Congressional Restraints on Executive Power*, ed. Thomas M. Franck (Washington Square, N.Y.: New York University Press, 1981), p. 128.
41. U.S. Department of State, Publication No. 8960, *Digest of the United States Practice in International Law 1977,* 376 (1979); cited in ibid.
42. For a discussion of Congress' efforts to change the Senate's treaty power, see F. M. Brewer, "The Treaty Power," *Editorial Research Reports*, Jan. 18, 1943, pp. 40-44; and *Congress and the Nation: 1945-1964*, I: 98.
43. *Congress and the Nation: 1945-1964,* I: 110.
44. For a general discussion of executive agreements, see Edward S. Corwin, *The President: Office and Powers, 1787-1957* (Washington Square, N.Y.: New York University Press, 1957), pp. 204-217; Schlesinger, *The Imperial Presidency,* pp. 86-88; Raoul Berger, *Executive Privilege* (Cambridge: Harvard University Press, 1974), pp. 140-162; Henkin, *Foreign Affairs*, pp. 176-186; Lehman, *The Executive, Congress and Foreign Policy,* pp. 78-83; and U.S., Congress, Senate, Judiciary Committee, Subcommittee on the Separation of Powers, *Congressional Oversight of Executive Agreements* (Washington, D.C.: U.S. Government Printing Office, 1973).
45. Thomas E. Cronin, "A Resurgent Congress and the Imperial Presidency," *Political Science Quarterly* (Summer 1980): 213.
46. Arthur M. Schlesinger Jr., "Congress and the Making of American Foreign Policy," in *The Presidency Reappraised,* 2d ed., edited by Thomas E. Cronin and Rexford G. Tugwell (New York: Praeger Publishers, 1977), p. 216.
47. *Congressional Quarterly Almanac 1972* (Washington, D.C.: Congressional Quarterly, 1973), p. 619.

## *Chapter 9*

# THE WAR POWER

The war power, like the treaty power, is split between Congress and the president and has been the subject of recurring controversy involving rival claims by the executive and legislative branches. The constitutional basis for the president's war power is Article II, Section 2: "The President shall be Commander in Chief of the Army and Navy of the United States, and of the Militia of the several States, when called into the actual Service of the United States." Article I, Section 8, of the Constitution sets forth Congress' authority in this area:

> The Congress shall have Power ... To declare War, grant Letters of Marque and Reprisal, and make Rules concerning Captures on Land and Water; To raise and support Armies. . . ; To provide and maintain a Navy; To make Rules for the Government and Regulation of the land and naval Forces; To provide for calling forth the Militia to execute the Laws of the Union, suppress Insurrections and repel Invasions; To provide for organizing, arming, and disciplining the Militia, and for governing such Part of them as may be employed in the Service of the United States, reserving to the States respectively, the Appointment of the Officers, and the Authority of training the Militia according to the discipline prescribed by Congress.

At the time the American Constitution was framed, the war-making power in all other countries was vested in the executive. When the Constitutional Convention at Philadelphia took up this question, at the session of Aug. 17, 1787, Pierce Butler, a delegate of South Carolina, proposed that the power to make war be granted to the president, "who will have all the requisite qualities and will not make war but when the nation will support it." But Elbridge Gerry of Massachusetts objected; he "never expected to hear in a republic a motion to empower the executive alone to declare war." George Mason of Virginia also opposed "giving the power of war to the executive, because he is not safely to be trusted with it." Charles Pinckney of South Carolina suggested placing the war power in the Senate, which would be "more acquainted with foreign affairs and most capable of proper resolutions." Pinckney felt that the proceedings of the House of Representatives were too slow and that it would be "too numerous for such deliberations. The convention nevertheless conferred the power on Congress as a whole. It changed the phrase "to make war," as reported by the Committee of Detail, to "to declare war," so as to leave the president the power to repel sudden attacks but not to commence war.[1]

The innovation of placing the war power in the legislative rather than the executive branch was hailed by Thomas Jefferson as a valuable restraint upon exercise of the power. He wrote to James Madison on Sept. 6, 1789: "We have already given, in example, one effectual check to the dog of war, by transferring the power of letting him loose from the executive to the legislative body, from those who are to spend to those who are to pay." Madison himself wrote: "The Constitution supposes what the history of all governments demonstrates, that the executive is the branch of power most interested in war and most prone to it. It has accordingly, with studied care, vested the question of war in the legislature." [2]

Writing in *The Federalist* (No. 69) against giving the war power to Congress, Alexander Hamilton noted that the powers of the president as commander in chief would be "much inferior" to that of the British King; "it would amount to nothing more than the supreme command and direction of the military and naval forces, as first general and admiral . . . while that of the British King extends to the declaring of war and to the raising and regulating of fleets and armies — all of which, by the Constitution . . . would appertain to the legislature." [3]

"Those who are to conduct a war cannot in the nature of things be proper or safe judges whether a war ought to be commenced, continued or concluded," wrote Madison. "They are barred from the latter functions by a great principle in free government, analogous to that which separates the sword from the purse, or the power of executing from the power of enacting laws." [4]

Thus was viewed the system of checks and balances on the war power at the time of the founding of the Republic. Writing in 1980, political scientist Cecil V. Crabb, Jr. noted: "As with other constitutional issues, the precise balance or allocation of the war powers between the two ends of Pennsylvania Avenue has been determined more by experience, precedents, and circumstances than by the intentions of the founders or by contending legal theories. On this front the overall tendency has been for legislative prerogatives to be eclipsed by forceful assertions of executive initiative and leadership." [5]

"With few exceptions, the power to initiate and wage war has shifted to the executive branch," wrote Louis Fisher, an American government specialist with the Library of Congress, in 1972. According to Fisher, the president's power as commander in chief has grown in response to three major developments:

> First, the President acquired the responsibility to protect American life and property abroad. He has invoked that vague prerogative on numerous occasions to satisfy much larger objectives of the executive branch. Second, the time boundaries of the "war period" have become increasingly elastic. The President may initiate military operations before congressional action, and he retains wartime powers long after hostilities have ceased. Third, the postwar period, which has been marked by nuclear weapons, the cold war, intercontinental missiles, military alliances, and greater U.S. world responsibilities, has accelerated the growth of presidential power. [6]

## Declared and Undeclared Wars

Beginning in 1950, a new dimension was injected into the question of congressional vs. presidential war powers: presidential commitments of American forces to combat without a declaration of war. U.S. combat troops were involved in full-scale war in Korea from 1950 to 1953 and in Indochina from 1965 to 1973 without a declaration of war in either conflict. In two other instances, Lebanon in 1958 and the Dominican Republic in 1965, U.S. combat troops were used to help maintain conditions of political stability in countries threatened by or undergoing civil strife.

Writing in the 1960s, before the United States went to war in Vietnam without formal congressional consent, constitutional historian C. Herman Pritchett concluded: Presidential powers are of "tremendous impact — so great in fact that to a considerable degree they cancel out the most important grant of external authority to Congress, the power to declare war." [7] Throughout the nation's history, only two major conflicts — the War of 1812 and the Spanish-American War — were clearly the product of congressional policy.

## Lincoln's Improvised War Powers . . .

In the early days of the Civil War, President Abraham Lincoln used to the fullest the war powers at his disposal. Without congressional authorization, he issued a proclamation on May 3, 1861, increasing the size of the regular Army and the Navy and calling for 80,000 volunteers. Moreover, he ordered 19 vessels added to the Navy and directed the secretary of the Treasury to advance $2 million to unauthorized persons to cover military and naval requisitions. When Congress convened July 4, 1861, the president declared that some of his emergency measures, "whether strictly legal or not, were ventured upon under what appeared to be a popular demand and a public necessity, trusting then, as now, Congress would readily ratify them."

And Congress did. On Aug. 6, 1861, it adopted a resolution providing that "All the acts, proclamations, and orders of the president respecting the Army and Navy of the United States, and calling out or relating to the militia or volunteers . . . are hereby approved and in all respects made valid . . . as if they had been issued and done under the previous express authority and direction of the Congress of the United States."

In 1863 the Supreme Court, in a group of rulings called *The Prize Cases* (2 Black 635), gave its blessing to another of Lincoln's improvised war powers. Early in the war, the president had proclaimed a blockade of Confederate ports. Vessels attempting to run the blockade were seized and condemned as "prizes" — that is, they were confiscated for having

Numerous U.S. administrations have justified the absence of a declaration of war by citing historical "precedents." Indeed, Congress declared war in only five conflicts: the War of 1812, the Mexican War, the Spanish-American War, World War I and World War II. No declaration was made or requested in the Naval War with France (1798-1800), the First Barbary War (1801-05), the Second Barbary War (1815), or the various Mexican-American clashes of 1914-17.[8] Categorizing the 1798-1800 war with France as "undeclared" may be disputed, according to Raoul Berger and Arthur M. Schlesinger Jr., because President John Adams took no independent action before Congress passed a series of

## ... Subsequently Validated by Congress

defied the president's order. The owners sued for redress on the ground that no war had ever been declared between North and South.

The court sustained the president's power to proclaim the blockade without a declaration of war. A state of war already existed, the majority said, and the president was obligated "to meet it in the shape it presented itself, without waiting for Congress to baptize it with a name. . . ." The court acknowledged that Congress had the power to declare war, but ruled that the president had to meet the challenge in the emergency until Congress could act:

> By the Constitution, Congress alone has the power to declare a national or foreign war. . . . [The President] has no power to initiate or declare a war either against a foreign nation or a domestic State. . . . If a war be made by invasion of a foreign nation, the President is not only authorized but bound to resist force, by force. He does not initiate the war, but is bound to accept the challenge without waiting for any special legislative authority. And whether the hostile party be a foreign invader, or States organized in rebellion, it is none the less a war, although the declaration be *"unilateral."*

Source: Richard L. Worsnop, "War Powers of the President," *Editorial Research Reports,* March 14, 1966, pp. 192-193; Arthur M. Schlesinger Jr., *The Imperial Presidency* (Boston: Houghton Mifflin Co., 1973), pp. 58 ff; Rexford G. Tugwell, *The Enlargement of the Presidency* (New York: Doubleday & Co. , 1960), pp. 150-164; Edward S. Corwin, *The President, Office and Powers* (New York: New York University Press, 1957), pp. 228-234; C. Herman Pritchett, *The American Constitution* (New York: McGraw-Hill, 1968), p. 376; Congressional Quarterly, *Guide to the U.S. Supreme Court* (Washington, D.C.: Congressional Quarterly, 1979), pp. 187-188.

acts which amounted, the Supreme Court ruled, to a declaration of "imperfect war." [9]

One study of the period from 1946 through 1975 cited 215 incidents in which the United States employed its armed forces for political purposes. The incidents ranged from a visit to a foreign port by a single warship, to deployment of major ground, air and naval units, to mobilizing reserves and placing strategic nuclear forces on alert. (Among the military activities excluded from the study were those related to the Korean and Indochina wars, those in defense of U.S. property and citizens, and routine training exercises and maneuvers.)[10]

The 19th century, according to Berger, offers no example of a president who plunged the United States into war in order to repel an attack by one foreign country on another. Indeed, this did not occur until the Korean War; both Woodrow Wilson and Franklin Roosevelt obtained a declaration of war before sending troops to engage in hostilities on foreign soil.[11]

During the congressional debate on presidential war powers in the 1960s and 1970s, some contended that declarations of war were outmoded, given the existence of nuclear weapons and the need to commit troops overseas in emergencies on a limited war basis. Testifying before the Foreign Relations Committee in 1971, Alpheus T. Mason, professor of political science at Princeton University, commented:

> The Framers, with deliberate care, made war-making a joint enterprise. Congress is authorized to "declare war"; the President is designated "commander in chief." Technology has expanded the President's role and correspondingly curtailed the power of the Congress. Unchanged are the joint responsibilities of the President and Congress. The fact that a congressional declaration of war is no longer practical does not deprive Congress of constitutionally imposed authority in war-making. On the contrary, it is under obligation to readjust its power position.[12]

Congress attempted to do just that in 1973 by passing the War Powers Resolution. *(Details, pp. 117-120.)*

## Congress and the World Wars

Once Congress has declared war and voted the necessary funds, presidents have vastly enlarged the scope of their authority, both in domestic and foreign affairs. By the turn of the century, the federal government had become increasingly active in regulating the economy, and when the United States entered World War I Congress delegated far-reaching powers to President Wilson over the economy and domestic affairs.

The foreign policy and domestic powers exercised by President Roosevelt in World War II were even more considerable, as the concept of a national emergency expanded with the necessity of placing the entire country on a war footing. Historian Edward S. Corwin has noted: "In the First World War, as in the Civil War, the emergency that constitutional interpretation set itself to meet was a *war* emergency in the narrow, palpable sense. In the Second World War the emergency preceded the war and continued beyond it — a fact of special significance when it is considered in relation to the effect of wartime practices on the constitutional law of peacetime. [13]

Corwin added that "No more sweeping delegation of legislative power has ever been made to an American President than that represented in the enactment of . . . the Lend-Lease Act of March 11, 1941, nearly nine months before our actual entry into a 'shooting war.' " [14] The act authorized the president to manufacture any defense article and to "sell, transfer title to, exchange, lease, lend or otherwise dispose of" the defense articles to any country whose defense he deemed vital to the defense of the United States.

After Congress declared war on Dec. 8, 1941, the president's war mobilization authority was expanded to include sweeping powers over the economy, specifically authority to regulate industry needed in the war effort and the power to reopen and operate plants closed by strikes. Under the Emergency Price Control Act of 1942, the president appointed a price administrator who was authorized to set maximum rents.[15] By April 1942 some 42 new agencies had been created to oversee the war effort, 35 of which were of "purely presidential creation" whose constitutional and legal status became a source of controversy.[16]

Both world wars, as well as the Civil War, highlighted the problems of ending a national emergency. "The change-over from emergency war powers to normal executive responsibilities," says Fisher, " is by no means a rapid process. Long after hostilities have ended, many economic controls remain in force." [17] On July 25, 1947, Congress terminated certain temporary emergency and war powers involving about 175 statutory provisions, some of which dated back to World War I. Nonetheless, 103 war or emergency statutes remained in effect.[18]

In 1973 the United States had been living under a state of national emergency for 40 years — ever since President Roosevelt declared in 1933 that a national emergency existed as a result of the Depression. The Special Senate Committee on the Termination of the National Emergency (created in 1973 and later re-formed as the Special Committee on National Emergencies and Delegated Emergency Powers) recommended ending the 1933 national emergency and three other emergency conditions still in existence. In 1976 Congress approved legislation officially terminating these states of national emergency and providing for congressional oversight and review of future emergency declarations.

Taking as a model the 1973 War Powers Resolution, the bill provided that any future national emergency proclaimed by the president could be terminated by Congress through a concurrent resolution — not subject to presidential veto — or by presidential proclamation.[19]

In 1977 Congress approved a bill restricting the authority of the chief executive to impose economic controls during presidentially declared national emergencies. The legislation did not weaken the wartime powers of the president, but it amended the Trading With the Enemy Act to remove the state of national emergency as the basis for the imposition of controls by the president. Authority under the 1917 act had been used over the years to justify actions ranging from the declaration of a bank holiday to the imposition of controls on foreign investments.[20]

## Expanded View of President's War Powers

In his book *President and Congress,* Fisher noted that the war powers of the president were drawn originally from "1) his responsibilities as commander in chief, 2) his oath to preserve, protect and defend the Constitution, 3) his duty to protect the nation from sudden attack, and 4) the inherent powers derived from the general heading 'executive power.' " However, "in recent decades, the definition of inherent and implied powers has become increasingly generous because of treaty commitments, vaguely worded congressional resolutions, and an accumulation of emergency statutes. Moreover, the President's constitutional responsibility for repelling sudden attacks and waging defensive war has expanded in scope until it is now used to justify involvement in full-scale wars without legislative approval." [21]

The wars in Korea and Indochina are cases in point. According to Schlesinger, President Truman "dramatically and dangerously enlarged the power of future Presidents to take the nation into major war," and Presidents Lyndon B. Johnson and Richard M. Nixon "surpassed all their predecessors in claiming that inherent and exclusive presidential authority, unaccompanied by emergencies threatening the life of the nation, unaccompanied by the authorization of Congress or the blessing of an international organization, permitted a President to order troops into battle at his unilateral pleasure." [22]

**Korea.** The war in Korea began with an attack on South Korea by North Koreans on June 25, 1950, and continued for three years at a cost of more than 150,000 U.S. casualties. On June 26 President Truman ordered American air and sea forces in the Far East to aid South Korea.

## National Emergencies

In an assertion of congressional authority over the executive branch, Congress passed legislation in 1976 providing for congressional oversight and review of states of national emergency declared by the president. The bill also formally terminated four existing states of emergency, dating back to 1933, that remained technically in force although the relevant crises long had passed.

HR 3884 was the product of a two-year study by the Senate Special Committee on National Emergencies and Delegated Emergency Powers, co-chaired by Charles McC. Mathias Jr., R-Md., and Frank Church, D-Idaho (1957-81). The panel was born of a concern in Congress that, to expedite dramatic action in times of emergency, it had granted the president extraordinary powers largely unchecked by Congress. The emergency powers, Church said in Senate debate, included the right to seize property and commodities, control the means of production, institute martial law, send troops abroad, and regulate private enterprise. "And the President can exercise all these extraordinary powers," Church pointed out, "without so much as asking leave of Congress."

To correct the situation, HR 3884 provided for automatic congressional review, every six months, of all future national emergencies and congressional review and accountability for all presidential actions taken under emergency powers. The purpose of the bill, sponsors stressed, was not to alter the president's emergency powers, but to provide procedures for invoking such powers under the multitude of laws—some 470 of them—that provided for emergency action.

The four national emergencies that would be ended by HR 3884 were declared:

— By Franklin D. Roosevelt on March 4, 1933, to deal with the Depression.

— By Harry S Truman on Dec. 16, 1950, to react to North Korea's invasion of South Korea.

— By Richard Nixon on March 23, 1970, to respond to a national postal strike.

— By Nixon on Aug. 15, 1971, to implement currency restrictions following an international monetary crisis.

The next day the U.N. Security Council called on U.N. members for help in repelling the attack. The president on June 30 ordered ground troops into South Korea and sent the 7th Fleet to act as a buffer between China and Taiwan.[23]

Secretary of State Dean Acheson recommended to Truman that he "should not ask [Congress] for a resolution of approval, but rest on his constitutional authority as commander in chief." [24] Truman never did ask Congress for a declaration of war in Korea, and he waited until Dec. 16, 1950 — six months after the outbreak of hostilities — to proclaim the existence of a national emergency. In defense of this course, it was argued that the Russians or Chinese, or both, had violated post-World War II agreements on Korea and that emergency powers authorized during World War II still could be applied. Provisions in the U.N. Charter also were used to justify Truman's action. A legal memorandum by the State Department in 1950 offered this defense: "Both traditional international law and Article 39 of the U.N. Charter and the resolution pursuant thereto authorize the United States to repel the armed aggression against the Republic of Korea." [25] However, the legality of that argument was questioned on the ground that U.S. armed forces were ordered to South Korea before the U.N. Security Council authorized the action.[26]

Although there was never a formal declaration of war or congressional resolution supporting Truman's decision, Congress implicitly ratified the action by consistently appropriating the requested funds for the war. Not until 1951 were the president's war powers seriously challenged by Congress. Sen. Robert A. Taft, R-Ohio (1939-53), opened a three-month-long "great debate" on Jan. 5, 1951, by asserting that Truman had "no power to agree to send American troops to fight in Europe in a war between the members of the Atlantic Pact and Soviet Russia." [27] The debate ended on April 4, when the Senate adopted two resolutions approving the dispatch of four divisions to Europe. One of the resolutions stated that it was the sense of the Senate that "no ground troops in addition to such four divisions should be sent to Western Europe . . . without further congressional approval."

Truman hailed the action as a "clear endorsement" of his troop plans, saying "there has never been any real question" about the United States doing its part in the defense of Europe. But he ignored the Senate's claim to a voice in future troop commitments. Neither resolution had the force of law. In essence, the "great debate" had confirmed both the president's power to commit U.S. forces without prior congressional approval and the decision to defend Western Europe.

Truman overstepped his powers as commander in chief when he relied on them, April 8, 1952, to take possession and control of all facilities, plants and properties of 86 steel companies involved in a dispute with the United Steelworkers. Congress ignored the president's request to approve the seizure order. Then, on June 2, the Supreme Court ruled (*Youngstown Sheet & Tube Co. v. Sawyer,* 343 U.S. 579) that his action was without statutory authority and that it violated the concept of separation of powers by usurping functions of Congress.

**Vietnam.** U.S. military aid to Vietnam was initiated by the Truman administration. In 1951 military aid to that country amounted to more than $500 million. Although President Dwight D. Eisenhower barred a U.S. combat role in Vietnam, in 1954 the United States sent 200 Air Force technicians to aid the French in their fight against the Viet Minh. The Foreign Relations Committee subsequently expressed concern at the lack of congressional consultation in that decision, and the State Department pledged to consult with Congress before making any other moves in Vietnam.[28]

In March 1954, at the beginning of the 56-day battle at Dienbienphu that ended with France's defeat, the White House tentatively approved a plan for immediate U.S. air intervention, but members of Congress, including Sens. Lyndon B. Johnson, D-Texas (1949-61), who was minority leader at the time, and Richard B. Russell, D-Ga. (1933-71), the highest-ranking Democrat on the Armed Services Committee, rejected the proposal.

North Vietnamese attacks on U.S. Navy destroyers in the Gulf of Tonkin solidifed congressional support for the war. The Tonkin Gulf Resolution of August 1964, later called by the Johnson administration the equivalent of a congressional declaration of war and used to justify its policies, was opposed by only two members of the Senate, Wayne Morse, D-Ore. (1945-69), and Ernest Gruening, D-Alaska (1959-69); and it received unanimous backing in the House. After adoption of the resolution, neither the Johnson nor Nixon administrations returned to Congress to seek additional authority for stepping up military activity. Nixon ordered U.S. troops into Cambodia in 1970, provided air support for South Vietnam's 1971 invasion of Laos, ordered Haiphong harbor mined in 1972 and launched the heaviest bombing of North Vietnam in December 1972 — all without seeking congressional consent.

As the war dragged on in the period spanning the 1964 Tonkin resolution and the 1973 Vietnam cease-fire, complaints about aggrandizement of presidential war powers began to surface. Increasing criticism of U.S. involvement was followed by outright disaffection in Congress. But once Congress committed itself to the war it was unable to bring itself to force an end to the conflict. Shortly before the Jan. 27, 1973, signing of the Vietnam peace agreement, Senate Majority Leader Mike Mansfield, D-Mont. (1953-77), insisted that Congress "can't end the war." "It's really up to the President," Mansfield said. "We shouldn't fool ourselves in that respect."At the peak of anti-war strength in Congress, only one out of three House members voted to back end-the-war proposals. On the few bills to reach House-Senate conference deliberations, House conferees almost invariably were responsible for deleting or emasculating Senate-passed anti-war amendments.

The picture of the Johnson and Nixon administrations carrying on military activities in Indochina without congressional consent often was overdrawn by critics of the war, who tended to overlook the frequent votes in Congress in favor of military appropriations. While critics often spoke of a constitutional crisis over war powers, there never was a constitutional confrontation between the president and Congress because Congress always was willing to appropriate the necessary funds. Once a president had committed men and materiel to battle, it became much harder for lawmakers to deny the forces the money they needed to wage the war.

Yet, from another viewpoint, the increasing number of anti-war votes in Congress — from five in 1969 to 35 in 1972 — may well have served to reinforce President Nixon's decision to continue troop withdrawals from Indochina, a policy Nixon had announced in June 1969. The votes were a constant signal that slowing down, or reversing, the troop withdrawals would involve heavy political costs.

In the spring of 1973, there was a postscript to Congress' response to the Vietnam War. Although it had pulled out of Vietnam two months after the January peace agreement, the Nixon administration continued its bombing of Cambodia and Laos. In action on a supplemental appropriation bill, the House for the first time voted to cut off funds for U.S. military activity in Southeast Asia. Final provisions of that measure, signed by Nixon, barred the use of any past or existing funds for financing directly or indirectly U.S. combat activities in, over or off the shores of North Vietnam, South Vietnam, Laos or Cambodia.

Congress did not stop with a bombing ban in finally challenging presidential power. In July 1973 Congress passed a tough war powers measure that set a 60-day limit on any presidential commitment of U.S. troops to hostilities abroad or in situations where hostilities might be imminent unless Congress declared war, authorized continuation of the commitment or was unable to meet the requirements because of an armed attack upon the United States.

## Policy Resolutions as War Authority

Since 1945 Congress on five occasions has passed joint resolutions authorizing or approving the president's determination to use such armed forces as he deemed necessary to repel armed attacks or threats against certain nations or geographical areas. Four of the resolutions were initiated by the president, who sought congressional approval for military actions either contemplated or already undertaken. The five resolutions were:

— Formosa Resolution, signed into law Jan. 29, 1955, authorizing the president to use U.S. forces to protect Taiwan (which until the 1960s was called "Formosa" by most westerners) and the Pescadores Islands against "armed attack" from Communist China.

— Middle East Resolution, signed into law March 9, 1957, proclaiming U.S. policy to defend Middle East countries "against aggression from any country controlled by international communism."

— Cuban Resolution, signed into law Oct. 3, 1962, authorizing the president to take whatever steps were necessary to defend Latin America against Cuban aggression or subversion and to oppose the deployment of Soviet weapons in Cuba capable of endangering U.S. security.

— Berlin Resolution, adopted in October 1962, reaffirming U.S. determination to use armed force, if necessary, to defend West Berlin and the access rights of the Western powers to West Berlin.

— Tonkin Gulf Resolution, signed into law Aug. 10, 1964, authorizing the president to use U.S. armed forces to repel attacks against U.S. forces and affirming U.S. determination to defend any Southeast Asia Treaty Organization (SEATO) member or protocol state (this included Vietnam) requesting assistance.

## 1973 War Powers Resolution

Increasingly frustrated with its ineffectual influence on American involvement in Indochina and on the scope of U.S. military commitments abroad, Congress in 1973 responded by passing — over a Nixon veto — legislation designed to limit the president's powers to commit U.S. forces abroad without congressional approval. Known as the War Powers Resolution (H J Res 542 — PL 93-148), the bill was heralded by its supporters as a major step in reasserting Congress' war-making powers. Said Jacob K. Javits, R-N.Y. (1957-81), chief architect of the Senate version of the legislation: "With the war powers resolution's passage, after 200 years, at last something will have been done about codifying the implementation of the most awesome power in the possession of any sovereignty and giving the broad representation of the people in Congress a voice in it. This is critically important, for we have just learned the hard lesson that wars cannot be successfully fought except with the consent of the people and with their support."

In vetoing the legislation, Nixon declared that the resolution would impose restrictions on the authority of the president that would be "both unconstitutional and dangerous to the best interests of our nation." The major provisions of the bill, he contended, would "purport to take away, by a mere legislative act, authorities which the president has properly exercised under the Constitution for almost 200 years." Many of the act's provisions were unconstitutional, he asserted, because "the only way in which the constitutional powers of a branch of the government can be altered is by amending the Constitution — and any attempt to make such alterations by legislation alone is clearly without force." [29]

The president's position was argued by some conservatives and administration supporters during debate on the bill. In their assertions that the bill was unconstitutional they were joined by a small group of liberals, but for different reasons. Thomas F. Eagleton, D-Mo., an author of the Senate's original war powers bill, branded the final version as "the most dangerous piece of legislation" he had seen in his five years in the Senate. Eagleton warned his colleagues: "We are going to give him [Nixon] more authority, and legalize it, than perhaps he ever dreamed he had. Not only President Nixon, but every president of the United States will have at least the color of legal authority, the advance blessing of Congress, given on an open, blank-check basis, to take us to war. It is a horrible mistake."

The war powers resolution was put to a test in May 1975, when Gerald R. Ford ordered the use of U.S. troops to free the American mer-

## War Powers Provisions

As enacted into law, the 1973 War Powers Resolution:

— Stated that the president could commit U.S. armed forces to hostilities or situations where hostilities might be imminent only pursuant to a declaration of war, specific statutory authorization or a national emergency created by an attack upon the United States, its territories or possessions, or its armed forces.

— Urged the president "in every possible instance" to consult with Congress before committing U.S. forces to hostilities and to consult Congress regularly after such a commitment.

— Required the president to report in writing within 48 hours to the Speaker of the House and president pro tempore of the Senate on any commitment or substantial enlargement of U.S. combat forces abroad, except for deployments related solely to supply, replacement, repair or training; required supplementary reports at least every six months while such forces were being engaged.

— Authorized the Speaker of the House and the president pro tempore of the Senate to reconvene Congress if it were not in session to consider the president's report.

— Required the termination of a troop commitment within 60 days after the president's initial report was submitted, unless Congress declared war, specifically authorized continuation of the commitment, or was physically unable to convene as a result of an armed attack; allowed the 60-day period to be extended for up to 30 days if the president determined and certified to Congress that unavoidable military necessity respecting the safety of U.S. forces required their continued use in bringing about a prompt disengagement.

— Allowed Congress at any time U.S. forces were engaged in hostilities without a declaration of war or specific congressional authorization by concurrent resolution to direct the president to disengage such troops.

— Set up congressional procedures for consideration of any resolution or bill introduced pursuant to the provisions of the resolution.

— Provided that if any provision of the resolution was declared invalid, the remainder of the resolution would not be affected.

chant ship *Mayaguez* and its crew of 39, seized May 12 by Cambodian communist troops off the disputed island of Poulo Wai in the Gulf of Siam. In this case there was general agreement in Congress that the president had the authority to commit U.S. troops without regard to the war powers law, even though the president complied with it by issuing a report on his action to Congress May 15 in accordance with the bill's 48-hour reporting requirement.

Although congressional reaction to Ford's use of force was generally favorable, some criticized the way Congress had been consulted. Pat M. Holt, chief of staff of the Foreign Relations Committee at the time of the incident, observed that, although the White House tried to keep key members informed of what was happening, ". . . the controlling fact is that members of Congress did not feel that they had been consulted." [30] Senate Majority Leader Mansfield said, "I did not give my approval or disapproval because the decision had already been made." He said he had questions about the whole affair and called for greater consultation, as did other congressional leaders.

On April 25, 1980, President Jimmy Carter announced that the U.S. had made a military attempt to rescue the 52 American hostages in Iran but the mission had failed. A few members of Congress charged that the president had violated the war powers resolution by not consulting Congress before launching the operation, but most accepted the administration's contention that the consultation provision did not apply to a rescue mission and that the need for absolute secrecy and surprise overrode the congressional need to know.[31]

## Secrecy vs. an Informed Public

In the executive-legislative struggle over the formulation of foreign policy, "Information manipulation — both suppression and selective release — is . . . one of the most powerful weapons employed. . . ," stated Harry L. Wrenn in a 1978 Library of Congress study. "Among participants in the policymaking process there is a near universal tendency toward *confidentiality* — the selective withholding of information from 'enemies' or competitors — and *salesmanship* — the structuring of that portion of information that is released in such a way as to strengthen one's own position to the utmost and to weaken that of the opposition correspondingly." [32]

The requirement of an informed citizenry in a democratic society, and the need for secrecy in certain government operations, is a modern dilemma about which Madison and the other Founding Fathers could not have been prescient. World War I saw the growth of the system of classifying documents, and the system was considerably strengthened during World War II. On March 22, 1940, President Roosevelt by executive order conferred presidential recognition for the first time on the military classification system. The system rapidly spread to the State Department and other executive branch agencies until, in Schlesinger's words, "a legitimate system of restriction grew ... into an extravagant and indefensible system of denial." [33]

By the 1970s Congress and the public had begun to lose confidence in the integrity of the secrecy system. "Illegitimate secrecy," wrote Schlesinger, "had corrupted the conduct of foreign affairs and had on occasion deprived voters of information necessary for democratic control of foreign policy." [34]

In Congress, committees in both chambers held extensive hearings on the subject of government secrecy. In August 1972 the Senate established a special 10-member Committee to Study Questions related to Secret and Confidential Government Documents, co-chaired by the majority and minority leaders. In its report, filed in October 1973, the committee stated that Congress should take a second look at the broad grant of power it had given presidents to classify government documents and thus put them beyond the reach even of members of Congress.[35]

Publication of the Pentagon Papers by the *New York Times* in June 1971 — two years after the Nixon administration had denied them to the Foreign Relations Committee — dramatically highlighted the secrecy issue. And the reading of the classified documents by Sen. Mike Gravel, D-Alaska (1969-81), during a special subcommittee meeting June 29 fueled the fire. The issue was greater than just the propriety of the Times' publication or Gravel's action. Some of the disclosures in the Pentagon Papers raised serious questions about the propriety of the secrecy system itself and of government claims to secrecy in the name of national security.

In his book *Executive Privilege* Berger commented on the revelations concerning U.S. Vietnam policy:

> However the impact on the national interest of disclosure to the public may be viewed, withholding of the Pentagon Papers from the Senate Foreign Relations Committee and from Congress is something else again. Congress ... was intended to be the senior partner in the new federal government, the chief agent in waging,

> continuing and terminating war. It was therefore entitled to be advised of all the relevant facts.... It is a measure of executive arrogance that refusal of this study to Congress was made in the name of the "national interest." Nowhere in the Constitution ... does it appear that the Founders looked to the President to protect the "national interest" against the Congress. [36]

Francis O. Wilcox, writing in 1971, discussed the "crucial" need for Congress to obtain adequate information — much of which is available only from the executive — if it is to have a voice in foreign policy-making. Traditionally, the executive branch has been reluctant, Wilcox argued, "to give Congress access to its policy-planning documents at an early enough stage to be significant.... The result is virtually to deny Congress effective access to the policy-making process until it has been completed." [37]

Use of its own professional staff is one method whereby Congress can obtain information. In 1969 and 1970 the newly created Senate Foreign Relations Subcommittee on U.S. Security Agreements and Commitments Abroad sent a two-man team on fact-finding missions to 25 countries. The staff investigations — followed by detailed, closed-door hearings — revealed a host of U.S. commitments — some express, some implied, some secret, some not — which might lead, in Wilcox's words, to U.S. involvement "in a thousand ways in countries around the world." [38]

The committee's probe revealed that the Johnson administration had agreed to special payments for Filipino, Thai and Korean troops in Vietnam. There also were secret military contingency plans with Thailand and previously undisclosed U.S. participation in the war in Laos.[39] (The panel's hearings on Laos were published in heavily censored form.) In 1975 and 1976 congressional investigations brought to light many illegal activities of the intelligence community, particularly the CIA.

In his study Wrenn concluded that congressional information problems were in large measure a direct consequence of Congress' role in shaping foreign policy:

> In a sense, there is a sort of natural fit between the power Congress exercises and the information it receives; it gets what in a political sense it deserves and can fruitfully use. This consequential link between the role Congress plays in foreign affairs and the information it has on those affairs is sometimes overlooked. Thus, in

> the Korean and Vietnam wars, both of which produced sharp information controversies between the two branches, congressional disputants readily recognized that in the past a lack of information had been a crippling deficiency, and that if they were to play a larger role in policymaking they would need to be better informed, but were less clear in noting the reciprocal of this, which was that their lack of information was to an important degree the consequence of a congressional abdication of an active role in the policy process.[40]

"Restraining the secrecy system would not automatically restore a congressional voice in foreign policy," wrote Schlesinger. "But it would at least deprive Congress of a favorite alibi: that, because it did not have the facts, it had no choice but to let Presidents make the decisions."[41]

## Notes

1. For a discussion of proceedings at the Constitutional Convention in Philadelphia, see Edward S. Corwin, *The President: Office and Powers, 1787-1957* (Washington Square, N.Y.: New York University Press, 1957), pp. 194 ff; and Raoul Berger, *Executive Privilege* (Cambridge: Harvard University Press, 1974), pp. 65 ff.
2. Berger, *Executive Privilege,* p. 64.
3. Ibid., p. 63.
4. Ibid., p. 64.
5. Cecil V. Crabb, Jr. and Pat M. Holt, *Invitation to Struggle: Congress, the President, and Foreign Policy* (Washington, D.C.: CQ Press, 1980), p. 45.
6. Louis Fisher, *President and Congress* (New York: The Free Press, 1972), p. 175.
7. C. Herman Pritchett, *The American Constitution* (New York: McGraw-Hill Book Co., 1959), pp. 357-358.
8. Fisher, *President and Congress,* p. 179.
9. Berger, *Executive Privilege,* p. 75; and Arthur M. Schlesinger, Jr., *The Imperial Presidency* (Boston: Houghton Mifflin Co., 1973), p. 21.
10. Barry M. Blechman and Stephen S. Kaplan, *Force Without War: U.S. Armed Forces as a Political Instrument* (Washington, D.C.: The Brookings Institution, 1978).
11. Berger, *Executive Privilege,* p. 82.
12. U.S., Congress, Senate, Foreign Relations Committee, *Hearings on War Powers Legislation,* 91st Cong., 1st sess., 1971 (Washington, D.C.: U.S. Government Printing Office, 1972), p. 254.
13. Corwin, *The President: Office and Powers,* p. 237.
14. Ibid.
15. Fisher, *President and Congress,* p. 189.

16. Corwin, *The President: Office and Powers,* p. 242.
17. Fisher, *President and Congress,* p. 190.
18. Ibid., p. 193.
19. *Congressional Quarterly Almanac 1973* (Washington, D.C.: Congressional Quarterly, 1974), p. 778; *Congressional Quarterly Almanac 1976* (Washington, D.C.: Congressional Quarterly, 1977), p. 521.
20. *Congressional Quarterly Almanac 1977* (Washington, D.C.: Congressional Quarterly, 1978), p. 412.
21. Fisher, *President and Congress,* p. 193.
22. Schlesinger, *The Imperial Presidency,* pp. 135, 193.
23. For a discussion of the Korean War, see ibid., chapter 6; and James A. Robinson, *Congress and Foreign Policy Making* (Homewood, Ill.: Dorsey Press, 1962), pp. 48-50.
24. Berger, *Executive Privilege,* p. 76.
25. Fisher, *President and Congress,* p. 194.
26. Ibid.; and Thomas J. Eagleton, *War and Presidential Power* (New York: Liveright, 1974), pp. 70-72.
27. Congressional Quarterly, *Global Defense* (Washington, D.C.: Congressional Quarterly, 1969), pp. 72-73.
28. For a discussion of the Vietnam War, see *Congress and the Nation*, 5 vols., *Congress and the Nation: 1973-1976,* vol 4. (Washington, D.C.: Congressional Quarterly, 1977), IV: 889-912.
29. On the War Powers Resolution, see Thomas M. Franck and Edward Weisband, *Foreign Policy by Congress* (New York and Oxford: Oxford University Press, 1979), pp. 61-82; *Congressional Quarterly Almanac 1973,* pp. 905-917; Eagleton, *War and Presidential Power*; Schlesinger, *The Imperial Presidency,* pp. 301-307; Pat M. Holt, *The War Powers Resolution: The Role of Congress in U.S. Armed Intervention* (Washington, D.C.: American Enterprise Institute for Public Policy Research, 1978); and W. Stuart Darling and D. Craig Mense, "Rethinking the War Powers Act," *Presidential Studies Quarterly,* 7 (Spring-Summer 1977): 126-136.
30. Holt, *The War Powers Resolution,* p. 19.
31. *Congresssional Quarterly Weekly Report,* April 26, 1980, pp. 1067-1068; May 17, 1980, p. 1371.
32. U.S., Congress, Senate, Committee on Foreign Relations, *Congress, Information and Foreign Affairs,* prepared by the Library of Congress, Congressional Research Service, Foreign Affairs and National Defense Division, committee print, 95th Cong., 2d Sess., 1978, pp. 2, 99.
33. Ibid., pp. 338-339.
34. Ibid., p. 359.
35. *Congressional Quarterly Almanac 1973,* p. 787.
36. Ibid., p. 284.

37. Francis O. Wilcox, *Congress, the Executive and Foreign Policy* (New York: Harper & Row, 1971), pp. 48-49.
38. Ibid., p. 136.
39. See Roland A. Paul, *American Military Commitments Abroad* (New Brunswick, N.J.: Rutgers University Press, 1973).
40. Senate Committee on Foreign Relations, *Congress, Information and Foreign Affairs*, p. 98.
41. Schlesinger, *The Imperial Presidency*, p. 372.

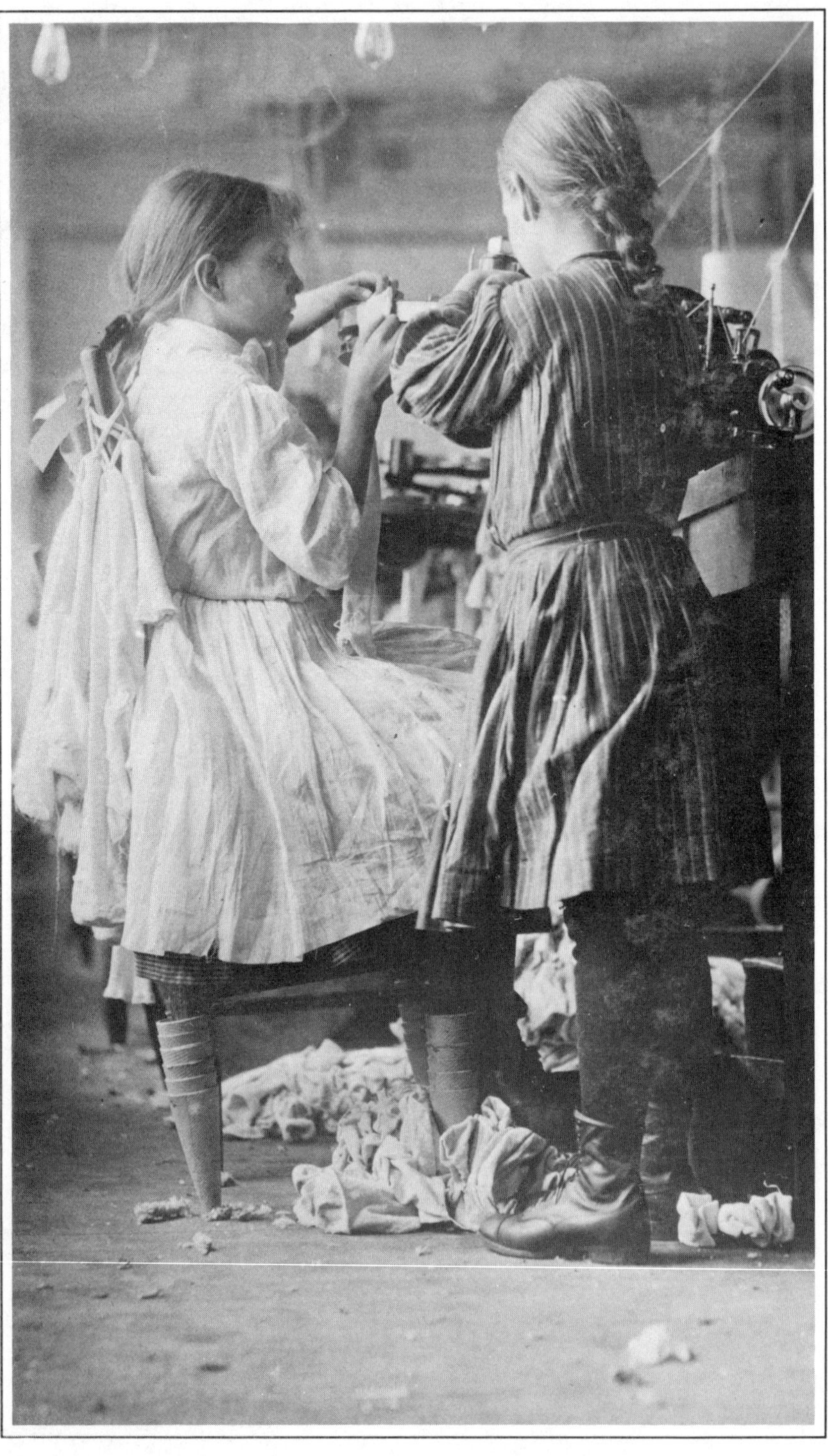

*Part III*

# Commerce Power

In 1918 the Supreme Court struck down an act of Congress that sought to prevent employment of children, such as in the textile mill pictured here. Congress had exceeded its power to regulate interstate commerce, the court ruled in *Hammer v. Dagenhart*.

## *Chapter 10*

# HISTORY OF COMMERCE CLAUSE

*"The Congress shall have Power . . . To regulate Commerce with foreign Nations, and among the several States, and with the Indian Tribes."*
(U.S. Constitution: Article I, Section 8, Clause 3)

With this simple grant of authority the Founding Fathers attempted to remedy one of the basic weaknesses of the federal government under the Articles of Confederation. The lack of a national power over commerce had been in large part responsible for the drafting of the Constitution, and the need for such a power was widely accepted.

The constitutional formula in Section 8, Clause 3, is a broad and general one: the positive grant of power to Congress is not coupled with a statement of the powers, if any, reserved to the states, and no definition of terms is offered. Four express limitations on the commerce power are contained in Article I, Section 9, but only one — forbidding Congress to lay a tax or duty on articles exported from any state — has had much practical significance. Thus the extent of Congress' power over commerce has been established by experience and judicial determination.

The basic Supreme Court decision involving the scope of the commerce clause was *Gibbons v. Ogden* in 1824. In a landmark opinion, Chief Justice John Marshall opted for a broad construction of the term "commerce" and emphatically asserted the supremacy of the federal power over it. But he rejected the argument — advanced by Daniel Webster, counsel for Gibbons — that the congressional power over commerce was "complete and entire," holding instead that "the completely internal commerce of a state . . . may be considered as reserved for the state itself." [1] From this acceptance of a divided authority over commerce has stemmed the concept of *interstate* as opposed to *intrastate* commerce, with movement across state lines as the basic test of the distinction.

Although Congress exercised its authority over foreign commerce from its earliest days, for nearly a century it failed to exploit its powers over commerce among the states. Most early Supreme Court decisions in the field dealt with state regulations that were challenged as infringements on the constitutional powers of Congress. The scope of state regulatory authority is still a problem for the courts today.

With enactment of the Interstate Commerce Act in 1887, Congress moved into the domestic regulatory field, and in the 20th century the scope of the commerce clause expanded to apply to almost any activity that affected interstate commerce. For years the Supreme Court held to the view that manufacturing and production were not a part of interstate commerce and that the commerce power extended only to activities that affected such commerce directly. By the 1940s, however, the court had come around to the view that the commerce power embraced activities that had an "effect upon commerce," however indirectly. Application of this doctrine led to a substantial expansion of congressional authority, and in the late 1930s and early 1940s the court concluded that the federal commerce power "is as broad as the need that evokes it." [2] That view, with one narrow exception, has prevailed since.

## Control of Commerce by the States

The necessity for national control over interstate and foreign commerce was the immediate occasion for the calling of the Constitutional Convention in 1787. "Most of our political evils," James Madison had written to Thomas Jefferson the previous year, "may be traced to our commercial ones." [3] Under the Articles of Confederation, adopted during the Revolutionary War, Congress had power to regulate trade only with the Indians; the control of interstate and foreign commerce was left to the states.

But commercial regulation by the several states proved increasingly chaotic after the Revolutionary War. Each state attempted to build up its own prosperity at the expense of its neighbors'. Justice William Johnson, in a concurring opinion in *Gibbons v. Ogden,* thus described the situation that had developed:

> For a century the states had submitted, with murmurs, to the commercial restrictions imposed by the parent state; and now, finding themselves in the unlimited possession of those powers over their own commerce, which they had so long been deprived of and

> so earnestly coveted, that selfish principle which, well controlled, is so salutary, and which, unrestricted, is so unjust and tyrannical, guided by inexperience and jealousy, began to show itself in iniquitous laws and impolitic measures, from which grew up a conflict of commercial regulations, destructive to the harmony of the states, and fatal to their commercial interests abroad. [4]

State legislatures imposed tariffs upon goods coming in from other states as well as from foreign countries. Thus, New York levied duties on firewood from Connecticut and cabbages from New Jersey. "The commerce which Massachusetts found it to her interest to encourage," wrote J. B. McMaster, "Virginia found it to hers to restrict. New York would not protect the trade in indigo and pitch. South Carolina cared nothing for the success of the fur interests." [5] Moreover, seaport states financed their governments through imposts on European goods passing through their harbors but destined for consumption in neighboring states. Madison described the plight of those states not having seaports: "New Jersey placed between Philadelphia and New York was likened to a cask tapped at both ends; and North Carolina, between Virginia and South Carolina, to a patient bleeding at both arms." [6]

Different currencies in each of the 13 states likewise hampered commercial intercourse. And if merchants were able to carry on an interstate business in spite of tariff and currency difficulties, they often had trouble in collecting their bills. Local courts and juries were less zealous in protecting the rights of distant creditors than those of their neighbors and friends.

The chaotic condition of interstate trade prompted the General Assembly of Virginia in 1786 to adopt a resolution proposing a joint meeting of commissioners appointed by each of the states "to take into consideration the trade of the United States; to examine the relative situations and trade of the said states; [and] to consider how far a uniform system in their commercial regulations may be necessary to their common interest and their permanent harmony." [7] The action of the Virginia Assembly led to a meeting at Annapolis later in the year of commissioners from five states: Delaware, New Jersey, New York, Pennsylvania and Virginia. The members of the Annapolis convention, however, thought it inadvisable to act with so few of the colonies represented and instead recommended a general meeting of all the colonies at Philadelphia in 1787.

## Adoption of the Commerce Clause

The desirability of uniform regulation of interstate and foreign commerce was so generally recognized that the proposal to give Congress blanket authority in this field occasioned comparatively little discussion at the Philadelphia convention. Some controversy did arise over an attempt by the South to limit the power of a congressional majority to regulate commerce. The southern states feared that the North might seek to dominate their commerce. Charles Pinckney of South Carolia proposed, therefore, that "all laws regulating commerce shall require the assent of two-thirds of the members present in each house," but this proposal was defeated by a vote of seven states to four, Maryland, Virginia, North Carolina and Georgia voting in the affirmative. If Pinckney's proposal had been adopted, says historian Charles Warren, "Enactment of protective tariffs might have been practically impossible. The whole political relations between the South and North growing out of commercial legislation would have been changed. The Nullification movement in the 1830s, which arose out of opposition to a Northern tariff, might not have occurred." [8]

In return for the South's acceptance of the unlimited power of a majority in Congress to regulate commerce, the northern states agreed to a ban on export taxes and to a provision that importation of slaves would not be prohibited before the year 1808. This was one of the important compromises reached at Philadelphia.

Many persons consider it remarkable that so important a part of the Constitution as the commerce clause should be so briefly expressed and should leave so much to future determination. But as Charles Warren has observed: "The violent differences of opinion which arose during the first half of the 19th century as to what the term 'commerce' included, and as to whether the power to 'regulate' was exclusive in Congress or exercisable by the states until Congress should act, were apparently not in the least foreseen by the members of the Convention." It is generally agreed that nothing more was immediately intended than that Congress should be empowered to prevent commercial wars among the states. Yet it is not to be doubted that the framers were aware of the scope of the power granted to Congress. James Monroe pointed out that the commerce clause involved "a radical change in the whole system of our government." [9]

## Supreme Court Interpretation

Although the federal government's power over interstate commerce was to become one of the most important and conspicuous it possesses, it was so little exercised in the first years of the nation's history that there was no need to define precisely what was meant by commerce "among the several States." Not until 1824, 35 years after the adoption of the Constitution, did a case involving the scope of this power reach the Supreme Court.

The circumstances leading to the court's decision in *Gibbons v. Ogden* involved precisely the sort of commercial warfare that had prompted the drafting of the Constitution in the first place. New York in 1798 granted to Robert R. Livingston, chancellor of the state, a monopoly over all steamboat operations in New York waters. In partnership with the inventor Robert Fulton, Livingston turned the monopoly into a viable transportation system and in 1811 was granted similar exclusive rights to operate in the waters of the territory of New Orleans.

Those grants prompted the other states to fight back. Connecticut, New Jersey and Ohio enacted retaliatory measures closing their waters to ships licensed by the New York monopoly while five other states granted steamship monopolies of their own. The result was navigational chaos.

The case that broke the monopoly involved Aaron Ogden, a former New Jersey governor (1812-13), and his partner Thomas Gibbons. Together the men ran a steam-driven ferry between Elizabethtown, N.J., and New York City. Ogden in 1815 had acquired a license from the Livingston-Fulton monopoly, and Gibbons held a permit under the federal Coastal Licensing Act of 1793 for his two boats. Despite their partnership, Gibbons ran his boats to New York in defiance of the monopoly rights that Ogden held, and in 1819 Ogden sued for an injunction to stop Gibbons' infringement of his rights under the monopoly. New York courts sided with Ogden, ordering Gibbons to halt his ferry service. Gibbons appealed to the Supreme Court, arguing that his federal license took precedence over the state-granted monopoly license and that he should be allowed to continue his ferrying in New York waters.

Delivering the court's opinion on March 2, 1824, Chief Justice John Marshall refused to construe the federal commerce power narrowly or to omit navigation from its scope: "Commerce undoubtedly is traffic,

## Congress Uses Its Commerce Powers . . .

From the beginning, the congressional power to regulate foreign commerce has been complete. The constitutional grant encompasses "every species of commercial intercourse between the United States and foreign nations. No sort of trade can be carried on between this country and any other, to which this power does not extend," wrote Chief Justice John Marshall in *Gibbons v. Ogden* (1824), in the classic interpretation of the commerce clause.[1]

The power to regulate commerce is inextricably tied to the powers over foreign relations and fiscal policies. Using these powers, Congress may set tariffs; regulate international shipping, aviation and communications; and establish embargoes against unfriendly countries. In conjunction with its powers to coin money, regulate its value and borrow funds for government activities, Congress may authorize U.S. participation in and appropriate contributions for international financing, banking and monetary systems such as the International Development Association and the World Bank.

The commerce power may be used to promote, inhibit or simply make rules for trade with other nations. It may be implemented by treaty or executive agreement as well as by acts of Congress.

### Tariffs

Historically, the predominant mechanism to restrict foreign trade has been the protective tariff. The first major business of the House in 1789 was to devise a tariff schedule. Unlike many later tariff laws, this one had as its chief objective the raising of revenue to finance the new government. Congress was not four days old, however, when a member of the House of Representatives from Philadelphia offered an amendment proposing additional duties on imported manufactured articles "to encourage the production of our country and to protect our infant manufacturers."

but it is something more; it is intercourse. It describes the commercial intercourse between nations, and parts of nations, in all its branches, and is regulated by prescribing rules for carrying on that intercourse. The mind can scarcely conceive a system for regulating commerce

## . . . To Promote or Restrict Foreign Trade

The Roosevelt administration's economic recovery program in 1934 included expansion of American exports, and the president proposed that Congress delegate some of its constitutional powers by authorizing him to negotiate trade agreements with other nations. The administration asked authority to cut tariffs by as much as 50 percent in return for equivalent concessions from other nations. Prodded by Secretary of State Cordell Hull, the Democratic-controlled 73rd Congress, over the nearly unanimous Republican opposition, made this grant of authority in the Trade Agreements Act of 1934. Since then, no serious efforts have been made to restore congressional tariff-making in place of presidential negotiation of bilateral and, after World War II, multilateral trade agreements.

### Non-tariff Barriers

Non-tariff barriers to the free flow of trade range from import quotas to embargoes. Although export taxes are forbidden under the Constitution, Congress can control export trade through licensing or other means. Thus it may bar shipment of strategic materials to hostile countries or restrict exports that would deplete essential domestic supplies. Congress has curbed imports that would interfere with domestic regulatory programs (such as agricultural commodities under production-control and price-support programs). It also has enacted "Anti-dumping," "Buy American" and "Ship American" legislation.

The ultimate restraint on foreign commerce is the embargo, which suspends commerce completely with specified countries. A recent example was the grain embargo President Carter imposed on the Soviet Union in 1980 after that country invaded Afghanistan. President Reagan imposed economic sanctions on both Poland and the Soviet Union in 1981 and 1982 after government officials declared martial law in Poland.

1. *Gibbons v. Ogden,* 9 Wheat. 1 at 193-194 (1824).

between nations, which shall exclude all laws concerning navigation. . . ."[10]

Congress' power applied to commerce with foreign nations, Marshall argued, and it also applied to commerce "... 'among the several states.' The word 'among' means intermingled with. A thing which is among others, is intermingled with them. Commerce among the states cannot stop at the external boundary line of each state, but may be introduced into the interior." [11] But Marshall did not find that the commerce power foreclosed all state regulation. "Such a power would be inconvenient and is certainly unnecessary," he said.[12]

With regard to the supremacy of the federal power, Marshall said:

> This power, like all others vested in Congress, is complete in itself, may be exercised to its utmost extent, and acknowledges no limitations, other than are prescribed in the constitution. . . . If, as has always been understood, the sovereignty of Congress, though limited to specified objects, is plenary as to those objects, the power over commerce with foreign nations, and among the several states, is vested in Congress as absolutely as it would be in a single government, having in its constitution the same restrictions on the exercise of the power as are found in the Constitution of the United States. [13]

Marshall did not address the question whether states could regulate areas Congress had not regulated. Nor did he answer the question whether the states could regulate commerce simultaneously with Congress. His opinion settled only two points — first, that navigation was commerce, and, second, that where state exercise of its power conflicts with federal exercise of the commerce power, the state must give way. In reaching the latter pronouncement, Marshall laid the groundwork for extending the commerce power to forms of transportation and communications not yet contemplated. By leaving the power to regulate wholly internal commerce to the states only so long as that commerce did not "extend to or affect" other states, he planted the seeds that eventually would allow Congress to regulate manufacture of goods and matters that themselves were not in commerce but were deemed to affect interstate commerce.

Congress did not make much use of the power claimed for it by Marshall until later in the century. Between 1824, when *Gibbons v. Ogden* was decided, and the 1880s, when the need for federal regulation of the nation's railroads and interstate corporations became apparent, the court's rulings on the commerce power focused primarily on determining when state actions impinged unconstitutionally on the federal commerce power.

## Notes

1. *Gibbons v. Ogden,* 9 Wheat. 1 (1824).
2. *Carter v. Carter Coal Co.,* Cardozo dissent, 298 U.S. 238 at 328 (1936).
3. Charles Warren, *The Making of the Constitution* (Boston: Little, Brown & Co., 1928), p. 16.
4. Bryant Putney, "Federal Powers Under the Commerce Clause," *Editorial Research Reports,* Oct. 4, 1935, p. 292.
5. Ibid., p. 293. See also J. B. McMaster, *History of the People of the United States* (1893), p. 206.
6. Putney, "Federal Powers," p. 293.
7. Ibid.
8. Warren, *Making of the Constitution,* pp. 585-586.
9. Ibid., p. 570.
10. *Gibbons v. Ogden,* 9 Wheat. 1 at 189-190 (1824).
11. Id. at 194.
12. Id. at 194-195.
13. Id. at 196-197.

## *Chapter 11*

# CONGRESS REGULATES INTERSTATE COMMERCE

For the first 100 years or so of the nation's life, most commerce was carried by water and so congressional regulation of interstate commerce primarily concerned navigation. But with the westward expansion of the country, a vast network of interstate railroads developed, and Congress, as a result, extended its commerce powers. Both before and after the Civil War the states attempted in various ways to curb increasing abuses by the railroads. These efforts were generally ineffective, however. Then, in 1886, the Supreme Court ruled in *Wabash, St. Louis & Pacific Railway Co. v. Illinois* that any enterprise engaged in interstate commerce could not be regulated by the states through which it passed. Such regulation, the court held, was barred by the commerce clause of the Constitution. The scope of the decision not only nullified state regulation of railroads but also precluded state action in such fields as the curbing of monopolies.[1]

### Creation of the ICC

The *Wabash* decision virtually forced Congress to provide for federal regulation of interstate railroads. The Interstate Commerce Act of 1887 stipulated that all rates should be reasonable and just, and prohibited rebate and price-fixing practices. To enforce the law, the act set up the Interstate Commerce Commission (ICC), which was given authority to issue cease-and-desist orders to halt any railroad found in violation of the act's provisions. The ICC was not given specific power to set rates or adjust those it found to be unreasonable, and it was unclear whether Congress intended the commission to have those powers. That determination fell to the Supreme Court.

At the time the ICC was created and for several years thereafter, a majority of the Supreme Court justices adhered to the principles of economic *laissez-faire*, opposing most government regulation — federal or state — that would impinge on the free development of business and industry. Moreover, many of the justices had been corporation lawyers before coming to the court; three of them — including Chief Justice Melville W. Fuller — numbered major interstate railroads among their clients. Thus, it was not surprising that the court viewed the ICC with little pleasure.

In 1894 the court upheld the ICC as an appropriate delegation of congressional powers. But three years later the court stripped the fledgling commission of its essential regulatory authority, holding that Congress had granted it no rate-fixing powers. The court majority also thought that the power to establish rates was a legislative function that constitutionally could not be delegated to an executive agency without violating the separation of powers.[2]

These cases left the ICC toothless and the abuses that led to its formation resumed with full force. Renewed demands from the public as well as from some of the rail companies encouraged Congress to attempt to revive the ICC as an enforcement mechanism. In 1906 Congress passed the Hepburn Act, which specifically authorized the commission to adjust rates it deemed to be unreasonable, and four years later it passed the Mann-Elkins Act of 1910, giving the ICC authority to set the entire railroad rate structure.

## Antitrust and Commerce

Simultaneous with development of the railroads into interstate networks was the growth of combinations or trusts in many areas of business and industry. The trusts were spurred during the depression of the mid-1870s when bigger companies bought up smaller, economically troubled firms. With the return of prosperity the trusts did not dissolve but instead grew even bigger, often using unsavory methods to drive smaller competitors out of business and consolidate their hold on the industry involved. By the turn of the century, trusts dominated the steel, oil, sugar, meatpacking, leather, electrical and tobacco industries.

This threat to the traditional concept of the free enterprise, competitive system was not popular. The public outcry led political party platforms to call on the federal government to control the trusts, and before the congressional elections of 1888 several antitrust bills were offered in Congress. But it was not until 1890 that Congress approved an antitrust measure, sponsored by Sen. John Sherman, R-Ohio.

Even as they worked on the measure, the national legislators expressed concern about its constitutionality. The law was based on Congress' authority to regulate interstate commerce. But many of the trusts involved only the manufacturing phase of commerce, an aspect that was not considered by many to be part of interstate commerce. In its final form, the Sherman Antitrust Act made illegal "[e]very contract, combination in the form of trust or otherwise, or conspiracy, in the restraint of trade or commerce among the several states, or with foreign nations. . . ." With that vague language Congress again left it to the courts to determine whether the law reached manufacturing trusts.[3]

## Federal Police Power

Congress has no explicit constitutional mandate to protect public health, public welfare and public morals. Such protections traditionally have been the responsibility of the states acting through their police powers. Nonetheless, Congress by the 1890s had begun to develop a federal police power to deal with a growing list of social and economic problems that were no longer local but national in scope.

This was the period of the progressive movement when farmers, laborers and consumers reacted against their exploitation by those who held the nation's wealth and power. Unemployment and poverty created by a series of economic depressions were widespread. Women and children worked long hours under wretched conditions for low pay. Immigrants and other poor people were crowded into filthy city ghettoes. Local governments were rife with corruption. As three prominent historians described it:

> Against the crowding evils of the time there arose a full-throated protest which distinguished American politics and thought from approximately 1890 to World War I. It demanded the centralization of power in the hands of a strong government and the extension of regulation or control over industry, finance, transportation, agriculture, labor and even morals. It found expression in a new concern for the poor and underprivileged, for women and children, for the immigrant, the Indian and the Negro. It called for new standards of honesty in politics and in business. It formulated a new social and political philosophy, which rejected laissez-faire and justified public control of social and economic institutions on the principles of liberal democracy.[4]

The national legislature used its constitutional grant of authority over interstate commerce to justify much of this regulation, claiming the power to regulate any matter that at some point was a part of interstate commerce. "Where the commerce power had previously been used primarily to regulate, foster or promote commerce for its own sake, . . . it now seemed that Congress might seek to regulate social and economic practices within the states, provided only that at some point they involved a crossing of state lines," wrote constitutional historian Robert K. Carr.[5]

Between 1903 and 1917 Congress enacted laws prohibiting the interstate transportation of explosives, diseased livestock, insect pests, falsely stamped gold and silver articles, narcotics, prostitutes and adulterated or misbranded foods and drugs. The Supreme Court sustained every one of these acts, and the federal police power appeared well-entrenched. Then, in 1918, the Supreme Court handed down a decision that left further expansion of the police power temporarily in doubt.

**Child Labor Case.** In *Hammer v. Dagenhart*, the court struck down a 1916 act of Congress that sought to discourage employment of children by prohibiting the shipment in interstate commerce of any product made in factories or mines that employed children under 14 or allowed children aged 14 to 16 to work more than a limited number of hours a week. By a 5-4 vote, the court declared that Congress had exceeded its authority. The power to regulate commerce is the authority "to control the means by which commerce is carried on, and not the "right to forbid commerce from moving," Justice William R. Day wrote for the majority.[6]

That statement required Day to distinguish his holding in the child labor case from the court's earlier decisions in which it had sanctioned congressional prohibition against the movement of lottery tickets and adulterated food in interstate commerce. He did so by declaring these latter articles to be harmful in themselves and asserting that their regulation "could only be accomplished by prohibiting the use of the facilities of interstate commerce to effect the evil intended." That "element is wanting in the present case," he said; the goods manufactured by children "are of themselves harmless." [7]

Day did not stop at this point but went on to examine the reasons why Congress enacted the law. "The act in its effect does not regulate transportation among the states," Day said, "but aims to standardize the ages at which children may be employed in mining and manufacturing within the states." Retreating to the earlier distinction the court made between commerce and manufacture, Day said mining and manufacture were subject only to state regulation.[8]

Justice Oliver Wendell Holmes' dissenting opinion left little doubt that the four minority justices believed the majority's ruling had been motivated in large part by the justices' personal views opposing the child labor act. On its surface, Holmes said, the act was indisputably within the federal commerce power. That being the case, he said, "it seems to me that it is not made any less constitutional because of the indirect effects it may have (that is, the discouragement of child labor), however obvious it may be that it will have those effects." [9]

Nor was it important that the evil was not itself in interstate transportation. "It does not matter whether the supposed evil precedes or follows the transportation," Holmes said. "It is enough that in the opinion of Congress the transportation encourages the evil." [10]

Furthermore, the federal commerce power could not be limited by its potential to interfere with intrastate regulation of commerce. States, Holmes wrote, ". . . may regulate their internal affairs and their domestic commerce as they like. But when they seek to send their products across the State line they are no longer within their rights. . . . Under the Constitution such commerce belongs not to the States but to Congress to regulate. It may carry out its views of public policy whatever indirect effect they may have upon the activities of the States." [11]

**Effect of Dagenhart.** With one major exception, the invalidation of a child labor tax law, the court did not rely heavily on the *Dagenhart* ruling as a precedent. In fact, the justices continued to sanction use of the commerce power as a police tool when it was applied to universally recognized social evils. The court let stand federal statutes prohibiting the interstate transportation of stolen cars, making transportation of kidnapped persons in interstate commerce a federal crime, and preventing the interstate shipment of convict-made goods to those states that prohibited them.[12] Like child labor, the goods involved in these three cases — cars, kidnapped persons and horse collars — were not in themselves harmful. Yet the court upheld the federal regulation in all three cases.

The court sanctioned use of the police power as recently as 1971 when it sustained provisions of the 1968 Consumer Credit Protection Act designed to prohibit loan-sharking. Although individual loan-sharking activities might be wholly intrastate, the court said that it was in a "class of activity" that affected intrastate commerce and thus could be regulated under the commerce power.[13]

## A New Deal for the Commerce Power

Congress made little use of the commerce power as a tool for regulating business between the court's 1918 ruling in the *Dagenhart* child labor case and the economic crisis of the Great Depression. Then, under President Franklin D. Roosevelt's forceful guidance, Congress in the 1930s attempted to use its commerce and fiscal powers to stimulate recovery. But the Supreme Court, still dominated by a small majority strongly disposed toward protection of private property rights and states' rights, resisted. The resulting collision, dramatized by Roosevelt's threat to increase the size of the court and fill the new seats with justices who would approve his New Deal legislation, ultimately led to the birth of the modern commerce power.

**Black Monday.** The centerpiece of Roosevelt's recovery program was the National Industrial Recovery Act (NIRA) of 1933. To speed industrial recovery, the NIRA authorized the president to approve codes of fair competition. Each of those codes, among other conditions, had to contain wage and hours standards for workers in the particular industry. In May 1935, on what came to be known as "black Monday," the Supreme Court declared the entire NIRA invalid. *Schechter Poultry Corp. v. United States* was a test case brought by the Roosevelt administration in the hope that a favorable response from the court would encourage industry compliance, which had been flagging. The circumstances involved, however, made it less than an ideal test.

The Schechter brothers bought live poultry that had been shipped into New York City largely from points out of the state, slaughtered it, then sold it locally. They were accused of violating several provisions of the New York City live poultry industry code, including the wage and hours standards and the prohibition against "straight killing" — allowing a customer to select individual poultry for slaughter. They also were charged with selling an "unfit chicken" to a local butcher. Wags quickly dubbed the suit the "Sick Chicken case."

The Supreme Court held that the Schechter brothers' operation was a local concern that did not directly affect interstate commerce. Instituting federal regulation through the fair competition codes was, therefore, an unconstitutional abridgement of states' rights. The court noted that the provisions of the code that the Schechters were charged with violating applied to the slaughtering operation and subsequent sale in local markets, activities the court said were not interstate commerce.

The court acknowledged that Congress had power not only to regulate interstate commerce but also to protect interstate commerce from burden or injury imposed by those engaged in intrastate activities. The effect of the burden must be direct, however, said the court. While the "precise line [between direct and indirect effects] can be drawn only as individual cases arise," the court said, the distinction was essential to maintenance of the federal system. Without it the federal government would have complete power over domestic affairs of the states.[14]

**Coal Codes.** The opinion in *Schechter* was unanimous, but no such unanimity marked the next New Deal decision. In *Carter v. Carter Coal Co.* (1936), the court declared the 1935 Bituminous Coal Conservation Act unconstitutional. That act said the production and distribution of coal so closely affected interstate commerce that federal regulation was necessary to stabilize the industry. Passed by Congress despite the adverse ruling in *Schechter*, the act authorized fixed prices for coal, provided for collective bargaining rights for coal miners, allowed a two-thirds majority of the industry to establish wage and hours standards for the entire industry and established a tax scheme to ensure compliance with the regulations.

Speaking for the majority, Justice George Sutherland focused first on the labor relations provisions. He declared that mining was production, not commerce, and that the relationship between a mine operator and mine workers was purely local in character. Since mining itself was not in interstate commerce, Sutherland contended, the next step was to determine if its effect on that commerce was direct. Sutherland then set forth a definition of direct effect that turned not on the degree to which a thing affected interstate commerce but on the manner in which the affect occurred. It made no difference whether one man or several men mined coal for sale in interstate commerce. Labor problems were local controversies affecting local production. "Such effect as they have upon commerce, however extensive it may be, is secondary and indirect," Sutherland said.[15]

But Justice Benjamin N. Cardozo declared that the distinction between direct and indirect effect was one of degree rather than kind. The federal commerce power, he maintained, was "as broad as the need that evokes it." [16] In this instance, the need was great, said Cardozo:

> Congress was not condemned to inaction in the face of price wars. . . . Commerce had been choked and burdened; its normal flow had been diverted from one state to another; there had been

> bankruptcy and waste and ruin alike for capital and for labor. . . . After making every allowance for difference of opinion as to the most efficient cure, the student of the subject is confronted with the indisputable truth that there were ills to be corrected, and ills that had a direct relation to the maintenance of commerce among the states without friction or diversion. An evil existing, and also the power to correct it, the lawmakers were at liberty to use their own discretion in the selection of the means.[17]

Cardozo's dissenting opinion recognized what the majority failed to acknowledge — that the many thousands of local economic problems of the Depression, taken together, were national in scope. In protecting state sovereignty and private property rights, the majority between January 1935 and June 1936 found unconstitutional eight of 10 major New Deal statutes. In addition to the NIRA and the coal codes, those statutes included the Agricultural Adjustment Act, the Municipal Bankruptcy Act, a federal farm mortgage relief act and the Railroad Retirement Act. In these cases, the majority time and again rejected the concept of national supremacy and the theory that Congress might act to protect the general welfare. It was this attitude that led to Roosevelt's attempt to moderate the conservative voice of the court through his controversial plan to fill the court with justices of his choosing.

The president, to use an appropriate cliché, lost the battle but won the war. Congress rejected his court-packing scheme, but not before one of the justices who generally voted with the conservative majority, Owen J. Roberts, did an about-face to convert the more liberal minority into a majority. In April 1937 Cardozo's reasoning in the *Carter* dissent became the majority opinion in a case upholding the 1935 National Labor Relations Act (NLRA).

**National Labor Law.** Passed in 1935, the NLRA declared that the denial of the rights of workers to organize and bargain collectively caused strikes and other labor problems that directly obstructed interstate commerce. To eliminate the obstruction and guarantee workers' rights, Congress prohibited both employees and employers from engaging in certain unfair labor practices. The act also established a National Labor Relations Board (NLRB) to administer the law.

The case of *NLRB v. Jones & Laughlin Steel Corp.* arose after the steel company fired 10 union employees from one of its Pennsylvania factories. The employees claimed they had been let go solely because they were union members. The NLRB agreed and ordered the steel company to stop discriminating against its union workers. When the company failed to comply, the NLRB asked a court of appeals to enforce its orders. Relying on the *Carter* decision, that court refused the petition, saying Congress did not have the power to regulate local labor relations.

By a 5-4 vote the Supreme Court reversed the lower court, sustaining the National Labor Relations Act. Affirming that Congress had the authority to regulate intrastate matters that directly burdened or obstructed interstate commerce, Chief Justice Charles Evans Hughes said the fact that the employees were engaged in the local activity of manufacturing was not "determinative." The question was what effect a labor strike of the factory would have on interstate commerce. He argued:

> In view of respondent's far-flung activities, it is idle to say that the effect would be indirect or remote. It is obvious that it would be immediate and might be catastrophic. We are asked to shut our eyes to the plainest facts of our national life and to deal with the question of direct and indirect effects in an intellectual vacuum. . . . When industries organize themselves on a national scale, making their relation to interstate commerce the dominant factor in their activities, how can it be maintained that their industrial labor relations constitute a forbidden field into which Congress may not enter when it is necessary to protect interstate commerce from the paralyzing consequences of industrial war? [18]

The court upheld the NLRB in four other cases decided the same day. Two of the cases involved a large trailer manufacturing company and a men's clothing manufacturer. Although these businesses sold a large portion of their products interstate, a labor strike against either one would not have had devastating effects on the national economy.[19] The third case involved the Associated Press; the court held that interstate communication of any kind was interstate commerce subject to regulation by Congress.[20] In the fourth case, the court held that a small company running buses between Virginia and the District of Columbia was an instrumentality of interstate commerce subject to the labor relations act.[21] With these decisions, the court declared that labor problems in almost any industry that depended in any way on interstate commerce for a portion of its business might sufficiently injure or burden interstate commerce as to demand compliance with the national labor relations law.

**Wages and Hours.** Given the new-found willingness of the court to construe the commerce power broadly, Congress decided to try again to set federal minimum wage and maximum hours standards. Since the court in 1918 had held that national hours limitations for child workers was an unwarranted federal intrusion into intrastate matters, reform attempts had been restricted to the individual states. Although the Supreme Court consistently upheld state maximum hours statutes, it did not approve a state minimum wage law until 1937.

Taking that as a signal, Congress passed the Fair Labor Standards Act of 1938, which set a 40-hour work week and an eventual minimum wage of 40 cents an hour, with time and a half for overtime. The act covered most workers "engaged in commerce or in the production of goods for commerce." It barred production of goods by workers paid less or working more than the standards prescribed, and, in a provision almost identical to that struck down in the child labor case (*Hammer v. Dagenhart*), it barred the shipment in interstate commerce of any products made in violation of the standards.

A test of the 1938 statute came to the court in 1941 after the government charged Fred W. Darby with violations of the standards. Darby ran a lumber company in Georgia, processing logs into finished lumber and selling a large part of it in other states. The court unanimously upheld the federal minimum wage statute in the case of *United States v. Darby Lumber Co*, overruling its decision in the child labor case. The court also held that the prohibition on the actual production of goods in violation of the standards was a proper means of protecting interstate commerce.

As several legal scholars have noted, the *Darby* opinion brought back to prominence the nationalistic interpretation of the commerce power first outlined in *Gibbons v. Ogden*, and the court ever since has not swerved significantly from this interpretation. Writing in 1942, Robert K. Carr said that after the *Darby* decision, "about the only further step the Court might take in its general reasoning concerning the commerce power would be to cease denying that manufacture is not of itself commerce and conclude that where goods are produced for, or affect, interstate trade, the act of production is a phase of the total process of commerce." [22] The court took that step the same year.

**Commerce Includes Production.** To replace the Agricultural Adjustment Act, which was declared unconstitutional in 1936 as an infringement on state power, Congress passed a new act in 1938. Rather than paying farmers to produce less of certain commodities, as the first bill had, the revised act established marketing quotas for the various commodities and penalized producers who exceeded them.

In 1939 the court upheld the act against a challenge that, like the 1936 measure, it infringed on the reserved powers of the states by attempting to regulate production. The 1938 law did not regulate production, the court said, but, rather, marketing, which was at the "throat" of interstate commerce.[23]

The same broad interpretation was given to the 1937 Agricultural Marketing Act, which established milk marketing agreements to control milk prices. With regard to that act, the court in 1942 stated:

> The power of Congress over interstate commerce is plenary and complete in itself, may be exercised to its utmost extent, and acknowledges no limitations other than are prescribed in the Constitution.... It follows that no form of a State activity can constitutionally thwart the regulatory power granted by the commerce clause to Congress. Hence the reach of that power extends to those intrastate activities which in a substantial way interfere with or obstruct the exercise of the granted power.[24]

Just how "substantial" the intrastate activity had to be was tested later in 1942 in the case of *Wickard v. Filburn.* Under the 1938 Agricultural Adjustment Act, Wickard had been allotted 11 acres of wheat. He planted 23 acres and harvested 269 bushels more than his quota permitted. He intended to sell what he was allowed and use the excess for feed and for seed for future crops. Although he did not sell the excess in either intrastate or interstate commerce, he still was penalized for raising more than his quota. Wickard challenged the penalty.

The court upheld Congress' authority to regulate Wickard's production, pointing out that by growing his own wheat, Wickard would not buy wheat and thus would reduce the market demand. This had a potentially substantial effect on interstate commerce, the court said. Thus the court found a rationale to uphold regulation by Congress of production that was not in commerce. Constitutional historian C. Herman Pritchett has called this case the "high-water mark of commerce clause expansionism."[25]

## The Modern Commerce Power

Since the late 1930s, Congress has had little difficulty in the courts in incorporating a broadly construed commerce clause in legislation. Not only has the commerce clause been the foundation for more detailed supervision of the commercial life of the nation by Congress and executive agencies. It was used in the 1960s to prohibit racial discrimination in public accommodations and in the 1970s to justify federal regulation of environmental pollutants.

**Racial Discrimination.** Early in the nation's history slaveholders feared that Congress might use its power over interstate commerce to prohibit racial discrimination, but the commerce power never was wielded against the traffic in human beings. After the Civil War, however, Congress attacked racial discrimination in public accommodations through several different means, all with little success. The most important tool was the 14th Amendment, but the court held in the 1883 *Civil Rights Cases* that the amendment applied only to discriminatory acts by states, not individuals, and thus the amendment could not be used to reach discrimination on railroads and other privately owned public carriers and accommodations.[26]

Opponents of racial segregation also tried to use the commerce power to reach discriminatory practices. The Interstate Commerce Commission, however, dismissed a challenge to segregated railroad facilities based on a section of the Interstate Commerce Act that prohibited "undue or unreasonable prejudice or disadvantage" in such facilities. "The disposition of a delicate and important question of this character, weighted with embarrassments arising from antecedent legal and social conditions, should aim at a result most likely to conduce to peace and order . . . ," said the commission, in effect ruling that it would not enforce the prohibition.[27]

Congressional concern as well as public interest in resolving the problem of segregation waned in the first decades of the 20th century. Then in 1946 the Supreme Court ruled that segregation on a public carrier burdened interstate commerce. The case involved a black woman who traveled on a bus from Virginia to Maryland. She refused to move to the back of the bus to make her seat available to a white; the court upheld her refusal.[28]

In 1950 the court ruled that separate dining facilities on interstate trains were a violation of the Interstate Commerce Act provision that had gone unenforced for so long.[29] Five years later the ICC announced that it was prohibiting racial discrimination on all trains and buses that crossed state lines. But it was not until the 1964 Civil Rights Act that Congress again attempted to prohibit racial discrimination in all public accommodations. Title II of the 1964 law barred discrimination on grounds of race, color, religion or national origin in public accommodations if the discrimination was supported by state law or official action, if lodgings were provided to transient guests, or if interstate travelers were served or if a substantial portion of the goods sold or entertainment provided moved in interstate commerce.

This portion of the act was immediately challenged as unconstitutional by a motel in downtown Atlanta, Ga., that served out-of-state travelers. The motel claimed that Congress had exceeded its power to regulate interstate commerce. In a unanimous ruling in *Heart of Atlanta Motel v. United States* (1964), the court upheld the validity of Title II, explaining that Congress' power to regulate interstate commerce gave it the authority to regulate local enterprise that "might have a substantial and harmful effect" on that commerce.[30]

**Insurance.** In one instance, the Supreme Court used the commerce clause to give Congress control of a field of trade it did not want. Ever since its 1869 decision in *Paul v. Virginia*, the Supreme Court had held consistently that purely financial or contractual transactions such as insurance were not in commerce, even if the transactions involved parties in different states.[31] This left to the states full authority to regulate the insurance business.

In 1944 the Justice Department sought to use the Sherman Act to break up a conspiracy of insurance companies that sought to monopolize fire insurance sales in six southern states. Using the precedent established by *Paul v. Virginia*, the companies, all members of the South-Eastern Underwriters Association, contended that they could not be reached by the antitrust act since their business was not in commerce. Overturning *Paul v. Virginia*, the court ruled against them. "No commercial enterprise of any kind which conducts its activities across state lines has been held to be wholly beyond the regulatory power of Congress under the Commerce Clause," wrote the court. "We cannot make an exception for the business of insurance." Congress, not the court, must make the exceptions to the antitrust act.[32]

**Environmental Law.** Congress' police power to protect the public health and welfare, derived primarily from its commerce power, has become the constitutional basis for federal legislation regulating air and water pollution. The Water Quality Improvement Act of 1970, the primary federal vehicle for water pollution prevention and control programs, states in its declaration of policy that Congress stepped into the environmental area "in connection with its jurisdiction over the waterways of the Nation and in consequence of the benefits resulting to the public health and welfare by the prevention and control of water pollution." Likewise, the primary purpose given for passage of the Air Quality Act of 1967 was "to promote health and welfare and the productive capability of [the nation's] population."

While various regulations promulgated under these statutes have been challenged in the courts, the Supreme Court has heard no case challenging the authority of Congress to act in these areas.

**State Governments.** In 1976 a divided Supreme Court placed the first restrictions in 40 years on congressional exercise of the commerce power. The court struck down the portion of a 1974 act extending minimum wage and overtime requirements to state and local government employees. Congress was delving too far into the essential functions of state and local governments, the court declared in *National League of Cities v. Usery*. Determination of its employees' wages and hours was an attribute of state sovereignty with which the federal government had no constitutional right to interfere, the five-man majority said. "Congress may not exercise that [commerce] power so as to force directly upon the states its choices as to how essential decisions regarding the conduct of integral governmental functions are to be made." [33]

Although Justice William J. Brennan Jr., in his minority opinion, charged that the majority's reasoning was not far different from the pre-1937 court's "overly restrictive construction of the commerce power," it seemed unlikely that the majority opinion in the 1976 case signified such a retreat.[34] For six years following the 1976 decision, the court did not invalidate any other federal law on the ground that Congress exceeded its power to regulate interstate commerce. In fact, in 1981 the court unanimously upheld a federal strip-mining regulation act against a challenge from strip-mine operators, landowners, mining industry groups and the states of Indiana and Virginia. (*Hodel v. Indiana, Hodel v. Virginia Surface Mining and Reclamation Assn.*) By 1982, constitutional issues surrounding the scope of the commerce power appeared largely resolved, giving Congress almost unlimited discretion to regulate commercial intercourse in the United States. "[I]f we moved into an era of novel economic measures or major nationalization programs, the Court might reassert its authority," wrote constitutional scholars Alan F. Westin and C. Herman Pritchett, "but the decades since 1937 have been years of consolidation rather than innovation in economic regulation, and the Court's withdrawal from constitutional intervention is therefore not likely to change in the immediate future." [35]

## Notes

1. *Wabash, St. Louis & Pacific Railway Co. v. Illinois,* 118 U.S. 577 (1886); Frederic A. Ogg and P. Orman Ray, *Introduction to American Government* (New York: Appleton-Century-Crofts, 1951), p. 563.
2. *Interstate Commerce Commission v. Brimson,* 154 U.S. 447 (1894); *Interstate Commerce Commission v. Cincinnati, New Orleans and Texas Pacific Railway Co.,* 167 U.S. 479 (1897); *Interstate Commerce Commission v. Alabama-Midland Railway Co.,* 168 U.S. 144 (1897).
3. Samuel Eliot Morison, Henry Steele Commager, William E. Leuchtenburg, *The Growth of the American Republic,* 2 vols., 6th ed. (New York: Oxford University Press, 1969), II: 64-80, 298-303.
4. Morison et al., *Growth of the American Republic,* II: 268.
5. Robert K. Carr, *The Supreme Court and Judicial Review* (New York: Farrar & Rinehart, 1942), p. 108.
6. *Hammer v. Dagenhart,* 247 U.S. 251 at 268-269 (1918).
7. Id. at 271.
8. Id. at 271-272.
9. Id. at 277.
10. Id. at 279-280.
11. Id. at 281.
12. *Brooks v. United States,* 267 U.S. 432 (1925); *Gooch v. United States,* 297 U.S. 124 (1936); *Kentucky Whip & Collar Co. v. Illinois Central Railroad Co.,* 299 U.S. 334 (1937).
13. *Perez v. United States,* 402 U.S. 146 (1971).
14. *Schechter Poultry Corp. v. United States,* 295 U.S. 495 at 546 (1935).
15. *Carter v. Carter Coal Co.,* 298 U.S. 238 at 309 (1936).
16. Id. at 328.
17. Id. at 331-332.
18. *National Labor Relations Board v. Jones & Laughlin Steel Corp.,* 301 U.S. 1 at 41-42 (1937).
19. *National Labor Relations Board v. Fruehauf Trailer Co.,* 301 U.S. 49 (1937); *National Labor Relations Board v. Friedman-Harry Marks Clothing Co.,* 301 U.S. 58 (1937).
20. *Associated Press v. National Labor Relations Board,* 301 U.S. 103 (1937).
21. *Washington, Virginia & Maryland Coach Co. v. National Labor Relations Board,* 301 U.S. 142 (1937).
22. Carr, *Supreme Court and Judicial Review,* p. 135.
23. *Mulford v. Smith,* 307 U.S. 38 at 47 (1939).

24. *United States v. Wrightwood Dairy Co.,* 315 U.S. 110 at 118-119 (1942).
25. C. Herman Pritchett, *The American Constitution,* 3rd ed. (New York: McGraw-Hill Book Co., 1977), p. 198.
26. *Civil Rights Cases,* 109 U.S. 3 (1883).
27. C. Herman Pritchett, *The American Constitution,* 1st ed. (New York: McGraw-Hill Book Co., 1959), p. 604.
28. *Morgan v. Virginia,* 328 U.S. 373 (1946).
29. *Henderson v. United States,* 339 U.S. 816 (1950).
30. *Katzenbach v. McClung,* 379 U.S. 294 (1964).
31. *Paul v. Virginia,* 8 Wall. 168 (1869).
32. *United States v. South-Eastern Underwriters Association,* 322 U.S. 533 at 553 (1944).
33. *National League of Cities v. Usery,* 426 U.S. 833 at 855 (1976).
34. Id. at 868.
35. C. Herman Pritchett and Alan F. Westin, *The Third Branch of Government: 8 Cases in Constitutional Politics* (New York: Harcourt, Brace & World, 1963), p. 3.

*Part IV*

# Impeachment

*Harper's Weekly* cover shows Rep. John A. Bingham, R-Ohio, before the Senate at President Andrew Johnson's 1868 impeachment trial. The defendant did not attend.

# Chapter 12

# CONSTITUTIONAL BACKGROUND

Impeachment is perhaps the most awesome, although least used, power of Congress. In essence it is a political action, couched in legal terminology, directed against a ranking official of the federal government. The House of Representatives is the prosecutor. The Senate chamber is the courtroom, and the Senate, the judge and jury. The final penalty is removal from office and disqualification from further office. There is no appeal.

Impeachment proceedings have been initiated in the House more than 60 times since 1789, but only 13 officers have been impeached: one president, one Cabinet officer, one senator and 10 federal judges.[1] Of these 13, 12 cases reached the Senate. Of the 12 cases reaching the Senate, two were dismissed before trial after the person impeached left office, six resulted in acquittal and four in conviction. (In the 13th case, federal Judge Mark H. Delahay was impeached in 1873, but resigned before the House sent the matter to the Senate.)[2]

All the convictions involved federal judges: John Pickering of the district court for New Hampshire, in 1804; West H. Humphreys of the eastern, middle and western districts of Tennessee, in 1862; Robert W. Archbald of the Commerce Court, in 1913; and Halsted L. Ritter of the southern district of Florida, in 1936.

Two impeachments stand out from the rest. They involved Supreme Court Justice Samuel Chase in 1805 and President Andrew Johnson in 1868, the two most powerful federal officials ever impeached. Both were impeached by the House: Chase for partisan conduct on the bench; Johnson for violating the Tenure of Office Act. Both were acquitted by the Senate after sensational trials. Behind both impeachments lay intensely partisan politics. Chase, a Federalist, was a victim of attacks on the Supreme Court by Jeffersonian Democratic-Republicans. If Chase had been convicted, the Democratic-Republicans then planned to move against Chief Justice John Marshall, also a Federalist. President Johnson was a victim of Radical Republicans opposed to his reconstruction policies after the Civil War.

The impeachment power was demonstrated dramatically in 1974 when the House of Representatives initiated an inquiry into President Richard Nixon's conduct as a result of charges arising out of a 1972 break-in at Democratic National Headquarters in the Watergate office building in Washington, D.C. The House Judiciary Committee adopted three articles of impeachment against Nixon late in July 1974. The articles charged him with abuse of his presidential powers, obstruction of justice, and contempt of Congress. Before the full House voted on these articles, Nixon resigned, on Aug. 9, after being told by Republican House and Senate leaders that the evidence against him virtually assured that he would be impeached, convicted and removed from office.[3]

## 'A Method of National Inquest'

As outlined in the Constitution, the impeachment process was designed "as a method of national inquest into the conduct of public men," according to Alexander Hamilton in *The Federalist* No. 65.[4] The Constitution provides that impeachment proceedings may be brought against "the President, Vice President and all civil officers of the United States," without explaining who is, or is not, a "civil officer." In practice, however, the overwhelming majority of impeachment proceedings have been directed against federal judges, who hold lifetime appointments "during good behavior" and cannot be removed by any other method. Nine of the 12 impeachment cases that have reached the Senate have involved federal judges. Federal judges also have been the subject of most House resolutions and investigations failing to result in impeachment.[5]

Impeachments also have been sought against Cabinet members, diplomats, customs collectors, a senator and a U.S. district attorney. These officials are subject to impeachment, yet it seldom has been necessary to resort to full-scale impeachment proceedings to bring about their removal. Proceedings against the only senator to be impeached, William Blount of Tennessee, were dismissed in 1799 after Blount had been expelled from the Senate in 1797. Secretary of War William W. Belknap, the only Cabinet member to be tried by the Senate, was acquitted in 1876 largely because senators questioned their authority to try Belknap, who had resigned several months before the trial.

The House Judiciary Committee twice has ruled that certain federal officials were not subject to impeachment. In 1833, the committee determined that a territorial judge was not a civil officer within the Constitution's meaning because he held office for only four years and could be removed at any time by the president.[6] In 1926 the committee said that a commissioner of the District of Columbia was immune from impeachment because he was an officer of the District and not a civil officer of the United States.[7]

## Historical Precedents for Impeachment

Impeachment as a constitutional process dates from 14th-century England when the fledgling Parliament sought to make the King's advisers accountable. The monarch, who was considered incapable of wrongdoing, was immune. Impeachment was used against ministers and judges whom the legislature believed guilty of breaking the law or carrying out the unpopular orders of the king. The system was based on the common law and the House of Lords could inflict the death penalty on those it found guilty.

Grounds for impeachment included both criminal and non-criminal activity. Joseph Story, in his *Commentaries on the Constitution of the United States*, wrote: "Lord chancellors and judges and other magistrates have not only been impeached for bribery and acting grossly contrary to the duties of their office, but for misleading their sovereign by unconstitutional opinions and for attempts to subvert the fundamental laws and introduce arbitrary power." [8]

In the mid-15th century, impeachment fell into disuse, largely due to the Tudor monarchs' ability to force Parliament to remove unwanted officials by bills of attainder or pains and penalties. But in the early 17th century, the excesses and absolutist tendencies of the Stuart kings prompted Parliament to revive its impeachment power to curb the monarch by removing his favorite aides.

The struggle between the king and the Commons came to a head with the impeachment of Charles the First's minister, the earl of Strafford, in 1642. The earl was impeached by the House of Commons for subverting the fundamental law and introducing an arbitrary and tyrannical government. While the charge was changed to a bill of attainder in the House of Lords, Raoul Berger wrote that "his impeachment may be regarded as the opening gun in the struggle whereby the Long Parliament 'prevented the English monarchy from hardening into an absolutism of the type then becoming general in Europe.' "[9]

More than 50 impeachments were brought to the House of Lords for trial between 1620 and 1787, the year in which the American Constitution was adopted. As the framers toiled in Philadelphia, the long impeachment and trial of Warren Hastings progressed in London. Hastings was charged with oppression, cruelty, bribery and fraud as colonial administrator and first governor general in India. The trial before the House of Lords lasted from Feb. 13, 1788, to April 23, 1795. Hastings was acquitted but, by that time, impeachment was considered overly cumbersome and unnecessary because of ministerial responsibility to Parliament. The last impeachment trial in Britain occurred in 1806.

Under the English system, an impeachment (indictment) was preferred by the House of Commons and decided by the House of Lords. In America, colonial governments and early state constitutions followed the British pattern of trial before the upper legislative body on charges brought by the lower house.

Despite these precedents, a major controversy arose in the Constitutional Convention over whether the Senate should try impeachments. Opposing that role for the Senate, James Madison and Charles Pinckney asserted that it would make the president too dependent on the legislative branch. Suggested alternative trial bodies included the "national judiciary," the Supreme Court or the assembled chief justices of state supreme courts. It was argued, however, that such bodies would be too small and perhaps even susceptible to corruption. In the end, the Senate was selected as the trial forum. Hamilton (a Senate opponent during the Convention) asked later in *The Federalist:* "Where else than in the Senate could have been found a tribunal sufficiently dignified, or sufficiently independent?"[10]

A lesser issue was the definition of impeachable crimes. In the original proposals, the president was to be removed on impeachment and conviction "for mal or corrupt conduct," or for "malpractice or neglect of duty." After several revisions, the final wording made impeachable crimes "treason, bribery or other high crimes and misdemeanors."[11] Debate over the meaning of this phrase has resumed during every serious impeachment inquiry.

The Constitution's impeachment provisions are scattered through the first three articles. To the House is given the "sole power of

## Impeachment Clauses

**Article I, Section 2.** "The House of Representatives . . . shall have the sole Power of Impeachment."

**Article I, Section 3.** "The Senate shall have the sole Power to try all Impeachments. When sitting for that Purpose, they shall be on Oath or Affirmation. When the President of the United States is tried, the Chief Justice shall preside: And no Person shall be convicted without the Concurrence of two-thirds of the Members present.

"Judgment in Cases of Impeachment shall not extend further than to removal from Office, and disqualification to hold and enjoy any Office of honor, Trust or Profit under the United States: But the Party convicted shall nevertheless be liable and subject to Indictment, Trial, Judgment and Punishment, according to Law."

**Article II, Section 2.** "The President . . . shall have Power to grant Reprieves and Pardons for Offenses against the United States, except in Cases of Impeachment."

**Article II, Section 4.** "The President, Vice President and all civil Officers of the United States, shall be removed from Office on Impeachment for, and Conviction of, Treason, Bribery, or other high Crimes and Misdemeanors."

**Article III, Section 2.** "The Trial of All Crimes, except in cases of Impeachment, shall be by Jury. . . ."

impeachment"; to the Senate, "the sole power to try all impeachments." Impeachments may be brought against "the President, Vice President, and all civil officers of the United States." Conviction is automatically followed by "removal from office" and possibly by "disqualification to hold" further public office.

The first attempt to use the impeachment power was made in 1796. Northwest Territory residents submitted to the House a petition accusing Judge George Turner, of the territorial supreme court, of arbitrary conduct. The petition was referred briefly to a special House committee and then was referred to Attorney General Charles Lee. Impeachment proceedings were dropped after Lee said that the territorial government would prosecute Turner in the territorial courts.[12]

## The Impeachment Procedure

The first impeachment proceedings, against Turner, provided no precedents for later impeachments. In fact, the process has been used so infrequently and under such widely varying circumstances that no uniform practice has emerged.

**The House of Representatives.** The House has no standing rules dealing with its impeachment role, which the Constitution describes in fewer than a dozen words.

At various times impeachment proceedings have been initiated by the introduction of a resolution by a member, by a letter or message from the president, by a grand jury action forwarded to the House from a territorial legislature, by a memorial setting forth charges, by a resolution authorizing a general investigation, or by a resolution reported by the House Judiciary Committee. The five cases to reach the Senate between 1900 and 1982 were based on Judiciary Committee resolutions.[13]

Before the Judiciary Committee's creation in 1813, the matter was referred to a special committee established for that purpose. Judge James H. Peck's impeachment in 1830 was the first referred to the Judiciary Committee.[14]

After submission of the charges, a committee investigation begins. The committee decides in each case whether the inquiry's subject has the right to be present at committee proceedings, to be represented by counsel, as well as to present and question witnesses.[15]

If the investigation supports the charges, the committee reports an impeachment resolution. Since 1912, articles of impeachment have been reported by the committee simultaneously with the resolution. Before that time, the articles were drawn up after the House had approved the impeachment resolution.[16]

The House is no more bound by a committee's recommendation on impeachment than it is by a committee's recommendation and action on any legislative matter. In 1933 the House Judiciary Committee found insufficient grounds to recommend impeachment of Judge Harold Louderback, but the House impeached the judge anyway.[17] The target of an impeachment resolution is impeached if the House adopts a resolution of impeachment by majority vote. The articles of impeachment may be approved by a simple majority and may be amended on the House floor.

After the resolution and the articles have been adopted by the House, the House managers are selected to present the case for impeachment to the Senate, acting as prosecutors in the Senate trial. An odd number — ranging from five to 11 — traditionally has been selected, including members from both parties who voted in favor of impeachment. They have been selected in various ways: by ballot, with a majority vote necessary for election; by resolution naming the slate; or by the Speaker of the House.[18] The full House may attend the trial, but the House managers are its official representatives in the Senate proceedings.

**The Senate.** In 1868, for President Johnson's impeachment trial, the Senate adopted a set of 25 rules for those proceedings. One new rule was added in 1935.

The trial is conducted in a fashion similar to a criminal trial. Both sides may present witnesses and evidence, and the defendant is allowed counsel, the right to testify in his own behalf and the right of cross-examination. If the president or the vice president is on trial, the Constitution requires the chief justice of the United States to preside. The Constitution is silent on a presiding officer for lesser defendants, but Senate practice has been for the vice president or the president pro tempore to preside.

The presiding officer can issue all orders needed to compel witnesses to appear or to enforce obedience to Senate orders. The presiding officer administers the oath to all the senators before they take part in the trial. The presiding officer rules on all evidence questions and his ruling stands unless he decides to submit the question to a Senate vote or unless a senator requests such a vote. Custom dictates that most questions concerning the admissibility of evidence are submitted to the Senate for decision. The presiding officer questions witnesses, asking questions submitted in writing by various senators who do no direct questioning themselves.

All the Senate's orders and decisions during an impeachment trial are made by roll-call vote and without debate unless in secret session. On the final question, guilt or innocence, each senator is limited to 15 minutes of debate in secret session. The Senate votes separately on each article of impeachment; the Constitution requires a two-thirds vote for conviction. If no article is approved by two-thirds of the senators present, the impeached official is acquitted. If any article receives two-thirds approval, the person is convicted. The Senate then votes to remove the person from office. The Senate also may vote to disqualify the person from holding future federal offices. Only two of the four convictions have been accompanied by disqualification, which is decided by a majority vote.

## Records, Resignations and Recesses

The shortest time from House impeachment to Senate verdict was one month, in the impeachment of federal Judge Halsted Ritter in 1936. The longest time was one year, in the early impeachments of Pickering and Chase. Andrew Johnson's impeachment took three months from House action to Senate judgment.

The shortest Senate trial on record is that of Judge West H. Humphreys, which took only one day; the longest was the two months consumed in the Senate trial of President Johnson.

In general, the resignation of the official about to be impeached puts an end to impeachment proceedings because the primary objective, removal from office, has been accomplished. This was the case in the impeachment proceedings begun against President Nixon and two federal judges: Mark H. Delahay, impeached by voice vote Feb. 28, 1873, and George W. English, impeached by a 306 to 62 vote April 1, 1926. [19]

However, resignation is not a foolproof way of precluding impeachment. Secretary of War William W. Belknap, aware of the findings of a congressional committee implicating him in the acceptance of bribes, resigned at 10 o'clock on the morning of March 2, 1876. Sometime after 3 o'clock that afternoon, the House impeached him by voice vote. The Senate debated the question of its jurisdiction, in light of his resignation, and decided by a vote of 37 to 29 that he could be impeached and tried despite his no longer being in office. He was found not guilty of the charges.[20]

Historical precedent indicates that an impeachment proceeding does not die with adjournment. In 1890 and 1891 the Judiciary Committee investigated a federal judge's conduct and decided that he should be impeached; a resolution to that effect was reported in 1891 and the House began debate but did not conclude before adjournment. In the new Congress in 1892, the evidence taken in the first investigation was referred to the committee again, a second investigation was conducted and the committee decided against impeachment.[21]

In Judge Pickering's case, the House impeached him but adjourned before drawing up articles of impeachment, which a committee appointed in the next Congress did do.[22]

Whether impeachment would have to begin again if the House impeached a person in one Congress but the Senate trial could not begin until the next is unclear. However, the view of the Senate as a continuing body according to custom would indicate that the trial could begin in the new Congress without a repetition of the House procedures. The Senate did decide in 1876 that an impeachment trial could proceed only when Congress was in session. The vote was close, 21 to 19. [23]

## Controversial Questions

Three major questions have dominated the history of impeachment in the United States:

— What is an impeachable offense?

— Can senators serve as impartial jurors?

— Are there ways other than impeachment to remove a federal judge from office?

"Treason" and "bribery," as constitutionally designated impeachable crimes, have caused little debate, for treason is defined elsewhere in the Constitution and bribery is well defined in statutory law. "High crimes and misdemeanors," however, have been anything that the prosecution has wanted to make them. In the 1970 attempt to impeach Supreme Court Justice William O. Douglas, then-Rep. Gerald R. Ford, R-Mich., declared: "An impeachable offense is whatever a majority of the House of Representatives considers it to be at a given moment in history." [24] The phrase is the subject of continuing debate pitting broad constructionists, who have viewed impeachment as a political weapon, against narrow constructionists, who have regarded impeachment as being limited to offenses indictable at common law.

The constitutional debates seem to indicate that impeachment is to be regarded as a political weapon. Narrow constructionists quickly won a major victory, though, when Supreme Court Justice Samuel Chase was acquitted, using as his defense the argument that the charges against him were not based on any indictable offense. President Johnson also won acquittal using a similar defense. His lawyers argued that conviction could result only from commission of high criminal offenses against the United States.[25]

The only two convictions in the 20th century suggest that the arguments of the broad constructionists still carry considerable weight. Robert W. Archbald, associate judge of the U.S. Commerce Court, was convicted and removed from office in 1913, and Halsted L. Ritter, U.S. judge for the southern district of Florida, in 1936. Archbald was convicted of soliciting for himself and for friends valuable favors from railroad companies, some of which were litigants in his court. It was conceded, however, that he had committed no indictable offense.[26] Ritter was convicted for conduct in a receivership case that raised serious doubts about his integrity.[27]

This debate resumed in 1974 with the impeachment inquiry into the conduct of President Nixon. The impeachment inquiry staff of the House Judiciary Committee argued for a broad view of "high crimes and misdemeanors," while Nixon's defense attorneys argued for a narrow view. As adopted by the House Judiciary Committee, Article I charged the president with obstruction of justice, a charge falling within the narrow view of impeachable offenses. Articles II and III reflected the broader interpretation, charging Nixon with abuse of his presidential powers and contempt of Congress.

An equally controversial issue, particularly in earlier impeachment trials, concerned the partisan interests of senators, which raised serious doubts about their ability to sit as impartial jurors.

President Johnson's potential successor, for example, was the president pro tempore of the Senate because there was a vacancy in the vice presidency. Sen. Benjamin F. Wade, R-Ohio, president pro tempore, took part in the trial and voted — for conviction. On the other hand, Andrew Johnson's son-in-law, Sen. David T. Patterson, D-Tenn., also took part in the trial and voted — for acquittal.

In the Johnson trial and in others, senators have been outspoken critics or supporters of the defendant, yet have participated in the trial and have voted on the articles. Some senators who had held seats in the House when the articles of impeachment first came up, and had voted on them there, have not disqualified themselves during the trial. On occasion, intense outside lobbying for, and against, the defendant has been aimed at senators. Senators have testified as witnesses at some trials and then voted on the articles. Senators may request to be excused from the trial, and in recent cases some senators have disqualified themselves when possible conflicts of interest have arisen.

For most of the 20th century, Congress has been engaged in a continuing search for an alternative to impeachment as a method of removing federal judges. This search has been spurred by concern to free the Senate, faced by an enormous legislative workload, from the time-consuming process of sitting as a court of impeachment, and by the desire of some members to restrict judicial power by providing a simpler and swifter means of removal than the cumbersome and unwieldy impeachment process.

By mid-1982, the search still was unsuccessful. Efforts to revise and accelerate the impeachment process have failed. So, too, have attempts to amend the Constitution to limit the tenure of federal judges to a definite term of years. One approach was to seek legislation providing for a judicial trial and judgment of removal for federal judges violating "good-behavior" standards. The House passed such a bill on Oct. 22, 1941, by a 124 to 122 vote, but it died in the Senate.

## Notes

1. Paul S. Fenton, "The Scope of the Impeachment Power," *Northwestern University Law Review,* vol. 65, no. 5 (1970), pp. 719-758, reprinted in U.S., Congress, House, Committee on the Judiciary, *Impeachment: Selected Materials,* 93d Cong., 1st sess., October 1973, pp. 663-688.
2. Asher C. Hinds, *Hinds' Precedents of the House of Representatives of the United States,* 5 vols. (Washington, D.C.: U.S. Government Printing Office, 1907), IV: 1008-1011.
3. For further details, see *Congressional Quarterly Almanac 1974* (Washington D.C.: Congressional Quarterly, 1975), pp. 867-902; *Watergate: Chronology of a Crisis* (Washington D.C.: Congressional Quarterly, 1975), pt. 3.
4. Alexander Hamilton, James Madison, and John Jay, *The Federalist Papers,* with an introduction by Clinton Rossiter (New York: Mentor, 1961), no. 65, p. 397.
5. U.S., Congress, House, Committee on the Judiciary, *Impeachment: Selected Materials on Procedure,* 93d Cong., 2d sess., January 1974, pp. 687-740, 851-900.
6. *Impeachment: Selected Materials on Procedure,* p. 697.
7. Ibid., p. 892.
8. Joseph Story, *Commentaries on the Constitution of the United States* (Boston: Hilliard Gray & Co., 1833), vol. 2, sec. 798.
9. Raoul Berger, *Impeachment: The Constitutional Problems* (Cambridge: Harvard University Press, 1973), p. 31.

10. Hamilton, Madison, and Jay, *The Federalist Papers,* no. 65, p. 398.
11. Max Farrand, ed., *The Records of the Federal Convention of 1787*, 3 vols. (New Haven: Yale University Press, 1911), I: 78; II: 116, 185-186, 292, 495, 545, 550-552.
12. *Impeachment: Selected Materials on Procedure,* pp. 687-689, citing *Hinds' Precedents,* III: 981.
13. *Impeachment: Selected Materials,* pp. 21-22; see also Clarence Cannon, *Cannon's Precedents of the House of Representatives of the United States,* 3 vols. (Washington, D.C.: U.S. Government Printing Office, 1935), I: 657.
14. *Impeachment: Selected Materials on Procedure,* pp. 343, 381, 411, 475, citing *Hinds' Precedents,* III: 644, 681, 711, 772.
15. *Impeachment: Selected Materials on Procedure,* pp. 477-478, 509-510, 609, 655, 795, 821.
16. Ibid., pp. 345-347, 382-383, 416-417, 483-484, 511, 555, 607-609, 658-659, 797.
17. Ibid, pp. 821-822, citing *Cannon's Precedents,* I: 709.
18. Ibid., pp. 765-767, citing *Cannon's Precedents,* I: 657.
19. Ibid., pp. 716, 890.
20. Ibid., pp. 4-15, 607-652.
21. Ibid., pp. 733-737.
22. Ibid., p. 383.
23. Ibid., pp. 2-3.
24. *Congressional Record,* 91st Cong., 2d sess., April 15, 1970, p. 11913.
25. *Impeachment: Selected Materials on Procedure,* pp. 456-471, 597.
26. Ibid., pp. 795-818.
27. *Impeachment: Selected Materials on Procedure,* p. 688, citing *Proceedings of the United States Senate in the Trial of Impeachment of Halsted L. Ritter,* S. Doc. No. 200, 74th Cong., 2d sess., 1936.

*Chapter 13*

# HISTORY OF IMPEACHMENTS

Impeachment is the ultimate limitation on the power of the president. The only presidential impeachment occurred in 1868. President Andrew Johnson, a Democrat, was charged with violation of a federal statute, the Tenure of Office Act. But the procedure also was a profoundly political struggle. Issues such as controlling the Republican Party, dealing with the chaos of the post-Civil War South, and establishing monetary and economic policy all became implicated in the impeachment process.

Johnson had been the only member of the U.S. Senate from a seceding southern state (Tennessee) to remain loyal to the Union in 1861. Lincoln later made him military governor of Tennessee and chose him as his running mate in 1864. After Lincoln's assassination in 1865, this outsider without allies or connections in the Republican Party succeeded to the presidency. Johnson's ideas on what should have been done to reconstruct and readmit the southern states to representation clashed with the wishes of a majority of Congress, overwhelmingly controlled by the Republicans.

Johnson as president was an anomaly. He was a southerner at a time when the South was out of the Union, a Jacksonian Democrat who believed in states' rights, hard money, and minimal federal government activity, running with an incumbent president who was pursuing a policy of expansion both in the money supply and the role of government.

Congress was divided into roughly three groups. The small minority of Democrats supported the president. About half the Republicans were known as "radicals" because they favored strong action to revolutionize southern society, by harsh military means if necessary. The other half of the Republicans were more conservative; while unwilling to go as far as the radicals, they wanted to make sure the South did not return to the unquestioned control of those who ruled it before the Civil War.

Upon taking office, Johnson began to pursue Lincoln's mild and tolerant reconstruction plans. The new president felt that a few basics were all that needed to be secured: abolition of slavery; ratification of the 13th Amendment, which abolished slavery in all states; repudiation of all state debts contracted by the Confederate governments; nullification of secession. When the southern states had done these things, Johnson felt they should be readmitted.

But Republicans wanted more: a Freedmen's Bureau, to protect and provide services for the ex-slaves; a civil rights bill guaranteeing blacks their rights; and an overall plan of reconstruction providing for temporary military governments in the South. Throughout 1866, Johnson and Congress battled over these issues.

## President Johnson's Impeachment

The Tenure of Office Act, the violation of which was to be the legal basis for Johnson's impeachment, was passed over his veto March 2, 1867. The act forbade the president to remove civil officers (appointed with the consent of the Senate) without the approval of the Senate. Its purpose was to protect incumbent Republican officeholders from executive retaliation if they did not support the president.

**House Action.** About the time the Tenure of Office Act was being debated, the first moves toward impeachment began. On Jan. 7, 1867, Rep. James M. Ashley, R-Ohio (1859-69), rose and formally charged the president with high crimes and misdemeanors. Ashley made only general charges, mentioning no specific violations of law. Most members recognized the charges as basically political grievances rather than illegal acts. The matter was referred to the House Judiciary Committee, which reported on March 2, 1867, two days before the end of the 39th Congress, that it had reached no conclusion.

On March 7, 1867, the third day of the 40th Congress, Ashley again introduced his resolution, which was referred to the Judiciary Committee for further investigation. The committee studied the matter throughout the year and on Nov. 25, 1867, reported an impeachment resolution. When the House voted on the matter on Dec. 6, the radicals suffered a crushing defeat. The resolution calling for impeachment was turned down, 57 to 108.

Johnson had long wanted to rid himself of Secretary of War Edwin M. Stanton. Stanton was a close ally of the radical Republicans. After repeatedly trying to get him to resign, Johnson suspended him on Dec. 12,

1867. On Jan. 13, 1868, the Senate refused to concur, thus, under the terms of the Tenure of Office Act, reinstating Stanton.

Apparently flushed by his victory on the impeachment issue, Johnson decided to force the issue. He dismissed Stanton on Feb. 21, citing the power and authority vested in him by the Constitution. This action enraged Congress, driving conservative Republicans into alliance with the radicals on impeachment. A House resolution on impeachment was immediately offered and was referred to the Committee on Reconstruction, headed by Rep. Thaddeus Stevens of Pennsylvania, one of the radical Republican leaders. The next day, Feb. 22, the committee reported a resolution favoring impeachment. The House vote, taken two days later, was 126 to 47 in favor, on a strict party-line basis.

**Senate Trial.** The House March 2 and 3 approved specific articles of impeachment and appointed managers to argue the charges before the Senate. There were 11 articles in all, the main one concerning Johnson's removal of Stanton in contravention of the Tenure of Office Act.

Between the time of the House action and the beginning of the Senate trial, the conservative Republicans had time to reflect. One of the main objects of their reflection was fiery Ben Wade of Ohio, president pro tempore of the Senate and, under the succession law then in effect, next in line for the presidency. He was also one of the most radical of the radical Republicans, a hard-liner on southern reconstruction and a monetary expansionist.

The impeachment trial opened March 30, 1868. House managers were John A. Bingham, R-Ohio; George S. Boutwell, R-Mass.; James F. Wilson, R-Iowa; Benjamin F. Butler, R-Mass.; Thomas Williams, R-Pa.; John A. Logan, R-Ill.; and Stevens. The president did not appear at the trial. He was represented by a team of lawyers headed by Henry Stanbery, who had resigned as attorney general to lead the defense.

After weeks of argument and testimony, the Senate on May 16 took a test vote on Article XI, a general, catchall charge, thought by the House managers most likely to produce a vote for conviction. The drama of the vote has become legendary. With 36 "guiltys" needed for conviction, the final count was guilty, 35, not guilty, 19.

Seven Republicans joined the 12 Democrats in supporting Johnson. Stunned by the setback, Senate opponents of the president postponed further voting until May 26. Votes were taken then on Article II and Article III. By identical 35 to 19 votes, Johnson was acquitted. To head off further defeats for Johnson opponents, Sen. George H. Williams, Union

Republican-Ore., moved to adjourn *sine die,* and the motion was adopted 34 to 16, abruptly ending the trial.

The Tenure of Office Act was virtually repealed early in Ulysses S. Grant's administration, once the Republicans had control of the appointing power, and was entirely repealed in 1887. In 1926 the Supreme Court declared in its decision in *Myers v. United States*: "The power to remove . . . executive officers . . . is an incident of the power to appoint them, and is in its nature an executive power." The opinion, written by Chief Justice William Howard Taft, himself a former president, referred to the Tenure of Office Act and declared that it had been unconstitutional.

## President Nixon's Resignation

In the case of President Richard Nixon, the process of impeachment did not move beyond its first stage — and yet it realized its purpose. Ten days after the House Judiciary Committee recommended that Nixon be impeached for obstruction of justice, abuse of power and contempt of Congress, Nixon resigned. In the face of certain impeachment by the House and removal by the Senate, he chose to leave the White House voluntarily.

The impeachment inquiry was but one link in the chain of events that brought about Nixon's premature departure from the presidency — a chain that began on June 17, 1972, with a burglary at Democratic National Headquarters in the Watergate Office Building in Washington, D.C. But the work of the House Judiciary Committee and its dramatic conclusion, a televised debate involving all 38 members, were crucial in preparing the nation to accept the resignation of the man elected president by an overwhelming vote less than two years earlier.

Nixon precipitated the inquiry with the "Saturday night massacre" — his firing on Oct. 20, 1973, of the first Watergate special prosecutor, Archibald Cox. Cox was persisting in his effort to force Nixon to release tapes of certain of his conversations following and, Cox suspected, concerning, the Watergate break-in. On the Monday following the Cox firing, a number of impeachment resolutions were introduced in the House and referred to the House Judiciary Committee. On Feb. 6, 1974, the House formally authorized the committee "to investigate fully and completely whether sufficient grounds exist for the House of Representatives to exercise its constitutional power to impeach Richard M. Nixon, President. . . ." The vote was 410 to 4.

Aware of the import of their task, the committee approached it deliberately. From February to May the staff, led by former Assistant Attorney General John M. Doar, assembled evidence related to the various charges against the president, which ranged from Watergate-related matters to questions of his personal finances. The committee subpoenaed the president for additional material. Nixon refused to comply, although he did release edited transcripts of some tapes the committee had sought.

On May 9 the committee began considering the evidence in executive session, a process that continued until mid-July. President Nixon was represented at the proceedings by James D. St. Clair, his chief defense counsel and a noted Boston trial attorney. On July 18 and 19 the committee heard Doar and St. Clair summarize the arguments. Doar advocated impeachment, telling the committee that "reasonable men acting reasonably would find the president guilty" of abusing his presidential powers. Defending the president, St. Clair argued that there was a "complete absence of any conclusive evidence demonstrating presidential wrongdoing sufficient to justify the grave action of impeachment."

On July 24 a unanimous Supreme Court rejected Nixon's claim of executive privilege to withhold evidence sought by the Watergate special prosecutor. Nixon, the court ruled, must comply with subpoenas for certain tapes.

That evening, on nationwide television, the Judiciary Committee began the final phase of its inquiry. For the first time, all 38 members spoke publicly on the evidence. By the end of the evening the outcome was clear. Seven of the 17 Republicans indicated that they would support impeachment. All the Democrats agreed. The vote would be bipartisan.

Four days later, July 27, the decisive roll-call came. The committee approved 27 to 11 the first article of impeachment, charging Nixon with obstructing justice, primarily in the Watergate investigation. Six Republicans joined all 21 Democrats. The second article, charging abuse of power, was approved July 29, by the even wider margin of 28 to 10. The third, charging contempt of Congress, was approved July 30, 21 to 17. Two other proposed articles were rejected.

House debate on impeachment was to begin Aug. 19; the outcome was considered a certainty. The Senate began preparing for a trial. Public opinion swung heavily in favor of impeachment and, for the first time, polls showed a majority of the American people in favor of conviction and removal as well.

On Aug. 5 Nixon released transcripts of three of the taped conversations that the Supreme Court ruling forced him to turn over to the special prosecutor. These made clear his knowing participation in the cover-up of White House involvement in the Watergate burglary. Faced with this new evidence, even the members of the Judiciary Committee who had continued to defend Nixon called for his resignation or impeachment. On Aug. 7 Republican leaders told him he had no more than 10 supporters in the House and 15 in the Senate. On Aug. 8 Nixon told the nation he would resign. He made no mention of impeachment. On Aug. 9, his resignation effective, he left the White House. The House Aug. 20 accepted the report of the committee inquiry, 412 to 3, formally concluding the matter.

## Officials Impeached

The House has impeached 13 federal officers. Following are summaries of all the cases, with the exception of President Johnson's impeachment proceeding, discussed earlier in the chapter.[1]

**William Blount.** On July 3, 1797, President John Adams sent to the House and Senate a letter from Sen. William Blount of Tennessee to James Carey, a U.S. interpreter to the Cherokee Nation of Indians. The letter told of Blount's plans to launch an attack by Indians and frontiersmen, aided by a British fleet, against Louisiana and Spanish Florida to achieve their transfer to British control. Adams' action initiated the first proceedings to result in impeachment by the House and consideration by the Senate.

In the Senate Blount's letter was referred to a select committee, which recommended his expulsion for "a high misdemeanor, entirely inconsistent with his public trust and duty as a Senator." The Senate expelled Blount on July 8 by a 25 to 1 vote.

The House, meanwhile, on July 7 adopted a committee resolution impeaching Blount, and on the same day it appointed a committee to prepare articles of impeachment. On Jan. 29, 1798, the House adopted five articles accusing Blount of attempting to influence the Indians for the benefit of the British.

Senate proceedings did not begin until Dec. 17, 1798. Blount challenged the proceedings, contending that they violated his right to a trial by jury, that he was not a civil officer within the meaning of the

Constitution, that he was not charged with a crime committed while a civil officer, and that courts of common law were competent to try him on the charges. On Jan. 11, 1799, the Senate by a 14 to 11 vote dismissed the charges for lack of jurisdiction. Citing the Senate vote, Vice President Thomas Jefferson ruled Jan. 14 that the Senate was without jurisdiction in the case, thus ending the proceedings.

**John Pickering.** In a partisan move to oust a Federalist judge, President Thomas Jefferson on Feb. 4, 1803, sent a complaint to the House citing John Pickering, U.S. judge for the district of New Hampshire. The complaint was referred to a special committee, and on March 2 the House adopted a committee resolution impeaching the judge by a vote of 45 to 8. A committee was appointed Oct. 20 to prepare articles of impeachment, and the House on Dec. 30 by voice vote agreed to four articles charging Pickering with irregular judicial procedures, loose morals and drunkenness. The judge, known to be insane at the time, did not attend the Senate trial, which began March 8 and ended March 12, 1804, with votes of 19 to 7 for conviction on each of the four articles. The Senate then voted 20 to 6 to remove Pickering from office, but it declined to consider disqualifying him from further office.

**Samuel Chase.** In an equally partisan attack on another Federalist judge, the House on Jan. 7, 1804, by an 81 to 40 vote adopted a resolution for an investigation of Supreme Court Justice Chase and of Richard Peters, a U.S. district court judge in Pennsylvania. The investigation supposedly was intended to study their conduct during a recent treason trial. The House dropped further action against Peters by voice vote on March 12. On the same day, by a 73 to 32 vote, it adopted a committee resolution to impeach Chase. A committee was appointed to draw up articles, and the House in a series of votes on Dec. 4, 1804, agreed to the eight articles, charging Chase with harsh and partisan conduct on the bench and with unfairness to litigants.

The trial began Feb. 9, 1805; Chase appeared in person. The Senate, voting on March 1, failed to produce the two-thirds majority required for conviction on any of the eight articles; "not guilty" votes outnumbered the "guilty" votes on five of the articles.

**James H. Peck.** On Jan. 7, 1830, the House adopted a resolution authorizing an investigation of federal Judge Peck's conduct. On April 24 the House by a 123 to 49 vote adopted a Judiciary Committee resolution impeaching Peck, and later the same day it appointed a committee to prepare articles of impeachment. A single article was adopted May 1 by voice vote charging Peck with setting an unreasonable and oppressive penalty for contempt of court. The trial stretched from Dec. 20, 1830, to Jan. 31, 1831, when Peck was acquitted; 21 senators voted for conviction and 22 for acquittal.

**West H. Humphreys.** During the Civil War, Humphreys, a U.S. judge for the east, middle and west districts of Tennessee, accepted an appointment as a Confederate judge, without resigning from his Union judicial assignment. Aware of the situation, the House on Jan. 8, 1862, by voice vote adopted a resolution authorizing an inquiry. On May 6 the House, also by voice vote, adopted a Judiciary Committee resolution impeaching Humphreys. On May 19 seven articles of impeachment were adopted.

Humphreys could not be served personally with the impeachment summons because he had fled Union territory. He neither appeared at the trial nor contested the charges. In a one-day trial June 26, the Senate convicted Humphreys on all except one charge and unanimously voted to remove him from his judgeship and disqualify him from further office.

**Mark H. Delahay.** In 1872 the House adopted a resolution authorizing an investigation of federal district Judge Delahay. The Judiciary Committee in 1873 proposed a resolution of impeachment, charging Delahay with misconduct in office including intoxication, which the House adopted. Delahay resigned before the articles of impeachment were prepared, and the matter was not pursued further by the House or Senate.

**William W. Belknap.** Faced with widespread corruption and incompetence among high officers of the Grant administration, the House in 1876 initiated a number of general investigations of government departments. On March 2, 1876, the House adopted a resolution from the Committee on Expenditures in the War Department impeaching Secretary of War Belknap. He was charged with receiving money for appointing and continuing in office a post trader at Fort Sill, Okla. Belknap resigned his position, but the Judiciary Committee continued work on impeachment articles. On April 3 the House agreed to five articles of impeachment.

As pretrial maneuvering proceeded, the Senate on May 29 declared by a vote of 37 to 29 that it had jurisdiction over Belknap regardless of his resignation. The trial, which ran from July 6 to Aug. 1, 1876, ended in acquittal, with a substantial number of senators indicating that they had voted against conviction on the ground that the Senate lacked jurisdiction.

**Charles Swayne.** On Dec. 10, 1903, the House adopted a resolution for a Judiciary Committee investigation of Swayne, U.S. judge for the northern district of Florida. The charges against him included padding his expense accounts, using railroad property in receivership for his personal benefit and misusing the contempt power. Months later the committee recommended impeachment, and the House adopted the resolution by voice vote on Dec. 13, 1904. After the vote to impeach, 13 articles were drafted and approved by the House; however, only the first 12 articles were presented to the Senate. The Senate trial opened Feb. 10 and ended Feb. 27 when the Senate voted acquittal on all 12 articles.

**Robert W. Archbald.** On May 4, 1912, the House adopted a Judiciary Committee resolution authorizing an investigation of Archbald, associate judge of the U.S. Commerce Court. A committee resolution impeaching Archbald was adopted in the House July 11 by a 223 to 1 vote. In the 13 articles of impeachment, Archbald was charged with various forms of misconduct, including the improper appointment of a jury commissioner. The trial began Dec. 3, 1912, and ended Jan. 13, 1913, with Archbald convicted on five of the 13 articles. The Senate on the same day removed him from office by voice vote and, by a 39 to 35 vote, disqualified him from further office.

**George W. English.** A resolution asking for an investigation of English, U.S. judge for the eastern district of Illinois, was introduced Jan. 13, 1925. The House on April 1, 1926, adopted by a 306 to 62 vote a Judiciary Committee resolution to impeach English. The resolution also set forth five articles of impeachment, charging the judge with partiality, tyranny and oppression. The trial was set to begin Nov. 10, but on Nov. 4 English resigned; at the request of House managers the Senate dismissed the charges Dec. 13 by a vote of 70 to 9.

**Harold Louderback.** On June 9, 1932, the House by voice vote adopted a resolution for an investigation of Louderback, U.S. federal judge for the northern district of California. The Judiciary Committee's study produced mixed results. The majority recommended censuring but not impeaching Louderback. However, the House on Feb. 24, 1933, by a 183 to 142 vote adopted a minority resolution impeaching the judge and specifying five articles. They accused Louderback of favoritism and conspiracy in the appointment of bankruptcy receivers. A trial that lasted from May 15 to May 24 ended in acquittal, with the "not guilty" votes outnumbering the "guilty" votes on all except one of the five articles.

**Halsted L. Ritter.** On June 1, 1933, the House by voice vote adopted a resolution for an investigation of Ritter, U.S. federal judge for the southern district of Florida. A long delay followed. Then on March 2, 1936, the House by a 181 to 146 vote adopted a Judiciary Committee impeachment resolution, with four articles of impeachment (the four original articles subsequently were replaced with seven amended ones). The charges involved judicial improprieties, including receiving corrupt payments, practicing law while serving as a federal judge, and preparing and filing false income tax returns. The trial lasted from April 6 to April 17. Although there were more "guilty" than "not guilty" votes on all except two of the first six articles, the majorities fell short of the two-thirds required for conviction. However, on the seventh article, with 56 votes necessary for conviction, the vote was 56 guilty and 28 not guilty. Thus, Ritter was convicted. He was ordered removed from office by voice vote. An order to disqualify him from further office was defeated, 0 to 76.

## Impeachment Attempts

In addition to the Nixon investigation, other proposed impeachments have failed to come to a vote in the House because the defendant died or because he resigned or received another appointment, removing him from office. Among the other unsuccessful impeachment attempts have been moves against two presidents, a vice president, two Cabinet officers, and a Supreme Court justice.[2]

**John Tyler.** The House on Jan. 10, 1843, rejected by an 84 to 127 vote a resolution to investigate the possibility of initiating impeachment proceedings against President John Tyler. Tyler had become a political outcast, ostracized by both Democrats and Whigs, but impeachment apparently was too strong a measure to take against him.

**Schuyler Colfax.** A move developed in 1872 to impeach Vice President Schuyler Colfax because of his involvement in the Crédit Mobilier scandal. The matter was dropped when the Judiciary Committee recommended against impeachment on the ground that Colfax had purchased his Crédit Mobilier stock before becoming vice president.

**Harry M. Daugherty.** A similar move to impeach Attorney General Harry M. Daugherty in 1922 on account of his action, or lack of action, in the Teapot Dome oil leasing scandal was dropped in 1923 when a congressional investigation of the affair got under way. Daugherty was forced by President Calvin Coolidge to resign March 28, 1924.

**Andrew W. Mellon.** A running fight between Rep. Wright Patman, D-Texas, and Secretary of the Treasury Andrew W. Mellon over federal economic policy in the depression came to a head in 1932. Patman on Jan. 6 demanded Mellon's impeachment on the ground of conflicting financial interests. To put an end to that move, President Herbert C. Hoover on Feb. 5 nominated Mellon to be ambassador to Great Britain and the Senate confirmed the nomination the same day.

**Herbert C. Hoover.** Two depression-era attempts by Rep. Louis T. McFadden, R-Pa., to impeach President Hoover on general charges of usurping legislative powers and violating constitutional and statutory law were rejected overwhelmingly by the House on Dec. 13, 1932, and Jan. 17, 1933.

**William O. Douglas.** Associate Justice William O. Douglas of the Supreme Court was subjected to several impeachment attempts. The day after Douglas granted a stay of execution to convicted Soviet spies Julius and Ethel Rosenberg in June 1953, Rep. W. M. Wheeler, D-Ga., introduced a resolution to impeach the justice. The resolution was unanimously tabled by the Judiciary Committee. In April 1970 two resolutions for Douglas' impeachment were introduced in the midst of bitter conflict over Senate rejection of two Supreme Court nominations. Among the charges cited were possible financial conflicts similar to those that had led to Senate rejection of the Nixon nominees for the Court. A special House Judiciary Subcommittee on Dec. 3, 1970, voted 3 to 1 against impeachment.

## Notes

1. U.S., Congress, House, Committee on the Judiciary, *Impeachment: Selected Materials on Procedure,* 93rd Cong., 2nd sess., January 1974, pp. 682-688; Arthur C. Hinds, *Hinds' Precedents of the House of Representatives of the United States,* 5 vols. (Washington, D.C.: U.S. Government Printing Office, 1907), III: 644-980; Clarence Cannon, *Cannon's Precedents of the House of Representatives of the United States,* 3 vols. (Washington, D.C.: U.S. Government Printing Office, 1935), III: 684-742, 778-786; and *Proceedings of the United States Senate in the Trial of Impeachment of Halsted L. Ritter,* S. Doc. No. 200, 74th Cong., 2nd sess., 1936, pp. 343-524, 549-685, 795-850, 884-892.
2. *Impeachment: Selected Materials on Procedure,* pp. 525, 722-724, 876-882.

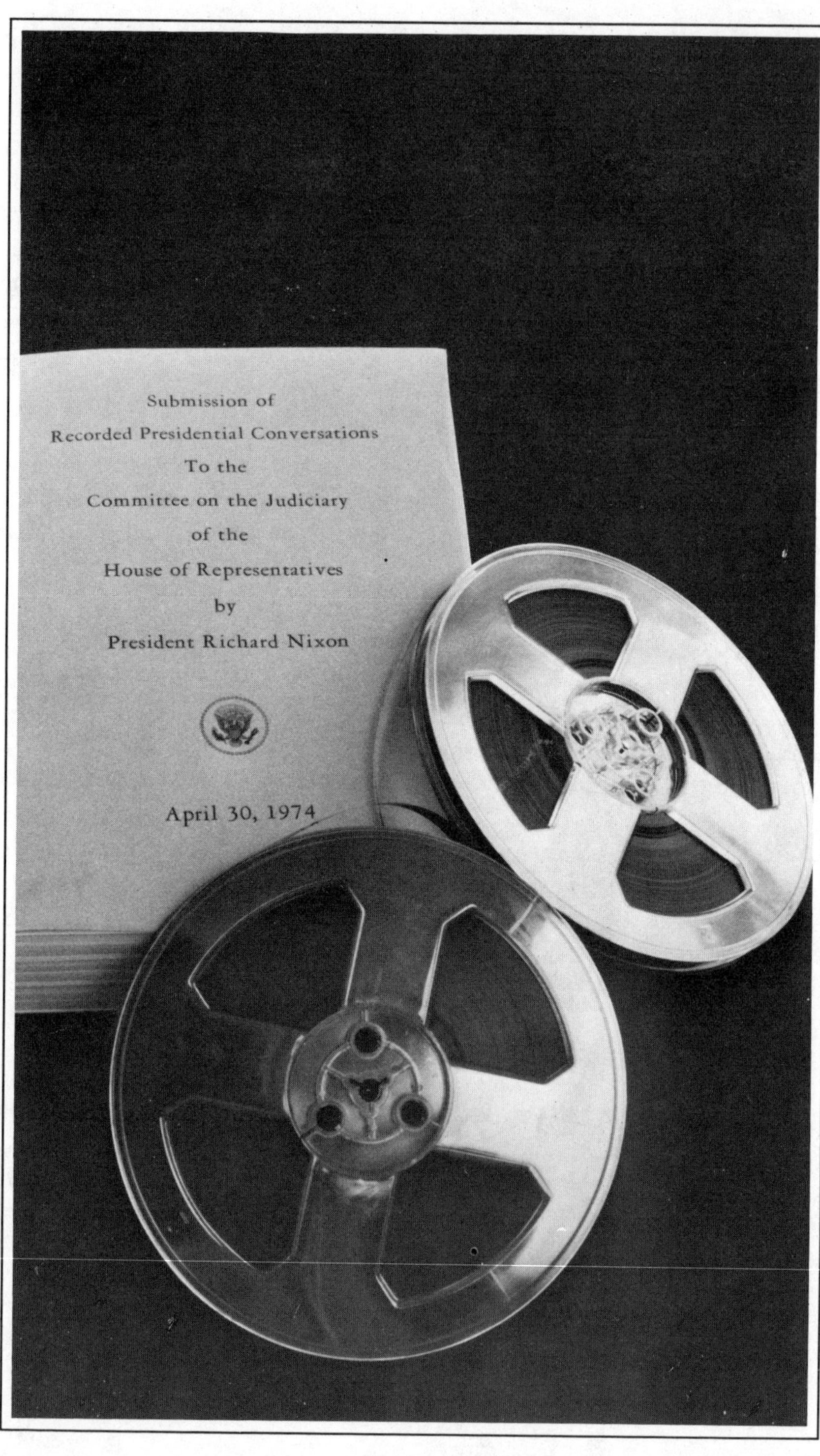
Submission of
Recorded Presidential Conversations
To the
Committee on the Judiciary
of the
House of Representatives
by
President Richard Nixon
April 30, 1974

# *Part V*

# Investigations

Congress' investigation of Watergate turned on evidence from tape recordings of President Richard Nixon's conversations in the White House.

## *Chapter 14*

# ORIGINS OF INVESTIGATIONS

The power of Congress to investigate — one of the most controversial and highly publicized powers of the national legislature — is not mentioned in the Constitution. Yet since it was first assumed by the House in 1792 — to investigate the massacre of U.S. soldiers in Indian territory — this power has been accepted as an inherent part of the power to legislate.

Since 1792, the trail of congressional investigations has been an erratic one, marked by some of the brightest and some of the darkest moments in congressional history. In the exercise of this power Congress has found itself time and again in direct confrontation with the executive and judicial branches, confrontations which produce new definitions of the separation of power among the three parts of the federal government. These investigations have transformed minor politicians into household words; they have broken the careers of important men. They have captured the attention of millions of readers and viewers, bringing home the function of Congress in a way no textbook or lecture can match.

Investigations gather information on the need for legislation, test the effectiveness of existing laws, inquire into the qualifications and character of members, and lay the groundwork for impeachment. Yet despite these valid functions, the practices of some committees have led critics to brand particular investigations as nothing more than political vehicles for publicity and an extravagant waste of time and money, producing few, if any, useful legislative results.

Nevertheless, the importance of this power is beyond question. It has been acknowledged again and again by judges and presidents as well as legislators and citizens. In 1957 Chief Justice Earl Warren wrote:

> The power of Congress to conduct investigations is inherent in the legislative process. That power is broad. It encompasses inquiries concerning the administration of existing laws as well as proposed or

> possibly needed statutes. It includes surveys of defects in our social, economic or political system for the purpose of enabling the Congress to remedy them. It comprehends probes into departments of the Federal Government to expose corruption, inefficiency or waste. . . . [1]

Woodrow Wilson, in his much-quoted graduate thesis on congressional government, wrote that "the informing function of Congress should be preferred even to its legislative function." [2] And Harry S Truman, who achieved national fame as chairman of the World War II Senate Special Committee to Investigate the National Defense Program, stated his belief in 1944 that "the power of investigation is one of the most important powers of Congress. The manner in which that power is exercised will largely determine the position and prestige of the Congress in the future." [3]

The power to investigate is a double-edged sword, however. As Sen. Sam J. Ervin Jr., D-N.C. (1954-74), chairman of the Senate Select Committee on Presidential Campaign Activities, has observed: "A legislative inquiry can serve as the tool to pry open the barriers that hide governmental corruption. It can be the catalyst that spurs Congress and the public to support vital reforms in our nation's laws. Or it can debase our principles, invade the privacy of our citizens, and afford a platform for demagogues and the rankest partisans." [4] An even gloomier view was once provided by Walter Lippmann, who described a congressional investigation as "that legalized atrocity . . . in which congressmen, starved of their legitimate food for thought, go on a wild and feverish manhunt and do not stop at cannibalism." [5]

## Subjects of Scrutiny

No period of American history has been without a congressional investigation. Only the Spanish-American war of 1898 — of all major U.S. military engagements — escaped congressional scrutiny. President William McKinley, a former member of the House, forestalled legislative inquiry by naming a commission to conduct that investigation.[6]

Many of the earliest congressional investigations concerned charges brought against a senator or representative, but most concerned the civil and military activities of the executive branch. For example, the Post Office Department was the target of probes in 1820, 1822 and 1830, the Bank of the United States in 1832 and 1834, the Smithsonian Institution in 1855 and the General Land Office in 1897.[7] In the late 19th century, a

## Investigations Defined

For purposes of this section, "investigation" has been defined as an inquiry by any congressional committee or subcommittee that uses investigative procedures (examining records, summoning and questioning witnesses) for one or more of the following reasons:

—Fact-finding for possible special and remedial legislation.

—Fulfilling Congress' function as a "watchdog" over government operations and programs.

—Informing the public.

—Resolving questions concerning membership or procedure such as conduct of elections or fitness of members of Congress.

Among committee activities not included in the definition: inquiries conducted by staff members without participation by members of Congress in formal hearings; routine hearings; and action on bills and resolutions.

new field for congressional investigation began to emerge — economic and social problems. There were studies of black migration from South to North (1880), strikebreaking by the railroads (1892) and the concentration of wealth in the "money trust" (1912-13).[8]

Government operations and social conditions served as the principal subjects of congressional investigation until the period between World Wars I and II, when the fear of subversion from foreign ideologies led to inquiries of a different sort. Investigations of social conditions and government operations continued while probes into possible subversion expanded rapidly. These hearings often involved broad-scale intrusions into the thoughts, actions and associations of all manner of persons and institutions, and raised searching legal and moral questions about the power and procedures of congressional inquiry. *(Box on investigations of un-Americanism, pp. 218-219)*

The expanded use of investigations made Congress' investigating power itself a major political issue. To some, the threat to national security posed by communist subversion was so great as to justify exceptional procedures. To others, the threat to individual liberties from the behavior and authority of some committees appeared a more real danger than that of communism. The conflict over the powers of the committees and the rights of witnesses continued, with shifting results and varying intensity into the 1960s. It was waged in Congress, in the courts, in the executive branch, in the councils of both parties and in public debates and election campaigns.

## Derivation of Investigative Power

Congress derives its power to investigate from Article I of the Constitution, which begins: "All legislative Powers herein granted shall be vested in a Congress of the United States. . . ." From this express grant of power is implied Congress' investigative power.[9]

The power of a legislative body to investigate was asserted as early as the 16th century by the British House of Commons. The Commons first used its investigative power in determining its membership. It then made increasing use of investigations to assist it in performing its lawmaking functions and in overseeing officials responsible for executing laws and spending the funds made available by Parliament. Investigating committees of the House of Commons had authority to summon witnesses and to examine documents, and the Commons could support its committees by punishing uncooperative witnesses for contempt. American colonial legislatures, the Continental Congress and state legislatures relied on these parliamentary precedents in carrying out their own investigations. Thus the power to investigate, to compel the attendance of witnesses and to demand the production of documents was regarded by most members of the early Congresses as an intrinsic part of the power to legislate.

There was some initial discussion, however, concerning the scope of this power. Strict constructionists asserted that limitation of the authority of Congress to specifically granted powers restricted investigations to clearly defined judicial functions, such as election disputes, impeachment proceedings or cases involving congressional privileges. Broad constructionists argued that the precedents supported an inherent investigative power as broad as the legislative function. The broad constructionists prevailed and won approval of the Army investigation in 1792. That first investigation served as a precedent for others. Since then, no serious challenge of the basic authority of Congress to investigate has ever been mounted. However, specific investigations have been challenged, with mixed results; opposition has arisen mainly in the case of investigations that have pried into private affairs, infringed on personal liberties or conflicted with executive branch prerogatives.

## Congress' Contempt Power

Like the investigative power which it reinforces, the congressional power to punish for contempt is based on parliamentary precedents dating from Elizabethan times.[10] No express power to punish for contempt, except in the case of a member, was granted Congress in the Constitution. But Congress assumed that it had inherent power to send persons in contempt to jail without a court order because it regarded such power as necessary for its own protection and for the integrity of its proceedings.[11]

The first use of the congressional power to punish a non-member for contempt was on Dec. 28, 1795, when Robert Randall was summoned to the bar of the House on a charge of having tried to bribe a member. Following debate, the House on Jan. 4, 1796, voted 78 to 17 to jail Randall for a week. Both chambers drew on precedents established in the Randall case to punish other non-members for contemptuous acts. The first committee witness cited for contempt was Nathaniel Rounsavell, editor of the Alexandria, Va., *Herald,* who refused in 1812 to answer questions before a House committee investigating a breach in the security of a secret House session. After a day's confinement in the custody of the House sergeant-at-arms, Rounsavell apologized and was discharged.[12]

The Senate first voted a contempt of Congress citation on March 20, 1800, when William Duane was ordered arrested for libeling a member. On May 14, the Senate by a 13-4 vote sentenced him to 30 days in jail and ordered him to pay costs. The first Senate committee witness to be cited was Thaddeus Hyatt, who had refused a summons by a committee investigating John Brown's raid on Harpers Ferry in 1859. The Senate March 12, 1860, by a 44-10 vote ordered Hyatt jailed. He was released June 15.[13]

The constitutionality of Congress' summary use of the contempt power was upheld by the Supreme Court in 1821 in the case of *Anderson v. Dunn.* The court declared that the power to punish contempts was assumed to be inherent in each chamber because without it, Congress could be "exposed to every indignity and interruption that rudeness, caprice, or even conspiracy may meditate against it." The power was limited, however, by the court "to the least power adequate to the end proposed," and imprisonment could not extend beyond the adjournment of Congress.[14]

The case grew out of an attempt by John Anderson to bribe a House member to help push a land claim through Congress. Anderson was given a summary trial at the bar of the House, at the end of which the Speaker reprimanded Anderson and then freed him. After his release, Anderson brought charges against Sergeant-at-Arms Thomas Dunn for assault and battery and for false arrest. A lower court ruled against Anderson, and he appealed. The Supreme Court likewise ruled against Anderson, but it upheld the constitutionality of the summary contempt power of Congress.[15]

Considering the sanction of imprisonment only to the end of a legislative session inadequate, Congress in 1857 passed a law, still in effect in amended form, making it a criminal offense to refuse information demanded by either chamber.[16] Even after passage of the 1857 law, Congress preferred to punish persons in contempt itself, reasoning that a few days of confinement might induce a witness to co-operate, while turning him over to a court would put him out of reach of the inquiring committee. Later, however, as the press of legislative business mounted and as court review of summary congressional punishment became more frequent, Congress increasingly relied on criminal prosecution for contempt under the 1857 law.

The last time either chamber punished someone for contempt was in 1932. Since then, all contempt of Congress citations have been prosecuted before the courts by the Justice Department. Congressional contempt cases fall into two general classes: (1) those involving positive acts, such as bribery or libel, which directly or indirectly obstruct the legislature in carrying out its function, and (2) those involving refusal to perform acts which the legislature claims authority to compel, such as testifying or producing documents. Few cases of the first type have occurred in recent years, and the courts have had little opportunity to define positive acts of contempt. The second type, while giving rise to much more extensive judicial interpretation, continues to raise many legal questions because of its greater complexity.

Exercising the inherent power of Congress itself to punish someone for contempt, a committee may introduce a resolution directing the presiding officer of the chamber to issue a warrant for arrest of the witness in contempt by the chamber's sergeant-at-arms. The witness is brought before the bar of the House, or Senate, and questioned.

## Contempt of Congress

Congress in 1857 enacted a statute that allowed it to turn over congressional contempt cases to the federal courts for indictment and trial. Under this statute, as it has been amended and interpreted, the courts are obligated to provide the defendant all the protections guaranteed defendants in other criminal actions. The statute (2 United States Code, Section 192) states:

> Every person who having been summoned as a witness by the authority of either House of Congress to give testimony or to produce papers upon any matter under inquiry before either House, or any joint committee established by a joint or concurrent resolution of the two Houses of Congress, or any committee of either House of Congress, willfully makes default, or who having appeared, refuses to answer any question pertinent to the question under inquiry, shall be deemed guilty of a misdemeanor, punishable by a fine of not more than $1,000 nor less than $100 and imprisonment in a common jail for not less than one month nor more than twelve months.

Subsequently, the full chamber may adopt a resolution ordering the confinement of the witness or his discharge, or the witness simply may be reprimanded by the chamber's presiding officer.

When a committee in either chamber wishes to institute criminal proceedings against a contumacious witness, it introduces a resolution in the parent body citing him for contempt. Only a simple majority vote is necessary for approval; such a resolution is seldom opposed. The matter is then referred to a U.S. attorney for presentation to a grand jury.

Between 1789 and 1976, Congress voted 384 contempt citations in cases where a witness refused to appear before a committee or refused to produce documents for a committee. Most of these citations have occurred since 1945, primarily as the result of activities by the House Un-American Activities Committee. In the period from 1792 until 1942, there were only 108 contempt citations.[17] Moreover, until 1945, Congress frequently refused to follow the recommendations of its committees on contempt citations. From 1796 to 1945, the House or Senate reversed the actions of committees in 34 cases.[18] But after 1945, the record was drastically altered. Of 226 contempt citations presented to both houses by 14 committees between 1945 and 1957, few cases were debated, few were discussed and none was defeated. After 1945, approval of a committee's contempt citation by the full House or Senate was "almost automatic." [19] In 1972, the House cited Watergate conspirator G. Gordon Liddy for contempt of Congress. The case was turned over to the U.S. attorney in the District of Columbia for presentation to a grand jury. Liddy, a former member of the "plumbers" special investigative unit at the White House, was cited for his refusal to be sworn in to testify before the House Armed Services Committee's Special Intelligence Subcommittee in July. The subcommittee and then the full committee approved the resolution citing him for contempt. The House approved the resolution by a vote of 334 to 11 on Sept. 10, 1972. Liddy was found guilty of contempt of Congress May 10, 1974. U.S. District Judge John H. Pratt, who heard the case without a jury in Washington, gave Liddy a suspended six-month sentence.[20]

## Notes

1. *Watkins v. United States,* 354 U.S. 178 at 187 (1957).
2. Woodrow Wilson, *Congressional Government,* reprint ed. (Cleveland: World Publishing Co., 1967), p. 303.
3. *Congressional Record,* Aug. 7, 1944, 78th Cong., 2nd sess., p. 6747.
4. James Hamilton, *The Power to Probe* (New York: Random House, 1976), p. xii.
5. C. Herman Pritchett, *The American Constitution* (New York: McGraw-Hill Book Co., 1968), p. 214.
6. Joseph P. Harris, *Congressional Control of Administration* (Washington, D.C.: The Brookings Institution, 1964), p. 253; and Marshall E. Dimock, *Congressional Investigating Committees* (Baltimore: Johns Hopkins Press, 1929), p. 87.
7. Dimock, *Congressional Investigating Committees,* p. 104; and Telford Taylor, *Grand Inquest* (New York: Simon & Schuster, 1955), p. 33.
8. Taylor, *Grand Inquest,* p. 51; *Congress and the Nation,* 5 vols., *Congress and the Nation: 1945-1964,* vol. 1 (Washington, D.C.: Congressional Quarterly, 1965), I: 1679.
9. For a discussion of development of the investigative power and controversy surrounding it, see Dimock, *Congressional Investigating Committees,* pp. 46, 117-121; and Taylor, *Grand Inquest,* pp. 5-16.
10. For background, see Carl Beck, *Contempt of Congress* (New Orleans: Hauser Press, 1959); and Ronald L. Goldfarb, *The Contempt Power* (New York: Columbia University Press, 1963).

11. Goldfarb, *The Contempt Power*, p. 25.
12. Ibid., p. 30; Beck, *Contempt of Congress,* p. 3; Ernest J. Eberling, *Congressional Investigations* (New York: Columbia University Press, 1928), pp. 37-42, 66-85.
13. Eberling, *Congressional Investigations,* pp. 161-167; Beck, *Contempt of Congress,* p. 191.
14. Dimock, *Congressional Investigating Committees,* pp. 121-123; Pritchett, *The American Constitution,* p. 217.
15. Goldfarb, *The Contempt Power,* p. 163.
16. Taylor, *Grand Inquest,* p. 35; *Congress and the Nation: 1945-1964,* I: 1783.
17. Goldfarb, *The Contempt Power,* p. 196; Beck, *Contempt of Congress,* appendix.
18. Beck, *Contempt of Congress,* p. 185.
19. Ibid., pp. 185-186, 189.
20. *Watergate: Chronology of a Crisis* (Washington, D.C.: Congressional Quarterly, 1975), pp. 311, 637.

## *Chapter 15*

# INVESTIGATIVE PROCEDURES

From the beginning, Congress has delegated its power to investigate to committees. And, after preliminary investigation of a subject by committee staff, committees generally have conducted most of their investigations by calling citizens knowledgeable on the matter to testify. Committees can request that testimony, using a subpoena *ad testificundum,* to make clear the seriousness of the request, or a subpoena *duces tecum,* if they wish the witness to bring certain documents or other materials. Either type of subpoena is ignored only at the risk of a contempt citation. A reluctant witness can be granted immunity; an immunized witness must then testify.

When witnesses appear before the committee, they are often sworn in before testifying. Any member of an investigating committee may, by law, administer this oath. Witnesses under oath may be prosecuted for perjury if they do not tell the truth in their testimony. Even unsworn witnesses are subject to prosecution for false statements. A federal law makes it a felony to make false statements or representations regarding "any matter within the jurisdiction of any department or agency of the United States." [1]

Prior to passage of the Legislative Reorganization Act of 1946, the majority of investigations were carried out by special or select committees established and given subpoena power to conduct the inquiry. When an investigation was concluded, the committee went out of existence. The first attempt to give subpoena power to a standing committee — the House Committee on Manufactures, for a tariff investigation — was strongly opposed but was approved Dec. 31, 1827, by a 102-88 vote. Opponents said the proposal was unheard of because subpoena power previously had been used only by committees acting as judicial bodies.[2]

The spectacular growth of the executive branch during the New Deal and World War II years led to a proliferation of congressional investigating committees as Congress struggled to fulfill its traditional function of overseeing the administration of laws and the spending of appropriations. Between 1945 and passage of the reorganization act in 1946, at least 50 investigations had been voted.[3]

The 1946 act reduced the number of standing committees from 48 to 19 in the House and from 33 to 15 in the Senate. It authorized standing committees of both chambers to "exercise continuous watchfulness of the execution by the administrative agencies concerned of any laws, the subject matter of which is within the jurisdiction" of the respective committees. The act also extended permanent subpoena power to all standing committees of the Senate and authorized $10,000 in investigating funds for each committee during each Congress.

### House Subpoena Power

The House in 1974 gave its committees and subcommittees general subpoena power to compel the attendance and testimony of witnesses and the production of books, records and any other documents considered necessary to an investigation. For many years, Speaker Sam Rayburn, D-Texas (1913-61), and Minority Leader Joseph W. Martin, R-Mass (1925-67), had opposed this grant of general subpoena power to House Committees because they feared that such power would make the committees uncontrollable and lead to sensational inquiries motivated by political ambitions. As a result of Rayburn's and Martin's opposition, individual House committees prior to 1974 had to seek specific House approval for authority to compel testimony and documents. In such cases, the House normally authorized broad committee investigatory power and use of the subpoena. But after 1974, specific subpoena authority no longer had to be given to each committee. However, the 1974 change required that a majority of a committee or subcommittee approve a subpoena before it was issued. In addition, compliance with a subpoena could be enforced only by action of the full House.

The House Banking Committee was the first congressional committee to attempt to use its subpoena power to investigate the 1972 break-in of the Democratic National Headquarters, located in the Watergate office-hotel complex in Washington, D.C. On Oct. 3, 1972, the committee rejected a resolution backed by Chairman Wright Patman, D-Texas, to call 40 individuals and organizations to testify about possible violations of banking laws and irregularities in Republican campaign financing suggested by the break-in.[4] The following year, on December

18th, the Senate Select Committee on Presidential Campaign Activities (Watergate Committee) construed its subpoena power broadly when it sought a large but unspecified number of White House tapes and documents. (The committee had issued earlier subpoenas in July.)[5]

The House Judiciary Committee, responsible for conducting the inquiry into charges against President Richard M. Nixon, was one of the standing committees granted general subpoena power by resolution at the beginning of the 93rd Congress in 1973. At that time, however, the official list of subjects under the committee's jurisdiction did not include impeachment. But on Feb. 6, 1974, with only four members voting "nay," the House formally granted the committee power to investigate the conduct of President Nixon to determine whether there were grounds for his impeachment.[6] The resolution gave explicit authorization for the committee to conduct the investigation, which was already under way, and granted it special subpoena power during the inquiry.

The committee's issuance of subpoenas to Nixon in the spring and summer of 1974 was an unprecedented action. In the only other impeachment proceedings against a president, Andrew Johnson in 1867 and 1868, Johnson himself was not subpoenaed.[7] *(See History of Impeachments Chapter, pp. 169-172)*

Before Nixon was served with subpoenas for tapes and documents July 23, 1973, two from the Senate Watergate investigating committee and one from the Watergate special prosecutor, the only president in office to be subpoenaed was Thomas Jefferson in 1807. When former Vice President Aaron Burr was on trial for treason, Burr asked Chief Justice John Marshall, who was presiding over the trial at the circuit level, to subpoena the president. Burr contended that Jefferson had a letter which would contradict testimony that had been given against Burr. Marshall found that the court could issue a subpoena to the president requiring the letter to be issued. Jefferson did not testify in person, but he said he would — and in fact did — produce the letter.[8]

## Cost of Investigations

The combined effect of the 1946 Legislative Reorganization Act and executive branch expansion beginning with the New Deal period in the 1930s was an explosion of investigative activity following World War II. Compared to approximately 500 investigations in almost 150 years from 1789 to 1938, the 90th Congress (1967-69) alone authorized 496 investigations.

The number and cost of the studies rapidly outdistanced the $10,000 per committee authorized in the 1946 act, and the committees in most cases were again required to seek special funds for investigative activities. In 1973, the Senate Watergate investigating committee alone was authorized $2 million to conduct its inquiry.[9] Four years later, the House Select Committee on Assassinations spent more than $3 million to reinvestigate the assassinations of President John F. Kennedy and the Rev. Martin Luther King Jr.

Although Congress continued to establish special investigating committees in postwar years, most major investigations were carried on by a handful of standing committees or their subcommittees: the House and Senate committees on government operations, the Internal Security Subcommittee of the Senate Judiciary Committee, the Senate Government Operations Permanent Investigations Subcommittee and the House Internal Security Committee.

## Procedural Stages

Congressional investigations proceed through three stages: authorization, staff preparation and public hearings.[10] A senator or representative may propose an investigation for a variety of reasons: to gather facts on widely known public occurrences such as an airline crash; to probe reports of improper conduct in the government, labor unions or business; or to pursue a personal interest such as government monetary policy or fees charged ranchers for grazing cattle on federal range land. Whatever the reason, the authority and scope of the inquiry are incorporated in a resolution for introduction in the House or Senate. Once introduced, the resolution is referred to a committee. The life of a special House investigation committee expires with a Congress, but that of a Senate committee depends upon its authorization.

**Authorization.** In the Senate, resolutions to authorize and fund investigations are considered by the Rules and Administration Committee and by the standing legislative committee having jurisdiction over the subject to be studied. In the House, the Administration Committee considers the funding of investigations. Prior to January 1975, House resolutions for investigations also had to be considered by the Rules Committee before being sent to the floor. However, this requirement has been eliminated, and in 1975 all standing committees were given direct authority to conduct investigations.

After being reported by the committees, a resolution is voted on by the full chamber. Joint House-Senate investigating committees are authorized by a concurrent resolution adopted by both chambers. Many resolutions to authorize investigations, like bills and resolutions on other matters, are never acted upon by a committee and die. But if a resolution authorizing an investigation is approved by a committee and adopted on the floor, an investigation almost always follows. One exception occurred in 1933 when an authorized investigation of the Reconstruction Finance Corporation by the Senate Banking and Currency Committee did not occur; the committee reported later that it had had no specific inquiry in mind and had asked for the investigatory power only as a precautionary step.[11]

It has long been a matter of courtesy in both the House and Senate that the sponsor of the resolution for an investigation shall preside over the inquiry. When the study is to be made by a standing committee, a subcommittee generally is appointed by the chairman of the full committee, with the sponsor of the resolution being named subcommittee chairman. When a select committee is authorized, the members are chosen by consultation between the vice president, or the Speaker of the House, and the majority and minority leaders.

**Staff Preparation.** Early congressional investigative committees had no staff and inquiries were undertaken informally. The investigating committee frequently knew little about the subject under study and simply struck out blindly, asking questions and considering evidence, hoping that something might be found that would be useful to the investigation. It was in the late 1800s and early 1900s that committee staffs first came into use by investigating committees. By the 1920s and 1930s the practice of relying on staff members to gather information was firmly established. Trained investigators, examining files and records before the start of public hearings, generally have accumulated most of the information produced by investigations. Occasionally an investigating committee has been authorized access to income tax returns, customarily by executive order. Until the Legislative Reorganization Act of 1946 authorized professional committee staffs, investigating committees frequently borrowed personnel from the administrative agencies. Trained investigators from government agencies still are used by many committees.

At its peak in 1973, the Senate Watergate committee had a total staff of 64, including 17 attorneys; the House Judiciary Committee's

## Investigations: A Road to Fame

Throughout history, some men have found congressional investigations to be a road to national recognition.

Sen. Gerald P. Nye, R-N.D. (1925-45), was considered a possible Republican presidential or vice presidential nominee in 1936, after he presided over the work of the Senate Special Committee Investigating the Munitions Industry.

Harry S Truman achieved national prominence as chairman of the World War II Senate Special Committee to Investigate the National Defense Program.

Richard M. Nixon first won recognition through his activities on the House Un-American Activities Committee, particularly in its investigation of Alger Hiss.

Sen. Estes Kefauver, D-Tenn. (House 1939-49; Senate 1949-63), became a leading presidential contender after the widely viewed televised hearings of his Senate Special Committee to Investigate Organized Crime in Interstate Commerce. In 1956, Kefauver was the Democratic nominee for vice president.

Sen. Robert F. Kennedy, D-N.Y. (1965-68), first achieved a measure of popular recognition while chief counsel of the Senate Select Committee on Improper Activities in the Labor or Management Field.

None of these politicians, however, derived as much authority from congressional investigations as Sen. Joseph R. McCarthy, R-Wis. (1947-57), whose power was felt — and feared — in Congress, in two administrations, in the State Department, in the armed forces, in universities, and in many other public and private institutions throughout the country.

impeachment inquiry staff in 1974 numbered close to 100 and included 43 attorneys.[12] In 1981, the staff of the Senate Government Operations Permanent Investigations Subcommittee included a chief counsel, a minority chief counsel, four assistant counsels, a deputy chief counsel, two executive assistants, six investigators, a staff editor, a chief clerk, an assistant chief clerk and three clerical assistants.[13]

**Public Hearings.** Public hearings are the most visible and controversial element of investigations, but as a rule they bring forth little material not already uncovered or suggested by staff work.[14] Hearings give the investigated person a chance to present his case. Procedures vary from committee to committee, but a witness usually is allowed to present a prepared statement and to be accompanied by and to consult with a lawyer. Questioning of witnesses is conducted by members of the committee, and by the committee's staff.

The widespread television and radio coverage afforded the Senate Watergate Committee during its first phase of hearings in the summer of 1973 illustrates the controversial impact of publicity. The committee's live audience was strongly anti-Nixon, and in the early months of the hearings made its feelings known with laughter and applause. Chairman Sam J. Ervin Jr. received a standing ovation when he entered the room. Finally, during the testimony of John D. Erlichman in July, the audience became so abusive that the chairman put an end to demonstrations of opinion.

The publicity led the first Watergate special prosecutor, Archibald Cox, on June 4, 1973, to urge the committee to call off its public hearings for one to three months. One of his reasons for doing so was that witnesses might be less likely to make full disclosures before television cameras than privately to prosecutors. However, Judge John J. Sirica of the U.S. District Court in Washington, denied Cox's request, declaring that "the court lacks completely any power of intervention" with the committee's proceedings.

## Notes

1. 18 U.S.C. 1001 (1970); see James Hamilton, *The Power to Probe* (New York: Random House, 1976), Chapter 3.
2. Marshall E. Dimock, *Congressional Investigating Committees* (Baltimore: Johns Hopkins Press, 1929), pp. 58, 73-74.
3. Joseph P. Harris, *Congressional Control of Administration* (Washington, D.C.: The Brookings Institution, 1964), p. 264.
4. *Watergate: Chronology of a Crisis* (Washington, D.C.: Congressional Quarterly, 1975), p. 514.
5. Ibid., p. 467.
6. Ibid., p. 518, for text of resolution.
7. Ibid., p. 356.
8. Ibid., p. 333; Raoul Berger, *Executive Privilege* (Cambridge: Harvard University Press, 1974), p. 187-194.

9. *Watergate: Chronology of a Crisis*, p. 652; *Congress and the Nation*, 5 vols., *Congress and the Nation: 1977-1980,* vol. 5 (Washington, D.C.: Congressional Quarterly, 1981), V: 734-735.
10. For a good discussion of procedure, see M. Nelson McGeary, *The Development of Congressional Investigative Power* (New York: Octagon Books, 1966), Chapter 3; and Donald H. Riddle, *The Truman Committee* (New Brunswick: Rutgers University Press, 1964), Chapter 2.
11. McGeary, *The Development of Congressional Investigative Power,* pp. 51-52.
12. *Watergate: Chronology of a Crisis*, p. 543.
13. Charles B. Brownson, *1981 Congressional Staff Directory* (Mount Vernon, Va.: Congressional Staff Directory, Ltd., 1981), p. 193.
14. McGeary, *The Development of Congressional Investigative Power,* pp. 73-81.

*Chapter 16*

# THE RIGHTS OF WITNESSES

The potential for conflict between the right of Congress to seek information and the right of a witness to protect his privacy has been present since the earliest days of congressional investigations; but not until the late 1930s did the rights of witnesses before a congressional investigating committee become a live issue.

Early legislative investigations were conducted in a comparatively low-key atmosphere, free from the instant publicity of television. Witnesses were often allowed to call their own supporting witnesses and to cross-examine hostile witnesses.[1] The advent in the 1930s of the inquisitorial congressional panel, typified by the House Special Committee to Investigate Un-American Activities (Dies Committee), aroused new concern. The low-key atmosphere had vanished, replaced by relentless probing questions before massed newsmen and newsreel cameras. Complaints mounted that the procedures of congressional investigators were exceeding their powers and violating the rights of witnesses.

In fact, as witnesses — and the courts — discovered, investigating committees had virtually free rein to determine their procedures. Challenges of the legality of committee procedures raised sensitive questions that courts studiously sought to avoid. They attempted to rule on narrow points of law rather than on the central point, the power of a committee to set its own procedures. "It would be an unwarranted act of judicial usurpation ... to assume for the courts the function of supervising congressional committees," wrote Justice Robert Jackson in 1949. "I should ... leave the responsibility for the behavior of its committees squarely on the shoulders of Congress." [2]

The result of the courts' evasiveness was that witnesses were at the mercy of the investigating committee, protected only by the general constitutional limitations on congressional authority and by the Bill of

Rights. A 1954 study of congressional investigative power by the Legislative Reference Service of the Library of Congress concluded: "There are few safeguards for the protection of a witness before a congressional committee. . . . In committee, his treatment usually depends upon the skill and attitude of the chairman and the members." [3] That conclusion was underscored by an earlier comment by House Un-American Activities Committee Chairman John Parnell Thomas, R-N.J. (1937-50): "The rights you have are the rights given you by this committee. We will determine what rights you have and what rights you have not got before the committee." [4]

During the postwar era, the growing number and broadened scope of investigations, and the increasing use of committee hearings for the purpose of edifying the public rather than informing the legislature, led to pressure for more precise definitions of committee powers. Television coverage of hearings, first used spectacularly during House Un-American Activities Committee investigations of communism in 1948, exposed witnesses to vast publicity, jeopardizing their privacy, their reputations and often their careers. In search of protection, witnesses turned to the Constitution. Their efforts to invoke the First Amendment in refusing to provide committees with information, on the ground that Congress had no right to probe their private convictions or their political views or propaganda activities, had mixed results. The Fourth Amendment guarantee against unreasonable search and seizure likewise offered uncertain protection. The arbitrary power of committees to demand the production of documents was the most used — and disputed — authority in the history of congressional investigations.

Once the courts upheld the right of congressional committee witnesses to invoke the Fifth Amendment's protection against self-incrimination, use of the amendment to avoid answering questions became highly controversial. The Fifth Amendment generally stood up as a defense against prosecution for contempt of Congress. However, witnesses could not invoke the privilege partially, answering as to incriminating facts and then refusing further explanation. For this reason, some witnesses repeatedly pleaded the Fifth Amendment, refusing to answer apparently innocuous questions. Because of the uncertainty of these constitutional safeguards for witnesses, pressure mounted for reform of committee procedures to protect the rights of witnesses and to give greater assurance that the purposes for which the investigations were instituted would, in fact, be accomplished.

## Rules Reforms

Proposals for "fair play" rules for investigations were numerous in the 83rd Congress. Both the House Rules Committee and the Senate Rules and Administration Committee in 1954 held hearings on a variety of proposed codes of committee procedure.[5]

**House.** The House March 23, 1955, adopted by voice vote a resolution amending House Rules to establish a minimum standard of conduct for House committees. The resolution:

—Required a quorum of at least two members when committees take testimony and receive evidence.

—Allowed witnesses at investigations to be accompanied by counsel.

—Required a committee, if it found that evidence "may tend to defame, degrade, or incriminate any person," to receive the evidence in secret session and to allow the person injured to appear as a witness and to request subpoenas of other witnesses.

—Required committee consent for release of evidence taken in secret session.

**Senate.** The Senate prescribed no "fair play" code for its committees. However, the Senate Republican Policy Committee on March 10, 1954, offered as "suggestions" a set of rules for investigations and sent the proposals to all Senate committee chairmen. The Republican proposals would have allowed counsel for witnesses, prohibited release of executive testimony except by majority vote, and strengthened the control of investigations by the majority of the committee.

The Rules Subcommittee of the Senate Rules and Administration Committee on Jan. 6, 1955, issued a report recommending 12 rules to protect witnesses and to ensure greater control of investigations. The report said "elaborate procedural devices" would be unnecessary if there were "courtesy and understanding on the part of committee members and staff." Among the recommendations were those to:

—Allow a person who felt his reputation had been damaged by other testimony to testify in his own behalf or file a sworn statement.

—Ban public release of testimony given in closed session, except by authorization of the committee.

—Advise each witness, in advance, of the subject of the investigation.

—Allow witnesses to request that television and other cameras and lights not be directed at him during his testimony, and have committee members present at the time to rule on the request.

The Senate left investigative procedures to the discretion of individual committees, whose practices varied considerably. After Sen. John L. McClellan, D-Ark. (1943-77), replaced McCarthy as chairman in 1955, the Permanent Investigations Subcommittee of the Senate Government Operations Committee adopted rules requiring the presence of two committee members when testimony was being taken, permitting anyone who was the subject of an investigation to submit questions in writing for cross-examination of other witnesses and allowing any person adversely affected by testimony to request an appearance or file a statement.

In the last analysis the actions of committees are determined by its members. For as Sen. J. W. Fulbright, D-Ark. (1945-1974), pointed out in 1951: "As a practical matter . . . the power to investigate is wielded by individuals, not by institutions. . . . This is . . . at once both the weakness and the strength of our legislative processes." [6]

## Immunity

To obtain testimony from individuals who would otherwise claim their constitutional right to remain silent rather than to incriminate themselves, Congress has authorized grants of immunity from prosecution.[7] When it approved the federal statute providing for punishment of recalcitrant witnesses before congressional committees, Congress in 1857 added a second section that contained an automatic and sweeping grant of immunity to witnesses testifying under the compulsion of congressional power. As enacted, the law provided that:

> . . . [N]o person examined and testifying before either House of Congress or any committee of either House, shall be held to answer criminally in any court of justice, or subject to any penalty or forfeiture, for any fact or act touching which he shall be required to testify before either House of Congress, or any committee of either House, as to which he shall have testified, whether before or after this act; . . . . Provided, that nothing in this act shall be construed to exempt any witness from prosecution and punishment for perjury committed by him in testifying as aforesaid. [8]

The disadvantages of this sort of immunity "bath" became evident in 1862 when it was revealed that embezzlers of millions in Indian trust bonds would escape prosecution because they had testified about their crime to a congressional committee and so, under the 1857 law, could not be prosecuted for it. Congress repealed the 1857 law and replaced it in 1862 with a narrower immunity statute. Under the new law, a witness' own testimony could not be used as evidence to convict him, but there was nothing to prevent its being used as a lead in discovering other evidence of crime.

An 1892 Supreme Court ruling raised questions about the adequacy of the 1862 immunity law, but that law remained unchanged until 1954, when the Eisenhower administration proposed, and Congress adopted, the Immunity Act of 1954.[9] The new law permitted either chamber of Congress by majority vote, or a congressional committee by two-thirds vote, to grant immunity to witnesses in national security investigations, provided an order was first obtained from a U.S. district court judge and also provided the attorney general was notified in advance and given an opportunity to offer objections. The bill also permitted the U.S. district courts to grant immunity to witnesses before the court or grand juries. The act granted immunity from prosecution for criminal activity revealed during compelled testimony. In a 1956 decision, the Supreme Court upheld the 1954 immunity statute as applied to grand jury witnesses, but made clear that it was proffering no opinion on its provisions granting immunity to congressional witnesses.[10]

In 1970, Congress wrote a whole new immunity law as part of the Organized Crime Control Act. It set out the rules for granting immunity to witnesses before congressional committees, courts, grand juries and administrative agencies. Under the new law, witnesses who received immunity to waive their Fifth Amendment rights and testify were guaranteed that their testimony and the information it contained would not be used against them in any criminal prosecution except one for perjury, should they lie in their testimony. It did not, however, immunize them from all prosecutions for matters mentioned in their testimony, if the government had other evidence of those crimes which was independent of their testimony.[11]

U.S. District Judge John J. Sirica approved grants of limited immunity — under the 1970 law — to White House Counsel John W. Dean III and Jeb Stuart Magruder, a former White House aide who was serving as deputy director of the Committee for the Re-Election of the President. Both were known to be under consideration for indictment in connection with the Watergate scandal and were reportedly prepared to offer evidence of the involvement of top White House officials, including the president. Both later served prison terms after pleading guilty to Watergate-related charges.

## Judicial Review

Not until late in the 19th century did the Supreme Court declare that congressional investigations were subject to judicial review. In its 1821 ruling on the contempt power of Congress, the court said that the action of the House must be "presumed" to be in accordance with the law. For 60 years, this statement shielded congressional investigations from any serious legal challenges.[12] Then, in 1881, the court's decision in a contempt of Congress case, *Kilbourn v. Thompson*, brought congressional investigations within the ambit of judicial review. In subsequent decisions concerning congressional investigations, the court has applied varying standards to such cases, but on the major point established by *Kilbourn*, that these investigations are subject to review by the federal courts, the court has not wavered.

**Kilbourn v. Thompson.** Hallet Kilbourn, manager of a real estate pool involved in the failure of the banking firm of Jay Cooke, was subpoenaed to appear and produce certain papers sought by a select House committee investigating the firm's failure. He refused, challenging the subpoena as exceeding the scope of the committee's investigation and representing nothing more than an attempt to exercise "the naked, arbitrary power of the House to investigate private business in which nobody but me and my customers have concern." [13] Kilbourn was arrested and held by the House in contempt. He subsequently sued the Speaker, members of the committee and the sergant-at-arms, John G. Thompson, for false arrest.

When his case reached the Supreme Court, the justices agreed with Kilbourn's challenge. The court ruled that Congress did not have a general power to punish for contempt. A recalcitrant committee witness could only be punished for contempt, held the court, if the inquiry for which he had been called was within the "legitimate cognizance" of Congress. Neither chamber, stated the court, "possesses the general power of making inquiry into the private affairs of the citizen."

The court's decision appeared to restrict congressional investigations to subjects that were clearly related to specifically granted powers, such as the impeachment power or the commerce power. Later rulings by the court blurred this restriction considerably.[14] In 1897, the Supreme Court held that investigations were "legitimate" inquiries within the meaning of the *Kilbourn* decision so long as they involved the conduct of members of Congress. Committees investigating the involvement of senators in sugar speculation could compel testimony about matters which would be considered outside the scope of congressional investigations were it not for the fact of senatorial involvement.[15]

**McGrain v. Daugherty.** In 1927, the court issued a decision that swept away nearly all the restrictions on the investigating power of Congress which *Kilbourn* had seemed to impose. In *McGrain v. Daugherty,* the court upheld the power of Congress to conduct broad-ranging legislative and oversight investigations. Together with inquiries into its membership, these two types of investigations comprise the vast majority of congressional investigations.

Following its inquiry in 1922 and 1923 into the "Teapot Dome scandal," the Senate created a select committee to investigate the failure of the Justice Department to uncover that scandal and to act against the officials involved. (The Secretary of the Interior had been accused, and was later convicted, of accepting more than $300,000 from private oil company executives in return for leasing the Teapot Dome naval oil reserve in Wyoming as well as other naval oil reserves. The Justice Department's failure to prosecute the Interior Secretary and others implicated in the affair prompted the investigation.) Mally S. Daugherty, brother of Attorney General Harry M. Daugherty (1921-24), was subpoenaed to testify before the select committee. He refused. The Senate issued a warrant ordering Deputy Sergeant-at-Arms John J. McGrain to arrest Mally Daugherty. Daugherty in turn challenged the Senate's power to compel him to testify. The court sustained the Senate's power.

The court held that the Senate and the House had the power to compel private citizens to appear before their committees and to answer pertinent questions to aid the legislative function. "The power of inquiry — with process to enforce it — is an essential and appropriate auxiliary to the legislative function," the court said. "A legislative body cannot legislate wisely or effectively in the absence of information respecting the conditions which the legislation is intended to affect or change; and where the legislative body does not itself possess the requisite information . . . recourse must be had to others who do possess it. Experience has taught that mere requests for information often are availing, and also that information which is volunteered is not always accurate or complete; so some means of compulsion are essential to obtain what is needed."

The court indicated further that it would presume a legislative purpose to lie behind a congressional investigation, whether indeed that was the purpose of the inquiry or not. "The only legitimate object the

Senate could have in ordering the investigation was to aid it in legislating, and we think the subject-matter was such that the presumption should be indulged that this was the real object," the court said. "An express avowal of the object would have been better; but in view of the particular subject-matter was not indispensable," the court added.

After giving this broad sanction to congressional investigations, the court appended two reservations. It cautioned, first, that "neither house is invested with 'general' power to inquire into private affairs and compel disclosures" and second, that "a witness rightfully may refuse to answer where the bounds of the power are exceeded or the questions are not pertinent to the matter under inquiry." [16]

**Sinclair v. United States.** In 1929 the Supreme Court held that a witness who refused to answer questions asked by a congressional committee could be punished if he were mistaken as to the law on which he based his refusal.[17] The fact that the witness acted in good faith on the advice of counsel was no defense, the court held. This precedent made any challenge of committee powers a risky proposition.

This case — *Sinclair v. United States* — also grew out of an investigation of the Teapot Dome scandal. The Interior Department had leased the public lands containing oil to the Mammoth Oil Co., of which the president and sole stockholder was Harry F. Sinclair. Sinclair had refused to answer questions of a Senate investigating committee on the ground that the whole matter was of exclusively judicial concern and therefore beyond the Senate's legitimate range of inquiry. He was convicted of contempt. In upholding the conviction, the Supreme Court declared that the naval oil reserves and their disposition were clearly a proper matter for congressional scrutiny.

In 1935, the court ruled that an investigating committee had authority to punish for contempt a witness who destroyed papers after the service of a subpoena for them.[18]

**United States v. Rumely.** Following World War II, the Supreme Court showed more concern for the rights of witnesses than the rights of congressional committees. In the 1953 case of *United States v. Rumely* the Supreme Court upheld a Court of Appeals decision reversing the contempt of Congress conviction of Edward A. Rumely. Rumely, a book publisher, had refused to tell the House Select Committee on Lobbying Activities the names of individuals making bulk purchases of books distributed by the Committee for Constitutional Government, an archconservative organization. He had asserted to the committee that "under the Bill of Rights, that is beyond the power of your committee to investigate." [19]

A majority of the court avoided the constitutional questions by narrowly construing the authority granted by the resolution establishing the committee. It held that the mandate to investigate "lobbying activities" was limited to "representations made directly to the Congress, its members, or its committees," and excluded attempts to influence Congress indirectly through public dissemination of literature. Interpreting the authorizing resolution to include attempts to influence Congress indirectly, dissenting Justices William O. Douglas and Hugo L. Black contended that to require a publisher to disclose the identity of book purchasers would violate the First Amendment guarantees of freedom of speech and the press.

## Postwar Quests and Questions

The postwar quest to uncover subversive elements in the United States produced a new style of congressional investigation and a new line of court decisions concerning those investigations. This new style of investigation sometimes involved broad-scale intrusions into the everyday lives of private citizens. The result was described in 1957 by Chief Justice Earl Warren: "Prior cases, like *Kilbourn, McGrain* and *Sinclair,* had defined the scope of investigative power in terms of the inherent limitations of the sources of that power. In the more recent cases, the emphasis shifted to problems of accommodating the interest of the Government with the rights and privileges of individuals. The central theme was the application of the Bill of Rights as a restraint upon the assertion" of the investigative power of the Congress.[20]

**The Right to Silence.** One line of these postwar rulings concerned the use of the privilege guaranteed by the Fifth Amendment — the privilege to avoid self-incrimination by remaining silent in the face of potentially incriminatory questions. Not until 1955 did the Supreme Court consider any contempt of Congress cases against witnesses who had invoked this privilege. But before that time, it had handed down two important rulings dealing with the invocation of the privilege of a witness before a grand jury. In the first case, *Blau v. United States* (1950), the court acknowledged that admission of communist activity might be incriminating. And in the second, *Rogers v. United States* (1951), the court held that a witness who had already answered questions about materially incriminating facts could not then invoke the Fifth Amendment.[21]

The usefulness of the Fifth Amendment as a defense against a contempt of Congress citation was addressed by the court in two cases decided on the same day in 1955. The circumstances from which the cases of *Quinn v. United States* and *Emspak v. United States* arose were similar. Both men had refused to answer certain questions from congressional committees pertaining to their affiliation with the Communist Party. Neither expressly invoked the Fifth Amendment privilege, but the court held that the intent of each man to base his refusal to answer on that privilege was clear.

There is no "ritualistic formula" involved in invoking this protection, wrote Chief Justice Warren in the *Quinn* case. "If an objection to a question is made in any language that a committee may reasonably be expected to understand as an attempt to invoke the privilege, it must be respected. . . ." [22]

**The Power to Expose.** The overriding purpose of some of the antisubversive hearings was exposure, as indicated in the comments of Rep. Martin Dies Jr., D-Texas (1931-45; 1953-59), chairman of the House Special Committee to Investigate Un-American Activities: "I am not in a position to say whether we can legislate effectively in reference to this matter, but I do know that exposure in a democracy of subversive activities is the most effective weapon that we have in our possession." [23]

Not until the late 1950s did the court speak to the issues raised by this assertion of power to investigate solely for the purpose of exposure. There was no such power, declared the court in the case of *Watkins v. United States* decided in 1957. "There is no congressional power to expose for the sake of exposure," stated the court. "The public is, of course, entitled to be informed concerning the workings of its government," continued the decision, but "that cannot be inflated into a general power to expose where the predominant result can only be an invasion of the private rights of individuals." [24]

The court's pronouncement came in the case of John T. Watkins, a labor organizer for the United Auto Workers, convicted of contempt of Congress after refusing to disclose certain information to the House Un-American Activities Committee. Watkins refused, saying that the committee was exceeding its power to demand the particular information at issue. The Supreme Court agreed and reversed his conviction.

Two years later, however, the court upheld a similar contempt conviction and watered down its *Watkins* declaration. The case of *Barenblatt v. United States* arose after Lloyd Barenblatt, a college professor, refused to answer questions from the House Un-American Activities Committee concerning his present or past membership in the Communist Party. He challenged the committee's right to ask such questions and asserted that the questions violated his First Amendment right to associate with persons who held similar beliefs. Citing the court's criticism, in *Watkins,* of the committee's mandate as too vague, Barenblatt argued that the committee was not authorized to inquire into his associations.

But the Supreme Court did not accept this argument. The inquiry was not unlawful simply because its purpose was exposure of such associations, held the court. "So long as Congress acts in pursuance of its constitutional power, the judiciary lacks authority to intervene on the basis of the motives which spurred the exercise of that power," the court said.[25]

Citing *Barenblatt,* the court in two 1961 cases affirmed the contempt citations of witnesses who contended they had been subpoenaed simply because they had criticized the Un-American Activities Committee.[26] Since 1961, however, the court has reversed almost every contempt conviction which has come before it.

## Notes

1. For background on rights of witnesses, see Telford Taylor, *Grand Inquest* (New York: Simon & Schuster, 1955), Chapter 6; and Library of Congress, Legislative Reference Service, *Congressional Power of Investigation* (Washington, D.C.: U.S. Government Printing Office, 1954), pp. 15-20.
2. *Eisler v. United States,* 338 U.S. 189 at 196 (1949).
3. Library of Congress, *Congressional Power,* p. 15.
4. Taylor, *Grand Inquest,* p. 240.
5. *Congress and the Nation,* 5 vols., *Congress and the Nation: 1945-1964,* vol. 1 (Washington, D.C.: Congressional Quarterly, 1965), I: 1683-1685.
6. J. W. Fulbright, "Congressional Investigations: Significance for the Legislative Processes," *University of Chicago Law Review,* 1951, p. 442.
7. James Hamilton, *The Power to Probe* (New York: Random House, 1976), pp. 78-85.
8. Taylor, *Grand Inquest,* pp. 215-216.
9. *Counselman v. Hitchcock,* 142 U.S. 547 (1892).
10. *Ullmann v. United States,* 350 U.S. 422 (1956).

11. *Congress and the Nation: 1969-1972,* vol. 3 (Washington D.C.: Congressional Quarterly, 1973), III: 274.
12. *Anderson v. Dunn,* 6 Wheat. 204 (1821); Taylor, *Grand Inquest; Congress and the Nation: 1945-1964,* I: 1680-1681, 1684.
13. *Kilbourn v. Thompson,* 103 U.S. 168 (1881).
14. Marshall E. Dimock, *Congressional Investigating Committees* (Baltimore: Johns Hopkins Press, 1929), pp. 131-136; C. Herman Pritchett, *The American Constitution,* (New York: McGraw Hill Book Co., 1968), p. 159.
15. *In re Chapman,* 166 U.S. 661 (1897).
16. *McGrain v. Daugherty,* 273 U.S. 135 at 173-174, 175, 176, 178 (1927).
17. *Sinclair v. United States,* 279 U.S. 263 (1929); M. Nelson McGeary, *The Development of Congressional Investigative Power* (New York: Octagon Books, 1966), pp. 97-100.
18. *Jurney v. MacCracken,* 294 U.S. 125 (1935).
19. *United States v. Rumely,* 345 U.S. 41 (1953); *Congress and the Nation: 1945-1964,* I: 1686; Taylor, *Grand Inquest,* pp. 140-146.
20. *Watkins v. United States,* 354 U.S. 178 at 195 (1957).
21. *Blau v. United States,* 340 U.S. 332 (1950); *Rogers v. United States,* 340 U.S. 367 (1951).
22. *Quinn v. United States,* 349 U.S. 155 at 162-63 (1955); *Emspak v. United States,* 349 U.S. 190 (1955).
23. August Raymond Ogden, *The Dies Committee* (Washington, D.C.: The Catholic University of America Press, 1945), p. 44.
24. *Watkins v. United States,* 354 U.S. 178 at 200 (1957); *Congress and the Nation: 1945-1964,* I: 1684.
25. *Barenblatt v. United States,* 360 U.S. 109 at 132 (1959).
26. *Wilkinson v. United States,* 365 U.S. 399 (1961); *Braden v. United States,* 365 U.S. 431 (1961).

*Chapter 17*

# EXECUTIVE PRIVILEGE

Congressional investigations have often sparked conflict with the executive branch, most frequently because a president has refused to comply with congressional demands for information. Practically every administration since 1792 has clashed with Congress over the question of "executive privilege," a term first used only in 1958,[1] and the issue has yet to be resolved as of 1982.

It can be argued that executive departments, established by Congress and maintained by its appropriations, are the creatures of the legislature and cannot deny it information regarding their activities. Congress may back up its demands by arousing public support for disclosure, especially if there is any suspicion that an administration is seeking to protect its political reputation by hiding mistakes or malfeasance. However, the long list of precedents in which presidents have successfully defied congressional demands for information, and Congress' reluctance to settle the issue by forcing it into the courts, support claims that the constitutional separation of powers permits the president, at his discretion, to withhold information sought by Congress.

Presidents have used a variety of reasons to justify denying information to Congress. Perhaps the most common has been the need for secrecy in military and diplomatic activities. Presidents also have sought to avoid unwarranted exposure of individuals to unfavorable publicity, especially when documents or files requested contain incomplete, inaccurate, misleading or unsubstantiated information. The need for confidential exchange of ideas between members of an administration has been cited as justifying refusal to provide records or describe conversations in the executive branch. Fears that disclosures would interfere with criminal or security investigations sometimes have prompted administrative secrecy. Critics of an administration frequently have charged that its real motive for refusing to divulge information was to escape criticism or scandal.

"Clearly, the president cannot turn over documents to Congress so that Congress can then decide whether or not they should have been turned over," wrote Telford Taylor in 1955. "If there is an executive privilege to withhold information when disclosures would not be 'in the public interest,' then the president must be the one to determine in any particular case whether the public interest permits disclosure or requires nondisclosure. Just as clearly, this leaves open the possibility that the president may abuse his prerogative, especially in instances where the information would reflect unfavorably on him or his administration of the nation's affairs." [2]

Taylor was writing during a period when critics of the congressional investigating power were pointing to what they considered abuses of the power by Joseph McCarthy's panel in the 1950s. Twenty years later, however, following clashes between President Lyndon B. Johnson and Congress over Vietnam War information and between President Richard M. Nixon and Congress over Watergate documents and testimony by members of the administration, the weight of opinion seemed to shift against use of the "privilege." Harvard Professor Raoul Berger, writing in 1974, described "executive privilege" as a "constitutional myth" — "a product of the nineteenth century, fashioned by a succession of presidents who created 'precedents' to suit the occasion. . . ." [3]

Presidents who refused demands from investigating committees have included Washington, Jefferson, Monroe, Jackson, Tyler, Polk, Fillmore, Lincoln, Grant, Hayes, Cleveland, Theodore Roosevelt, Coolidge, Hoover and all subsequent presidents or members of their administrations.[4] In some cases committees have accepted the president's refusal without comment; in others the refusal has led to a full-scale constitutional confrontation. Summaries of selected cases follow.

### Washington

The "precedent" of executive privilege was first established in 1792 when a select House committee conducting the first congressional inquiry investigated an Indian victory over Maj. Gen. Arthur St. Clair and his men in the Northwest Territory. The committee wrote to War Secretary Henry Knox and asked him to turn over all the documents relating to the St. Clair expedition. Knox asked President George Washington for advice; the president raised the subject at a Cabinet meeting. The Cabinet agreed that the House could conduct such an investigation and could call for such papers. It decided, according to the report of Thomas Jefferson, "that the executive ought to communicate such papers as the public good would permit, and ought to refuse those, the disclosure of which would endanger the public." As it developed, none of the St. Clair papers were regarded as confidential, and the president on April 4 directed Knox to make the papers available to the committee.[5]

(Four years later, in 1796, Washington claimed executive privilege when he refused a House request for correspondence relating to the intensely controversial Jay Treaty with Great Britain. The House was debating a bill to implement portions of the treaty; the bill eventually was passed.)

### Jackson

A House committee appointed "to examine into the conditions of the executive departments" adopted on Jan. 23, 1837, a series of resolutions that directed President Andrew Jackson and members of his Cabinet to furnish lists of federal appointments made without the concurrence of the Senate. Information concerning the salaries of the appointees and whether they were being paid without having taken office also was requested. Jackson, backed by a large majority in the House, categorically refused, in what was to become one of the most successful efforts of a president to resist congressional investigators.[6]

"According to the established rules of law," Jackson replied on Jan. 27, "you request myself and the heads of departments to become our own accusers, and to furnish the evidence to convict ourselves." The president continued: "If you either will not make specific accusations, or if, when made, you attempt to establish them by making free men their own accusers, you will not expect me to countenance your proceedings."[7] He then invoked "the principles of justice" as well as the Constitution in refusing the congressional request.[8]

After three months of fruitless questioning of Cabinet officers and others, the committee concluded that it had overstepped its authority in submitting a blanket request for documents, and it dropped the inquiry.

### Tyler

The House on May 18, 1842, adopted a resolution requesting War Secretary J. C. Spencer to make available to the Indian Affairs Committee reports on the Cherokee Indians and alleged frauds committed against them. After consulting with President John Tyler, Spencer on June 3 refused, asserting that negotiations to settle claims with the Indians still were in progress. The committee persisted in its request, and on Aug. 13 the House adopted a committee resolution requesting the information from Tyler. Tyler took no action on the request. On Dec. 30, the House adopted another resolution asking when the president was going to act.[9]

Tyler replied, Jan. 31, 1843, that the claims negotiations had been concluded in the meantime, and information dealing with the alleged frauds would be submitted. However, the president withheld portions of the reports containing personal comments about Indian negotiators and about recommendations for future action. In doing so, the president argued that the House could not demand information, even if relevant to a House debate, if the information would interfere with the discretion of the executive branch. "It cannot be that the only test is whether the information relates to a legitimate subject of deliberation," Tyler said. Also to be considered, he added, were the protection of confidential sources of government officials and the protection of officials from malicious publicity. The president's message was referred to the Indian Affairs Committee, which submitted a report, Feb. 25, criticizing the president's position but recommending no action.

**Cleveland**

President Grover Cleveland in 1885 was the first Democrat in the White House since James Buchanan in 1861. Democrats also controlled the House, but Republicans had a majority in the Senate. As the new president began replacing holdover Republican officeholders with Democrats, the Senate committees to which the nominations were referred repeatedly requested the information that had led to removal of the Republican incumbents. The standard department reply was that at the direction of the president it refused, on the ground that the public interest would not be served or that the removal had been a purely executive action.[10] Some 650 Republican officeholders were replaced.

On Dec. 26, 1885, the Senate Judiciary Committee asked Attorney General A. H. Garland for information on the dismissal of George N. Durskin, U.S. district attorney for the Southern District of Alabama. There being no response from Garland, the Senate on Jan. 26, 1886, adopted a committee resolution directing the attorney general to furnish the papers. In his reply, Feb. 1, Garland said the president had directed him to report that "the public interest would not be prompted by compliance with the resolution." The Senate responded, Feb. 18, by adopting a resolution refusing to concur in the removal of office-holders when the documents on which the removal was based were withheld.

In a message to the Senate, March 1, Cleveland disclaimed any intent to withhold official papers and asserted that the letters and reports leading to the dismissals were inherently private and confidential. He continued: "I do not suppose that the public offices of the United States are regulated or controlled in their relations to either house of Congress by the fact that they were created by laws enacted by" Congress.[11]

Cleveland's argument raised the recurring question of whether government departments are creatures of the executive branch, because they carry out executive functions, or creatures of the legislative branch, because they are established and financed through congressional action. From March 9 to 26 the Senate debated the issue. It concluded by adopting a resolution citing the attorney general for being "in violation of his official duty and subversive of the fundamental principles of the government. . . ." President Cleveland stood his ground, however, and the Senate ultimately confirmed his nominee to replace Durskin, John D. Burnett.

## Hoover

During Senate consideration of the London Naval Treaty of 1930, the Foreign Relations Committee asked for the papers relating to the London Conference at which the treaty had been negotiated. Secretary of State Henry L. Stimson submitted some of the papers but withheld others, explaining June 6, 1930, that he had been "directed by the president to say" that their production "would not in his opinion be compatible with the public interest."

The committee adopted a resolution, June 12, asserting that the documents were "relevant and pertinent when the Senate is considering a treaty for the purpose of ratification." On July 10, the Senate, supporting the committee, adopted a resolution requesting the president to submit the material, "if not incompatible with the public interest." Pleading the next day that the papers were confidential, Hoover again declined to produce them. The Senate on July 21 consented to ratification of the treaty, with "the distinct and explicit understanding" that it contained no secret agreements.[12]

## Truman

President Harry S Truman in 1948 became involved in a head-on clash between the executive branch and an investigating committee of Congress. On March 1 the House Un-American Activities Special Subcommittee on National Security issued a report that called Dr. Edward U. Condon, director of the Bureau of Standards, "one of the weakest links in our national security." The subcommittee promptly subpoenaed Commerce Department records of loyalty investigations of Condon, but Secretary of Commerce W. Averell Harriman refused to release them on the ground that their publication would be "prejudicial to the public interest." [13]

President Truman became personally involved in the controversy on March 13 when he issued the following directive barring disclosure of any loyalty files to Congress:

> Any subpoena or demand or request for information, reports or files of the nature described, received from sources other than those persons in the executive branch ... who are entitled thereto by reason of their special duties, shall be respectfully declined on the basis of this directive, and the subpoena or demand or other request shall be referred to the office of the president for such response as the president may determine to be in the public interest in the particular case. There shall be no relaxation of this directive except with my express authority. [14]

On April 22 the House adopted a resolution demanding that Harriman surrender an FBI report on Condon. The disputed documents were transferred to the White House, and the president refused to release them — despite Condon's request that they be made public. The following month the House passed a bill "directing all executive departments and agencies of the federal government to make available to any and all standing, special or select committees of the House of Representatives and the Senate, information which may be deemed necessary to enable them to properly perform the duties delegated to them by Congress." Refusal to comply was to be considered a misdemeanor, punishable by a fine of up to $1,000 or imprisonment for up to one year, or both.

In the Senate, the bill was referred to the Committee on Expenditures in the Executive Departments (Government Operations), where it died upon expiration of the 80th Congress.[15]

## Investigations of 'Un-Americanism': . . .

One of the most significant expansions of congressional investigative powers beyond direct legislative matters was the study of subversive movements after World War II. Instead of pursuing traditional lines of congressional inquiry — government operations and national social and economic problems — the committee probed into the thoughts, actions and associations of persons and institutions.

The abolition in January 1975 of the House Committee on Un-American Activities, renamed the Internal Security Committee in 1969, ended 30 years of controversy over the committee's zealous pursuit of subversives. From the outset the committee was attacked by liberals and civil libertarians. Through the 1960s it withstood court suits challenging the constitutionality of its mandate and attempts in the House to end its funding. As late as 1974 it appeared that the committee was still invincible when the House voted 246-164 to retain it. But a year later the committee died when the House Democratic Caucus, by voice vote, transferred its functions to the Judiciary Committee.

### Early History

The first congressional investigation of un-American activities was authorized Sept. 19, 1918, two months prior to the armistice in World War I. Its original mandate was to investigate the activities of German brewing interests. The investigation, conducted by the Senate Judiciary Committee, was expanded in 1919 to cover "any efforts . . . to propagate in this country the principles of any party exercising . . . authority in Russia . . . and . . . to incite the overthrow" of the U.S. government.

The House on May 12, 1930, set up a Special Committee to Investigate Communist Activities in the United States — the Fish Committee, so-called after its chairman, Rep. Hamilton Fish Jr., R-N.Y. (1920-45). On March 20, 1934, the House created a Special Committee on Un-American Activities, under Chairman John W. McCormack, D-Mass. (1928-71). On May 26, 1938, three years after the McCormack Committee submitted its report, which covered Nazi as well as Communist activities in the United States, the House set up another Special Committee on Un-American Activities, under Chairman Martin Dies Jr., D-Texas (1931-45; 1953-59). The committee, whose chairman was avowedly anti-Communist and anti-New Deal, was given a broad mandate to investigate subversion.

# . . . Congress Stretches Its Powers

## Postwar Developments

The Dies Committee was reconstituted in succeeding Congresses until 1945. At the beginning of the 79th Congress, Jan. 3, 1945, Rep. John E. Rankin, D-Miss. (1921-53), offered an amendment to the House rule to make the Dies Committee a standing committee and to rename it the House Committee on Un-American Activities. Opponents of the committee lost, 208-186.

The next five years marked the peak of the committee's influence. In 1947 it launched an investigation into communism in the motion picture industry, with repercussions that lasted almost a decade. Its hearings resulted in the Hollywood blacklist that kept many writers and actors suspected of Communist leanings out of work.

It was the committee's investigation in 1948 of State Department official Alger Hiss, and Hiss' subsequent conviction for perjury, that established communism as a leading political issue and the committee as an important political force. The case against Hiss, which at one point appeared flimsy to other committee members, was vigorously developed by a young member of the committee, Richard M. Nixon. The committee's tactics during this period included extensive use of contempt citations against unfriendly witnesses, some of whom pleaded the Fifth Amendment right against self-incrimination.

The Internal Security Subcommittee of the Senate Judiciary Committee, set up in 1951, also regularly conducted probes of Communist activities. Many state legislatures emulated Congress by undertaking investigations of subversion. The most famous national investigations of communism were conducted by Sen. Joseph R. McCarthy, R-Wis. (1947-57), as chairman (1953-54) of the Permanent Investigations Subcommittee of the Senate Government Operations Committee. His behavior in this role intensified concern over the use by Congress of its investigating powers and led in 1954 to his censure by the Senate. After McCarthy's censure, investigations of communism attracted less public attention.

Source: August R. Ogden, *The Dies Committee* (Washington D.C: The Catholic University of America Press, 1945); Walter Goodman, *The Committee* (New York: Farrar, Straus and Giroux, 1968); *Congress and the Nation,* 5 vols., *Congress and the Nation: 1945-1964,* vol. 1 (Washington D.C.: Congressional Quarterly, 1965), I: 1679-1680.

## Eisenhower

During the Army-McCarthy hearings before the Senate Government Operations Permanent Investigations Subcommittee, President Dwight D. Eisenhower on May 17, 1954, forbade testimony about a Jan. 12 meeting between Attorney General Herbert Brownell Jr. and Army Counsel John Adams. Developments in the aggressively anti-communist hearings being conducted by Subcommittee Chairman Joseph R. McCarthy, R-Wis. (1947-57), had been discussed at the meeting. In a letter to Defense Secretary Charles E. Wilson imposing the ban on testimony about the meeting, Eisenhower stressed the importance of candid, private communication within the executive branch and the "proper separation of power between the executive and legislative branches." When Adams cited the president's order in refusing to answer a question on May 24, McCarthy accused him of using "a type of Fifth Amendment privilege."

McCarthy said three days later that he wanted all federal workers to know "that I feel it's their duty to give us any information which they have about graft, corruption, Communists, treason, and that there is no loyalty to a superior officer which can tower above and beyond their loyalty to their country." The senator promised to shield the identity of informants. The Democrats on the subcommittee protested McCarthy's call for informers, and Brownell on May 28, with the president's approval, issued a statement: "The executive branch . . . has the sole and fundamental responsibility under the Constitution for the enforcement of our laws and presidential orders. . . . That responsibility cannot be usurped by an individual who may seek to set himself above the laws of our land or to override orders of the president of the United States to federal employees of the executive branch." [16]

## Kennedy and Johnson

President Eisenhower's May 17, 1954, letter and accompanying memorandum soon became the basis for an extension of the claim of "executive privilege" far down the administrative line from the president. After that time, according to a 1973 report prepared by the Government and General Research Division of the Library of Congress, "the executive branch answer to nearly every question about the authority to withhold information from the Congress was 'yes,' they had the authority." [17]

The pattern of invoking the privilege by executive branch officials was altered, but not broken, by President John F. Kennedy in 1962. The previous year, a special Senate subcommittee had opened hearings on the

Pentagon's system for editing speeches of military leaders. When the panel asked the identity of the editors, the president directed the secretary of defense, in a Feb. 8, 1962, letter, "not to give any testimony or produce any documents which would disclose such information." He added, however: "The principle which is at stake here cannot be automatically applied to every request for information. Each case must be judged on its own merits." And on March 7, 1962, the president wrote, "Executive privilege can be invoked only by the president and will not be used without specific presidential approval." [18] Nonetheless, after the Kennedy directive, executive branch officials in his administration refused to provide information to congressional committees at least three times, apparently without presidential authorization.[19]

President Lyndon B. Johnson continued this trend, despite a letter of April 2, 1965, in which he stated that "the claim of 'executive privilege' will continue to be made only by the president." Although he did not personally invoke the privilege, there were at least two refusals by appointees in his administration to provide information to congressional committees.

## Nixon

In addition to Watergate-related information, President Richard Nixon personally and formally invoked the claim of "executive privilege" against congressional committees four times. In a memorandum issued March 24, 1969, Nixon stated that the privilege would not be used without specific presidential approval. But between 1969 and 1973, there were at least 15 other instances in which documents or testimony were refused to congressional committees without direct presidential approval. "In fact, the presidential statements [on executive privilege] have been limitations in name only," concluded the Library of Congress report.[20]

**Watergate and Executive Privilege.** The most dramatic clash over executive privilege came during the inquiry into the Watergate scandal. It pitted Nixon against two congressional committees, the special prosecutor (both Archibald Cox and his successor, Leon Jaworski) and a grand jury. The confrontation began with establishment of the Senate Select Committee on Presidential Campaign Activities (known as the Watergate Committee) in February 1973. At first, Nixon pleaded executive privilege, refusing to allow his aides to appear before the panel. But in April he reversed himself, stating that government employees and particularly White House employees "are expected fully to cooperate in this matter. I condemn any attempts to cover up in this case, no matter who is involved."

On May 3, the White House issued new guidelines on the privilege: "The President desires that the invocation of executive privilege be held to a minimum." The privilege should be invoked only in connection with conversations with the president, conversations among aides involving communications with the president, and with regard to presidential papers and national security.

On May 29, Nixon said he would not provide information through oral or written testimony to the Watergate grand jury or to the Senate committee. For him to do so would be "constitutionally inappropriate" and a violation of the separation of powers. Nixon repeated his refusal to appear before the committee or to hand over presidential papers in a letter to Chairman Sam J. Ervin Jr., D-N.C., July 6. "No president could function if the private papers of his office, prepared by his personal staff, were open to public scrutiny," he said. "Formulation of sound public policy requires that the president and his personal staff be able to communicate among themselves in complete candor. . . . If he were to testify before the committee irreparable damage would be done to the constitutional principle of separation of powers." [21]

**Battle for the Tapes.** Nixon's declaration assumed new dimensions later in July, however, when it was revealed that tape recordings had been made of many presidential conversations in the White House during the period under investigation. Immediately, a struggle for the tapes began. The legal battle lasted almost exactly a year, from July 23, 1973, when the Senate committee and the Watergate grand jury subpoenaed the first group of tapes, to July 24, 1974, when the Supreme Court ruled against Nixon and ordered that he hand over the tapes sought by the special prosecutor. But the Senate investigating committee never obtained the tapes it sought. The administration's argument prevailed in that case.

On Aug. 29, U.S. District Court Judge John J. Sirica ruled that the president should give him the tapes subpoenaed by Special Prosecutor Archibald Cox so that he could review them. On Oct. 12, the U.S. Court of Appeals for the District of Columbia Circuit upheld Sirica's decision.[22] Five days later, Oct. 17, Sirica refused to enforce the Senate Watergate Committee's request for the same tapes. In dismissing the case, Sirica said Congress had never enacted any law giving federal courts jurisdiction in such a case.

Moving quickly to rectify the situation, Congress by Dec. 3 sent to the White House legislation specifically granting the federal district court in the District of Columbia jurisdiction over suits brought by the Senate Watergate Committee to enforce subpoenas. The bill became law (PL 93-190) without Nixon's signature. The Senate committee Dec. 19 approved new subpoenas for nearly 500 presidential tapes and documents; Nixon Jan. 4 refused to comply.

Deciding to seek enforcement of the original subpoenas before litigating Nixon's refusal to comply with the more recent demands, the committee Jan. 7, 1974, renewed its original suit and asked Sirica to reconsider it in light of PL 93-190. Sirica referred the case to U.S. District Court Judge Gerhard A. Gesell. Again, the White House asked the court to dismiss the suit.

On Jan. 25 Gesell issued his ruling, quashing the July 23 subpoena for documents, but directing Nixon to respond more directly to the July 23 subpoena for the five tapes. The judge asked Nixon to provide a detailed statement explaining what parts of the subpoenaed tapes he considered covered by executive privilege. On Feb. 6, Nixon sent Gesell a letter stating simply that disclosure of the tapes "would not be in the public interest." Two days later Gesell refused to require the White House to turn over the tapes to the Senate panel. The committee's use of the tapes might make it difficult to obtain an unbiased jury for the trials arising out of the Watergate matter, he explained. "The committee's role as a 'grand inquest' into governmental misconduct is limited," wrote Gesell. "It may only proceed in aid of Congress' legislative function . . . the time has come to question whether it is in the public interest for the criminal investigative aspects of its work to go forward in the blazing atmosphere of . . . publicity." The Senate Watergate Committee Feb. 19 agreed to terminate its public hearings, but also decided to appeal the Feb. 8 ruling. The bid was lost May 23, when a U.S. court of appeals rejected the appeal.[23]

Meanwhile, Cox's successor, Leon Jaworski, and the House Judiciary Committee (which was authorized to begin an impeachment inquiry in February 1974) issued their subpoenas for tapes and documents. Again, Nixon and his lawyers, arguing presidential confidentiality, refused to comply. However, Nixon announced April 29, 1974, the day before the deadline set by the Judiciary Committee subpoena, that he would make public the transcripts of 46 tapes the next day. The committee was not satisfied. Divided closely along party lines, the committee voted May 1 to inform the president that "you have failed to comply with the committee's subpoena. . . ." Jaworski, whose subpoena for evidence Nixon had also rejected, took his case to the Supreme Court late in May.

"Inherent in the executive power vested in the president under Article II of the Constitution is executive privilege, generally recognized as a derivative of the separation of powers doctrine," argued Nixon's lawyer James D. St. Clair.[24]

"The qualified executive privilege for confidential intra-governmental deliberations, designed to promote the candid interchange between officials and their sides, exists only to protect the legitimate functioning of the government," said Jaworski. "Thus, the privilege must give way where, as here, it has been abused. There has been a *prima facie* showing that each of the participants in the subpoenaed conversations, including the president, was a member of the conspiracy to defraud the United States and to obstruct justice. . . . The public purpose underlying the executive privilege for governmental deliberations precludes its application to shield alleged criminality." [25]

On July 24, hours before the Judiciary Committee began public debate on impeachment, the Supreme Court ruled unanimously against the president and ordered him to give up the tapes.[26] Within a week of the Supreme Court's decision, the Judiciary Committee adopted three articles of impeachment, among them one citing Nixon for contempt of Congress for failing to comply with the panel's subpoenas. Nixon began surrendering the tapes to Sirica on July 30. On Aug. 2, Nixon made public the transcript of some of the tapes that showed his participation in a cover-up after the Watergate break-in and his approval of the use of the Central Intelligence Agency to block an FBI investigation of the event. These revelations led directly to his resignation Aug. 9.

## Ford, Carter, Reagan

In November 1975 the House Intelligence Committee issued three subpoenas for information concerning national security affairs. Secretary of State Henry A. Kissinger refused to turn over the State Department documents on the orders of President Gerald R. Ford, who cited executive privilege. The material requested involved "highly sensitive military and foreign affairs assessments and evaluations" as well as consultations and advice to former Presidents Kennedy, Johnson and Nixon, according to the White House letter to Kissinger ordering withholding of the material.

Committee Chairman Otis G. Pike, D-N.Y. (1961-79), countered that executive privilege could not be invoked by Ford for the documents of previous administrations. The committee voted to cite Kissinger in contempt, but subsequently dropped the action after receiving "substantial compliance" with two of the subpoenas when the White House agreed to turn over documents dating back to 1961.[27] The Kissinger incident was the first time that a full committee of Congress had voted to hold a Cabinet member in contempt.

A second instance occurred in 1982, when the House Energy and Commerce Committee approved a contempt resolution against Interior Secretary James G. Watt. President Ronald Reagan had invoked executive privilege and refused to allow Watt to give the panel documents concerning the administration's consideration of the impact of Canadian energy policies on American firms. The administration contended that the papers related to sensitive foreign policy matters. After the committee vote, however, the White House agreed to turn over the documents temporarily for examination by the committee members. In return the committee dropped the contempt move.

President Jimmy Carter invoked executive privilege against Congress only once — in 1980. He invoked the privilege to withhold documents concerning his unsuccessful effort to impose an oil import fee. But after a House subcommittee voted to hold Carter's energy secretary, Charles Duncan, in contempt, the White House agreed to allow the committee to see the sought-after documents.[28]

## Notes

1. Raoul Berger, *Executive Privilege* (Cambridge: Harvard University Press, 1974), p. 1.
2. Telford Taylor, *Grand Inquest* (New York: Simon & Schuster, 1955), p. 101.
3. Berger, *Executive Privilege,* pp. 1, 14.
4. *Congress and the Nation*, 5 vols, *Congress and the Nation: 1945-1964,* vol. 1 (Washington, D.C.: Congressional Quarterly, 1965), I: 1681.
5. Taylor, *Grand Inquest,* p. 99; Berger, *Executive Privilege,* pp. 166-179.
6. Marshall E. Dimock, *Congressional Investigating Committees* (Baltimore: Johns Hopkins Press, 1929), pp. 105-107; Library of Congress, Legislative Reference Service, *Congressional Power of Investigation* (Washington, D.C.: U.S. Government Printing Office, 1954), p. 51.
7. Taylor, *Grand Inquest,* p. 193.
8. Ernest J. Eberling, *Congressional Investigations* (New York: Columbia University Press, 1928), p. 135.

9. Berger, *Executive Privilege,* pp. 183-185; Asher C. Hinds, *Hinds' Precedents of the House of Representatives of the United States,* 5 vols. (Washington, D.C.: U.S. Government Printing Office, 1907), III: 181-186.
10. Taylor, *Grand Inquest,* p. 101; Eberling, *Congressional Investigations,* pp. 256-258; *Hinds' Precedents,* III: 190-192.
11. Eberling, *Congressional Investigations,* p. 258.
12. Clarence Cannon, *Cannon's Precedents of the House of Representatives of the United States,* 3 vols. (Washington, D.C.: U.S. Government Printing Office, 1935), I: 597-599.
13. Taylor, *Grand Inquest,* p. 102; Walter Goodman, *The Committee* (New York: Farrar, Straus & Giroux, 1968), pp. 226-237.
14. Taylor, *Grand Inquest,* p. 102; *Federal Register,* March 16, 1948.
15. *Congress and the Nation,* I: 1693.
16. Taylor, *Grand Inquest,* p. 133.
17. Berger, *Executive Privilege,* pp. 373-386.
18. Ibid., p. 377.
19. Ibid., p. 381.
20. Ibid., p. 384.
21. *Watergate: Chronology of a Crisis* (Washington, D.C.: Congressional Quarterly, 1975), pp. 47, 103, 189.
22. Ibid., pp. 297, 341-344.
23. Ibid., pp. 513, 523, 640.
24. Ibid., p. 680.
25. Ibid., pp. 678-679.
26. Ibid., pp. 718.
27. *Congressional Quarterly Almanac, 1975* (Washington, D.C.: Congressional Quarterly, 1976), pp. 404-407.
28. *Congressional Quarterly Almanac, 1980* (Washington, D.C.: Congressional Quarterly, 1981), pp. 273-274.

BRANDEIS
THE LAW
SUPREME COURT
MONOPLY
PRIVILEGE

*Part VI*

# Confirmations

Uproar over President Woodrow Wilson's Supreme Court nomination of Louis Brandeis prompted this ***Puck*** cartoon. Caption reads: "THAT BRANDEIS APPOINTMENT. Chorus of Grief-Stricken Conservatives: Oh, what an associate for such a pure and innocent girl! And we have tried to bring her up so carefully, too!"

## *Chapter 18*

# THE CONFIRMATION PROCESS

The authors of the Constitution spent considerable time debating how appointments to government posts should be made before deciding that the president would appoint them with the advice and consent of the Senate. Senatorial confirmation of executive appointments is a distinctly American political and legislative phenomenon.

If the Founding Fathers were alive today, one feature of the contemporary political system that probably would surprise them would be the number of nominations that pass through the Senate. Although the mechanics of the confirmation process have remained much the same, the federal government's growth has dramatically increased the number of appointments requiring confirmation.

In the 23 Congresses spanning the 46 years between 1935 and 1981, the number of nominations received by the Senate has grown almost sevenfold — from 22,487 in the 74th Congress (1935-37) to 154,797 in the 96th (1979-81). Numbers alone do not give an accurate picture of the nominations process. The vast majority of nominations sent annually to the Senate involve the routine confirmation of appointments and promotions for military officers and officers of specialized services such as the Foreign Service and Public Health Service. These nominations usually are passed en bloc and confirmation is a formality. In *The Advice and Consent of the Senate*, Joseph P. Harris placed 99 percent of the nominations in this category.

It is the remaining 1 percent of the nominations, involving those persons who will occupy top policy-making positions in government, that sometimes locks the president and Senate in battle. These include nominations to Cabinet and sub-Cabinet posts, the federal judiciary, major diplomatic and military positions and top positions on independent boards and regulatory agencies.

Senate consent to an executive appointment came to mean simply that a majority of the Senate approved the president's nomination. Although most nominations are confirmed by the Senate, pro forma approval is not always certain. Political considerations always have been a part of the nomination and confirmation process, and in recent years the Senate often has examined carefully a nominee's economic views, social philosophy and personal finances. Once the Senate has approved a nominee and ordered the resolution of confirmation sent to the president, it cannot reverse its decision without the president's approval.

## Cabinet Nominations

Most Cabinet nominations are confirmed with little difficulty, on the theory that presidents should have great leeway in selecting the members of their official "family." Between 1789 and 1982 only eight men nominated to the Cabinet have been rejected by the Senate. The last Cabinet-level rejection was the 1959 nomination by Dwight D. Eisenhower of Lewis L. Strauss to be secretary of commerce.

Nominations to sub-Cabinet positions, which have multiplied dramatically in the 20th century, are treated much like Cabinet nominations, although the president is expected to consult in advance with key members of Congress on appointments of particular interest to them. Sub-Cabinet posts frequently are used to reward various party factions. Since 1933 none has been rejected outright by the Senate, although a few have been turned down in committee, withdrawn or never acted upon.

Independent board and commission appointments offer a somewhat different situation. Usually created by act of Congress and not subordinate to any executive department, the boards and commissions frequently are viewed as an arm of Congress rather than as part of the executive branch, and members of Congress expect to play a larger role in the selection process. Typically, the act of Congress creating an independent agency may require a bipartisan membership or impose geographical or other limitations on the president's selection flexibility. Contests with the Senate over these nominations have been frequent, although, considering the numbers involved, few nominees have been rejected outright. Independent agencies with single administrators have had fewer problems; these nominations tend to be treated more like Cabinet nominations.

## The Constitutional Mandate

"The President . . . shall nominate, and by and with the Advice and Consent of the Senate, shall appoint Ambassadors, other public Ministers and Consuls, Judges of the Supreme Court, and all other Officers of the United States, whose Appointments are not herein otherwise provided for, and which shall be established by Law; but the Congress may by Law vest the Appointment of such inferior Officers, as they think proper, in the President alone, in the Courts of Law, or in the Heads of Departments.

"The President shall have Power to fill up all Vacancies that may happen during the Recess of the Senate, by granting Commissions which shall expire at the End of their next Session."

The above words — Article II, Section 2, of the Constitution — provided four methods of appointment: presidential appointment with Senate confirmation, presidential appointment without Senate confirmation, appointment by courts of law and appointment by heads of departments. Congress exercises no power to appoint executive officers, though it may set qualifications for offices established by statute. Congressional requirements usually pertain to citizenship, salary level, residence, age, political affiliation in the case of bipartisan commissions and boards and professional competence. Congress must also approve the funds to pay the salaries of executive branch officers.

### Diplomatic, Judicial, and Other Nominations

Major diplomatic nominations usually encounter little opposition. Although the Senate attempted to exercise extensive authority over diplomatic appointments in the Republic's early days, in modern practice presidents have been allowed wide discretion in their selection of ambassadors and other persons to assist them in the conduct of foreign relations.

Appointments to lower federal courts are another matter. Presidents customarily have consulted individual senators of their own political party on matters of district court appointments related to the senators' home states. If the senators and president are of different parties, the president is expected to consult with state party leaders before making a selection. Senatorial dictation of judicial appointments was reinforced by the institution of senatorial courtesy; this unwritten custom calls for the Senate to refuse to confirm a nomination to a federal court position within a particular state if the senators belonging to the president's party from that state opposed the nomination. But policy considerations, as well as political ones, sometimes take precedence over the practice of senatorial courtesy. The chief executive has wider discretion in making appointments to circuit court judgeships, since these jurisdictions embrace several states, and to other specialized courts such as those dealing with certain tax matters and customs.

Appointees in one broad classification until recently were selected by the legislative branch of the government. Postmasters of the first, second and third classes at one time constituted the largest group of civilian employees requiring Senate confirmation. Although it was the Senate that gave its advice and consent, custom decreed that members of the House — if they were of the same party as the president — made the actual selection of appointees in their districts.

That patronage system survived until 1970 when Congress created an independent U.S. Postal Service. The postal reorganization set up an independent government agency to take over operations of the Post Office Department. The 1970 law ended congressional influence over appointment of postmasters. U.S. attorneys and marshals have continued to be patronage appointments. Appointed with Senate confirmation for four-year terms, they serve at the pleasure of the president.

## Marbury v. Madison

The Supreme Court has decided only a few cases involving the appointment process, but the decisions handed down in those instances, beginning with *Marbury v. Madison* in 1803, control the president's power to nominate and appoint in addition to limiting his authority to remove appointees. The most famous decision made by Chief Justice John Marshall, and perhaps the most famous in the court's history, began as a relatively unimportant controversy over a presidential appointment. William Marbury sought delivery of his commission of appointment as a justice of the peace.

In addition to the political significance of the case in constitutional history as the means by which the court established the principle of judicial review, *Marbury v. Madison* had something to say about the appointment process. The Supreme Court held that Marbury should have received his commission, which had been duly signed and sealed but not delivered. But Chief Justice Marshall held that the court lacked the power to issue the order commanding Secretary of State James Madison to deliver it. The effect of the *Marbury* decision was that, in making appointments, the president was under no enforceable obligation to deliver a commission, even after the nominee was confirmed by the Senate. *(Court decisions discussion, p. 244)*

## Nomination Procedures

It has been customary since the time of George Washington for the chief executive to submit nominations in written form. But President Warren G. Harding in 1921 proceeded directly from his inaugural ceremonies to the Senate chamber to present his Cabinet nominations.

Before submitting a nomination, the president normally consults with key members of Congress, political organizations and special interest groups in an effort to obtain informal clearance for his candidate. Because the president prefers to avoid a confirmation fight, serious opposition at this stage may lead him to choose another person for the post.

"The President rarely announces a nomination without first assessing the sentiments of those individuals and interests most likely to be affected by the nomination," wrote G. Calvin Mackenzie in his book, *The Politics of Presidential Appointments*. "The Senate uses the confirmation process not simply as an opportunity to reject or support a nominee, but also to identify the areas in which its members disagree with the nominee and to attempt to narrow those areas of disagreement so that it can feel comfortable in confirming him." [1]

The basic purpose of the congressional confirmation proceedings is to determine the character and competence of the nominee: whether there is any conflict of interest, particularly financial, and whether his qualifications are deemed appropriate for the job. Senators also use confirmation hearings to voice their constituents' concerns and, when relevant, to find out what the nominee may do for their states or regions. However, Mackenzie emphasized that public policy issues continue to dominate Senate confirmation proceedings.

**Confirmation Hearings.** Since 1868 most nominations have been referred to committee. The committee, or a subcommittee, holds hearings at which the nominee and others may testify. Most of these hearings are routine, although some have turned into gruelling inquisitions. Nominees have been known to ask the president to withdraw their names rather than face such an ordeal.

Until about 1950, it was unusual for Supreme Court nominees to be invited to appear before the Senate Judiciary Committee. Felix Frankfurter, who received such an invitation in 1939, noted that on only one previous occasion had a high court nominee testified before the committee. Frankfurter originally declined the committee's invitation but later appeared at its request. Ten years later the committee, by a 5 to 4 vote, invited court nominee Sherman Minton to appear before it. When Minton questioned the propriety of such an appearance, the committee reversed itself and reported the nomination favorably to the Senate. Despite these precedents, in recent years Supreme Court nominees have been expected to testify at hearings on their nominations. Justice Abe Fortas in 1968 became the first nominee for chief justice ever to appear before the committee and the first sitting justice, except for recess appointees, ever to do so.

When hearings on a nomination have been completed, the full committee may report the nomination favorably, unfavorably or without recommendation, or it may simply take no action at all. Nominations that fail to gain approval usually meet defeat at this stage. The confirmation burden is unevenly distributed among Senate committees. Judiciary (judges, U.S. attorneys and U.S. marshals), Commerce (regulatory agencies), Foreign Relations (ambassadors) and Armed Services (primarily military) are among those committees with major confirmation duties. At least 14 committees have some confirmation responsibility.

In his book *A Government of Strangers*, Hugh Heclo concluded, "In affecting the everyday work of the government, these hundreds of personnel selections add up to a cumulative act of choice that may be at least as important as the electorate's single act of choice for president every four years." [2]

**Final Senate Action.** Nominations that reach the floor are called up on the executive calendar, frequently en bloc, and usually are approved without objection. The question takes the following form: "Will the Senate advise and consent to this nomination?" Controversial nominations may be debated at length, but few are brought to the floor unless sufficient votes for confirmation can be mustered.

Since 1929 Senate rules (Rule 31) have provided that nominations shall be considered in open session unless the Senate, by a majority vote in open session, decides to go into closed session to consider a nomination. Before 1929 the customary practice was to consider nominations in closed session (also called executive session), and votes taken in executive session were not supposed to be made public.

Pending nominations may not be put to a Senate vote on the day they are received or on the day they are reported from committee, except by unanimous consent. They may be approved, rejected or returned (recommitted) to the committee that considered the nominee.

Pending nominations technically expire at the end of each congressional session. In practice, they normally are carried forward to the next year by unanimous consent. Opponents of a nomination may block them, however, forcing the administration to formally resubmit the nominations or make new ones. And after a presidential election in which a new administration takes office, members of the new president's party in the Senate (particularly if they become the majority, as occurred with the Republicans in 1981) can be expected to object to pending nominations being held over until the next Congress.

Senate rules permit a move for reconsideration and recall of a confirmation resolution within two legislative days after its passage if the resolution of confirmation has not been sent to the president, thereby passing the jurisdiction over the issue to the chief executive. A case involving this issue reached the Supreme Court in 1932.

In December 1930 President Herbert Hoover nominated George O. Smith to be chairman of the Federal Power Commission. The Senate on Dec. 20 confirmed Smith and ordered the resolution of confirmation sent to the president. Later that same day, the Senate adjourned until Jan. 5, 1931. The president, notified of Smith's confirmation, delivered the commission of appointment, and Smith took office.

On Jan. 5, the next day the Senate was in seesion, it voted to reconsider Smith's nomination. A month later it voted again and refused to confirm Smith. President Hoover refused to return the confirmation resolution as requested by the Senate, describing the maneuver as an effort by the legislative branch to exercise the power of removal. The Senate then took the matter to court to test Smith's right to continue in office. When the matter came before the Supreme Court, Smith's right to the position was upheld on the grounds that Senate precedent did not support Senate reconsideration of a confirmation after the nominee had taken the oath of office.

## Recess Appointments

Recess appointments present special problems. Article II, Section 2, of the Constitution provides that "the president shall have power to fill up all vacancies that may happen during the recess of the Senate, by granting commissions which shall expire at the end of their next session." The section's ambiguities have produced repeated controversies between the president and the Senate. The chief point of contention is the constitutional meaning of the word "happen." If it means "happen to occur," then the president can only fill offices that become vacant after the Senate adjourns. If it means "happen to exist," he can fill any vacancy existing while the Senate is in recess, whatever the cause.[3]

President Washington, taking a strict view of his powers, sought specific Senate authorization to make recess appointments of military officers whose positions were created by a bill enacted near the end of a session. President James Madison opted for a broad construction. His recess appointment of envoys to negotiate a peace treaty with Great Britain brought outcries from the Senate that a recess appointment could not be made to an office never before filled. However, resolutions protesting Madison's action never came to a vote, and the appointments ultimately were confirmed.

Although the recess appointment debate continued for years, it gradually became accepted practice that the president could make recess appointments to fill any vacancies, no matter how they arose. However, federal law prohibits payment of salary to any person appointed during a recess of the Senate if the vacancy existed while the Senate was in session, until the appointee has been confirmed by the Senate. But this prohibition does not apply if the vacancy occurred during the last 30 days of a congressional session or if the Senate failed to act on a nomination the president had submitted to it before adjournment.

The nominees who were appointed by President Jimmy Carter while the Senate was in recess at the time of the 1980 elections legally could have served without Senate confirmation until the end of Congress' 1981 session. However, they probably would have resigned if the new president had so requested. According to the White House Records Office, Carter made 18 civilian recess appointments in the last year of his term, including his nominations for chairman and four members of the board of directors of the multibillion-dollar Synthetic Fuels Corporation.[4]

## Weaknesses in the Process

One of the most damaging episodes during the Carter administration, involving Bert Lance, forced the Senate to take stock of the way it considered executive nominations.

Lance, Carter's first director of the Office of Management and Budget, resigned eight months after being confirmed by the Senate. His confirmation hearings in January 1977 failed to turn up questionable banking practices by the former Georgia banker. This and other cases early in the Carter years demonstrated the pitfalls for both the executive and legislative branches in the way appointments to high government offices were made, and they led to a general tightening up of committee procedures for evaluating nominees. One result was that committees began to require more detailed financial disclosures than ever before. Another consequence was greater congressional attention to actual and potential conflicts of interest.

Common Cause, the public citizen lobbying group, in November 1977 published a report calling the process a "rubber-stamp machine." The study was based on consideration of 50 Carter nominations. It concluded that the Senate inadequately examined the background and qualifications of most nominees, failed to build an adequate public record for the confirmation decision and rushed to confirmation without any affirmative finding that the caliber of the nominees met the requirements of their offices.

Senators Abraham Ribicoff, D-Conn. (1963-81) and Charles H. Percy, R-Ill, both among those most stung by the handling of the Lance affair, proposed legislation to standardize and centralize Senate confirmations. But these criticisms reflected the complexity of the confirmation task, which presents several distinct difficulties:

—Confirmation to high office increasingly must focus on potential conflicts of interest that turn on complex evaluations of financial information about both individuals and corporations for which they have worked.

—Traditional FBI inquiries into arrest records, youthful associations and other personal background data must be carefully weighed to avoid unfairly penalizing an individual for conduct that may be constitutionally protected even though not approved by many in society.

—Appointment to high office is patronage by any other name, and removing politics from patronage is no easier today than in the 19th century.

—In addition to being affected by partisan politics, the appointment process is enmeshed constantly in conflict between the legislative and executive branches over both patronage and substantive policy.

Remarking on the complexities of the nomination procedure confronting the Senate, Mackenzie wrote:

> If it [the Senate] is too assertive in applying what it collectively believes to be appropriate standards for presidential appointees, it is criticized for interfering with the president's right to run the government. But if it is too deferential to the president, challenging only the very worst of his nominations, it is criticized for being a rubber stamp, for not effectively carrying out its responsibilities in the appointment process.[5]

## Power of Removal

Controversy over the role of the Senate in the removal of government officers began in the early days of the Republic and continued intermittently into the 20th century. The Constitution contained no language governing removals except for the impeachment provisions of Article II, Section 4. Alexander Hamilton, writing in *The Federalist* (No. 77), contended that the consent of the Senate "would be necessary to displace as well as to appoint," but this view soon was challenged.[6]

Debate over the removal power began in the First Congress, during consideration of a bill to establish the Department of Foreign Affairs. Two principal theories were advanced. One group insisted that since the Constitution gave the Senate a share in the appointment power, the Senate must also give its advice and consent to removals. The other group, led by James Madison, maintained that the removal power was an executive function, necessarily implied in the power to nominate, and that Senate participation would violate the principle of separation of powers.

Madison's view prevailed in the House, which passed the bill by a 29 to 22 vote after deleting language specifically vesting removal power in the president and substituting a provision that implied recognition of the president's exclusive removal power under the Constitution. After a lengthy and spirited debate in closed session, the Senate narrowly acceded to the House interpretation. That the Senate agreed to limit its own powers was attributed widely to senatorial respect for President Washington.

Early presidents exercised great restraint in use of the removal power, even after the enactment in 1820 of the "Four Years" law. This law established a fixed, four-year term for district attorneys, customs collectors and many other officers who previously had served at the pleasure of the president. Presidents James Monroe and John Quincy Adams followed a policy of renominating all such persons when their terms expired unless they had been guilty of misconduct. However, senatorial pressure for patronage was on the rise, and Adams' self-restraint was met by Senate demands for a broader role in appointments and removals.

## Jackson's Clashes With Senate

Andrew Jackson's sweeping and partisan use of the removal power soon brought fresh Senate demands for a larger share in the patronage pie. Controversy over the issue led to a series of Senate resolutions requesting the president to inform the Senate of his reasons for removing various officials. Jackson complied with several of these requests, but by 1835 he had had enough. A Senate resolution, adopted by a 23 to 22 vote, requesting information on the "charges, if any," against the recently removed surveyor general of south Tennessee brought the following response:

> It is . . . my solemn conviction that I ought no longer, from any motive, nor in any degree, to yield to these unconstitutional demands. Their continued repetition imposes on me, as the representative and trustee of the American people, the painful but imperious duty of resisting to the utmost any further encroachment on the rights of the Executive. . . . The President in cases of this nature possesses the exclusive power of removal from office; and under the sanctions of his official oath, and of his liability to impeachment, he is bound to exercise it whenever the public welfare shall require. On no principle known to our institutions can he be required to account for the manner in which he discharges this portion of his public duties, save only in the mode and under the forms prescribed by the Constitution. [7]

Meanwhile, the Senate had appointed a committee to look into the matter. The committee reported a bill to repeal the first two sections of the "Four Years" law and to require the president to submit to the Senate the reasons for each removal. Supported by John C. Calhoun, Daniel Webster, and Henry Clay, the measure won Senate approval but never was taken up in the House. Webster and Clay disputed the interpretation of the removal power established by the First Congress. Attributing that interpretation largely to congressional confidence in President Washington, Clay said it had not been reconsidered only because it had not been abused prior to the Jackson administration.

## Opposition to Tenure Act

The next great clash between the Senate and the chief executive over the removal power occurred during President Andrew Johnson's administration. Among its consequences were the Tenure of Office Act of 1867 and Johnson's impeachment. The conflict grew out of Johnson's fight with the radical Republican leaders of Congress over Reconstruction policy and his use of the removal power to provide jobs for his own followers. The act forbade the president to remove civil officers (appointed with the advice and consent of the Senate) without the approval of the Senate. It was intended to protect incumbent Republican officeholders from executive retaliation if they did not support the Democratic president.

President Johnson vetoed the bill on the ground that it was unconstitutional to restrict the president's power of removal, but Congress enacted the measure over the veto by a 35 to 11 vote in the Senate and a 133 to 37 vote in the House. Johnson promptly put the Tenure of Office Act to the test. First, he suspended Secretary of War Edwin M. Stanton, but the Senate refused to concur in the suspension. Johnson then attempted to dismiss Stanton and make another appointment to the post. The House immediately initiated impeachment proceedings and on Feb. 24, 1868, adopted 11 articles of impeachment. The principal charge against President Johnson was that he had violated the new law by dismissing Stanton. A two-thirds majority was required to convict. By a margin of only one vote, Johnson was acquitted in the Senate. *(History of Impeachments chapter, pp. 169-172)*

Early in President Ulysses S. Grant's administration, Congress amended the Tenure of Office Act by repealing its provisions regulating suspensions. The amended law in 1869 provided that the president might suspend officers "in his discretion" without reporting to the Senate the reasons for his action; but it required prompt nomination of successors.[8] A subsequent dispute between President Grover Cleveland and the Republican-controlled Senate finally led to repeal of what was left of the Tenure of Office Act.

While Congress was in recess in the summer of 1885, Cleveland suspended 643 government officers whose positions were subject to senatorial confirmation. When Congress reconvened, he submitted to the Senate the names of their replacements, to whom he had given recess appointments. The committees handling these nominations then called upon the executive departments for information on the reasons for the suspensions, information the departments refused to give.

The Senate responded with two resolutions. One censured a state attorney general for refusal to transmit the desired papers and a second resolution said it was "the duty of the Senate to refuse its advice and consent to proposed removals of officers" in cases where information requested by the Senate was withheld.[9]

Cleveland then sent a special message to the Senate reasserting the president's authority:

> I am solely responsible to the people from whom I have so lately received the sacred trust of office.... The pledges I have made were made to the people, and to them I am responsible. I am not responsible to the Senate, and I am unwilling to submit my actions and official conduct to them for judgment.... [10]

Public opinion responded to the president's message, and the nomination logjam was broken. The following year Sen. George F. Hoar, R-Mass. (1877-1904), introduced legislation to repeal the Tenure of Office Acts, and the bill speedily was enacted into law.

## Other Controversies

Another major controversy over the removal power occurred in 1920 when President Woodrow Wilson vetoed the forerunner of the Budget and Accounting Act of 1921. That measure, as transmitted to Wilson, provided that the comptroller general and assistant comptroller general were to be appointed by the president subject to Senate confirmation, but were to be subject to removal by concurrent resolution of Congress. A concurrent resolution does not require the president's approval to take effect and thus the president would have had no control over the removal of these officers. Wilson's veto message was emphatic: "I am convinced that the Congress is without constitutional power to limit the appointing power and its incident power of removal derived from the Constitution." [11]

The following year, the Budget and Accounting Act of 1921 became law with the signature of President Warren G. Harding. The enacted legislation, however, differed from the 1920 version in providing for removal of the comptroller general and assistant comptroller general by joint resolution, which, like a bill, requires the signature of the president, or passage over his veto, to take effect.

## Court Decisions

The courts have upheld the president's right unilaterally to remove government officials. After nearly 140 years of controversy over the issue, the Supreme Court met the issue head on in 1926. In the words of Chief Justice William Howard Taft, the court had "studiously avoided deciding the issue until it was presented in such a way that it could not be avoided." [12]

The case involved a postmaster who had been removed from office by President Wilson in 1920, without consultation with the Senate, although the 1876 law under which the man had been appointed stipulated: "Postmasters of the first, second and third classes shall be appointed and may be removed by the president, by and with the advice and consent of the Senate, and shall hold their offices for four years, unless sooner removed or suspended according to law." [13]

In a 6-3 decision, the court upheld the president's unrestricted power of removal as inherent in the executive power invested in the office by the Constitution. In the decision of *Myers v. United States,* the court concluded:

> It therefore follows that the Tenure of Office Act of 1867, in so far as it attempted to prevent the president from removing executive officers who had been appointed by him by and with the consent of the Senate was invalid, and that subsequent legislation of the same effect was equally so. . . . The provision of the law of 1876, by which the unrestricted power of removal of first-class postmasters is denied to the president, is in violation of the Constitution and invalid.[14]

In a unanimous 1935 decision, *Humphrey's Executor v. United States,* the court modified this position. The 1935 case involved a federal trade commissioner whom President Franklin D. Roosevelt had tried to remove because, as he told the commissioner, "I do not feel that your mind and my mind go along together on either the policies or the administration" of the FTC.[15] The court held that the FTC was "an administrative body created by Congress to carry into effect legislative policies" and thus could not "in any proper sense be characterized as an arm or an eye of the Executive." In ruling that Roosevelt had exceeded his authority in removing the commissioner, the court indicated that except for officials immediately responsible to the president and those exercising non-discretionary or ministerial functions, Congress could apply such limitations on removal as it saw fit.

In a later decision, *Wiener v. United States,* the court built on the *Humphrey's* decision. That case involved the refusal of a member of the War Claims Commission appointed by President Harry S Truman to resign when the Eisenhower administration came to power. Congress created the commission with "jurisdiction to receive and adjudicate according to law" certain damage claims resulting from World War II. The law made no provision for removal of commissioners.

Wiener was removed by Eisenhower, and the commission member sought his pay in court. The Supreme Court agreed with him. It noted the similarity between the *Wiener* and *Humphrey's* cases: in both situations, presidents had removed persons from quasi-judicial agencies without showing cause for the sole purpose of naming persons of their own choosing.

The court said it understood the *Humphrey's* decision to

> . . .draw a sharp line of cleavage between officials who were part of the executive establishment and were thus removable by virtue of the president's constitutional powers, and those who are members of a body "to exercise its judgment without the leave or hindrance of any other official or any department of the government,". . . as to whom a power of removal exists only if Congress may fairly be said to have conferred it. This sharp differentiation derives from the difference in functions between those who are part of the executive establishment and those whose tasks require absolute freedom from executive interference.

The court also noted the "intrinsic judicial character" of the commission. As a result of this case and of the *Myers* and *Humphrey's* cases, the rule has developed that a president can remove a member of a quasi-judicial agency only for cause, even if Congress has not so provided.

## Notes

1. G. Calvin Mackenzie, *The Politics of Presidential Appointments* (New York: Free Press, 1981), p. xix.
2. Hugh Heclo, *A Government of Strangers* (Washington, D.C.: Brookings Institution, 1977), p. 88.

3. *President Carter 1980* (Washington, D.C.: Congressional Quarterly, 1981), p. 91.
4. *Inside Congress* (Washington, D.C.: Congressional Quarterly, 1979), p. 95.
5. Mackenzie, *The Politics of Presidential Appointments,* p. 186.
6. Alexander Hamilton, James Madison, and John Jay, *The Federalist Papers,* with an introduction by Clinton Rossiter (New York: Mentor, 1961), p. 459.
7. George H. Haynes, *The Senate of the United States: Its History and Practice* (Boston: Houghton-Mifflin, 1938), p. 796.
8. Ibid., p. 805.
9. Ibid., pp. 807-808.
10. Ibid., p. 808.
11. Ibid., p. 810.
12. Ibid., p. 828.
13. Ibid.
14. Ibid., p. 829.
15. Ibid., p. 831.

*Chapter 19*

# HISTORY OF APPOINTMENTS

The president "shall nominate, and by and with the Advice and Consent of the Senate, shall appoint. . . ." [1] The constitutional language governing the appointment power, drafted and agreed to in the final weeks of the Constitutional Convention of 1787, represented a compromise between delegates who favored vesting in the Senate sole authority for appointing principal government officers and those who held that the president alone should control appointments as an executive function.

As finally adopted, the Constitution required Senate confirmation of principal officers of the government — "Ambassadors, other public Ministers and Consuls, Judges of the Supreme Court" were mentioned specifically — but provided that Congress could "by Law vest the Appointment of such inferior Officers, as they think proper, in the President alone, in the Courts of Law, or in the Heads of Departments."

Approval of that compromise language did not, however, settle the controversy over the Senate's role in the appointment process. To Alexander Hamilton, writing in *The Federalist* (No. 66), the Senate's function did not appear significant: "It will be the office of the President to *nominate*, and with the advice and consent of the Senate to *appoint*. There will, of course, be no exertion of *choice* on the part of the Senate. They may defeat one choice of the Executive and oblige him to make another; but they cannot themselves *choose* — they can only ratify or reject the choice he may have made." [2]

John Adams saw it differently. "Faction and distraction," he wrote, "are the sure and certain consequences of giving to the Senate a vote on the distribution of offices." [3] Looking ahead to the emergence of political parties, Adams foresaw the rise of the spoils system and the use of the appointive power as a senatorial patronage tool. President George Washington regarded the appointment power as "the most irksome part of the executive trust," [4] but his exercise of that power was widely acclaimed; the Senate withheld its consent only five times during his administration.

## Precedents Established by Washington

Methods of handling presidential nominations had to be instituted early in the new government. Washington established the precedent of submitting nominations to the Senate in writing, and the Senate after debate on the propriety of the secret ballot determined to take voice votes on nominations. The president rejected suggestions that he be present during Senate consideration of appointments: "It could be no pleasing thing, I conceive, for the President, on the one hand to be present and hear the propriety of his nominations questioned; nor for the Senate on the other hand to be under the smallest restraint from his presence from the fullest and freest inquiry into the character of the person nominated." [5]

Uncertainty over the extent of the Senate's role in executive appointments surfaced early in Washington's administration. Could the Senate decide only whether or not to give its consent to the person named, or could it also rule on the necessity of the post and the grade of the appointee? Washington's nominations of ministers to Paris, London and The Hague in December 1791 were blocked for weeks by Senate debate on a resolution opposing the appointment of "ministers plenipotentiary to reside permanently at foreign courts." [6] Washington's nominations finally were approved, by narrow votes, on the ground of special need for representation at those three capitals.

Washington maintained high standards for selection of appointees, and although he consulted widely both with members of Congress and other persons, he rebuffed all attempts at encroachment on his prerogatives. Thus he refused to appoint Aaron Burr as minister to France in 1794, despite such a recommendation by a caucus of Democratic-Republican senators and representatives, because he questioned Burr's integrity.

Washington was not always successful in resisting senatorial pressure. Early in the First Congress the Senate rejected his nomination of Benjamin Fishbourn to the post of naval officer (a customs official handling manifests, clearances, etc.) for the Port of Savannah out of courtesy to the two Georgia senators, who had a candidate of their own. Washington yielded, nominating the senators' choice, and senatorial courtesy was born. *(Box, p. 255)*

The practice of inquiring into the political views of a presidential nominee also had its beginning in the Washington administration. John Rutledge of South Carolina, nominated in 1795 to succeed John Jay as chief justice of the United States, was rejected by the Senate on a 10 to 14 vote, primarily because of his opposition to the Jay Treaty with Great Britain. Rutledge, one of the original six Supreme Court justices (1789-91), already was serving as chief justice on a recess appointment.

## Injection of Politics

John Adams, that vigorous critic of the Constitution's appointment provisions, found nothing in his experience as president to make him change his view. The Federalist Senate cleared his appointments with Federalist leader Alexander Hamilton, at the time a private citizen, and Adams later complained that he "soon found that if I had not the previous consent of the heads of departments, and the approbation of Mr. Hamilton, I ran the utmost risk of a dead negative in the Senate." [7]

During Adams' tenure, appointments became increasingly determined by political considerations. The practice of consulting, and bowing to the wishes of, state delegations in Congress in making appointments from a member's state also was solidified.

Thomas Jefferson had far less trouble with appointments than his predecessor. He was the acknowledged leader of his party, and for most of his term that party was in control of Congress. Unlike Jefferson, James Madison soon found that he had to submit to Senate dictation in the matter of appointments. A small clique of senators was able to force the appointment of Robert Smith as secretary of state, although Madison had wanted to give the post to his secretary of the Treasury, Albert Gallatin.

Gallatin's subsequent appointment as envoy to negotiate a peace treaty with Great Britain also met with difficulty in the Senate. Gallatin was already in Europe when the Senate adopted a resolution declaring that the duties of envoy and secretary of the Treasury were incompatible. Subsequently, Gallatin resigned his Treasury post and was confirmed as envoy.

That nomination led to a controversy over the propriety of consultation between the president and a Senate committee on pending nominations. Although previous presidents had agreed to consult with committees appointed by the party caucus or by the Senate itself, Madison decided to put an end to the practice. In a message to the Senate he insisted that if the Senate wanted information on nominations, the correct procedure was to confer with appropriate department heads, not the president. "The appointment of a committee of the Senate to confer immediately with the executive himself," he said, "appears to lose sight of the coordinate relation between the executive and the Senate, which the Constitution has established, and which ought therefore to be maintained." [8] In spite of this message, the president received a special committee appointed by the Senate to confer with him about the Gallatin nomination, but Madison refused to discuss the nomination with it.

## Growth of the 'Spoils System'

The administrations of James Monroe and John Quincy Adams were marked by the growth of the so-called spoils system, as members of the Senate increasingly insisted on control of federal appointments in their states. Legislation referred to as the "Four Years" law, enacted in 1820, greatly increased the number of appointments available. This law provided fixed four-year terms for many federal officers who previously had served at the pleasure of the president. Although its ostensible purpose was to ensure the appointees' accountability, its value as a patronage tool soon became clear. Commented Adams: "The Senate was conciliated by the permanent increase of their power, which was the principal ultimate effect of the act, and every senator was flattered by the power conferred upon himself of multiplying chances to provide for his friends and dependents. . . ." [9]

Both Monroe and John Quincy Adams resisted pressure to use the "Four Years" law as a means of introducing rotation in office. They followed the policy of renominating officers upon expiration of their terms, unless they had been guilty of misconduct. Upon taking office as president in 1825, Adams resubmitted all of Monroe's nominations on which the Senate had failed to act. President Andrew Jackson did not follow that policy, however, and withdrew all of Adams' nominations.

Jackson, to whom rotation in office was a leading principle, made full use of the "Four Years" law to find places for his supporters. Although he was in constant conflict with the Senate over appointments, he was so popular in the country that relatively few were rejected.

The Senate twice rejected Jackson's renomination of four incumbent directors of the Bank of the United States. Senate opposition stemmed from reports critical of the bank that had been submitted to the president by the directors. After efforts to recommit the nominations failed, the Senate rejected them by a 20 to 24 vote. Jackson renominated the same persons, only to have them rejected once again.

The Bank of the United States also figured in controversy over the nomination of Roger B. Taney as secretary of the Treasury in 1834. Taney was rejected on an 18 to 28 vote after having served for nine months under a recess appointment. Opposition rested on his withdrawal of federal funds from the bank, an action he had recommended as attorney general. In fact, it was to carry out that policy that he had been appointed Treasury secretary. Taney's nomination was the first outright Senate rejection of a Cabinet appointee in U.S. history, although Madison had been prevented from appointing Gallatin as secretary of state in 1809 because he feared Gallatin would be rejected.

Early in 1835 Jackson nominated Taney to the Supreme Court. The Senate did not take up that nomination until the closing days of its session, when it voted, 24 to 21, for an indefinite postponement. Undaunted, the president in December 1835 named Taney to be chief justice, a position made vacant by the death of John Marshall. Notwithstanding charges that the selection was an insult to the Senate, because it had twice rejected the nominee, Taney's appointment was confirmed in March 1836 by a vote of 29 to 15.

## Patronage at a Peak

The 40-year period from 1837 to 1877 marked the high point of Senate efforts to control executive appointments. During this period, the spoils system reached its peak and all presidents were subject to intense pressure for patronage appointments. Senatorial courtesy was firmly entrenched.

President John Tyler, a dissident Democrat who had accepted the Whig nomination for vice president in 1840 and then repudiated the Whigs upon succeeding William Henry Harrison as president, was peculiarly unfortunate in his relations with the Senate. Since he was without a following in either party, both Whigs and Democrats were anxious to embarrass him, and many of his nominees — including four to the Cabinet and four to the Supreme Court — were rejected. In 1843 his nomination of Caleb Cushing as secretary of the Treasury was rejected three times in one day.

Nine months after succeeding Tyler in 1845, President James K. Polk offered a vacant Supreme Court seat to Secretary of State James Buchanan. Buchanan declined, and Polk then named to the court an obscure but able Pennsylvania judge, George W. Woodward. Polk interpreted the Senate's 20-29 rejection of the nomination as an attempt to weaken his administration.

In the tension-filled decade of the 1850s, President Millard Fillmore was unable to persuade the Senate to approve his southern nominees to the court. In 1852 the Senate refused to act upon the nomination of Edward A. Bradford of Louisiana. In 1853 Democratic opposition forced the postponement, on a 26 to 25 vote, of Senate action on the nomination of Sen. George E. Badger of North Carolina. The Democratic Senate that year also failed to act on the Whig president's nomination to the court of William C. Micou of Louisiana.

Weakened by resignations of senators from seceding states, the Senate in 1861 rejected, 25 to 26, President James Buchanan's nomination of Jeremiah S. Black of Pennsylvania to the Supreme Court. Black, a former attorney general and secretary of state, was opposed by the Republicans, who wished the newly elected President Abraham Lincoln to fill the court seat with his own choice.

Lincoln, a shrewd politician, made masterful use of the appointment power to hold the divided factions of his party together and to advance his legislative goals. Early in his administration he devoted much of his time to patronage. Most officers subject to presidential appointment had been removed after the 1860 election, and Lincoln tried to distribute these offices equitably among his various supporters. Only for major posts was a high standard of qualification deemed essential.

Andrew Johnson's bitter struggle with the Senate over appointments, a byproduct of the fight over the post-Civil War Reconstruction policy, led to curbs on the president's removal powers in the Tenure of Office Act of 1867 and to Johnson's impeachment trial. *(Details, p. 170)*

Senate hostility to Johnson blocked the elevation in 1866 of Attorney General Henry Stanbery of Ohio to the Supreme Court. The Senate never acted directly on the nomination but instead passed a bill to reduce the size of the court from 10 to eight justices. The purpose of the bill was to kill the Stanbery nomination by abolishing the seat to which he was named. Stanbery resigned as attorney general in 1868 to serve as Johnson's chief counsel during the impeachment proceedings. When Johnson subsequently renominated him to the post of attorney general, the Senate refused, 11 to 29, to confirm the appointment.

## Civil Service Reform

Senatorial ascendancy over the presidency in the matter of appointments and the excesses of the spoils system led to public pressure for civil service reform during the presidency of Ulysses S. Grant. In response to that pressure, Congress in 1871 enacted a civil service law but failed to appropriate funds to implement it.

Three of Grant's appointments to the Supreme Court failed to win Senate approval. The first was his attorney general, Ebenezer Rockwood Hoar, who had earned the Senate's enmity by refusing to bow to political pressure in filling new judgeships created under an 1869 law. After Hoar's rejection, 24 to 33, Sen. Simon Cameron of Pennsylvania exclaimed: "What could you expect for a man who has snubbed 70 senators!" [10] In 1874 Grant was forced to withdraw two successive nominations for chief justice.

The accession to the presidency of Rutherford B. Hayes in 1877 marked the beginning of presidential efforts to curb senatorial control over nominations. Hayes' selection of his own Cabinet members without consulting Senate leaders was viewed as presumptuous by them, and they countered with an unprecedented delay in acting upon his nominations. However, when public opinion came to the aid of the president, the nominations were confirmed quickly.

Unable to obtain from Congress the civil service reform legislation he recommended, Hayes nevertheless attempted throughout his one term of office to curb patronage abuses. Meanwhile, the spoils system's heyday was drawing to a close. Previous efforts at significant civil service reform had ended in failure, but public revulsion over President James A. Garfield's assassination by a disappointed office-seeker in 1881 provided new impetus for change. With the endorsement of President Chester A. Arthur, who had been Garfield's vice president, a civil service system was established by the Pendleton Act of 1883.

## Resistance to Patronage

A key test of the president's right to suspend federal officers, which occurred during President Grover Cleveland's first term, was followed by repeal of the Tenure of Office Act. After that, few Cleveland nominations were rejected. However, in his second term, two conservative appointees to the Supreme Court were rejected upon appeal to the rule of courtesy by Sen. David B. Hill, D-N.Y. (1892-97). William B. Hornblower and Wheeler H. Peckham, respected New York attorneys but of a political faction opposed to Hill, were rejected by votes of 24 to 30 and 32 to 41, respectively. Cleveland then nominated a Louisiana senator, Edward Douglass White, D-La. (1891-94), who was confirmed immediately — an example of the courtesy traditionally accorded by the Senate to one of its own members.

President Theodore Roosevelt, like William McKinley before him, tried to avoid patronage fights with Congress. However, Roosevelt, an advocate of civil service reform, insisted on high qualification for federal office. Members of Congress, he said, "may ordinarily name the man, but I shall name the standard, and the men have got to come up to it." [11] His care in the matter of judicial appointments twice led him to refuse to nominate candidates recommended by Sen. Thomas C. Platt, R-N.Y. (1897-1909). On one of these occasions he wrote to Platt, "It is, I trust, needless to say that I fully appreciate the right and duty of the Senate to reject or to confirm any appointment according to what its members conscientiously deem their duty to be; just as it is my business to make an appointment which I conscientiously think is a good one." [12]

President William H. Taft recommended a dramatic extension of the civil service system that would have included postmasters and other field officers then subject to Senate confirmation, but Congress did not enact the necessary legislation.

President Woodrow Wilson accepted Treasury Secretary William G. McAdoo's suggestion that he allow his department heads to handle distribution of patronage, a chore that traditionally had been undertaken by the president himself. Wilson generally tried to get along with the Senate and on occasion yielded to it in the interests of party harmony, but he suffered several notable rejections in contests over local offices.

## Nominations Under Wilson

Two national controversies over nominations during Wilson's administration involved George Rublee, to head the Federal Trade Commission, and Louis D. Brandeis, to fill a Supreme Court vacancy. Rublee was rejected in 1916 following a two-year fight led by Sen. Jacob H. Gallinger, R-N.H. (1891-1918), who opposed the nomination on the ground that it was "personally obnoxious" to him. Republican Sen. Robert M. La Follette, R-Wis. (1906-25), deplored Gallinger's use of the "personally obnoxious" formula against a national appointment. It was the first such application of the rule, he said, since he had been in the

## Senatorial Courtesy

Under the unwritten custom of senatorial courtesy, the Senate generally will refuse to confirm a nomination to an office within a particular state unless the nominee has been approved by the senators of the president's party from that state. The rule is not usually applied to nominations to national office. Moreover, the importance of senatorial courtesy has diminished as patronage positions have been brought into the Civil Service and as new professional requirements have been established.

A senator typically invokes the rule of courtesy by stating that the nominee is "personally obnoxious" to him. This may mean that the senator and the nominee are personal or political foes, or simply that the senator has another candidate for the post. In effect, the custom permits the senators of the party in office to control selection of local federal officials — district court judges, U.S. attorneys, marshals and the like. In states where neither senator belongs to the president's party the president has greater freedom of choice, although state party leaders usually make recommendations to him.

The custom of senatorial courtesy had its beginnings in the administration of George Washington.* The custom of senatorial courtesy, however, did not become firmly established until many years later. Under early practice, the objecting senator had only to voice the customary formula, but since 1930 he has been expected to explain the reasons for his opposition to the nominee.

The Senate does not invariably sustain appeals to the rule of courtesy. It depends on whether the objecting senator is in good standing with his colleagues, the nature of his objection and whether the nomination is to a local or national office.

A specialized form of senatorial courtesy decrees that the nomination of a senator or former senator will be confirmed at once, without even being referred to committee. This tradition is not always honored, however. The nominations to the Supreme Court of Sen. Hugo L. Black in 1937 and of former Sen. Sherman Minton in 1949 were referred to committee.

*Joseph P. Harris, *The Advice and Consent of the Senate* (New York: Greenwood Press, 1968), pp. 40-41, 216-17; James D. Richardson, ed., *A Compilation of the Messages and Papers of the Presidents* (New York: Bureau of National Literature, 1897), Vol. I, pp. 50-51.

Senate. During the fight, Rublee served on the FTC for a year and a half on a recess appointment.

The nomination and subsequent confirmation of Brandeis in 1916 ended one of the most bitter appointment struggles in the nation's history. The opposition to Brandeis was led by New England business groups that considered him a radical and a crusader because of his unpaid public activities. Industrial interests charged that he was anti-business and guilty of unethical conduct, but four months of unusual open hearings by a Senate Judiciary subcommittee — hearings that were reopened twice — failed to turn up any valid grounds for rejection. One supporter, Arthur Hill of the Harvard Law School, attributed the opposition to the fact that "Mr. Brandeis is an outsider, successful and a Jew." The committee procrastinated, despite the fast approaches of Congress' adjournment and the national political conventions. Finally, after personal appeals by Brandeis and the president to wavering senators, the committee cleared the nomination by a 10 to 8 party-line vote. When the Senate voted June 1, Brandeis was confirmed, 47 to 22, with the vote following party lines.

Early in President Warren G. Harding's administration, the White House announced that Republican senators would select nominees for local offices and that the president would "hold Republican senators to account for appointments made by him on their recommendations." Should the appointees prove unworthy or incompetent, he said, the senators would bear "the responsibility for whatever trouble arises through this means." [13] Probably to his detriment, few nominees during his administration were rejected. Three of his Cabinet members later became involved in scandals, and his Veterans Administration administrator was convicted of fraud.

Although President Calvin Coolidge had few clashes with the Senate over appointments, he became the first president since 1868 to have a Cabinet nominee rejected. Coolidge in 1925 nominated Charles Beecher Warren, a prominent Michigan attorney, to be his attorney general. Little opposition was expected. However, when the nomination reached the Senate floor, where it was considered in unusual open session (until 1929 most nominations were considered in closed session), opponents attacked Warren for his association with the "Sugar Trust." Such a man, they said, could not be relied upon to enforce the antitrust laws.

The Senate vote on Warren ended in a 40 to 40 tie, thus rejecting the nominee. Vice President Charles G. Dawes, napping at his hotel, was not present to cast the deciding vote. While efforts were being made to get Dawes to the floor, a Republican senator changed his vote so he could offer a motion to reconsider the nomination. His motion then was tabled (rejected) 41 to 39, effectively killing the nomination of Warren. A furious Coolidge promptly renominated Warren, who was again defeated, 39 to 46. A contributing factor to the second defeat was the president's announcement as debate was in progress that if Warren was not confirmed, he would be given a recess appointment. Warren declined that honor.

President Herbert C. Hoover took a firm line on patronage abuses and refused to nominate candidates simply because they were recommended by GOP party organizations. Hoover also instituted the practice of making public the endorsers of judicial nominees.

Hoover met one notable nomination defeat: the rejection of Judge John J. Parker to the Supreme Court in 1930 — the first such rejection in 36 years. The Parker case marked the third effort in five years by Senate liberals to block appointments to the court of persons they thought to be too conservative. They had failed to block the confirmation of Harlan Fiske Stone in 1925 and of Charles Evans Hughes as chief justice earlier in 1930. But, with the aid of a campaign mounted by organized labor and the National Association for the Advancement of Colored People, they were able to defeat Parker, 39 to 41.

## Controversial Roosevelt Appointments

President Franklin D. Roosevelt had few problems with appointments in his first years in office, but following the defeat of his court-packing plan and his unsuccessful effort to purge Democratic opponents in the 1938 primaries, difficulties increased.

The only major appointment controversy of his first term involved Rexford G. Tugwell, a member of the president's "brain trust" who was nominated in 1934 to the newly created post of under secretary of agriculture. Despite opposition based on his liberal views, Tugwell was confirmed, 53 to 24. In Roosevelt's second term, many more appointees came under attack because of their allegedly radical positions. Perhaps the most notable of the second-term controversies involved Harry Hopkins, who won confirmation as secretary of commerce in 1939 only after a fight in which politics in the Works Progress Administration was the central issue. Hopkins was confirmed, 58 to 27, but a number of Democrats abstained.

Roosevelt's efforts to cut off patronage of Democratic senators who opposed his New Deal programs had mixed success. He succeeded in disciplining senators Huey P. Long, D-La. (1932-35), and Rush D. Holt, D-W.Va. (1935-41). But he failed with Harry F. Byrd, D-Va. (1933-65); Carter Glass, D-Va. (1920-46); Pat McCarran, D-Nev. (1933-54); and W. Lee O'Daniel, D-Texas (1941-49). All successfully invoked senatorial courtesy to defeat nominations they had opposed.

Of Roosevelt's eight nominees to the Supreme Court, only one — Sen. Hugo L. Black, D-Ala. (1927-37) — faced serious opposition. Roosevelt appointed Black, who had vigorously supported New Deal programs, in 1937 after defeat of the president's court-packing plan. Although it was traditional for the Senate to confirm one of its own members immediately without reference to committee, the Black nomination was sent to the Judiciary Committee. The nomination was cleared by the committee, 13 to 4, and by the Senate, 63 to 16, after a debate punctuated by charges that Black had been a member of the Ku Klux Klan and had received Klan support in his 1926 election campaign. Black's confirmation did not end this controversy, and he finally made a public statement that he had once been a member of the Klan but had resigned and severed all ties with the organization.

Partisanship declined during World War II, and the president, in the interests of national unity, tried to avoid controversial nominations. Most emergency agencies were created by executive order, and their heads did not require Senate confirmation. Controversy erupted anew in 1945 with Henry A. Wallace's appointment as secretary of commerce to succeed Jesse Jones. Wallace, vice president in Roosevelt's third term, had been dumped from the Democratic ticket in 1944 because of conservative opposition to his "radical" economic views; but he had participated vigorously in the fall campaign and was expected to be rewarded with a Cabinet post. On Inauguration Day 1945 Roosevelt wrote to Jones asking him to step aside for Wallace. "Henry Wallace deserves almost any service which he believes he can satisfactorily perform," the letter said.[14]

Wallace's chief reason for wanting the commerce post was that it would give him control of the vast lending powers of the Reconstruction Finance Corporation. However, before acting on the Wallace nomination, Congress passed legislation removing the RFC from the Commerce Department and giving it independent status. Jones, testifying on the bill, said the RFC should not be directed by a man who was "willing to jeopardize the country's future with untried ideas and idealistic schemes." [15] Wallace, replying to charges that he was not qualified to supervise the RFC, said, "[I]t is not a question of my lack of experience. Rather, it is a case of not liking the experience I have." [16] After enactment of the RFC removal bill, the Senate on March 1, 1945, confirmed Wallace as secretary of commerce by a 56 to 32 vote. Ten Republicans joined 45 Democrats and one independent in voting for confirmation; five Democrats and 27 Republicans voted against him.

Three weeks later the Senate rejected another Roosevelt appointee charged with radical views. Aubrey W. Williams, nominated to be Rural Electrification administrator, had a background as social worker, administrator of the National Youth Administration and organization director of the National Farmers Union. Opposition was based on his racial positions and on charges that he was an atheist and a communist sympathizer. Nineteen Democrats joined 33 Republicans to defeat Williams, 36 to 52.

## Truman's Battles With the Senate

President Harry S Truman had difficulty with the Senate over appointments. Early in his administration he was widely criticized for appointing "cronies" to important offices. After the 1946 midterm election, in which the Republicans won control of Congress, Truman tried to avoid controversy by nominating men who would be acceptable to the Senate. The Republican 80th Congress did not reject any of Truman's nominees, although 153 names were withdrawn. In 1948 the Senate did not act on some 11,122 nominations, apparently in the expectation that a Republican president would be elected who would fill the vacancies with Republicans.

The two most explosive contests that did occur in the 80th Congress concerned nominees who had been named before the 1946 election, David E. Lilienthal and Gordon R. Clapp. In the autumn of 1946, Truman gave Lilienthal, chairman of the Tennessee Valley Authority (TVA), a recess appointment to the chairmanship of the newly created Atomic Energy Commission. Truman appointed Clapp, who had served under Lilienthal, to replace him as TVA chairman.

The opposition to both nominations was led by Sen. Kenneth McKellar, D-Tenn. (1917-53), who for years had been engaged in a patronage dispute with the TVA management. During the mid-1940s,

McKellar had made several unsuccessful efforts to require Senate confirmation of all TVA employees earning $4,500 a year or more, and he resented TVA's insistence on a merit employment policy. Further, he had locked horns with TVA in 1941 over the location of a dam to be constructed in his state. Although he was not a member of the committees that considered the two nominations, McKellar conducted lengthy interrogations of witnesses and accused both Lilienthal and Clapp of having communist sympathies. When the nominations finally reached the floor in April 1947, Lilienthal was confirmed, 50 to 31, as was Clapp, 36 to 31. During the debate on Clapp, McKellar complained that the president had appointed him "without saying beans to me," and declared that he was "hurt beyond expression" that his colleagues should vote for nominees he opposed.[17]

Senatorial courtesy played a role in several of Truman's defeats. In 1950 the Senate rejected, 14 to 59, the nomination of Martin A. Hutchinson to be a member of the Federal Trade Commission. Hutchinson, a foe of Sen. Harry F. Byrd, D-Va. (1933-65), and his Virginia political machine, was opposed by Sens. Byrd and A. Willis Robertson, D-Va. (1946-67). In 1951 Sen. Paul H. Douglas, D-Ill. (1949-67), successfully appealed to the courtesy tradition to defeat two of Truman's choices for federal district judgeships in Illinois. Douglas said the president should have nominated two candidates recommended by him.

But one plum of congressional patronage came to an end in 1952. President Truman proposed, and Congress accepted, a reorganization plan putting all Internal Revenue Bureau (later renamed the Internal Revenue Service) jobs, except that of commissioner, under civil service. The action followed congressional hearings in 1951 on scandals in the agency. The Senate, however, defeated other reorganization plans to put postmasters, customs officials and U.S. marshals under civil service.

## Eisenhower, Kennedy Appointments

At the outset of his administration in 1953, President Dwight D. Eisenhower was criticized by conservative Republicans who contended that his Cabinet selections failed to give appropriate recognition to the wing of the Republican Party led by Sen. Robert A. Taft, R-Ohio (1939-53). The president also gave his department and agency heads free rein to select their own subordinates, but when Republican leaders in the Senate complained that their suggestions were being ignored and that even the customary clearances were not being obtained, the senators were invited to take their recommendations directly to the department heads. Subsequently, more appointments went to conservative Republicans.

Several of Eisenhower's early nominations were opposed on conflict-of-interest grounds. The most celebrated was that of Charles E. Wilson as secretary of defense. Wilson, former president of General Motors, was required to divest himself of all GM stock before the Senate Armed Services Committee consented to recommend his confirmation. Wilson had not planned to give up his stock. Similar issues arose with the nominations of Harold E. Talbott as secretary of the Air Force and Robert T. Stevens as secretary of the Army. From this time on, the Senate showed a greater interest in conflict-of-interest questions in the consideration of presidential nominations.

One of Eisenhower's subsequent Cabinet nominations was rejected — the first such rejection since 1925. Lewis L. Strauss already was serving under a recess appointment when, after months of hearings, the Senate rejected his nomination as secretary of commerce by a 46 to 49 vote. Opponents accused Strauss of a lack of integrity and criticized his conservative approach to government. Specific issues raised against him included his role in the Dixon-Yates power contract, viewed by public power advocates as an attempt to undermine the Tennessee Valley Authority; his actions in the J. Robert Oppenheimer security case; and his alleged withholding of information from Congress and the public while chairman of the Atomic Energy Commission.

Of Eisenhower's five appointees to the Supreme Court, three took their seats on the court under recess appointments before they had been confirmed by the Senate. Chief Justice Earl Warren was unanimously confirmed in 1954 despite publication of a 10-point summary of charges against him, including allegations that at one time he was connected with a liquor lobbyist and that he lacked judicial experience. William J. Brennan Jr. was confirmed in 1957 by voice vote, although Sen. Joseph R. McCarthy, R-Wis. (1947-57), had protested Brennan's comparison of congressional investigations of communism to Salem witch hunts. Potter Stewart was confirmed in 1959 by a 70 to 17 vote, with the opposition coming entirely from Southern Democrats who criticized his concurrence in the Supreme Court's 1954 school desegregation decision.

In 1960 the Senate adopted a Democratic-sponsored resolution that the president should not make recess appointments to the Supreme Court except to prevent or end a breakdown in the administration of the court's business, and that a recess appointee should not take his seat on the court until the Senate had "advised and consented" to the nomination. Proponents claimed it was difficult to investigate the qualifications of a person already sitting on the court. Opponents charged that the Democrats hoped for a victory in the 1960 presidential election and feared that a vacancy might occur on the court in time for Eisenhower to give a recess appointment to a Republican.

Efforts of the Democratic-controlled 86th Congress to keep judicial appointments out of a Republican president's hands also led to a four-year delay in enacting legislation to create an unprecedented number of new circuit and district court judgeships. Proposed by Eisenhower in 1957, the bill did not become law until after President John F. Kennedy took office in 1961. The 73 judgeships created by this law, in addition to 42 judgeship vacancies created by death or resignation, gave Kennedy in his first year in office the largest number of judicial appointments ever available to a president in a single year. Kennedy participated far more actively than had Eisenhower in the selection of appointees. None of Kennedy's nominations was rejected by the Senate, and few were contested. His two nominees to the Supreme Court — Byron R. White and Arthur J. Goldberg in 1962 — were confirmed without difficulty.

Racial issues figured in several of Kennedy's nominations. Despite opposition from southerners, Robert C. Weaver was confirmed in 1961 by voice vote as administrator of the Housing and Home Finance Agency. Weaver, a black, had been national chairman of the National Association for the Advancement of Colored People. Similarly, Spottswood W. Robinson III, a black dean of the Howard University Law School, was confirmed as a member of the Civil Rights Commission. But Kennedy's nomination of Thurgood Marshall, a black civil rights lawyer, to the Second Circuit Court of Appeals was held up by the Senate Judiciary Committee for a year. Marshall was confirmed in 1962, 54 to 16, with the dissenting votes again coming from Southern Democrats. (Marshall in 1967 became the first black member of the Supreme Court.)

## Fight Over Fortas

President Lyndon B. Johnson, with one dramatic exception, had very little trouble with the Senate over nominations. His Cabinet appointees were confirmed without difficulty, and his first two Supreme Court appointments encountered only routine opposition.

The nomination of Abe Fortas to be an associate justice of the Supreme Court was confirmed by voice vote in 1965, although three Republicans charged that Fortas had asked Washington newspaper editors to delay release of a story that presidential aide Walter W. Jenkins had been arrested on a morals charge shortly before the 1964 presidential election. In 1967, President Johnson nominated Thurgood Marshall, then solicitor general, to the Supreme Court. Despite criticism from some senators about Marshall's belief in an activist judiciary, his nomination was confirmed 69 to 11. Ten Southern Democrats and one Northern Democrat voted against him.

In 1968 Johnson was unsuccessful in his effort to elevate Fortas to chief justice of the United States as the replacement for Earl Warren, who sought to retire. After a controversial fight centering on Fortas' extra-judicial activities involving the White House, Fortas asked the president to withdraw his name. Terming the action of the recalcitrant Senate "tragic," Johnson consented.

Another diminution of senatorial patronage occurred during the Johnson administration when Congress acceded to a presidential reorganization plan placing the Customs Bureau on a career, civil service basis. Previously, appointments of customs collectors and other officers had been made by the president, generally on senators' recommendations. Johnson's reorganization plan, submitted in 1965, went into effect after a Senate resolution disapproving the plan was rejected, 17 to 64.

## Nixon's Appointments

Early in his first year in office, President Richard M. Nixon cut off another source of congressional patronage. He said he was ending the patronage system of appointing postmasters and rural letter carriers and that henceforth high scores on competitive examinations would be the sole criterion for filling the posts.

**Postal Reform.** The system of choosing postmasters from among the three highest scorers on competitive examinations already was in effect. However, under past practice the preferred candidate of a member of Congress or party official was allowed to repeat the test until he gained a place among the top three. Under the new system, the test would be given only once, and the postmaster general would select from among the three leading scorers. Members of Congress still would be consulted, but their recommendations would not necessarily be followed.

Nixon also sought congressional approval of legislation to end presidential appointment and senatorial confirmation of first-, second- and third-class postmasters. The Senate passed the bill in 1969, but the House did not act. This goal was achieved in the Postal Reorganization Act of 1970, however, which eliminated all political influence in the selection of postal employees, including postmasters.

Nixon's early appointments to major policy posts were confirmed with little difficulty. Yet appointments that never were made generated some controversy. Dr. John H. Knowles was slated to get the job of assistant secretary for health and scientific affairs in the Health, Education and Welfare Department, but the proposed nomination was blocked after strong opposition from Senate Minority Leader Everett Dirksen, R-Ill. (1951-69), and the American Medical Association.

For the first time since 1950, the Senate in 1973 struck down a nomination to a major independent federal regulatory agency. By a vote of 51 to 42, the Senate June 13 rejected the nomination of Robert H. Morris to be a member of the Federal Power Commission. Opponents based their criticism of Morris on his background as an attorney for 15 years with Standard Oil of California, an industry regulated by the commission.

**Supreme Court Struggle.** The previously cited nomination controversies under Nixon paled by comparison with the struggles that arose over the president's efforts to fill a vacancy on the Supreme Court. His first nominee to the court, Warren E. Burger, as the replacement for Chief Justice Earl Warren, was confirmed quickly by a 74 to 3 vote in 1969. Burger, a judge of the Court of Appeals for the District of Columbia Circuit, was little known outside of legal circles at the time of his nomination, but he appeared to meet Nixon's standard of judicial conservatism.

It was with his next court nomination that Nixon ran into opposition in the Democratic-controlled Senate. In May 1969 Justice Fortas resigned under fire for accepting an outside fee from the family foundation of a convicted stock manipulator. To fill the vacancy, Nixon in August nominated Clement F. Haynsworth Jr. of South Carolina, chief judge of the Fourth Circuit Court of Appeals.

Haynsworth was opposed by labor and civil rights leaders. As in the Fortas case, however, the debate centered on judicial ethics. Opposition to the nomination was led by Democratic Sen. Birch Bayh, D-Ind. (1963-81). He and others said they did not question Haynsworth's honesty or integrity but, rather, his sensitivity to the appearance of ethical impropriety and his judgment regarding participation in cases in which his financial interests could be said to be involved, if only indirectly.

During committee hearings, Haynsworth's financial affairs and judicial record were scrutinized more thoroughly and extensively than those of any other court nominee. The Judiciary Committee approved the nomination Oct. 9 by a 10 to 7 vote. The 10-man majority asserted that Haynsworth was "extraordinarily well qualified" for the court post and that the objections raised to his nomination were without substance.[18]

Despite the Judiciary Committee's support, opposition to Haynsworth continued, and the president refused to withdraw the nomination. After a week's debate, the Senate on Nov. 21, 1969, rejected the nomination. Republican defections played a decisive role in the outcome. Seventeen Republicans, including the three top GOP leaders in the Senate, joined 38 Democrats in voting against confirmation. Twenty-six Republicans and 19 Democrats voted to confirm.

In 1970 Nixon tried once more to fill the Supreme Court vacancy. He nominated another southerner, G. Harrold Carswell of Florida, a judge of the Fifth Circuit Court of Appeals. Few senators wanted a repetition of the Haynsworth fight, and opposition to Carswell developed slowly. However, when it came to light that Carswell in a 1948 campaign speech had pledged himself to the principle of white supremacy, resistance to the nomination began to build. Carswell repudiated the views he had expressed more than 20 years earlier, but further charges of a continuing racist attitude were raised against him. Other critics, including many within his own profession, contended that Carswell was a man of mediocre abilities who lacked the judicial competence requisite for service on the high court.

Carswell won the Judiciary Committee's approval Feb. 16 by a vote of 13 to 4. But when the nomination moved to the Senate in March 1970, opponents succeeded in delaying the vote. In this atmosphere, Nixon wrote a letter to a Republican senator supporting Carswell and said:

> What is centrally at issue in this nomination is the constitutional responsibility of the president to appoint members of the court — and whether this responsibility can be frustrated by those who wish to substitute their own philosophy or their own subjective judgment for that of the one person entrusted by the Constitution with the power of appointment. The question arises whether I, as president of the United States, shall be accorded the same right of

> choice in naming Supreme Court Justices which has been freely accorded to my predecessors of both parties. [19]

Nixon said he respected the right of any senator to differ with his selection but that the actual duty of appointing nominees belonged to the president, rather than to the Senate.

The first Senate vote on Carswell came on April 6 on a motion to recommit the nomination to the Judiciary Committee. Opponents had hoped to defeat the appointment indirectly by burying the matter in committee, but the recommittal effort became a preliminary skirmish won by the administration. The recommittal move was rejected, 44-52.

After two days of intensive lobbying, the final vote on Carswell was taken April 8, 1970, and the nomination was rejected 45 to 51. Thirteen Republicans joined 38 Democrats, five of them from the South, in opposition to Carswell. It was the first time since 1894 that a president had suffered consecutive rejections of two nominees for the same court seat.

Nixon then nominated Harry A. Blackmun of Minnesota, a judge of the Eighth Circuit Court of Appeals, to fill the Supreme Court vacancy. Blackmun had a reputation as a moderate and scholarly judge, and both liberals and conservatives praised the president's selection. The Senate Judiciary Committee unanimously reported the nomination, and the Senate confirmed it May 12, 1970, by a 94 to 0 vote.

In 1971 Nixon nominated and the Senate confirmed Lewis F. Powell Jr. and William H. Rehnquist as justices of the Supreme Court. Not since Warren G. Harding had one president, in his first term, had the opportunity to appoint so many members of the court.

The impact of Nixon's appointments to the courts and regulatory agencies was felt for many years after the Watergate crisis forced him to resign the presidency on Aug. 9, 1974. In addition to his Supreme Court appointments, he named 215 judges to the lower courts of the federal judicial system. Nixon appointees (or persons named by previous presidents whom he reappointed) dominated the 12 regulatory agencies. By the day of his resignation, Nixon had nominated every member of eight regulatory agencies: the five members of the Civil Aeronautics Board, the seven members of the Federal Communications Commission, the five members of the Federal Maritime Commission, the five members of the Federal Power Commission, the five members of the National Labor Relations Board, the three members of the National Mediation Board, the five members of the Securities and Exchange Commission and the five members of the Consumer Product Safety Commission.

## Ford's Appointments

President Gerald R. Ford withdrew four controversial nominations in 1974 after he succeeded President Nixon. The first was Andrew E. Gibson, to be administrator of the Federal Energy Administration (FEA). His name was withdrawn after publication of reports disclosing that Gibson had been promised $880,000 in severance pay from his former employer, an oil shipping company with interests related to matters he would have to monitor as head of FEA.

Ford did not resubmit three controversial nominations after the October-November congressional election recess that year. The nominations not resubmitted were those of Peter M. Flanigan to be ambassador to Spain, Stanton B. Anderson to be ambassador to Costa Rica and Daniel T. Kingsley to be a member of the Federal Power Commission. Anderson and Kingsley were holdovers from the Nixon administration.

Ford encountered no opposition strong enough to lead to the rejection of his Cabinet appointees or his one nominee to the Supreme Court. However, three of his appointments to government boards were rejected by Senate committees within two weeks in late 1975. The rejections in two cases were based upon objections to the nominees' social philosophy and in another to a conflict-of-interest charge.

Only one of Ford's Cabinet nominations was highly controversial. Stanley K. Hathaway, who was appointed secretary of the interior, was attacked by liberal senators and environmental groups for what they considered a pro-development and anti-conservation record as governor of Wyoming. Nevertheless, Hathaway was confirmed in June 1975 by a 60 to 36 vote after five days of hearings by the Senate Interior Committee. Shortly thereafter, on July 25, he resigned for health reasons.

Ford's selection for the Supreme Court, Federal Appeals Judge John Paul Stevens, to fill the seat left vacant by William O. Douglas' retirement, was confirmed without difficulty. But the Senate Commerce Committee killed the renomination of Isabel A. Burgess to a second five-year term on the National Transportation Safety Board. Opposition to her developed when a committee staff report showed she had purchased stock in an airline regulated by the board and accepted free transportation, meals and lodging from other regulated companies. She also had unusually high travel expenses and absenteeism.

At about the same time, the Senate Banking, Housing and Urban Affairs Committee rejected the nomination of former Rep. Ben B. Blackburn, R-Ga. (1967-75), to be chairman of the Federal Home Loan Bank Board. Foes of the nomination objected to his attitude toward blacks and public housing tenants and his opposition to civil rights legislation during his years in the House. Also rejected in committee (Senate Commerce) was the nomination of Colorado beer executive Joseph Coors to the board of the Corporation for Public Broadcasting. The question of a possible conflict of interest based upon Coor's membership on the board of Television News Inc. and his conservative political philosophy led to the decision.

The Senate Public Works Committee rejected two Ford nominations to the three-member board of directors of the Tennessee Valley Authority. By an 11 to 1 vote, the committee indefinitely postponed action on the nomination of Mississippi dairyman James F. Hooper III. Hooper's nomination had been protested by Sen. Bill Brock, R-Tenn. (1971-77), as well as labor unions, environmentalists and other officials from the seven states in which the TVA supplied electric power. Critics contended that his record of business failure made him unqualified for the post. Ford subsequently nominated Thomas L. Longshore, an executive with the Alabama Power Company, to the TVA post, but the committee also rejected that choice, by a 6 to 8 vote.

Conflict-of-interest charges led to the withdrawal, at the nominee's request, of Ford's nomination of Albert C. Hall as assistant secretary of the Air Force. Hall also resigned his position as assistant secretary of defense because of a controversy over his relationship with his previous employer, Martin-Marietta Corp.

The Senate Judiciary Committee tabled, and thus killed, the nomination of William B. Poff to a U.S. district court judgeship for the western district of Virginia. Poff fell victim to the tradition of senatorial courtesy; his nomination was opposed by Sen. William Lloyd Scott, R-Va. (1973-79). Scott's preferred candidate was Glen M. Williams, who subsequently got the nomination and was confirmed.

## Carter Nominations

Although none of President Jimmy Carter's nominations was rejected by the full Senate, several were killed in committee, either by vote or inaction. Opposition to some nominees was strong enough to force Carter to withdraw their names. Included in this category was

Theodore C. Sorensen, nominated in 1977 to be director of the Central Intelligence Agency.

From the first disclosure that Sorensen was President Carter's choice as CIA director, support for the former Kennedy aide was less than enthusiastic. Conservatives mobilized an intense campaign against the nomination, stressing Sorensen's inexperience in foreign affairs, his allegedly casual attitude toward the use of classified material and his request in 1948 for draft classification as a non-combatant. He also apparently was hurt in conservative circles by the revelation that he had argued the nation would not be harmed by publishing the "Pentagon Papers," classified government documents about the Vietnam War, in 1971. At Sorensen's request, Carter withdrew his name from consideration. Carter then nominated Adm. Stansfield Turner, who was confirmed.

Paul C. Warnke's nomination as chief U.S. delegate to the strategic arms limitation talks (SALT) with the Soviet Union and as director of the U.S. Arms Control and Disarmament Agency drew fire from defense hard-liners who objected to his so-called "soft" views on arms control. After four days of sometimes acrimonious debate, the Senate confirmed Warnke by a 58 to 40 vote. Senate approval was due in large measure to personal lobbying by President Carter.

Carter's nomination in 1977 of Samuel D. Zagoria to the bipartisan Federal Election Commission (FEC) proved particularly troublesome: it showed how the rules of the appointments game were expected to be played. A former aide to a Republican New Jersey senator, Zagoria had not been recommended for the Republican FEC slot by either the Senate or the House Republican leadership. They immediately charged that Carter had reneged on his pledge to pick Republican nominees from a leadership-approved list and refused to accept it.

Carter resubmitted Zagoria's nomination early in 1978, but Republicans still refused to accept a nominee who had not been recommended by them. Carter eventually withdrew Zagoria's name. (Zagoria subsequently won confirmation for a position on the Consumer Product Safety Commission.) To fill the GOP vacancy on the FEC, Carter nominated Max Friedersdorf, a former White House legislative liaison who had been recommended by GOP congressional leaders. The Senate confirmed Friedersdorf without opposition.

For the first time since 1938 the Senate Judiciary Committee in 1980 rejected a federal judgeship nominee. By a 9 to 6 vote in March, the panel refused to approve Charles B. Winberry, Carter's nominee for a district judgeship in North Carolina's eastern district. The state's Democratic senator, Robert Morgan, D-N.C. (1975-81), had recommended Winberry, a politically well-connected lawyer from Rocky Mount, N.C., who was the senator's longtime friend and former campaign manager. Opponents, led by Democrat Patrick J. Leahy of Vermont and Republican Orrin G. Hatch of Utah, contended Winberry was not qualified because of alleged ethical indiscretions and lack of experience. The two senators pointed to allegations that in handling a 1976 cigarette mail fraud case, Winberry knew his client had accomplices but failed to inform the presiding judge, as legal canons required. Senators also said Winberry violated ethical standards by writing a letter to a federal judge's law clerk during a pending case without notifying the opposing side.

Seventeen months elapsed between the time John W. McGarry was nominated to a Democratic Federal Election Commission vacancy and the date he was formally confirmed. Carter submitted McGarry's nomination in September 1977. Republicans and the public citizen lobby, Common Cause, criticized the former Boston lawyer's close ties to House Speaker Thomas P. O'Neill Jr., D-Mass. The Senate Rules Committee postponed hearings on McGarry. Carter resubmitted the nomination in 1978. The Rules Committee approved it by a 7 to 2 vote, even though committee hearings had exposed discrepancies between the financial disclosure statements McGarry, then special counsel for the House Administration Committee, had filed with the clerk of the House and his income tax returns. Still concerned by his friendship with O'Neill, the GOP leadership threatened a filibuster, thereby preventing Senate consideration of the nomination in the final days of the session.

Carter renewed the controversy in October 1978 by naming McGarry to a recess appointment, a move that brought an angry response from the commisssion member whom McGarry was to replace, former Michigan Democratic Chairman Neil Staebler. Staebler filed an unsuccessful lawsuit against McGarry, contending that Staebler should not be replaced until his successor was confirmed by the full Senate. The Senate ended the controversy in February 1979 by confirming McGarry by voice vote.

Senate Republicans, hoping to keep as many appointments as possible open for incoming President Ronald Reagan, managed to defer action on many presidential nominees at the end of the second session of the 96th Congress. Except for some vacancies that President Carter filled

## Patronage Plum for Carter, Reagan

Legislation establishing 152 new federal court judgeships — the largest number ever created by a single act of Congress — was approved in 1978. The Omnibus Judgeship Act of 1978 added 117 new district court judgeship positions and 35 new positions on the circuit courts of appeals to the existing 398 district court judgeships and 97 circuit court judgeships.

The bill provided President Jimmy Carter with the largest block of judicial patronage in the nation's history. Some Republicans complained that passage of the measure without a merit selection process in place could lead to a wave of partisan political appointments. Although the bill required the president to establish "standards and guidelines for the selection of judges on the basis of merit," the president was not required to follow those selection procedures.

Although Carter nominated more women, blacks and Hispanics to federal district and appellate judgeships than any other president, he, like his predecessors, primarily nominated members of his own political party.

In a memorandum made public by the Reagan administration soon after the inauguration, Attorney General William French Smith pledged to continue the principle of selecting federal judges "on the basis of merit and quality." But, in contrast to the Carter administration, the memo of March 6, 1981, made no mention of trying to secure judgeships for women and minorities.

Smith said the administration intended to respect the traditional role of senators in recommending candidates to the president. In states with no Republican senators, the administration would turn to GOP House members for recommendations, the attorney general said.

The memo also indicated that senators would be encouraged to submit three to five candidates for each vacancy, and that the attorney general could, "when appropriate," propose candidates that a senator could consider in making his recommendations.

In language similar to the Carter administration's, Smith "encouraged" members to use a screening process "to ensure that highly qualified candidates are identified and recommended."

through recess appointments, 113 nominations, including 17 prospective federal judges, were left unconfirmed by the Senate.

An ad hoc GOP committee was set up early in 1980 to screen Carter's nominees. The three-man committee, made up of Sens. Mark O. Hatfield of Oregon, Ted Stevens of Alaska and John Tower of Texas, was responsible for blocking many of Carter's nominations. According to Thomas Decker, minority staff director for the Senate Rules Committee, its goal was to see if there were nominees who, for policy reasons, should be deferred for Reagan's consideration.

By threatening to oppose them on the floor, the GOP senators successfully held up action on the five members of the Legal Services Corporation as well as nominees for the National Labor Relations Board. Also blocked were four appointments to the board of the Public Broadcasting Corporation, an appointment to the Equal Employment Opportunity Commission, a nomination to the U.S. Parole Commission and circuit and district judges. There were no Supreme Court vacancies during Carter's term.

## Reagan Nominations

Although President Reagan's Cabinet and top-level appointments were approved handily during his first year in office, three of his nominations ran into opposition in the Senate. Almost all of the opposition, however, was from the outnumbered Democrats, and eventual confirmation was never in doubt. Reagan's choice of James G. Watt as secretary of the interior was strongly opposed by environmentalists. As a lawyer, Watt had specialized in cases contesting the department's management of federal lands, environmental laws and conservation actions of various environmental groups. The Senate confirmed him 83 to 12, with all the votes against cast by Democrats.

There were two other controversial choices. For secretary of state, Reagan nominated Alexander M. Haig Jr., whose reputation as an efficient public servant was clouded by questions concerning his role in the Nixon White House on issues such as the Vietnam War and Watergate. Nevertheless, the Senate approved him by a 93 to 6 vote. For secretary of labor, Reagan appointed Raymond J. Donovan, whose nomination was delayed by allegations that his New Jersey construction firm had made payoffs to union officials. An FBI investigation failed to substantiate the charges, and Donovan was confirmed.

The most controversial nomination during Reagan's first year was that of Ernest W. Lefever as assistant secretary of state for human rights. At issue was Reagan's plan to downplay Carter's activist human rights policy abroad and return to "quiet diplomacy" in trying to persuade U.S. allies to respect human rights. The nomination generated controversy because the sincerity of Lefever's devotion to human rights was questioned by his opponents and because of connections between a non-profit public policy foundation Lefever headed and the Nestle Corp.

The Senate Foreign Relations Committee voted not to recommend him by a 13 to 4 vote, and Lefever withdrew his nomination hours later. The committee vote against Lefever was thought to be unprecedented in the committee's history. Nominees had been forced to withdraw before a committee vote was held, but committee staffers said Lefever's case was the first in recent memory in which Foreign Relations had formally rejected a nominee.

William M. Bell's nomination to head the Equal Employment Opportunity Commission led to the unusual situation of a black man being opposed by civil rights groups. Opposition to Bell's nomination grew after a hearing in which it was revealed that he had little experience in government, had never managed more than four employees and had run a job placement firm that had not found anyone a job in the preceding year. Support for Bell was so weak that the administration asked the committee to postpone its vote.

In another fight over nominations, tensions arose within the Senate Foreign Relations Committee when the panel defied one of its fellow members, conservative Republican Jesse Helms of North Carolina, who had opposed seven administration nominees for State Department posts. After much controversy, the committee approved three nominations bitterly opposed by Helms: Chester A. Crocker, assistant secretary of state for African affairs; Myer Rashish, under secretary of state for economic affairs; and Robert D. Hormats, assistant secretary of state for economic and business affairs.

After the committee action, Helms dropped his active opposition to Hormats and other nominees not yet cleared by the committee. But he continued to hold up Senate action on Crocker and Rashish until they answered written questions he had submitted, particularly on their attitudes toward détente with the Soviet Union.

Helms made an issue of the nominations by informing Majority Leader Howard H. Baker Jr., R-Tenn., he would place a "hold" on each one under senatorial courtesy. Traditionally, the Senate leadership usually honors such holds, delaying a Senate vote on a nomination in question until the "hold" is removed. However, as majority leader, Baker could have overridden Helms or placed a time limit on the Helms "hold." But there was no pressure on Baker to do so. Baker's reticence to override Helms was not a matter of weakness, but merely reluctance to rescue the nominations without support from Secretary of State Haig or the White House. Said a source close to the Republican leadership: "There's been no pressure from Haig or from the president. If the State Department wants those guys confirmed, Al Haig should call Baker, or Reagan should call Baker. He [Baker] doesn't have any direction from anyone downtown to push for them, so he's not going to buck Helms."

Meanwhile, the nominees went to work in their respective State Department jobs anyway, as paid "consultants." After the nominees had answered Helms' written questions, the senator released the nominations, and they were confirmed easily by 84 to 7 votes.

## Notes

1. For a comprehensive discussion of appointments see Joseph P. Harris, *The Advice and Consent of the Senate: A Study of the Confirmation of Appointments by the United States Senate* (Westport, Conn.: Greenwood Press, 1968).
2. Alexander Hamilton, James Madison, and John Jay, *The Federalist Papers*, with an introduction by Clinton Rossiter (New York: Mentor, 1961), p. 405.
3. Harris, *The Advice and Consent of the Senate*, p. 29.
4. George H. Haynes, *The Senate of the United States: Its History and Practice* (Boston: Houghton-Mifflin, 1938), p. 724.
5. Harris, *The Advice and Consent of the Senate*, p. 39.
6. Haynes, *The Senate*, p. 727.
7. Harris, *The Advice and Consent of the Senate*, p. 45.
8. Ibid., p. 50.
9. Ibid., p. 51.
10. Ibid., p. 75.
11. Ibid., p. 91.
12. Ibid.
13. Ibid., p. 116.
14. Ibid., p. 146.
15. Ibid., p. 148.
16. Ibid.
17. Ibid., p. 176.
18. *Congress and the Nation*, 5 vols., *Congress and the Nation: 1969-1972*, vol. 3 (Washington, D.C.: Congressional Quarterly, 1973), III: 294.
19. *Congressional Quarterly Almanac 1970* (Washington, D.C.: Congressional Quarterly, 1971), p. 160.

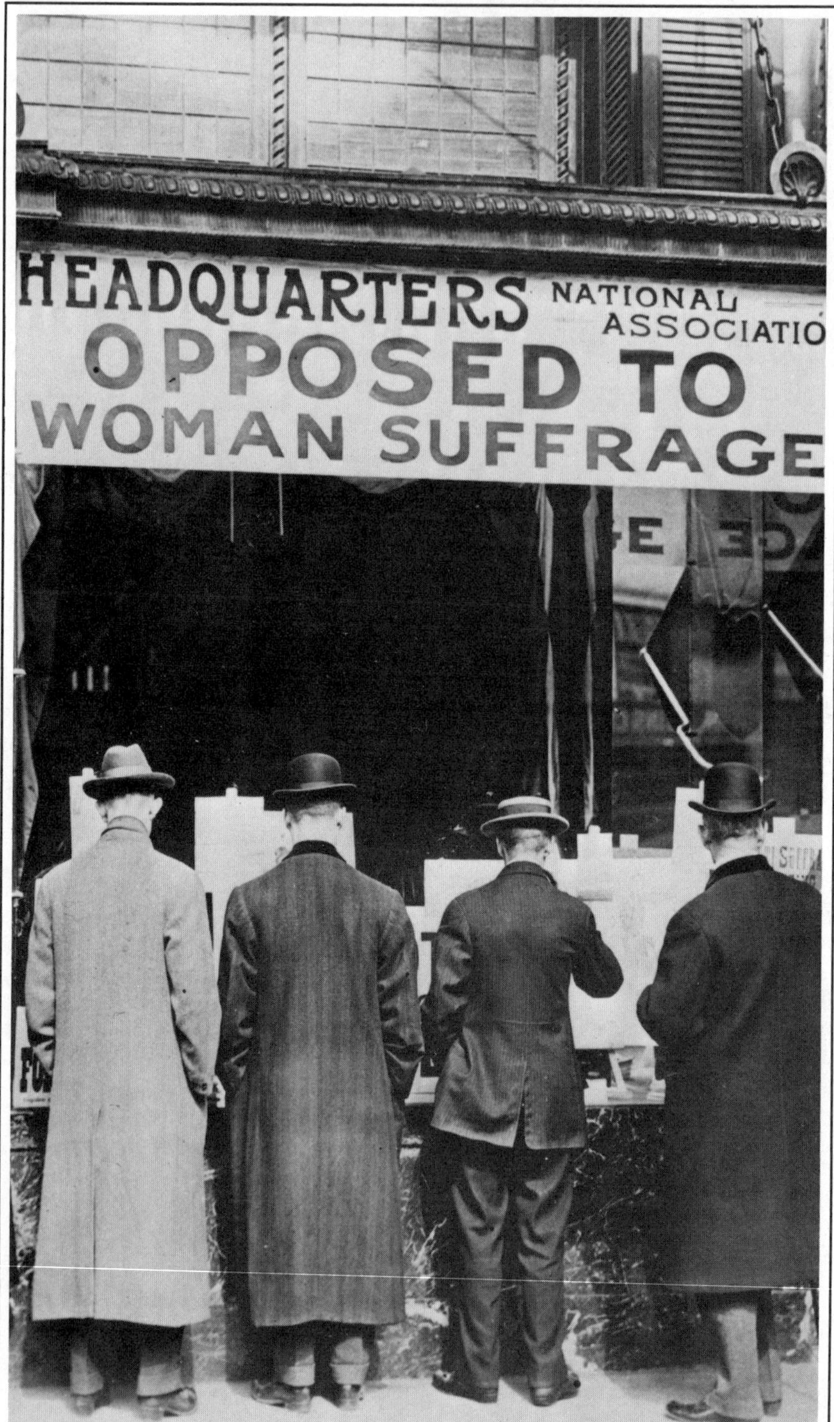
HEADQUARTERS NATIONAL ASSOCIATIO
OPPOSED TO
WOMAN SUFFRAGE

# *Part VII*

# Amending Power

Despite concerted opposition to women's suffrage, the 19th Amendment to the Constitution was ratified Aug. 18, 1920.

*Chapter 20*

# THE CONSTITUTIONAL CONVENTION

The Constitution as we know it would never have been written if it had been easy to amend the Articles of Confederation. But to make any change in that first charter required the consent of both the Continental Congress and every one of the states. In drafting a better amending procedure, delegates to the Philadelphia Convention in 1787 had little guidance. Six of the 13 state constitutions were written as "perpetual charters" without provision for amendment. Only three state legislatures were empowered to propose changes. In four, the amending power was vested solely in popular conventions. The unwritten British constitution could be altered by Parliament. Although British governmental principles did exist to contain and guide governing institutions, there was neither a document to define nor an agency to declare what was "unconstitutional." Acts of Parliament were the supreme law of the land.

America's Founding Fathers were unwilling to rely on so flexible a base. The 13 independent states would not surrender part of their newly won sovereignty without a clear, written understanding of the union they were joining. Furthermore, they would need guarantees that the new national government would not unilaterally alter the terms of the agreement, particularly to reduce the sovereignty retained by the states.

The reliance on separation of powers and checks and balances for protection against arbitrary government required that the arrangement not be subject to easy alteration, lest the separation and the balance be destroyed. Arbitrary acts of Parliament convinced the former colonists that certain rights must be inviolable by government and must be protected by a law that no one government agency could itself change. Consequently, the Constitutional Convention sought to write a document to embody the fundamental law of the land. And yet the delegates assembled in Philadelphia realized that they could not anticipate all the future needs of the new nation. They devised a Constitution that would be easier to amend than the Articles of Confederation but more difficult to revise than the British constitution. They built into the amendment process the principle of checks and balances basic to the Constitution itself and reserved to the states the ultimate power to alter the agreement into which the states had entered.

## Delegates' Amendment Proposals

The plan for a national government presented by Edmund Randolph of Virginia on May 29, 1787, the fourth day of the Convention, said that "provision ought to be made for the amendment of the Articles of Union whensoever it shall seem necessary" and that "the assent of the National Legislature ought not to be required thereto." A plan proposed by Charles Pinckney of South Carolina on the same day provided that amendments "to invest future additional Powers in the United States" should be proposed by conventions and ratified by an unspecified percentage of the state legislatures.[1]

When Randolph's proposal was raised in the Convention on June 5, Pinckney said he doubted its "propriety or necessity." But Elbridge Gerry of Massachusetts favored it: "The novelty and difficulty of the experiment requires periodical revision. The prospect of such a revision would also give intermediate stability to the Government." George Mason of Virginia, supporting the Randolph proposal, said: "The plan now to be formed will certainly be defective, as the Confederation has been found, on trial, to be. Amendments, therefore, will be necessary and it will be better to provide for them in an easy, regular and constitutional way, than to trust to chance and violence. It would be improper to require the consent of the National Legislature, because they may abuse their power and refuse their consent on that very account."

On June 20, Mason said that "the Convention, though comprising so many distinguished characters, could not be expected to make a faultless government," and that he would prefer "trusting to posterity the amendment of its defects, rather than to push the experiment too far."

The Convention agreed, on July 23, that "provisions ought to be made for future amendments . . . whensoever it shall seem necessary" and referred the matter to the Committee of Detail. In its report of Aug. 6, the committee recommended: "On the application of the legislatures of two-thirds of the states in the Union, for an amendment of this Constitution, the Legislature of the United States shall call a convention for that purpose." The Convention adopted this recommendation on

Aug. 30, in spite of the contention of Gouverneur Morris of Pennsylvania that "the Legislature should be left at liberty to call a convention, whenever they please."

On the motion of Gerry, the Convention Sept. 10 voted to reconsider the amendment provision. Gerry argued that because the Constitution was to be paramount to the state constitutions, "two-thirds of the states can bind the Union to innovations that may subvert the state constitutions altogether." Alexander Hamilton of New York also favored reconsideration, although not for Gerry's reason. According to Hamilton, "There was no greater evil in subjecting the people of the United States to the major voice than the people of a particular state." He continued:

> It had been wished by many and was much to have been desired that an easier mode for introducing amendments had been provided by the Articles of Confederation. It was equally desirable now that an easy mode should be established for supplying defects which will probably appear in the new system. The mode proposed was not adequate. The state legislatures will not apply for alterations but with a view to increase their own powers. The national Legislature will be most sensible to the necessity of amendments, and ought also to be empowered, whenever two-thirds of each branch should concur, to call a convention.

This was one of the few suggestions by Hamilton that found a place in the Constitution.

Roger Sherman of Connecticut moved to add this language: "or the Legislature may propose amendments to the several states for their approbation, but no amendments shall be binding until consented to by the several states." James Wilson of Pennsylvania moved to reduce the requirement of unanimous consent of the states to a two-thirds majority. Six states — Connecticut, Georgia, Massachusetts, New Jersey, North Carolina and South Carolina — voted against this motion, and five states — Delaware, Maryland, New Hampshire, Pennsylvania and Virginia — voted in favor. But a later motion by Wilson to permit three-fourths of the states to make an amendment effective was adopted without dissent.

Madison then proposed a substitute for the entire article, which was adopted with only one state dissenting. Madison's plan provided that amendments should be proposed by Congress when two-thirds of both houses considered it necessary or when two-thirds of the state legislatures made application, and would be ratified by three-fourths of the state legislatures or three-fourths of the state conventions, as Congress might designate.

When this provision was reported by the Committee on Style on Sept. 15, Morris and Gerry objected that both methods of amendment depended upon Congress. They urged a provision requiring Congress, when requested by two-thirds of the states, to call a convention to propose amendments. This provision was accepted without dissent.

John Rutledge of South Carolina protested that he "could never agree to give a power by which the articles relating to slaves might be altered by the states not interested in that property and prejudiced against it." The Convention consequently agreed to a provision prohibiting amendment before 1808 of the clauses concerned with slavery (the counting of slaves as three-fifths of the population for assessment of direct taxes and authorization of the slave trade). At the last minute, Sherman said he feared that "three-fourths of the states might be brought to do things fatal to particular states, as abolishing them altogether or depriving them of their equality in the Senate." He sought another proviso prohibiting any amendment by which any state would "be affected in its internal policy, or deprived of its equal suffrage in the Senate." Madison warned against adding special provisos restricting the amending power, lest every state insist on protecting its boundaries or exports. However, "the circulating murmurs of the small states" prompted Morris to propose protecting equal representation in the Senate from amendment, a proviso adopted unanimously. These were the only two limitations on the substance of amendments that could be approved.

## Constitutional Provision

As finally agreed upon, Article V of the Constitution provided that:

> The Congress, whenever two-thirds of both Houses shall deem it necessary, shall propose Amendments to this Constitution, or, on the Application of the Legislatures of two-thirds of the several States, shall call a Convention for proposing Amendments, which, in either Case, shall be valid to all Intents and Purposes, as Part of this Constitution, when ratified by the Legislatures of three-fourths of the several States, or by Conventions in three-fourths thereof, as the one or the other Mode of Ratification may be proposed by the Congress; Provided that no Amendment which may be made prior to the Year One thousand eight hundred and eight shall in any Manner affect the first and fourth Clauses in the Ninth Section of the first Article; and

## State Constitutional Conventions

The Constitution's provision allowing an amendment to be proposed by a convention requested by two-thirds of the states has never been successfully invoked.

A proposed amendment to limit the maximum rate of federal income, death and gift taxes to 25 percent was actively promoted among state legislatures before and after World War II. More than a score of state legislatures petitioned Congress to call a convention that would propose such an amendment, but a number of the states subsequently rescinded the resolutions and the movement then died out.

By 1969, 33 state legislatures, one short of the required number, had petitioned Congress for a convention to propose an amendment that would authorize states to apportion one house of a bicameral legislature on a basis of geography or political subdivisions, as well as population. This movement was prompted by the Supreme Court's 1964 decision in *Reynolds v. Sims*, which held that both houses of a state legislature must be apportioned on a basis of substantial equality of population. Led by Sen. Everett McKinley Dirksen, R-Ill. (House 1933-49; Senate 1951-69), many members of Congress vigorously attacked the court's interpretation of the Constitution on apportionment. Dirksen tried unsuccessfully in 1965 to secure a constitutional amendment. Despairing of congressional initiatives, supporters of the Dirksen proposal placed their hopes for an amendment on a convention. No additional states petitioned for this convention between 1970 and 1982, and the length of time for states to call never has been established. *(See box, pp. 292-293)*

Concerned about the economic impact of the growing federal deficit, 31 state legislatures by early 1982 had called for a constitutional convention to consider an amendment requiring that the federal budget be balanced. The actions of these legislatures spurred the 97th Congress in 1982 to give serious consideration to approving a more qualified amendment which would require a three-fifths vote of both chambers to unbalance any future federal budget. President Reagan, locked in a stalemate with Congress over looming budget deficits, endorsed the balanced budget amendment during a nationwide television address on April 29, 1982.

that no State, without its Consent, shall be deprived of its equal Suffrage in the Senate.

This provision allowed either Congress or the state legislatures to initiate the amending process, either Congress or a general convention to propose amendments, and either state legislatures or state conventions to ratify amendments. Congress determines which method of ratification will be employed, and what form a general convention would take if requested by the state legislatures. The president has no formal authority over constitutional amendments; his veto power does not extend to them. Nor can governors veto approval of amendments by their legislatures.

Notification of state ratification is transmitted by the states to the head of the General Services Administration. (Until 1950, the Secretary of State performed this function.) His action in proclaiming the adoption of an amendment on receipt is purely ministerial; the amendment is brought into effect by the ratifying action of the necessary number of states on the day when the required number of ratifications is reached. (However, the 18th Amendment had an unusual provision postponing its effectiveness for one year after ratification was completed.)

## Ratification of the Constitution

Omission of a Bill of Rights was the principal source of dissatisfaction with the new Constitution in the state ratifying conventions held in 1788. The demand for amendments to establish these rights, and to effect various other changes in the Constitution, made the provisions of Article V an issue in the struggle for ratification. In the Virginia convention, Patrick Henry and George Mason raised vehement objections to the amending process of Article V. "When I come to contemplate this part," Henry said, "I suppose that I am mad or that my countrymen are so." He continued: "The way to amendments is, in my conception, shut. . . . Two-thirds of Congress or of the state legislatures are necessary even to propose amendments. If one-third of these be unworthy men, they may prevent the application for amendments; but what is destructive and mischievous is that three-fourths of the state legislatures, or of the state conventions, must concur in the amendments when proposed. . . . A bare majority in four small states may hinder the adoption of amendments. . . . Is this an easy mode of securing the public liberty? It is, sir, a most fearful situation, when the most contemptible minority could prevent the alteration of the most oppressive government, for it may in many respects prove to be such." [2]

James Madison, on the other hand, praised the amendment process: "The mode [of amendment] preferred by the convention seems to be stamped with every mark of propriety. It guards equally against that extreme facility, which would render the Constitution too mutable; and that extreme difficulty which might perpetuate its discovered faults." [3]

## Change Without Amendment

Since the Constitution was drafted, the United States has been transformed beyond recognition. And yet this document remains the fundamental law of the land. The amending process has contributed to the remarkable durability of the Constitution. But basic changes in the nature of the Constitution are by no means limited to those achieved through the amendment process. Each branch of the national government has contributed to changes in the original arrangement of governmental power created at the Constitutional Convention.

The interpretation of the Constitution by the Supreme Court has been a major source of change. Early acceptance of the principle of judicial review established the high court as the authoritative interpreter of the Constitution. In the 1803 case of *Marbury v. Madison*, Chief Justice John Marshall asserted the Supreme Court's power to declare Acts of Congress unconstitutional: "It is emphatically the province and duty of the judicial department to say what the law is. . . . So if a law be in opposition to the Constitution; if both the law and the Constitution apply to a particular case, so that the Court must either decide that case conformably to the law, disregarding the Constitution; or conformably to the Constitution, disregarding the law, the Court must determine which of these conflicting rules governs the case. This is the very essence of judicial duty." [4]

The Constitution also has been effectively, if not literally, amended by Congress and the executive branch as they have responded to new national needs with actions and programs unthought of by the drafters of the Constitution in 1787. Perhaps the most dramatic expansion of power as a result of executive action has been in the area of war and national emergency. *(See Chapter 9, the section on the Expanded View of President's War Power, pp. 112-117.)*

## Notes

1. Bryant Putney, "Revision of the Constitution," *Editorial Research Reports,* April 21, 1937, pp. 285-303; Charles Warren, *The Making of the Constitution* (Boston: Little, Brown & Co., 1928), pp. 672-684.
2. Putney, "Revision of the Constitution," p. 293.
3. *The Federalist Papers,* with an Introduction by Clinton Rossiter (New York: Mentor, 1961), p. 278.
4. *Marbury v. Madison,* 1 Cr. 137 (1803).

*Chapter 21*

# USE OF AMENDING PROCESS

The Constitution has been amended 26 times. Some of the amendments, such as the 11th and 16th, reversed judicial interpretations of the Constitution; others made only technical adjustments in the mechanisms of government. For example, the 12th Amendment provided for separate balloting for president and vice president in the electoral college, and the 20th Amendment revised the dates for the beginning of presidential terms and the convening of Congress.

Other amendments advanced the course of democracy by extending the vote to blacks (15th) and women (19th), lowering the voting age from 21 to 18 (26th) and providing for the direct election of senators (17th). The economy was profoundly affected by the Income Tax Amendment (16th) and social mores by the Prohibition Amendment (18th, repealed by the 21st). The relationship between the national and state governments was altered by the 14th Amendment, the most fundamental formal revision of the Constitution. Relying largely on the amendment's guarantee of "equal protection of the laws," the Supreme Court has forced fundamental reforms in state policies of racial segregation and legislative malapportionment.

The constitutional amendments have come in clusters. The first 10, the Bill of Rights, were practically a part of the original Constitution. The 11th and 12th, designed to correct the functioning of the Constitution, were soon precipitated by a Supreme Court decision and by a crisis arising from a flaw in the procedure for electing the president and vice president. The Civil War prompted the 13th, 14th and 15th Amendments. Apart from those three, which grew out of the nation's gravest crisis, more than a century elapsed between constitutional amendments. From 1913 to 1920, largely as the culmination of the progressive movement, four amendments of fundamental importance were ratified — giving the United States the income tax, direct election of senators, Prohibition, and women's suffrage. The next two amendments, rescinding Prohibition and altering the dates for the beginning of a new Congress and of the presidential term, went into effect in 1933. There have been five amendments since the Second World War, none of them profoundly revising the system of government.

The best known amendment unsuccessfully pressed during the 1940s and 1950s was the so-called Bricker Amendment that would have limited the treaty-making power and the president's authority to enter into executive agreements. In 1950 the amendment came within one vote of securing the necessary two-thirds Senate majority. *(See Chapter 8, The Treaty Power, pp. 99-100.)*

After being proposed in every Congress since 1923, the Equal Rights Amendment was approved by Congress in 1972 and sent to the states for ratification. As of June 30, 1982, the deadline for approval, 35 states, three short of the required 38, had ratified the proposal. Pending before the Supreme Court in 1982 were cases questioning the validity of several states' rescissions of their approval of the ERA and Congress' right to extend the ERA ratification period, which it had done in 1978.

Constitutional amendments also have been sought by advocates of prayer in public schools, abolition of the electoral college for electing the president, banning abortion, prohibiting the use of busing to desegregate public schools and requiring a balanced federal budget.

## Leadership of Congress

Although the Constitutional Convention envisioned a substantial role for the states in the amendment process, Congress has dominated that procedure. The states never have been successful in calling for a convention to propose an amendment, as they are authorized to do, by petitions to Congress from two-thirds of the legislatures. During the first 100 years of its existence, Congress received only 10 such petitions from state legislatures. But between 1893 and 1974, more than 300 such petitions were received.[1] The states, while approving 26 amendments proposed by Congress, by mid-1982 had refused to ratify only seven.

Undoubtedly, the need to obtain the approval of three-fourths of the states has deterred Congress from proposing amendments. On at least one occasion, the prospect that the states might take the initiative prompted Congress to act. The 17th Amendment, providing for direct election of senators, was continually blocked in the Senate until the state legislatures were on the verge of requiring a convention. Even in this

## Equal Rights Amendment

Forty-nine years after it was first introduced, a constitutional amendment guaranteeing equal rights for men and women was approved by the Senate March 22, 1972, and sent to the states for ratification. A decade later, the amendment died, failing by three states to win ratification. The Senate vote was 84-8 — 22 more than the two-thirds majority required to adopt a proposed constitutional amendment. The House had approved it by a 354-24 roll-call vote on Oct. 12, 1971. The House margin was 102 more than was necessary.

As sent to the states, the amendment stated: "Equality of rights under the law shall not be denied or abridged by the United States or by any state on account of sex," and authorized Congress to enforce the provision by "appropriate legislation." The amendment would take effect two years after ratification.

Less than two hours after the Senate acted on March 22, 1972, Hawaii became the first state to ratify the measure. In the six months following congressional passage, 20 other states followed suit. Nine states endorsed the amendment in 1973, three in 1974, and only one — North Dakota — in 1975. By early 1978, 35 states had ratified the amendment, three short of the requisite number; several state legislatures, however, had either shelved or flatly rejected it. Moreover, some states that had ratified the amendment attempted to rescind their approval. The validity of this action was an issue pending before the Supreme Court in 1982.

In sending the amendment to the states, Congress provided that the legislatures had seven years, until 1979, to approve it. In 1978 Congress extended this ratification period by 39 months, until June 30, 1982. No state ratified after the extension, and the validity of the extension also was being challenged before the court.

Opponents of the Equal Rights Amendment argued that its passage would subject women to the draft, abolish protections women had from dangerous and unpleasant jobs, wipe out women's rights to privacy in public facilities and adversely affect marriage laws, property and divorce rights. Supporters responded that the ERA would not affect constitutional privacy rights, but would end unlawful discrimination, ensuring equal treatment for women and men in such areas as employment, pay, and criminal sentences.

## Length of Time for Ratification

The time elapsing between the submission by Congress of a constitutional amendment and its ratification by the requisite number of states has averaged about one and one-half years. The first 10 amendments were proposed and ratified as a group, the process taking two years and 81 days. The longest time of all — three years and 340 days — was needed to complete ratification of the 22nd Amendment. In contrast the 26th Amendment was ratified in 100 days, and eight other amendments were ratified in less than one year. The detailed record follows:

| Amendment | Passed Congress | Ratified | Time Elapsed Years | Time Elapsed Days |
|---|---|---|---|---|
| 1-10 (Bill of Rights) | Sept. 25, 1789 | Dec. 15, 1791 | 2 | 81 |
| 11 (Suits against states) | Mar. 4, 1794 | Feb. 7, 1795 | | 340 |
| 12 (Presidential electors) | Dec. 9, 1803 | June 15, 1804 | | 189 |
| 13 (Abolition of slavery) | Jan. 31, 1865 | Dec. 6, 1865 | | 309 |
| 14 (Civil rights: due process) | June 13, 1866 | July 9, 1868 | 2* | 26 |
| 15 (Black suffrage) | Feb. 26, 1869 | Feb. 3, 1870 | | 342 |
| 16 (Income tax) | July 12, 1909 | Feb. 3, 1913 | 3* | 206 |
| 17 (Direct election of senators) | May 13, 1912 | April 8, 1913 | | 330 |
| 18 (Prohibition) | Dec. 18, 1917 | Jan. 16, 1919 | 1 | 29 |
| 19 (Women's suffrage) | June 4, 1919 | Aug. 18, 1920 | 1* | 75 |
| 20 ("Lame duck") | Mar. 2, 1932 | Jan. 23, 1933 | | 327 |
| 21 (Prohibition repeal) | Feb. 20, 1933 | Dec. 5, 1933 | | 288 |
| 22 (Presidential tenure) | Mar. 24, 1947 | Feb. 27, 1951 | 3* | 340 |
| 23 (D.C. vote) | June 16, 1960 | Mar. 29, 1961 | | 286 |
| 24 (Poll tax) | Sept. 14, 1962 | Jan. 23, 1964 | 1 | 131 |
| 25 (Presidential disability) | July 6, 1965 | Feb. 10, 1967 | 1 | 219 |
| 26 (18-year-old vote) | Mar. 23, 1971 | July 1, 1971 | | 100 |

* Includes a leap year.

Source: Library of Congress, Congressional Research Service, *The Constitution of the United States of America: Analysis and Interpretation* (Washington D.C.: U.S. Government Printing Office, 1973).

case, however, Congress had for years provided the principal public arena for debate of the issue.

Congress has the power to determine by which of the two procedures the states shall ratify a proposed amendment. In every case except one, approval by the state legislatures has been prescribed. Only for the 21st Amendment (the repeal of Prohibition), did Congress call for ratification by state conventions. The exception occurred for three principal reasons: (1) a desire for speedy ratification; (2) the contention of repeal advocates that state legislatures ratifying the 18th Amendment had yielded to pressure from Prohibition forces, had overrepresented rural areas favoring Prohibition and had not represented the views of the majority of the people; and (3) the desire to remove permanently from the political arena a question that had divided states, regions and political parties. The 21st Amendment, submitted to the states in February 1933, was ratified by conventions in 36 of the then total of 48 states by December of that year.

The Supreme Court has spoken infrequently about the amending power of Congress. Most of the court's decisions came in the wake of the controversial Prohibition amendments. The court held that liquor was a proper subject for a constitutional amendment, that two-thirds of the members of the House or Senate present must approve a proposed amendment (not two-thirds of the entire membership), and that Congress has the power to set a time limit for ratification.[2]

## Unresolved Questions

Of the two methods of proposing amendments — a convention called by Congress at the request of the legislatures of two-thirds of the states, or by a two-thirds majority of each house of Congress — only the latter has been employed.

In the 1960s, however, the Council of State Governments mounted a campaign to secure a constitutional amendment that would allow one house of a state legislature to be apportioned on some basis other than population. In the early 1980s a similar drive for a convention to approve a balanced budget amendment highlighted the many uncertainties about use of the convention formula, questions that have not yet been resolved. Unresolved questions also exist about ratification of amendments. Constitutional authorities have disagreed about whether Congress or the state legislatures should determine the procedures for ratification by state conventions.

## Constitutional Convention Procedures: . . .

Because Congress never has been required through state legislative petitions to call a convention to amend the Constitution, important questions on the procedures that would be followed never have been answered.

The close call in the 1960s, when 33 states petitioned Congress for a convention to propose a reapportionment amendment, prompted constitutional law experts to urge preparation of procedural guidelines to avoid chaos should a convention be held. As a result, Sen. Sam J. Ervin Jr., D-N.C. (1954-74), chairman of the Senate Judiciary Subcommittee on Separation of Powers, introduced a bill to establish constitutional convention procedures. The bill passed the Senate in 1971 and 1973 but died when the House did not act. In 1981, the Senate Judiciary Subcommittee on the Constitution considered a similar measure after 30 states called for a convention to consider a balanced budget amendment. *(See box, p. 283)*

Among the questions about such a convention are:

**Valid Convention Call.** What constitutes a valid call of two-thirds of the legislatures? Must the resolutions to Congress be identical in all details or simply relate to one general subject?

**Length of Time to Call.** In what time span must the required two-thirds of the states submit their resolutions? The Constitution is silent on this point. In resolutions submitting proposed amendments to the states throughout most of the 20th century, Congress has stipulated a seven-year maximum period for ratification.

**Rescinding a Call.** Can a state rescind a previous call for a convention? The Constitution says nothing about the legality of a rescinding action. But in 1868, when New Jersey and Ohio attempted to withdraw their ratifications of the 14th Amendment, Congress refused to accept their withdrawals. The issue was before the Supreme Court in 1982.

**Forcing Congress to Act.** If the required two-thirds of the legislatures issue a convention call, is Congress obligated to call the convention? By the letter of the Constitution, it would appear to have no choice. But Congress might find pretexts for invalidating individual state petitions and the Supreme Court might consider Congress the final judge of those petitions.

## ... Congress Delves into the Unknown

**Procedures for a Call.** How would Congress act to call a convention? If there were no dispute, the Judiciary committees of the two houses probably would report appropriate resolutions which the two houses would approve. But what would happen if one of the committees refused to report such a resolution? The resolution might be considered a privileged proposition that could be referred to committee or considered directly without committee action or recommendation. But what if opponents of the resolution in the Senate blocked action with a filibuster?

**Restricting a Convention.** How should a congressional resolution calling a convention be worded? The fear of a "runaway convention" has been a major concern about this procedure for amending the Constitution. Should, or could, Congress limit the convention to proposing an amendment on the subject named in the petitions from the states?

The performance of state constitutional conventions raises serious doubts that a national convention to amend the Constitution could be bound in advance. Moreover, the convention that wrote the U.S. Constitution ignored its original mandate merely to amend the Articles of Confederation. But if amendments were submitted on subjects not specified in the summoning of a convention, they might be subjected to political attack on the ground that the convention had not been authorized, or its members elected, to act in other areas.

**Apportionment of a Convention.** What would be the apportionment of a constitutional convention? The Constitution is silent on this point. The Constitutional Convention of 1787 had different numbers of delegates from different states but accorded only one vote to each state. Congress presumably could require that a new constitutional convention be apportioned on the same basis as the existing U.S. House, or the House and Senate combined.

**Delegate Selection.** How would delegates be chosen? That question could be left to the discretion of the state legislatures, or Congress might attempt to lay down ground rules requiring the election either by congressional districts or by statewide balloting, or by a combination of the two.

Bills have been introduced in Congress to spell out procedures, but none has passed. State legislatures have been divided on this question. At least 21 legislatures provided by statute that state officials were to follow the procedures specified in a federal law if Congress should enact one. Sixteen legislatures, assuming that the procedural question was within their jurisdiction, passed laws applicable not merely to the convention summoned for the 21st Amendment, but for all future conventions called to ratify amendments to the U.S. Constitution. One state, New Mexico, claimed exclusive authority on the matter and directed its officials to resist any attempt at congressional encroachment on that authority. *(See box, Constitutional Convention Procedures, pp. 292-293)*

Another uncertainty concerns the definition of a "reasonable" time period for ratification, a question that the Supreme Court has left to Congress. The 18th Amendment (Prohibition) was the first to specify a period of years, seven, to complete ratification. In 1921 the court held that Congress had the power to fix a definite ratification period "within reasonable limits." In 1939 the court held that the definition of a "reasonable" period was essentially political and should be answered by Congress, rather than the court.[3]

The Child Labor Amendment proposed in 1924, with no time limit, might technically still be open for ratification. As of mid-1982, 28 states had ratified the amendment. Even if 10 more states were to ratify (the three-fourths requirement applies to the number of states presently in the Union, not the number at the time the amendment was proposed), it seems unlikely that Congress would consider this a "reasonable" time period. In March 1976 Kentucky ratified the 13th, 14th and 15th Amendments — more than 100 years after they became part of the Constitution. *(See box, Length of Time for Ratification, p. 290)*

Two major questions concerning the amending power were before the U.S. Supreme Court in mid-1982 in a pair of cases concerning the proposed Equal Rights Amendment. The first question in the cases *National Organization of Women v. Idaho* and *Carmen v. Idaho* concerned the power of Congress to extend the period for ratification of an amendment. This question arose after Congress in 1978 extended the ratification period for the ERA for 30 months beyond the original seven years. The second question concerned the power of states that have once ratified an amendment to rescind that approval. Five states that had ratified the ERA had subsequently moved to nullify that action. The court has recognized the power of a state that initially refuses to ratify subsequently to ratify, but it has not addressed the opposite question.

## The Amending Process: An Appraisal

As James MacGregor Burns, J. W. Peltason and Thomas E. Cronin noted in their book, *Government by the People,* "The entire amending procedure has been criticized because neither a majority of the voters at large nor even a majority of the voters in a majority of the states can formally alter the Constitution. But when a majority of the people are serious in their desire to bring about changes in our constitutional system, their wishes are usually implemented either by formal amendment or by the more subtle methods of interpretation and adaptation." [4]

C. Herman Pritchett commented in *The American Constitution*, "The adoption of four, possibly five amendments since 1961 is evidence that the amending machinery is not hard to operate if there is a genuine consensus on the need, and may even lead to some concern that amendments are too easy to achieve. . . . It is of prime importance that the Constitution retain its brevity and be limited to basic structural arrangements and the protection of individual liberties. It would be disastrous if it became, through the amending power, a vehicle by which pressure groups and crackpots could impose their nostrums on the nation." [5]

## Notes

1. James MacGregor Burns and J. W. Peltason, with Thomas E. Cronin, *Government by the People,* 9th ed. (New York: Prentice-Hall, 1975), p. 64.
2. *National Prohibition Cases,* 253 U.S. 350 (1920), *Dillon v. Gloss,* 256 U.S. 368 (1921).
3. *Dillon v. Gloss,* 256 U.S. 368 (1921), *Coleman v. Miller,* 307 U.S. 433 (1939).
4. Burns, et al., *Government by the People,* p. 67.
5. C. Herman Pritchett, *The American Constitution,* 3rd ed. (New York: McGraw-Hill Book Co., 1977), p. 29.

*Part VIII*

# Electing the President

Always the captivating candidate, Theodore Roosevelt displays the energy and zeal that caught the imaginations of the American people in the early 20th century.

## *Chapter 22*

# HISTORICAL BACKGROUND

Under the Constitution, Congress has two key roles in the election of the president and vice president of the United States. First, it is directed to receive and, in joint session, count the electoral votes after they have been certified by the states. Second, if no candidate has a majority of the electoral votes, it is the responsibility of the House of Representatives to choose the president and the Senate to choose the vice president.

Although many of the Constitution's framers apparently thought that most elections would be decided by Congress, the House actually has chosen a president only twice, in 1801 and 1825. But in the course of the nation's history a number of campaigns have been designed deliberately to throw elections into the House, where each state has one vote, and a majority of states is needed to elect the president. Apprehension over such an outcome has nurtured electoral reform efforts over the years.

In addition to its role in electing the president, Congress bears responsibility in the related areas of presidential succession and disability. The 20th Amendment empowers Congress to decide what to do if the president-elect and the vice president-elect both fail to qualify by the date prescribed for commencement of their terms; it also gives Congress authority to settle problems arising from the death of candidates in cases where the election devolves upon Congress. Under the 25th Amendment, Congress has ultimate responsibility for resolving disputes over presidential disability. It also has authority to confirm presidential nominations to fill vacancies in the vice presidency.

The president's power to appoint a new vice president under the terms of the 25th Amendment has been used twice since the amendment was ratified on Feb. 10, 1967. It was used for the first time in 1973 when Vice President Spiro T. Agnew resigned and President Richard M. Nixon nominated Gerald R. Ford to be vice president. It was used again in 1974 when Ford succeeded to the presidency upon Nixon's resignation and chose former New York Gov. Nelson A. Rockefeller as vice president.

## Constitutional Background

The method of selecting a president was the subject of long debate at the Constitutional Convention of 1787. Several plans were proposed and rejected before a compromise solution, which became Article II, Section 1, Clause 2 of the Constitution, was adopted.[1]

The convention considered several methods for selecting the chief executive: by direct popular election, by Congress, by state legislatures or by intermediate electors. Direct election was opposed by those who felt that the people lacked sufficient knowledge of the character and qualifications of potential candidates to make an intelligent choice. Many delegates also feared the citizens of the various states would be unlikely to agree on a single person, usually casting their votes for favorite-son candidates well known to them. Southerners opposed direct election for another reason: the suffrage was more widespread in the North than in the South, where the slaves did not vote.

The convention also considered giving Congress the power to pick the president. However, this plan also was rejected, largely out of concern that it would compromise executive independence. Similarly, a plan to let state legislatures choose the president was turned down because it was feared the president might feel so indebted to the states as to allow them to encroach on federal authority.

## Electoral Vote System

Unable to agree on a plan for selecting the president, the convention in August 1787 appointed a "Committee of Eleven" to propose a solution. The committee on Sept. 4 suggested a compromise under which each state would appoint presidential electors (known as the electoral college), equal to the total number of its representatives and senators. The electors, chosen in a manner set forth by each state legislature, would meet in their own states and cast votes for two persons. The votes would be counted in Congress, with the candidate receiving a majority elected president and the one receiving the second highest number becoming vice president.

No distinction was made between ballots for president and vice president. The subsequent development of national political parties and the nomination of tickets for president and vice president caused confusion in the electoral system. All the electors of one party tended to vote for the two nominees of their own party. But with no distinction between the presidential and vice presidential nominees, the danger arose of a tie vote between the two. This actually happened in 1800, leading to a change in the original electoral system by adoption of the 12th Amendment.

The committee's compromise plan was a great concession to the less populous states, since they were assured two extra votes (corresponding to their senators) regardless of how small their populations might be. The plan also left important powers with the states by giving complete discretion to state legislatures to determine the method of choosing electors.

Only one provision of the committee's plan aroused serious opposition — that giving the Senate the right to decide elections in which no candidate received a majority of electoral votes. Some delegates maintained that the Senate, which already had been given treaty ratification powers and the responsibility to "advise and consent" to all important executive appointments, might become too powerful. Therefore, a counterproposal was made, and accepted, allowing the House to decide the winner in instances when the electors failed to give a majority of their votes to a single candidate. The interests of the small states were preserved by giving each delegation only one vote in the House on the roll calls to elect the president.

The system adopted by the Constitutional Convention was a compromise born out of the necessity of overcoming major state and regional differences: diverse state voting requirements, the slavery issue, big- versus small-state rivalries and the complexities of the balance of power among different branches of the government. It also was apparently as close to direct popular election of the president as the men who wrote the Constitution thought possible and appropriate at the time. Some scholars have suggested that the electoral college, as it came to be called, was a "jerry-rigged improvisation" that really left to future generations the work of finding the best form of presidential selection.[2]

## Changes in Electoral System

Only once since ratification has the Constitution been amended substantially to alter the method of electing the president.

In the 1800 presidential election, the Democratic-Republican (anti-Federalist) electors inadvertently caused a tie in the electoral college by casting equal numbers of votes for Thomas Jefferson, whom they wished to be elected president, and Aaron Burr, whom they wished to elect vice president. The election was thrown into the House of Representatives and 36 ballots were required before Jefferson finally was elected president. The 12th Amendment, ratified four years later, sought to prevent a recurrence of this incident by providing that the electors would vote separately for president and vice president.[3]

Other changes in the system have evolved over the years.[4] The authors of the Constitution intended that each state choose its most distinguished citizens as electors and that they should deliberate and vote as individuals in electing the president. But as strong political parties began to appear, the electors came to be chosen merely as representatives of the parties. Independent voting by electors almost disappeared.

On a few occasions, however, an elector has broken ranks to vote for a candidate other than his party's. In none of these cases did the switch alter the election result. In 1796 a Pennsylvania Federalist elector voted for Democratic-Republican Thomas Jefferson instead of Federalist John Adams. And in 1820 the New Hampshire Democratic-Republican elector voted for John Quincy Adams instead of the party nominee, James Monroe.

There were no further defections until 1948, when Preston Parks, a Truman elector in Tennessee, voted for Gov. Strom Thurmond of South Carolina, the State Rights Democratic Party (Dixiecrat) presidential nominee. Since then, there have been the following switched votes:

— In 1956, when W. F. Turner, an Adlai E. Stevenson II elector in Alabama, voted for a local judge, Walter E. Jones.

— In 1960, when Henry D. Irwin, a Nixon elector in Oklahoma, voted for Sen. Harry F. Byrd, D-Va.

— In 1968, when Dr. Lloyd W. Bailey, a Nixon elector in North Carolina, voted for George C. Wallace, the American Independent Party candidate.

— In 1972, when Roger L. McBride, a Nixon elector in Virginia, voted for John Hospers, the Libertarian Party candidate.

— In 1976, when Mike Padden, a Ford elector, voted instead for former California Governor Ronald Reagan.

As democratic sentiment increased early in the 19th century, there arose a demand that electors be chosen by direct popular vote of the people instead of by the state legislatures. By 1804 the majority of state legislatures had adopted popular-vote provisions.

Initially, most "popular-election" states provided that electors should be chosen from districts similar to congressional districts, with the electoral vote of a state split if the various districts differed in their political sentiment. This "district plan" of choosing electors was supported by the leading statesmen of both parties, including Thomas Jefferson, Alexander Hamilton, James Madison, John Quincy Adams, Andrew Jackson and Daniel Webster.[5]

The district plan, however, tended to dilute the power of political bosses and the dominant majorities in state legislatures, who found themselves unable to "deliver" their states for one candidate or another. These groups brought pressure to change the electoral procedure, and the states moved toward a winner-take-all popular ballot. Under this system, all of a state's electoral votes go to the party that wins a plurality of popular votes statewide.

By 1804 six of the 11 "popular-election" states cast their electoral votes under the statewide popular ballot; by 1824, 12 out of 18. By 1836 all states except South Carolina had adopted the system of choosing electors statewide by popular vote. After the Civil War, South Carolina dropped the practice of having the state legislature select the electors and instead adopted a system of statewide, popular vote selection.

However, since no mention of a statewide, popular election system was ever written into the U.S. Constitution, state legislatures retain the power to specify any method of choosing presidential electors and determine how the electoral votes are divided. In 1969, for example, Maine adopted a partial district system, allotting one electoral vote to each of its two congressional districts (its other two electoral votes go to the statewide winner).

## Jefferson-Burr Deadlock

The election of 1800 was the first in which the contingent election procedures of the Constitution were put to the test and the president was elected by the House of Representatives.[6] The Federalists, a declining but still potent political force, nominated John Adams for a second term and chose Charles Cotesworth Pinckney as his running mate. A Democratic-Republican congressional caucus chose Vice President Thomas Jefferson for president and Aaron Burr, who had been instrumental in winning the New York legislature for the Jeffersonians earlier in 1800, for vice president.

The bitterly fought campaign was marked by efforts in several states to change for partisan advantage the method of selecting electors. In New York, where electors previously had been chosen by the legislature, Hamilton proposed that Governor John Jay call the lame-duck Federalist legislature into special session to adopt a proposal for popular election of electors under a district system, thus denying the incoming Democratic-Republicans an opportunity to appoint electors. Jay declined, and in the end the new legislature cast all 12 New York electoral votes for Jefferson and Burr.

The Federalists were more successful in Pennsylvania, another critical state. The state senate, where holdover members maintained Federalist control, refused to renew legislation providing for selection of electors by statewide popular vote. The state's house of representatives, in Democratic-Republican hands, was forced to accept a compromise that gave the Federalists seven electors and the Democratic-Republicans eight.

The electors met in each state on Dec. 4, and the results gradually became known throughout the country: Jefferson and Burr, 73 electoral votes each; Adams, 65; Pinckney, 64; John Jay, 1. The Federalists had lost, but because the Republicans had neglected to withhold one electoral vote from Burr, their presidential and vice presidential candidates were tied and the election was thrown into the House.

The lame-duck Congress, with a strong Federalist majority, was still in office for the electoral count, and the possibilities for intrigue were only too apparent. After toying with and rejecting a proposal to block any election until March 4 when Adams' term expired, the Federalists decided to throw their support to Burr and thus elect a cynical and pliant politician over a man they considered a dangerous radical. Alexander Hamilton opposed this move: "I trust the Federalists will not finally be so mad as to vote for Burr," he wrote. "I speak with intimate and accurate knowledge of his character. His elevation can only promote the purposes of the desperate and the profligate. If there be a man in the world I ought to hate, it is Jefferson. With Burr I have always been personally well. But the public good must be paramount to every private consideration." [7]

On Feb. 11, 1801, Congress met in joint session — with Jefferson in the chair — to count the electoral vote. This ritual ended, the House retired to its own chamber to elect a president. When the House met it became apparent that the advice of Hamilton had been rejected. A majority of Federalists in the House insisted on backing Burr over Jefferson, the man they despised more. Indeed, if Burr had given clear assurances he would run the country as a Federalist he might well have been elected. But Burr was unwilling to make those assurances, and, as one chronicler put it, "no one knows whether it was honor or a wretched indecision which gagged Burr's lips." [8]

In all, there were 106 members of the House at the time, consisting of 58 Federalists and 48 Democratic-Republicans. If the ballots had been cast individually, Burr would have been elected, but the Constitution provided that each state cast one vote, with a majority necessary for election. On the first ballot, Jefferson received the votes of eight states, one short of a majority of the 16 states then in the Union. Six states backed Burr, and the representatives of Vermont and Maryland were equally divided, so they lost their votes.

Thirty-six ballots were taken before the House came to a decision. Predictably, there were men who sought to exploit the situation for personal gain. Jefferson wrote on Feb. 15, "Many attempts have been made to obtain terms and promises from me. I have declared to them unequivocally that I would not receive the Government on capitulation; that I would not go in with my hands tied." [9]

The impasse finally was broken when Vermont and Maryland switched to support Jefferson. Delaware and South Carolina also withdrew their support from Burr by casting blank ballots. The final vote: 10 states for Jefferson, 4 (all from New England) for Burr. Thus Jefferson became president and Burr automatically became vice president.

Federalist James A. Bayard of Delaware, who had played a key role in breaking the deadlock, wrote to Hamilton: "The means existed of electing Burr, but this required his cooperation. By deceiving one man (a great blockhead) and tempting two (not incorruptible), he might have secured a majority of the states. He will never have another chance of being president of the United States; and the little use he has made of the one which has occurred gives me but an humble opinion of the talents of an unprincipled man." [10]

The Jefferson-Burr contest clearly illustrated the dangers of the double-balloting system established by the original Constitution, and pressure began to build for an amendment requiring separate votes for president and vice president. Congress approved the 12th Amendment in December 1803, and the states — acting with unexpected speed — ratified it in time for the 1804 election.

**John Quincy Adams' Election**

The only other time a president was elected by the House occurred in 1825. There were many contenders for the presidency in the 1824 election, but four predominated: John Quincy Adams, Henry Clay, William H. Crawford and Andrew Jackson. Crawford, secretary of the Treasury under Monroe, was the early front-runner, but his candidacy faltered after he suffered a paralytic stroke in 1823.[11]

When the electoral votes were counted, Jackson had 99, Adams 84, Crawford 41 and Clay 37. Jackson also led in the popular voting in the 18 states choosing their electors by popular vote, although the significance of the popular vote was open to challenge. Under the 12th Amendment, the names of the three top contenders — Jackson, Adams and the ailing Crawford — were placed before the House. Clay's support was vital to the two front-runners.

From the start, Clay apparently intended to support Adams as the lesser of two evils. But before the House voted, a great scandal erupted. A Philadelphia newspaper printed an anonymous letter alleging that Clay had agreed to support Adams in return for being made secretary of state. The letter alleged also that Clay would have been willing to make the same deal with Jackson. Clay immediately denied the charge and pronounced the writer of the letter "a base and infamous calumniator, a dastard and a liar." [12]

When the House met to vote, Adams was supported by the six New England states and New York and, in large part through Clay's backing, by Maryland, Ohio, Kentucky, Illinois, Missouri and Louisiana. Thus a majority of 13 delegations voted for him — the bare minimum he needed for election since there were then 24 states in the Union. The election was accomplished on the first ballot, but Adams took office under a cloud from which his administration never recovered.

Jackson had believed the charges and found his suspicions vindicated when Adams, after the election, did appoint Clay secretary of state. "Was there ever witnessed such a bare-faced corruption in any country before?" he wrote to a friend.[13] Jackson's successful 1828 campaign made much of his contention that the House of Representatives had thwarted the will of the people by denying him the presidency in 1825 even though he had been the leader in popular and electoral votes.

## Elections Decided by Senate, House

On only one occasion has the Senate had to decide a vice presidential contest. That was in 1837, when Martin Van Buren was elected president with 170 out of 294 electoral votes, while his vice presidential running mate, Richard M. Johnson, received only 147 electoral votes — one less than a majority. The discrepancy occurred because Van Buren electors from Virginia boycotted Johnson. (Johnson's nomination had been opposed by Southern Democrats because of his longstanding involvement with a mulatto woman.)[14] The Senate elected Johnson, 33 to 16, over Francis Granger of New York, the runner-up in the electoral vote for vice president.

Although only two presidential elections actually have been decided by the House, a number of others — including those of 1836, 1856, 1860, 1892, 1948, 1960 and 1968 — could have been thrown into the House by only a small shift in the popular vote.

The threat of House election was clearly present in 1968, when George C. Wallace of Alabama ran as a third-party candidate.[15] For the record, Wallace frequently asserted that he could win an outright majority in the electoral college by the addition of key Midwestern and Mountain states to his hoped-for base in the Deep South and border states. In reality, the Wallace campaign had a narrower goal: to win the balance of power in the electoral college voting, thus depriving either majority party of the clear electoral majority required for election. Wallace made it clear that in that situation he would expect one of the major party candidates to make concessions to the Wallace forces in return for enough votes from Wallace electors to win the election.

Wallace made it known that he expected the election to be settled in the electoral college — through switches to other candidates of some of the electoral votes won by Wallace — and not in the House of Representatives. At the end of the campaign it was disclosed that Wallace had obtained written affidavits from all of his electors in which they promised to vote for Wallace "or whomsoever he may direct" in the electoral college.

In response to the Wallace challenge, both major party candidates, Republican Richard M. Nixon and Democrat Hubert H. Humphrey, maintained that they would refuse to bargain with Wallace for his electoral votes. Nixon asserted that the House, if the decision rested there, should elect the popular-vote winner. Humphrey said the representatives should select "the President they believe would be best for the country." Bipartisan efforts to obtain advance agreements from House candidates to vote for the national popular-vote winner if the election should go to the House failed. Neither Nixon nor Humphrey responded to suggestions that they pledge before the election to swing enough electoral votes to the popular-vote winner to assure his election without help from Wallace.

In the end, Wallace received only 13.5 percent of the popular vote and 46 electoral votes (including the vote of one Republican defector), all from southern states. He failed to win the balance of power in the electoral college that he had hoped to use to wring policy concessions from one of the major party candidates. If Wallace had won a few border states, or if a few thousand more Democratic votes had been cast in northern states barely carried by Nixon, thus reducing Nixon's electoral vote below 270, Wallace would have been in a position to bargain off his electoral votes or to throw the election into the House for final settlement. The near-success of the Wallace strategy briefly provided new impetus in Congress for reform of the electoral college system.

## Counting the Electoral Vote

The dates for the casting of popular votes, for the meeting of the electors to cast ballots in the various states and for the official counting of the electoral votes before a joint session of Congress have been modified several times since 1788.[16] The Continental Congress established the procedure for the first election under the Constitution. On Sept. 13, 1788, Congress directed that each state choose its electors on the first Wednesday in January 1789. It further directed that these electors were to cast their ballots on the first Wednesday in February 1789.

In 1792 the Second Congress passed legislation setting up a permanent timetable for choosing electors. Allowing some flexibility in dates, the law directed that states choose their electors within the 34 days preceding the first Wednesday in December of each presidential election year. Then the electors would meet in their various states and cast their ballots on the first Wednesday in December. On the second Wednesday of the following February, the votes were to be opened and counted before a joint session of Congress. Provision also was made for a special presidential election in case of the removal, death, resignation or disability of both the president and vice president.

Under this system, states chose presidential electors at various times. For instance, in 1840 the popular balloting for electors in Pennsylvania and Ohio began on Oct. 30 and ended in North Carolina on Nov. 12. South Carolina, the only state still choosing presidential electors through the state legislature, appointed its electors on Nov. 26.

Congress modified the system in 1845, providing that each state choose its electors on the same day — the Tuesday following the first Monday in November — a provision that still remains in force. The next change occurred in 1887, when Congress provided that electors were to meet and cast their ballots on the second Monday in January instead of the first Wednesday in December. Congress also dropped the provision for a special presidential election.

## Current Practice

In 1934 Congress again revised the law. The new arrangements, still in force in 1982, directed the electors to meet on the first Monday after the second Wednesday in December. The ballots are opened and counted before Congress on Jan. 6 (the next day if Jan. 6 falls on a Sunday). The Constitution provides that "The President of the Senate shall, in the presence of the Senate and House of Representatives, open all the certificates, and the votes shall then be counted. . . ."

However, the document offers no guidance on handling disputed ballots. Before counting the electoral votes in 1865, Congress adopted the 22nd Joint Rule, which provided that electoral votes that had been challenged in the joint session could not be counted except by concurrent votes of both the Senate and House. The rule was pushed by congressional Republicans to ensure the rejection of electoral votes from the newly reconstructed states of Louisiana and Tennessee. Using that rule in 1873, Congress threw out the electoral votes of Louisiana and Arkansas and three from Georgia.

The rule lapsed at the beginning of 1876, when the Senate refused to readopt it because the House was controlled by the Democrats. Thus, after the 1876 election, when it became apparent that, for the first time, the outcome of an election would be determined by decisions on disputed electoral votes, Congress had no rules to guide it.

## Hayes-Tilden Contest

The 1876 campaign pitted Republican Rutherford B. Hayes against Democrat Samuel J. Tilden. Early election night returns indicated that Tilden had been elected. He had won normally Republican Indiana, New York, Connecticut and New Jersey. Those states, in addition to his expected southern support, would have given him the election. However, by the following morning it became apparent that if the Republicans could hold South Carolina, Florida and Louisiana, Hayes would be elected with 185 electoral votes to 184 for Tilden. But if a single elector in any of those states voted for Tilden, he would throw the election to the Democrats. Tilden led in the popular-vote count by more than a quarter of a million votes.[17]

The situation was much the same in each of the three contested states. Historian Eugene H. Roseboom described it as follows: "The Republicans controlled the state governments and the election machinery, had relied upon the Negro masses for votes and had practiced frauds, as in the past. The Democrats used threats, intimidation, and even violence when necessary, to keep Negroes from the polls; and where they were in a position to do so they resorted to fraud also. The firm determination of the whites to overthrow carpetbag rule contributed to make a full and fair vote impossible; carpetbag hold on the state governments made a fair count impossible. Radical reconstruction was reaping its final harvest." [18]

Both parties pursued the votes of the three states with a fine disregard for propriety or legality, and in the end double sets of electoral vote returns were sent to Congress from all three. Oregon also sent two sets of returns. Although Hayes carried that state, the Democratic governor discovered that one of the Hayes electors was a postmaster and therefore ineligible to be an elector under the Constitution, so the governor certified the election of the top-polling Democratic elector. However, the Republican electors met, received the resignation of their ineligible colleague, then reappointed him to the vacancy since he had in the meantime resigned his postmastership.

Had the 22nd Joint Rule remained in effect, the Democratic House of Representatives could have ensured Tilden's election by objecting to any of Hayes' disputed votes. But, since the rule had lapsed, Congress had to find some new method of resolving the electoral disputes. A joint committee was created to work out a plan, and the resulting Electoral

Commission law was approved by large majorities and signed into law Jan. 29, 1877 — only two days before the date scheduled for counting the electoral votes.

The law, which applied only to the 1876 electoral vote count, established a 15-member Electoral Commission that was to have final authority over disputed electoral votes, unless both houses of Congress agreed to overrule it. The commission was to consist of five senators, five representatives and five Supreme Court justices. Each chamber was to select its own commission members, with the understanding that the majority party would have three members and the minority two. Four justices, two from each party, were named in the bill, and these four were to select the fifth. It was expected that they would pick Justice David Davis, who was considered a political independent, but he was disqualified when the Illinois legislature named him to a seat in the Senate. Justice Joseph P. Bradley, a Republican, then was named to the 15th seat on the commission. The Democrats supported his selection because they considered him the most independent of the remaining justices, all of whom were Republicans.

The electoral vote count began in Congress on Feb. 1, and the proceedings continued until March 2. States were called in alphabetical order, and, as each disputed state was reached, objections were raised to both Hayes and Tilden electors. The question then was referred to the Electoral Commission, which in every case voted 8 to 7 for Hayes. In the end, Justice Bradley voted with the Republicans on every dispute. Subsequently, the Democratic House rejected the commission's decision, but the Republican Senate upheld it, so the decision stood.

As the count went on, Democrats in the House threatened to launch a filibuster to block resumption of joint sessions so that the count could not be completed before Inauguration Day. The threat never was carried out because of an agreement reached between the Hayes forces and southern conservatives. The southerners agreed to let the electoral count continue without obstruction. In return, Hayes agreed that, as president, he would withdraw federal troops from the South, end Reconstruction and make other concessions. The southerners, for their part, pledged to respect the rights of blacks, a pledge they proved unable to carry out.

Thus, at 4 a.m. on March 2, 1877, the president of the Senate was able to announce that Hayes had been elected president with 185 electoral votes, as against 184 for Tilden. Later that day Hayes arrived in

Washington. The following evening he took the oath of office privately at the White House because March 4 fell on a Sunday. His formal inauguration followed on Monday. The country acquiesced. Thus ended a national crisis that easily could have resulted in civil war.

Not until 1887 did Congress enact permanent legislation on the handling of disputed electoral votes. The Electoral Count Act of that year gave each state final authority in determining the legality of its choice of electors and required majorities of both the Senate and House to reject any disputed electoral votes. It also established procedures for counting electoral votes in Congress.

## Modern Test of Electoral Count Act

The procedures of the 1887 law relating to disputed electoral votes were used for the first time following the election of 1968. When Congress met in joint session Jan. 6, 1969, to count the electoral votes, Sen. Edmund S. Muskie, D-Maine (1959-80), and Rep. James G. O'Hara, D-Mich. (1959-77), joined by six other senators and 37 other representatives, filed a written objection to the vote cast by a North Carolina elector, Dr. Lloyd W. Bailey of Rocky Mount, who had been elected as a Republican but chose to vote for Wallace and Curtis E. LeMay instead of for Nixon and Spiro T. Agnew.

Acting under the 1887 law, Muskie and O'Hara objected to Bailey's vote on the grounds that it was "not properly given" because a plurality of the popular votes in North Carolina had been cast for Nixon-Agnew, and the state's voters had chosen electors to vote for Nixon and Agnew only. Muskie and O'Hara asked that Bailey's vote not be counted at all by Congress.

The 1887 statute, currently incorporated in the U.S. Code, Title 3, Section 15, stipulates that "no electoral vote or votes from any state which shall have been regularly given by electors whose appointment has been lawfully certified ... from which but one return has been received shall be rejected, but the two Houses concurrently may reject the vote or votes when they agree that such vote or votes have not been so regularly given. . . ." The statute did not define the term "regularly given," though at the time of its adoption concern centered on problems of dual sets of electoral vote returns from a state, votes cast on an improper day or votes disputed because of uncertainty about whether a state lawfully was in the Union on the day that the electoral vote was cast.

The 1887 statute provided that if written objection to any state's vote was received from at least one member of both the Senate and House, the two legislative bodies were to retire immediately to separate sessions, debate for two hours with a five-minute limitation on speeches, and that each chamber was to decide the issue by vote before resuming the joint session. Both the Senate and House had to reject a challenged electoral vote (or votes) before the vote was actually rejected.

At the Jan. 6 joint session, convened at 1 p.m. in the House chamber with Senate President Pro Tempore Richard B. Russell, D-Ga. (1933-71), presiding, the electoral vote counting proceeded smoothly through the alphabetical order of states until the North Carolina result was announced, at which time O'Hara rose to announce the filing of the complaint. The two houses then proceeded to separate sessions, at the end of which the Senate, by a 33 to 58 roll-call vote, and the House, by a 170 to 228 roll-call vote, refused to sustain the challenge to Bailey's vote. The two houses then reassembled in joint session and the results of the separate deliberations were announced. The remainder of the count of the electoral vote by state then proceeded without further incident. At the conclusion, Russell announced the vote and declared Nixon and Agnew elected. Although Congress did not sustain the challenge to Bailey's vote, the case of the "faithless" elector led to renewed pressure for electoral reform.

## Notes

1. Edward Stanwood, *A History of the Presidency from 1788 to 1897* (Boston: Houghton Mifflin Co., 1898), pp. 1-9.
2. Neal R. Peirce, *The People's President: The Electoral College and the Emerging Consensus for a Direct Vote* (New York: Simon & Schuster, 1968), p. 52.
3. Stanwood, *History of Presidency,* pp. 11-13, 77-82.
4. *Congressional Quarterly's Guide to U.S. Elections* (Washington, D.C.: Congressional Quarterly, 1975), pp. 202-205, 948-949.
5. Peirce, *People's President,* p. 76.
6. Stanwood, *History of Presidency,* pp. 54-73.
7. Ibid., p. 70.
8. Peirce, *People's President,* p. 69.
9. Arthur M. Schlesinger Jr., ed. *History of American Presidential Elections 1789-1968,* 4 vols. (New York: Chelsea House Publishers and McGraw-Hill Book Co., 1971), I: 133.

10. Eugene H. Roseboom, *A History of Presidential Elections* (New York: Macmillan Co., 1959), p. 47.
11. Stanwood, *History of Presidency,* pp. 123-141.
12. Ibid., p. 138.
13. Roseboom, *History of Presidential Elections,* p. 88.
14. Schlesinger, *History of American Presidential Elections,* I: 584, 596.
15. *Congressional Quarterly Weekly Report, 1968,* pp. 1811-1823, 2955-2956, 3171.
16. Stanwood, *History of Presidency,* pp. 20, 38, 203-204, 242, 452; Roseboom, *History of Presidential Elections,* pp. 246-247.
17. Stanwood, *History of Presidency,* pp. 356-393.
18. Roseboom, *History of Presidential Elections,* pp. 243-244.

# *Chapter 23*

# REFORM EFFORTS

From the very beginning, the constitutional provisions governing the selection of the president have had few defenders, and many efforts at electoral-college reform have been undertaken. In mounting a challenge to the electoral vote system after the 1968 presidential election, Rep. Hale Boggs, D-La. (1947-73), then the House majority whip, said there was a "crying need to amend the Constitution and once and for all get rid of this anachronistic system which every four years puts us in the position of playing Russian roulette with the election of the President of the United States." But all efforts to replace it with another system have failed.

## Electoral Reform Proposals

Since Jan. 6, 1797, when Rep. William L. Smith, Fed.-S.C. (1789-97), introduced the first proposed constitutional amendment for reform of the electoral college system, hardly a session of Congress has passed without the introduction of one or more resolutions of this nature. But only one — the 12th Amendment, ratified in 1804 — ever has been approved.

By the mid-20th century, public interest in a change in the electoral college system was spurred by the close 1960 and 1968 elections, by a series of Supreme Court rulings relating to apportionment and districting, and by the introduction of unpledged elector systems in some of the southern states during the height of the civil rights movement in the 1950s and 1960s. (In 1960, for example, uncommitted electors won in the states of Alabama and Mississippi, giving all eight of Mississippi's electoral votes and six of Alabama's 11 votes to Sen. Harry F. Byrd, D-Va. (1933-65).)

Early in 1969 President Richard M. Nixon asked Congress to take prompt action on electoral college reform. He said he would support any plan that would eliminate individual electors and distribute among the presidential candidates the electoral vote of every state and the District of Columbia in a manner more closely approximating the popular vote.[1]

Later that year the House approved, 338 to 70, a resolution proposing a constitutional amendment to eliminate the electoral college and to provide instead for direct popular election of the president and vice president. The measure set a minimum of 40 percent of the popular vote as sufficient for election and provided for a runoff election between the two top candidates for the presidency if no candidate received 40 percent of the vote. Under that plan the House of Representatives no longer could have been called upon to select a president. The proposed amendment also authorized Congress to provide a method of filling vacancies caused by the death, resignation or inability of presidential nominees before the election was held and a method of filling post-election vacancies caused by the death of the president-elect or vice president-elect.

Nixon, who had favored a proportional plan of allocating each state's electoral votes, endorsed the House-passed constitutional amendment and urged the Senate to adopt it. To become effective, the proposed amendment had to be approved by a two-thirds majority in both the Senate and House and be ratified by the legislatures of three-fourths of the states. When the proposal reached the Senate in September 1970, small-state and southern senators succeeded in blocking action on it. The resolution was put aside Oct. 5, following two unsuccessful efforts to cut off a filibuster.

In 1977 President Jimmy Carter recommended the adoption of a constitutional amendment abolishing the electoral college and replacing it with direct, popular election of the president. However, the Senate in 1979 refused to approve Carter's proposed constitutional amendment. The vote was 51 to 48, 15 short of the required two-thirds majority needed to approve a proposed amendment to the Constitution.[2]

As of 1982 no further efforts to change the electoral college system had made headway in Congress.

## Presidential Disability

A decade of congressional anxiety over the question of presidential disability was removed in 1967 with the ratification of the 25th Amendment to the Constitution. The amendment for the first time provided a specific method to ensure continuity in carrying out the

## House Election Thoughts

Except for the Founding Fathers, few Americans ever have found much to commend in the system of providing for the contingent election of a president by the House. Some comments:

Thomas Jefferson, 1823: "I have ever considered the constitutional mode of election ultimately by the Legislature voting by states as the most dangerous blot on our Constitution, and one which some unlucky chance will some day hit."

Martin Van Buren, 1826: "There is no point on which the people of the United States [are] more perfectly united than upon the propriety, not to say the absolute necessity, of taking the election away from the House of Representatives."

Sen. Oliver P. Morton of Indiana, a leading reform advocate, 1873: "The objections to this constitutional provision for the election of the President need only to be stated, not argued. First, its manifest injustice. In such an election each state is to have but one vote. Nevada, with its 42,000 population, has an equal vote with New York, having 104 times as great a population. It is a mockery to call such an election just, fair or republican."

Source: Neal Peirce, *The People's President: The Electoral College and the Emerging Consensus for a Direct Vote* (New York: Simon & Schuster, 1968), p. 132.

functions of the presidency in the event of presidential disability. It also spelled out procedures to be used in filling vacancies in the vice presidency.[3]

Congressional consideration of the problem of presidential disability had been prompted by President Dwight D. Eisenhower's heart attack in 1955. The ambiguity of the language of the disability clause (Article II, Section 1, Clause 5) of the Constitution had provoked occasional debate ever since the Constitutional Convention of 1787. But Congress had been unable to decide how far the term "disability" extended or who would be the judge of it.

Clause 5 provided that Congress should decide who was to succeed to the presidency in the event that both the president and the vice president died, resigned or became disabled. Congress enacted succession laws three times. By an Act of March 1, 1792, it provided for succession (after the vice president) of the president pro tempore of the Senate, then of the House Speaker. If those offices were vacant, states were to send electors to choose a new president.

That law stood until passage of the Presidential Succession Act of Jan. 19, 1886, which changed the line of succession to run from the vice president to the secretary of state, secretary of the Treasury and so on through the Cabinet in order of rank. Sixty-one years later, the Presidential Succession Act of 1947 — which still is in force — placed the Speaker of the House and the president pro tempore of the Senate ahead of Cabinet officers in the line of succession after the vice president.

The 25th Amendment was approved by the Senate and House in 1965. It took effect Feb. 10, 1967, after being ratified by 38 states. But before its ratification, no procedures had been established to govern situations arising from a presidential incapacity or a vacancy in the vice president's office. Two presidents had sustained serious disabilities — James A. Garfield, who was shot in 1881 and was confined to his bed until he died two and one-half months later, and Woodrow Wilson, who suffered a serious stroke in 1919 but served out his term of office. In each case the vice president did not assume any duties of the presidency for fear he would appear to be usurping the power of that office. As for a vice presidential vacancy, the United States has been without a vice president 18 times, for a total of 40 years through 1982, after the elected vice president either succeeded to the presidency, died or, on two occasions, resigned. (John C. Calhoun resigned as vice president Dec. 28, 1832, to become a U.S. senator and Spiro T. Agnew was forced to resign Oct. 10, 1973.)

Ratification of the 25th Amendment established procedures that clarified these areas of uncertainty in the Constitution. The amendment provided that the vice president should become acting president under either one of two circumstances. If the president informed Congress that he was unable to perform his duties, the vice president would become acting president until the president could resume his responsibilities. If the vice president and a majority of the Cabinet, or other body designated by Congress, found the president to be incapacitated, the vice president would become acting president until the president informed Congress that his disability had ended. Congress was given 21 days to resolve any dispute over the president's disability; a two-thirds vote of both chambers was required to overrule the president's declaration that he was no longer incapacitated.

Whenever a vacancy occurred in the office of vice president, the president was to nominate a vice president and the nomination was to be confirmed by a majority vote of both houses of Congress.

### Confusion After Reagan Shooting

In the aftermath of the attempted assassination of President Ronald Reagan in 1981, there was no need to invoke the presidential disability provisions of the 25th Amendment. However, some of the public statements made by administration officials immediately after the shooting reflected continuing confusion over the issue of who is in charge when the president temporarily is unable to function. Soon after word of the shooting became known, the members of the Reagan Cabinet gathered in the White House, ready to invoke the amendment's procedures, if necessary. Vice President George Bush was on an Air Force jet returning to Washington from Texas.

At a televised press briefing later that afternoon, Secretary of State Alexander M. Haig Jr. confirmed that Reagan was in surgery. Under anesthesia, it was clear that he temporarily was unable to make presidential decisions should the occasion — such as a foreign attack or other national emergency — require them. Attempting to reassure the country, Haig stated that he was in control in the White House pending the return of Vice President George Bush, with whom he was in contact.

This assertion was followed by the question, from the press, as to who was making administration decisions. Haig responded, "Constitutionally, gentlemen, you have the president, the vice president and the secretary of state in that order, and should the president decide he wants to transfer the helm to the vice president, he will do so. He has not done that."

Haig's response dealt with the old line of succession that predated the Presidential Succession Act. The Constitution does not spell out a line of succession. The 1947 law specifies that the line of succession is the vice president, the Speaker of the House, the president pro tempore of the Senate, the secretaries of state, Treasury, defense, the attorney general, the secretaries of interior, agriculture, commerce, labor, health and human services, housing and urban development, transportation, energy and education.

## Vice Presidential Vacancies

Since its ratification in 1967, the 25th Amendment has been used twice to fill a vacancy in the office of the vice president.[4] The first time was in 1973 after Vice President Agnew's resignation. Agnew, under investigation for multiple charges of alleged conspiracy, extortion and bribery, agreed to resign and avoided imprisonment by pleading *nolo contendere* (no contest) to a single charge of federal income tax evasion.

On Oct. 12 President Nixon nominated House Minority Leader Gerald R. Ford, R-Mich. (1949-73), to be vice president. Ford became the 40th vice president of the United States Dec. 6, an hour after the House of Representatives voted 387 to 15 to confirm him. The Senate had approved the nomination Nov. 27 by a 92 to 3 vote. Ford's confirmation followed hearings and approval by the House Judiciary and Senate Rules committees.

The 25th Amendment was used a second time in 1974 when Nixon resigned as president Aug. 9, 1974, to avoid impeachment because of the Watergate scandal. Ford succeeded to the presidency, becoming the first unelected president in American history, and on Aug. 20 he nominated former Gov. Nelson A. Rockefeller of New York as the new vice president.

Rockefeller became the 41st vice president of the United States Dec. 19, 1974, after the House confirmed his nomination 287 to 128. The Senate had given its approval to the nomination Dec. 10 by a 90 to 7 vote. Rockefeller's nomination had been approved by the House Judiciary and Senate Rules committees after several days of hearings.

With both the president and vice president holding office through appointment rather than election, members of Congress and the public expressed concern about the power of a president to, in effect, appoint his own successor. Among those proposing a change was Sen. John O. Pastore, D-R.I. (1950-76), who sponsored a resolution for a constitutional amendment to provide for a special national election for president whenever an appointed vice president became president with more than one year remaining in a presidential term.

Hearings on proposed changes were held in February 1975 by the Senate Judiciary Subcommittee on Constitutional Amendments. No further action was taken on the proposal.

## Notes

1. *Congress and the Nation,* 5 vols., *Congress and the Nation: 1969-1972,* vol. 3 (Washington, D.C.: Congressional Quarterly, 1973), III: 1012-1019.
2. *Congressional Quarterly Almanac 1979* (Washington D.C.: Congressional Quarterly, 1980), pp. 551-553.
3. *Congress and the Nation: 1965-1968,* vol. 2 (Washington D.C.: Congressional Quarterly, 1969), pp. 645-648.
4. *Congressional Quarterly Almanac 1973* (Washington D.C.: Congressional Quarterly, 1974), pp. 1061-1068; *Congressional Quarterly Almanac 1974* (Washington D.C.: Congressional Quarterly, 1975), pp. 917-935.

# CONSTITUTION OF THE UNITED STATES

We the People of the United States, in Order to form a more perfect Union, establish Justice, insure domestic Tranquility, provide for the common defence, promote the general Welfare, and secure the Blessings of Liberty to ourselves and our Posterity, do ordain and establish this Constitution for the United States of America.

## Article I

**Section 1.** All legislative Powers herein granted shall be vested in a Congress of the United States, which shall consist of a Senate and House of Representatives.

**Section 2.** The House of Representatives shall be composed of Members chosen every second Year by the People of the several States, and the Electors in each State shall have the Qualifications requisite for Electors of the most numerous Branch of the State Legislature.

No Person shall be a Representative who shall not have attained to the age of twenty five Years, and been seven Years a Citizen of the United States, and who shall not, when elected, be an Inhabitant of that State in which he shall be chosen.

Representatives and direct Taxes shall be apportioned among the several States which may be included within this Union, according to their respective Numbers, which shall be determined by adding to the whole Number of free Persons, including those bound to Service for a Term of Years, and excluding Indians not taxed, three fifths of all other Persons. The actual Enumeration shall be made within three Years after the first Meeting of the Congress of the United States, and within every subsequent Term of ten Years, in such Manner as they shall by Law direct. The Number of Representatives shall not exceed one for every thirty Thousand, but each State shall have at Least one Representative; and until such enumeration shall be made, the State of New Hampshire shall be entitled to chuse three, Massachusetts eight, Rhode-Island and Providence Plantations one, Connecticut five, New-York six, New Jersey four, Pennsylvania eight, Delaware one, Maryland six, Virginia ten, North Carolina five, South Carolina five, and Georgia three.

When vacancies happen in the Representation from any State, the Executive Authority thereof shall issue Writs of Election to fill such Vacancies.

The House of Representatives shall chuse their Speaker and other Officers; and shall have the sole Power of Impeachment.

**Section 3.** The Senate of the United States shall be composed of two Senators from each State, chosen by the Legislature thereof, for six Years; and each Senator shall have one Vote.

Immediately after they shall be assembled in Consequence of the first Election, they shall be divided as equally as may be into three Classes. The Seats of the Senators of the first Class shall be vacated at the Expiration of the second Year, of the second Class at the Expiration of the fourth Year, and of the third Class at the Expiration of the sixth Year, so that one third may be chosen every second Year; and if Vacancies happen by Resignation, or otherwise, during the Recess of the Legislature of any State, the Executive thereof may make temporary Appointments until the next Meeting of the Legislature, which shall then fill such Vacancies.

No Person shall be a Senator who shall not have attained to the Age of thirty Years, and been nine Years a Citizen of the United States, and who shall not, when elected, be an Inhabitant of that State for which he shall be chosen.

The Vice President of the United States shall be President of the Senate, but shall have no Vote, unless they be equally divided.

The Senate shall chuse their other Officers, and also a President pro tempore, in the Absence of the Vice President, or when he shall exercise the Office of President of the United States.

The Senate shall have the sole Power to try all Impeachments. When sitting for that Purpose, they shall be on Oath or Affirmation. When the President of the United States is tried the Chief Justice shall preside: And no Person shall be convicted without the Concurrence of two thirds of the Members present.

Judgment in Cases of Impeachment shall not extend further than to removal from Office, and disqualification to hold and enjoy any Office of honor, Trust or Profit under the United States: but the Party convicted shall nevertheless be liable and subject to Indictment, Trial, Judgment and Punishment, according to Law.

**Section 4.** The Times, Places and Manner of holding Elections for Senators and Representatives, shall be prescribed in each State by the Legislature thereof; but the Congress may at any time by Law make or alter such Regulations, except as to the Places of chusing Senators.

The Congress shall assemble at least once in every Year, and such Meeting shall be on the first Monday in December, unless they shall by Law appoint a different Day.

**Section 5.** Each House shall be the Judge of the Elections, Returns and Qualifications of its own Members, and a Majority of each shall constitute a Quorum to do Business; but a smaller Number may adjourn from day to day, and may be authorized to compel the Attendance of absent Members, in such Manner, and under such Penalties as each House may provide.

Each House may determine the Rules of its Proceedings, punish its Members for disorderly Behaviour, and, with the Concurrence of two thirds, expel a Member.

Each House shall keep a Journal of its Proceedings, and from time to time publish the same, excepting such Parts as may in their Judgment require Secrecy; and the Yeas and Nays of the Members of either House on any question shall, at the Desire of one fifth of those Present, be entered on the Journal.

Neither House, during the Session of Congress, shall, without the Consent of the other, adjourn for more than three days, nor to any other Place than that in which the two Houses shall be sitting.

**Section 6.** The Senators and Representatives shall receive a Compensation for their Services, to be ascertained by Law, and paid out of the Treasury of the United States. They shall in all Cases, except Treason, Felony and Breach of the Peace, be privileged from Arrest during their Attendance at the Session of their respective Houses, and in going to and returning from the same; and for any Speech or Debate in either House, they shall not be questioned in any other Place.

No Senator or Representative shall, during the Time for which he was elected, be appointed to any civil Office under the Authority of the United States, which shall have been created, or the Emoluments whereof shall have been encreased during such time; and no Person holding any Office under the United States, shall be a Member of either House during his Continuance in Office.

**Section 7.** All Bills for raising Revenue shall originate in the House of Representatives; but the Senate may propose or concur with amendments as on other Bills.

Every Bill which shall have passed the House of Representatives and the Senate, shall, before it become a Law, be presented to the President of the United States; If he approve he shall sign it, but if not he shall return it, with his Objections to that House in which it shall have originated, who shall enter the Objections at large on their Journal, and proceed to reconsider it. If after such Reconsideration two thirds of that House shall agree to pass the Bill, it shall be sent, together with the Objections, to the other House, by which it shall likewise be reconsidered, and if approved by two thirds of that House, it shall become a Law. But in all such Cases the Votes of both Houses shall be determined by yeas and Nays, and the Names of the Persons voting for and against the Bill shall be entered on the Journal of each House respectively. If any Bill shall not be returned by the President within ten Days (Sunday excepted) after it shall have been presented to him, the Same shall be a Law, in like Manner as if he had signed it, unless the Congress by their Adjournment prevent its Return, in which Case it shall not be a Law.

Every Order, Resolution, or Vote to which the Concurrence of the Senate and House of Representatives may be necessary (except on a question of Adjournment) shall be presented to the President of the United States; and before the Same shall take Effect, shall be approved by him, or being disapproved by him, shall be repassed by two thirds of the Senate and House of Representatives, according to the Rules and Limitations prescribed in the Case of a Bill.

**Section 8.** The Congress shall have Power To lay and collect Taxes, Duties, Imposts and Excises, to pay the Debts and provide for the common Defence and general Welfare of the United States; but all Duties, Imposts and Excises shall be uniform throughout the United States;

To borrow Money on the credit of the United States;

To regulate Commerce with foreign Nations, and among the several States, and with the Indian Tribes;

To establish an uniform Rule of Naturalization, and uniform Laws on the subject of Bankruptcies throughout the United States;

To coin Money, regulate the Value thereof, and of foreign Coin, and fix the Standard of Weights and Measures;

To provide for the Punishment of counterfeiting the Securities and current Coin of the United States;

To establish Post Offices and post Roads;

To promote the Progress of Science and useful Arts, by securing for limited Times to Authors and Inventors the exclusive Right to their respective Writings and Discoveries;

To constitute Tribunals inferior to the supreme Court;

To define and punish Piracies and Felonies commited on the high Seas, and Offences against the Law of Nations;

To declare War, grant Letters of Marque and Reprisal, and make Rules concerning Captures on Land and Water;

To raise and support Armies, but no Appropriation of Money to that Use shall be for a longer Term than two Years;

To provide and maintain a Navy;

To make Rules for the Government and Regulation of the land and naval Forces;

To provide for calling forth the Militia to execute the Laws of the Union, suppress Insurrections and repel Invasions;

To provide for organizing, arming, and disciplining, the Militia, and for governing such Part of them as may be employed in the Service of the United States, reserving to the States respectively, the Appointment of the Officers, and the Authority of training the Militia according to the discipline prescribed by Congress;

To exercise exclusive Legislation in all Cases whatsoever, over such District (not exceeding ten Miles square) as may, by Cession of Particular States, and the Acceptance of Congress, become the Seat of the Government of the United States, and to exercise like Authority over all Places purchased by the Consent of the Legislature of the State in which the Same shall be, for the Erection of Forts, Magazines, Arsenals, dock-Yards, and other needful Buildings; — And

To make all Laws which shall be necessary and proper for carrying into Execution the foregoing Powers, and all other Powers vested by this Constitution in the Government of the United States, or in any Department or Officer thereof.

**Section 9.** The Migration or Importation of such Persons as any of the States now existing shall think proper to admit, shall not be prohibited by the Congress prior to the Year one thousand eight hundred and eight, but a Tax or duty may be imposed on such Importation, not exceeding ten dollars for each Person.

The Privilege of the Writ of Habeas Corpus shall not be suspended, unless when in Cases of Rebellion or Invasion the public Safety may require it.

No Bill of Attainder or ex post facto Law shall be passed.

No capitation, or other direct, Tax shall be laid, unless in Proportion to the Census of Enumeration herein before directed to be taken.

No Tax or Duty shall be laid on Articles exported from any State.

No Preference shall be given by any Regulation of Commerce or Revenue to the Ports of one State over those of another; nor shall Vessels bound to, or from, one State, be obliged to enter, clear or pay Duties in another.

No Money shall be drawn from the Treasury, but in Consequence of Appropriations made by Law; and a regular Statement and Account of the Receipts and Expenditures of all public Money shall be published from time to time.

No Title of Nobility shall be granted by the United States: And no Person holding any Office of Profit or Trust under them, shall, without the Consent of the Congress, accept of any present, Emolument, Office, or Title, of any kind whatever, from any King, Prince or foreign State.

**Section 10.** No State shall enter into any Treaty, Alliance, or Confederation; grant Letters of Marque and Reprisal; coin Money; emit Bills of Credit; make any Thing but gold and silver Coin a Tender in Payment of Debts; pass any Bill of Attainder, ex post facto Law, or Law impairing the Obligation of Contracts, or grant any Title of Nobility.

No State shall, without the Consent of the Congress, lay any Imposts or Duties on Imports or Exports, except what may be absolutely necessary for executing it's inspection Laws: and the net Produce of all Duties and Imposts, laid by any State on Imports or Exports, shall be for the Use of the Treasury of the United States; and all such Laws shall be subject to the Revision and Controul of the Congress.

No State shall, without the Consent of Congress, lay any Duty of Tonnage, keep Troops, or Ships of War in time of Peace, enter into any Agreement or Compact with another State, or with a foreign Power, or engage in War, unless actually invaded, or in such imminent Danger as will not admit of delay.

## Article II

**Section 1.** The executive Power shall be vested in a President of the United States of America. He shall hold his Office during the Term of four Years, and, together with the Vice President, chosen for the same Term, be elected, as follows.

Each State shall appoint, in such Manner as the Legislature thereof may direct, a Number of Electors, equal to the whole Number of Senators and Representatives to which the State may be entitled in the Congress: but no Senator or Representative, or Person holding an Office of Trust or Profit under the United States, shall be appointed an Elector.

The Electors shall meet in their respective States, and vote by Ballot for two Persons, of whom one at least shall not be an Inhabitant of the same State with themselves. And they shall make a List of all the Persons voted for, and of the Number of Votes for each; which List they shall sign and certify, and transmit sealed to the Seat of the Government of the United States, directed to the President of the Senate. The President of the Senate shall, in the Presence of the Senate and House of Representatives, open all the Certificates, and the Votes shall then be counted. The Person having the greatest Number of Votes shall be the President, if such Number be a Majority of the whole Number of Electors appointed; and if there be more than one who have such Majority, and have an equal Number of Votes, then the House of Representatives shall immediately chuse by Ballot one of them for President; and if no Person have a Majority, then from the five highest on the list the said House shall in like Manner chuse the President. But in chusing the President, the Votes shall be taken by States, the Representation from each State having one Vote; a quorum for this Purpose shall consist of a Member or Members from two thirds of the States, and a Majority of all the States shall be necessary to a Choice. In every Case, after the Choice of the President, the Person having the greatest Number of Votes of the Electors shall be the Vice President. But if there should remain two or more who have equal Votes, the Senate shall chuse from them by Ballot the Vice President.

The Congress may determine the Time of chusing the Electors, and the Day on which they shall give their Votes; which Day shall be the same throughout the United States.

No Person except a natural born Citizen, or a Citizen of the United States, at the time of the Adoption of this Constitution, shall be eligible to the Office of President; neither shall any Person be eligible to that Office who shall not have attained to the Age of thirty five Years, and been fourteen Years a Resident within the United States.

In Case of the Removal of the President from Office, or of his Death, Resignation, or Inability to discharge the Powers and Duties of the said Office, the Same shall devolve on the Vice President, and the Congress may by Law provide for the Case of Removal, Death, Resignation or Inability, both of the President and Vice President, declaring what Officer shall then act as President, and such Officer shall act accordingly, until the Disability be removed, or a President shall be elected.

The President shall, at stated Times, receive for his Services, a Compensation, which shall neither be encreased nor diminished during the Period for which he shall have been elected, and he shall not receive within that Period any other Emolument from the United States, or any of them.

Before he enter on the Execution of his Office, he shall take the following Oath or Affirmation: — "I do solemnly swear (or affirm) that I will faithfully execute the Office of President of the United States, and will to the best of my Ability, preserve, protect and defend the Constitution of the United States."

**Section 2.** The President shall be Commander in Chief of the Army and Navy of the United States, and of the Militia of the several States, when called into the actual Service of the United States; he may require the Opinion, in writing, of the principal Officer in each of the executive Departments, upon any Subject relating to the Duties of their respective Offices, and he shall have Power to grant Reprieves and Pardons for Offenses against the United States, except in Cases of Impeachment.

He shall have Power, by and with the Advice and Consent of the Senate, to make Treaties, provided two thirds of the Senators present concur; and he shall nominate, and by and with the Advice and Consent of the Senate, shall appoint Ambassadors, other public Ministers and Consuls, Judges of the supreme Court, and all other Officers of the United States, whose Appointments are not herein otherwise provided for, and which shall be established by Law: but the Congress may by Law vest the Appointment of such inferior Officers, as they think proper, in the President alone, in the Courts of Law, or in the Heads of Departments.

The President shall have Power to fill up all Vacancies that may happen during the Recess of the Senate, by granting Commissions which shall expire at the End of their next Session.

**Section 3.** He shall from time to time give to the Congress Information of the State of the Union, and recommend to their Consideration such Measures as he shall judge necessary and expedient; he may, on extraordinary Occasions, convene both Houses, or either of them, and in Case of Disagreement between them, with Respect to the Time of Adjournment, he may adjourn them to such Time as he shall think proper; he shall receive Ambassadors and other public Ministers; he shall take Care that the Laws be faithfully executed, and shall Commission all the Officers of the United States.

**Section 4.** The President, Vice President and all Civil Officers of the United States, shall be removed from office on Impeachment for, and Conviction of, Treason, Bribery, or other high Crimes and Misdemeanors.

## Article III

**Section 1.** The judicial Power of the United States, shall be vested in one supreme Court, and in such inferior Courts as the Congress may from time to time ordain and establish. The Judges, both of the supreme and inferior Courts, shall hold their Offices during good Behaviour, and shall, at stated Times, receive for their Services, a Compensation, which shall not be diminished during their Continuance in Office.

**Section 2.** The judicial Power shall extend to all Cases, in Law and Equity, arising under this Constitution, the Laws of the United States, and Treaties made, or which shall be made, under their Authority; — to all Cases affecting Ambassadors, other public Ministers and Consuls; — to all Cases of admiralty and maritime Jurisdiction; — to Controversies to which the United States shall be a Party; — to Controversies between two or more States; — between a State and Citizens of another State; — between Citizens of different States; — between Citizens of the same State claiming Lands under Grants of different States, and between a State, or the Citizens thereof, and foreign States, Citizens or Subjects.

In all Cases affecting Ambassadors, other public Ministers and Consuls, and those in which a State shall be Party, the supreme Court shall have original Jurisdiction. In all the other Cases before mentioned, the supreme Court shall have appellate Jurisdiction, both as to Law and

Fact, with such Exceptions, and under such Regulations as the Congress shall make.

The Trial of all Crimes, except in cases of Impeachment, shall be by Jury; and such Trial shall be held in the State where the said Crimes shall have been committed; but when not committed within any State, the Trial shall be at such Place or Places as the Congress may by Law have directed.

**Section 3.** Treason against the United States, shall consist only in levying War against them, or in adhering to their Enemies, giving them Aid and Comfort. No Person shall be convicted of Treason unless on the Testimony of two Witnesses to the same overt Act, or on Confession in open Court.

The Congress shall have Power to declare the Punishment of Treason, but no Attainder of Treason shall work Corruption of Blood, or Forfeiture except during the Life of the Person attainted.

## Article IV

**Section 1.** Full Faith and Credit shall be given in each State to the public Acts, Records, and judicial Proceedings of every other State. And the Congress may by general Laws prescribe the Manner in which such Acts, Records and Proceedings shall be proved, and the Effect thereof.

**Section 2.** The Citizens of each State shall be entitled to all Privileges and Immunities of Citizens in the several States.

A Person charged in any State with Treason, Felony, or other Crime, who shall flee from Justice, and be found in another State, shall on Demand of the executive Authority of the State from which he fled, be delivered up, to be removed to the State having Jurisdiction of the Crime.

No Person held to Service or Labour in one State, under the Laws thereof, escaping into another, shall, in Consequence of any Law or Regulation therein, be discharged from such Service or Labour, but shall be delivered up on Claim of the Party to whom such Service or Labour may be due.

**Section 3.** New States may be admitted by the Congress into this Union; but no new State shall be formed or erected within the Jurisdiction of any other State; nor any State be formed by the Junction of two or more States, or Parts of States, without the Consent of the Legislatures of the States concerned as well as of the Congress.

The Congress shall have Power to dispose of and make all needful Rules and Regulations respecting the Territory or other Property belonging to the United States; and nothing in this Constitution shall be so construed as to Prejudice any Claims of the United States, or of any particular State.

**Section 4.** The United States shall guarantee to every State in this Union a Republican Form of Government, and shall protect each of them against Invasion; and on Application of the Legislature, or of the Executive (when the Legislature cannot be convened) against domestic Violence.

## Article V

The Congress, whenever two thirds of both Houses shall deem it necessary, shall propose Amendments to this Constitution, or, on the Application of the Legislatures of two thirds of the several States, shall call a Convention for proposing Amendments, which, in either Case, shall be valid to all Intents and Purposes, as Part of this Constitution, when ratified by the Legislatures of three fourths of the several States, or by Conventions in three fourths thereof, as the one or the other Mode of Ratification may be proposed by the Congress; Provided that no Amendment which may be made prior to the Year One thousand eight hundred and eight shall in any Manner affect the first and fourth Clauses in the Ninth Section of the first Article; and that no State, without its Consent, shall be deprived of its equal Suffrage in the Senate.

## Article VI

All Debts contracted and Engagements entered into, before the Adoption of this Constitution, shall be as valid against the United States under this Constitution, as under the Confederation.

This Constitution, and the Laws of the United States which shall be made in Pursuance thereof; and all Treaties made, or which shall be made, under the Authority of the United States, shall be the supreme Law of the Land; and the Judges in every State shall be bound thereby, any Thing in the Constitution or Laws of any State to the Contrary notwithstanding.

The Senators and Representatives before mentioned, and the Members of the several State Legislatures, and all executive and judicial Officers, both of the United States and of the several States, shall be bound by Oath or Affirmation, to support this Constitution; but no religious Test shall ever be required as a Qualification to any Office or public Trust under the United States.

## Article VII

The Ratification of the Conventions of nine States, shall be sufficient for the Establishment of this Constitution between the States so ratifying the Same. Done in Convention by the Unanimous Consent of the States present the Seventeenth Day of September in the Year of our Lord one thousand seven hundred and Eighty seven and of the Independence of the United States of America the Twelfth In witness whereof We have hereunto subscribed our Names, George Washington, President and deputy from Virginia.

| | |
|---|---|
| **New Hampshire:** | John Langdon,<br>Nicholas Gilman. |
| **Massachusetts:** | Nathaniel Gorham,<br>Rufus King. |
| **Connecticut:** | William Samuel Johnson,<br>Roger Sherman. |
| **New York:** | Alexander Hamilton |
| **New Jersey:** | William Livingston,<br>David Brearley,<br>William Paterson,<br>Jonathan Dayton. |
| **Pennsylvania:** | Benjamin Franklin,<br>Thomas Mifflin,<br>Robert Morris,<br>George Clymer,<br>Thomas FitzSimons,<br>Jared Ingersoll,<br>James Wilson,<br>Gouverneur Morris. |
| **Delaware:** | George Read,<br>Gunning Bedford Jr.,<br>John Dickinson,<br>Richard Bassett,<br>Jacob Broom. |

| | |
|---|---|
| **Maryland:** | James McHenry,<br>Daniel of St. Thomas Jenifer,<br>Daniel Carroll. |
| **Virginia:** | John Blair,<br>James Madison Jr. |
| **North Carolina:** | William Blount,<br>Richard Dobbs Spaight,<br>Hugh Williamson. |
| **South Carolina:** | John Rutledge,<br>Charles Cotesworth Pinckney,<br>Charles Pinckney,<br>Pierce Butler. |
| **Georgia:** | William Few,<br>Abraham Baldwin. |

## Amendments

### Amendment I

*(First ten amendments ratified Dec. 15, 1791.)*

Congress shall make no law respecting an establishment of religion, or prohibiting the free exercise thereof; or abridging the freedom of speech, or of the press; or the right of the people peaceably to assemble, and to petition the Government for a redress of grievances.

### Amendment II

A well regulated Militia, being necessary to the security of a free State, the right of the people to keep and bear Arms, shall not be infringed.

### Amendment III

No Soldier shall, in time of peace be quartered in any house, without the consent of the Owner, nor in time of war, but in a manner to be prescribed by law.

### Amendment IV

The right of the people to be secure in their persons, houses, papers, and effects, against unreasonable searches and seizures, shall not be violated, and no Warrants shall issue, but upon probable cause, supported by Oath or affirmation, and particularly describing the place to be searched, and the persons or things to be seized.

**Amendment V**

No person shall be held to answer for a capital, or otherwise infamous crime, unless on a presentment or indictment of a Grand Jury, except in cases arising in the land or naval forces, or in the Militia, when in actual service in time of War or public danger; nor shall any person be subject for the same offence to be twice put in jeopardy of life or limb; nor shall be compelled in any criminal case to be a witness against himself, nor be deprived of life, liberty, or property, without due process of law; nor shall private property be taken for public use, without just compensation.

**Amendment VI**

In all criminal prosecutions, the accused shall enjoy the right to a speedy and public trial, by an impartial jury of the State and district wherein the crime shall have been committed, which district shall have been previously ascertained by law, and to be informed of the nature and cause of the accusation; to be confronted with the witnesses against him; to have compulsory process for obtaining witnesses in his favor, and to have the Assistance of Counsel for his defence.

**Amendment VII**

In Suits at common law, where the value in controversy shall exceed twenty dollars, the right of trial by jury shall be preserved, and no fact tried by a jury, shall be otherwise re-examined in any Court of the United States, than according to the rules of the common law.

**Amendment VIII**

Excessive bail shall not be required, nor excessive fines imposed, nor cruel and unusual punishments inflicted.

**Amendment IX**

The enumeration in the Constitution, of certain rights, shall not be construed to deny or disparage others retained by the people.

**Amendment X**

The powers not delegated to the United States by the Constitution, nor prohibited by it to the States, are reserved to the States respectively, or to the people.

**Amendment XI** *(Ratified Feb. 7, 1795)*

The Judicial power of the United States shall not be construed to extend to any suit in law or equity, commenced or prosecuted against one of the United States by Citizens of another State, or by Citizens or Subjects of any Foreign State.

**Amendment XII** *(Ratified June 15, 1804)*

The Electors shall meet in their respective states and vote by ballot for President and Vice-President, one of whom, at least, shall not be an inhabitant of the same state with themselves; they shall name in their ballots the person voted for as President, and in distinct ballots the person voted for as Vice-President, and they shall make distinct lists of all persons voted for as President, and of all persons voted for as Vice-President, and of the number of votes for each, which lists they shall sign and certify, and transmit sealed to the seat of the government of the United States, directed to the President of the Senate; — The President of the Senate shall, in the presence of the Senate and House of Representatives, open all the certificates and the votes shall then be counted; — The person having the greatest number of votes for President, shall be the President, if such number be a majority of the whole number of Electors appointed; and if no person have such majority, then from the persons having the highest numbers not exceeding three on the list of those voted for as President, the House of Representatives shall choose immediately, by ballot, the President. But in choosing the President, the votes shall be taken by states, the representation from each state having one vote; a quorum for this purpose shall consist of a member or members from two-thirds of the states, and a majority of all the states shall be necessary to a choice. And if the House of Representatives shall not choose a President whenever the right of choice shall devolve upon them, before the fourth day of March next following, then the Vice-President shall act as President, as in the case of the death or other constitutional disability of the President — The person having the greatest number of votes as Vice-President, shall be the Vice-President, if such number be a majority of the whole number of Electors appointed, and if no person have a majority, then from the two highest numbers on the list, the Senate shall choose the Vice-President; a quorum for the purpose shall consist of two-thirds of the whole number of Senators, and a majority of the whole number shall be necessary to a choice. But no person constitutionally ineligible to the office of President shall be eligible to that of Vice-President of the United States.

**Amendment XIII** *(Ratified Dec. 6, 1865)*

**Section 1.** Neither slavery nor involuntary servitude, except as a punishment for crime whereof the party shall have been duly convicted, shall exist within the United States, or any place subject to their jurisdiction.

**Section 2.** Congress shall have power to enforce this article by appropriate legislation.

**Amendment XIV** *(Ratified July 9, 1868)*

**Section 1.** All persons born or naturalized in the United States and subject to the jurisdiction thereof, are citizens of the United States and of the State wherein they reside. No State shall make or enforce any law which shall abridge the privileges or immunities of citizens of the United States; nor shall any State deprive any person of life, liberty, or property, without due process of law; nor deny to any person within its jurisdiction the equal protection of the laws.

**Section 2.** Representatives shall be apportioned among the several States according to their respective numbers, counting the whole number of persons in each State, excluding Indians not taxed. But when the right to vote at any election for the choice of electors for President and Vice President of the United States, Representatives in Congress, the Executive and Judicial officers of a State, or the members of the Legislature thereof, is denied to any of the male inhabitants of such State, being twenty-one years of age, and citizens of the United States, or in any way abridged, except for participation in rebellion, or other crime, the basis of representation therein shall be reduced in the proportion which the number of such male citizens shall bear to the whole number of male citizens twenty-one years of age in such State.

**Section 3.** No person shall be a Senator or Representative in Congress, or elector of President and Vice President, or hold any office, civil or military, under the United States, or under any State, who, having previously taken an oath, as a member of Congress, or as an officer of the United States, or as a member of any State legislature, or as an executive or judicial officer of any State, to support the Constitution of the United States, shall have engaged in insurrection or rebellion against the same, or given aid or comfort to the enemies thereof. But Congress may by a vote of two-thirds of each House, remove such disability.

**Section 4.** The validity of the public debt of the United States, authorized by law, including debts incurred for payment of pensions and bounties for services in suppressing insurrection or rebellion, shall not be questioned. But neither the United States nor any State shall assume or pay any debt or obligation incurred in aid of insurrection or rebellion against the United States, or any claim for the loss or emancipation of any slave; but all such debts, obligations and claims shall be held illegal and void.

**Section 5.** The Congress shall have power to enforce, by appropriate legislation, the provisions of this article.

## Amendment XV *(Ratified Feb. 3, 1870)*

**Section 1.** The right of citizens of the United States to vote shall not be denied or abridged by the United States or by any State on account of race, color, or previous condition of servitude.

**Section 2.** The Congress shall have power to enforce this article by appropriate legislation.

## Amendment XVI *(Ratified Feb. 3, 1913)*

The Congress shall have power to lay and collect taxes on incomes, from whatever source derived, without apportionment among the several States, and without regard to any census or enumeration.

## Amendment XVII *(Ratified Apr. 8, 1913)*

The Senate of the United States shall be composed of two Senators from each State, elected by the people thereof, for six years; and each Senator shall have one vote. The electors in each State shall have the qualifications requisite for electors of the most numerous branch of the State legislatures.

When vacancies happen in the representation of any State in the Senate, the executive authority of such State shall issue writs of election to fill such vacancies: *Provided,* That the legislature of any State may empower the executive thereof to make temporary appointments until the people fill the vacancies by election as the legislature may direct.

This amendment shall not be so construed as to affect the election or term of any Senator chosen before it becomes valid as part of the Constitution.

**Amendment XVIII** *(Ratified Jan. 16, 1919)*

**Section. 1.** After one year from the ratification of this article the manufacture, sale, or transportation of intoxicating liquors within, the importation thereof into, or the exportation thereof from the United States and all territory subject to the jurisdiction thereof for beverage purposes is hereby prohibited.

**Section 2.** The Congress and the several States shall have concurrent power to enforce this article by appropriate legislation.

**Section 3.** This article shall be inoperative unless it shall have been ratified as an amendment to the Constitution by the legislatures of the several States, as provided in the Constitution, within seven years from the date of the submission hereof to the States by the Congress.

**Amendment XIX** *(Ratified Aug. 18, 1920)*

The right of citizens of the United States to vote shall not be denied or abridged by the United States or by any State on account of sex.

Congress shall have power to enforce this article by appropriate legislation.

**Amendment XX** *(Ratified Jan. 23, 1933)*

**Section 1.** The terms of the President and Vice President shall end at noon on the 20th day of January, and the terms of Senators and Representatives at noon on the 3d day of January, of the years in which such terms would have ended if this article had not been ratified; and the terms of their successors shall then begin.

**Section 2.** The Congress shall assemble at least once in every year, and such meeting shall begin at noon on the 3d day of January, unless they shall by law appoint a different day.

**Section 3.** If, at the time fixed for the beginning of the term of the President, the President elect shall have died, the Vice President elect shall become President. If a President shall not have been chosen before the time fixed for the beginning of his term, or if the President elect shall have failed to qualify, then the Vice President elect shall act as President until a President shall have qualified; and the Congress may by law provide for the case wherein neither a President elect nor a Vice President elect shall have qualified, declaring who shall then act as President, or the manner in which one who is to act shall be selected, and such person shall act accordingly until a President or Vice President shall have qualified.

**Section 4.** The Congress may by law provide for the case of the death of any of the persons from whom the House of Representatives may choose a President whenever the right of choice shall have devolved upon them, and for the case of the death of any of the persons from whom the Senate may choose a Vice President whenever the right of choice shall have devolved upon them.

**Section 5.** Sections 1 and 2 shall take effect on the 15th day of October following the ratification of this article.

**Section 6.** This article shall be inoperative unless it shall have been ratified as an amendment to the Constitution by the legislatures of three-fourths of the several States within seven years from the date of its submission.

**Amendment XXI** *(Ratified Dec. 5, 1933)*

**Section 1.** The eighteenth article of amendment to the Constitution of the United States is hereby repealed.

**Section 2.** The transportation or importation into any State, Territory or possession of the United States for delivery or use therein of intoxicating liquors, in violation of the laws thereof, is hereby prohibited.

**Section 3.** This article shall be inoperative unless it shall have been ratified as an amendment to the Constitution by conventions in the several States, as provided in the Constitution, within seven years from the date of the submission hereof to the States by the Congress.

**Amendment XXII** *(Ratified Feb. 27, 1951)*

**Section 1.** No person shall be elected to the office of the President more than twice, and no person who has held the office of President, or acted as President, for more than two years of a term to which some other person was elected President shall be elected to the office of the President more than once. But this Article shall not apply to any person holding the office of President when this Article was proposed by the Congress, and shall not prevent any person who may be holding the office of President, or acting as President, during the term within which this Article becomes operative from holding the office of President or acting as President during the remainder of such term.

**Section 2.** This Article shall be inoperative unless it shall have been ratified as an amendment to the Constitution by the legislatures of three-fourths of the several States within seven years from the date of its submission to the States by the Congress.

**Amendment XXIII** *(Ratified March 29, 1961)*

**Section 1.** The District constituting the seat of Government of the United States shall appoint in such manner as the Congress may direct:

A number of electors of President and Vice President equal to the whole number of Senators and Representatives in Congress to which the District would be entitled if it were a State, but in no event more than the least populous State; they shall be in addition to those appointed by the States, but they shall be considered, for the purposes of the election of President and Vice President, to be electors appointed by a State; and they shall meet in the District and perform such duties as provided by the twelfth article of amendment.

**Section 2.** The Congress shall have power to enforce this article by appropriate legislation.

**Amendment XXIV** *(Ratified Jan. 23, 1964)*

**Section 1.** The right of citizens of the United States to vote in any primary or other election for President or Vice President, for electors for President or Vice President, or for Senator or Representative in Congress, shall not be denied or abridged by the United States or any State by reason of failure to pay any poll tax or other tax.

**Section 2.** The Congress shall have power to enforce this article by appropriate legislation.

**Amendment XXV** *(Ratified Feb. 10, 1967)*

**Section 1.** In case of the removal of the President from office or of his death or resignation, the Vice President shall become President.

**Section 2.** Whenever there is a vacancy in the office of the Vice President, the President shall nominate a Vice President who shall take office upon confirmation by a majority vote of both Houses of Congress.

**Section 3.** Whenever the President transmits to the President pro tempore of the Senate and the Speaker of the House of Representatives his written declaration that he is unable to discharge the powers and duties of his office, and until he transmits to them a written declaration to the contrary, such powers and duties shall be discharged by the Vice President as Acting President.

**Section 4.** Whenever the Vice President and a majority of either the principal officers of the executive departments or of such other body as Congress may by law provide, transmit to the President pro tempore of the Senate and the Speaker of the House of Representatives their written declaration that the President is unable to discharge the powers and duties of his office, the Vice President shall immediately assume the powers and duties of the office as Acting President.

Thereafter, when the President transmits to the President pro tempore of the Senate and the Speaker of the House of Representatives his written declaration that no inability exists, he shall resume the powers and duties of his office unless the Vice President and a majority of either the principal officers of the executive department or of such other body as Congress may by law provide, transmit within four days to the President pro tempore of the Senate and the Speaker of the House of Representatives their written declaration that the President is unable to discharge the powers and duties of his office. Thereupon Congress shall decide the issue, assembling within forty-eight hours for that purpose if not in session. If the Congress, within twenty-one days after receipt of the latter written declaration, or, if Congress is not in session, within twenty-one days after Congress is required to assemble, determines by two-thirds vote of both houses that the President is unable to discharge the powers and duties of his office, the Vice President shall continue to discharge the same as Acting President; otherwise, the President shall resume the powers and duties of his office.

**Amendment XXVI** *(Ratified July 1, 1971)*

**Section 1.** The right of citizens of the United States, who are eighteen years of age or older, to vote shall not be denied or abridged by the United States or by any State on account of age.

**Section 2.** The Congress shall have power to enforce this article by appropriate legislation.

# SELECTED BIBLIOGRAPHY

## Part I Powers of the Purse

### Books


Berman, Larry. *The Office of Management and Budget and the Presidency, 1921-1979.* Princeton, N.J.: Princeton University Press, 1979.

Blough, Ray. *The Federal Taxing Process.* Englewood Cliffs, N.J.: Prentice-Hall, 1952.

Fenno, Richard F., Jr. *The Power of the Purse: Appropriation Politics in Congress.* Boston: Little, Brown & Co., 1973.

Findley, William. *Review of the Revenue System Adopted by the First Congress.* Philadelphia: T. Dobson, 1794; reprint ed., New York: A. M. Kelley, 1971.

Fisher Louis. *President and Congress.* New York: Free Press, 1972.

———. *Presidential Spending Power.* Princeton, N.J.: Princeton University Press, 1975.

Galloway, George B. *The Legislative Process in Congress.* New York: Thomas Y. Crowell Co., 1955.

Harris, Joseph P. *Congressional Control of Administration.* Washington, D.C.: The Brookings Institution, 1964.

Havemann, Joel. *Congress and the Budget.* Bloomington, Ind.: Indiana University Press, 1978.

Horn, Stephen. *Unused Power: The Work of the Senate Committee on Appropriations.* Washington, D.C.: The Brookings Institution, 1970.

Ippolito, D.S. *The Budget and National Politics.* San Francisco: W.H. Freeman, 1978.

Kimmel, Lewis H. *Federal Budget and Fiscal Policy, 1789-1958.* Washington, D.C.: The Brookings Institution, 1959.

LeLoup, Lance. *The Fiscal Congress.* Westport, Conn.: Greenwood Press, 1981.

Lewis, Wilfred, Jr. *Federal Fiscal Policy in the Postwar Recessions.* Washington, D.C.: The Brookings Institution, 1962.

MacLean, Joan C. *President and Congress: The Conflict of Powers.* The Bronx, N.Y.: H.W. Wilson, 1955.

Manley, John F. *The Politics of Finance: The House Committee on Ways and Means.* Boston: Little, Brown & Co., 1970.

McAllister, Eugene J., ed. *Agenda for Progress: Examining Federal Spending.* Washington, D.C.: Heritage Foundation, 1981.

———. *Congress and the Budget: Evaluating the Process.* Washington, D.C.: Heritage Foundation, 1979.

Ogg, Frederic A., and Ray, P. Orman. *Introduction to American Government.* New York: Appleton-Century-Crofts, 1951.

Ott, David J., and Ott, Attiat F. *Federal Budget Policy.* rev. ed. Washington, D.C.: The Brookings Institution, 1969.

Pechman, Joseph A. *Federal Tax Policy.* 3rd ed. Washington, D.C.: The Brookings Institution, 1977.

Pressman, Jeffrey L. *House vs. Senate: Conflict in the Appropriation Process.* New Haven, Conn.: Yale University Press, 1966.

Pritchett, C. Herman. *The American Constitution.* 3rd ed. New York: McGraw-Hill Book Co., 1977.

Schick, Allen. "The Battle of the Budget." In *Congress Against the President*, edited by Harvey C. Mansfield, Sr., pp. 51-70. New York: Praeger Publishers, 1975.

———. *Congress and Money: Budgeting, Spending and Taxing.* Washington, D.C.: The Urban Institute, 1980.

———. *The Congressional Budget Act of 1974: Legislative History and Analysis* Washington D.C.: Library of Congress, Congressional Research Service, 1976.

———. "The Three-Ring Budget Process: The Appropriations, Tax and Budget Committee in Congress." In *The New Congress,* edited by Thomas E. Mann and Norman J. Ornstein, pp. 288-328. Washington, D.C.: American Enterprise Institute for Public Policy Research, 1981.

Selko, Daniel T. *The Federal Financial System.* Washington, D.C.: The Brookings Institution, 1940.

Sharkansky, Ira. *The Politics of Taxing and Spending.* New York: Bobbs-Merrill Co., 1969.

Wallace, Robert Ash. *Congressional Control of Federal Spending.* Detroit: Wayne State University Press, 1960.

Weidenbaum, Murray L. *Federal Budgeting: The Choice of Government Programs.* Washington, D.C.: American Enterprise Institute for Public Policy Research, 1964.

Williams, Walter. *The Congressional Budget Office: A Critical Link in Budget Reform.* Seattle: Institute of Government Research, University of Washington, 1974.

Wilmerding, Lucius, Jr. *The Spending Power: A History of the Efforts of Congress to Control Expenditures.* New Haven, Conn.: Yale University Press, 1943.

**Government Publications**

President's Commission on Budget Concepts. *Report of th President's Commission on Budget Concepts.* Washington, D.C.: U.S. Government Printing Office, 1967.

U.S. Congress. House. Committee on the Budget. *Congressional Budget Reform, Committee Print, July 12, 1974.* Washington, D.C.: U.S. Government Printing Office, 1975.

U.S. Congress. Joint Study Committee on Budget Control. *Improving Congressional Control Over Budgetary Outlay and Receipt Totals, Report, February 7, 1973.* Washington, D.C.: U.S. Government Printing Office, 1973.

U.S. Congress. Senate. *The Authority of the Senate to Originate Appropriations Bills.* S. Doc. 17, 88th Cong., 1st sess., 1963.

——. Committee on Government Operations. *Financial Management in the Federal Government.* S. Doc. 11, 87th Cong., 1st sess., 1961.

## Part II Foreign Affairs

**Books**

Abshire, David M. *Foreign Policy Makers: President vs. Congress.* The Center for Strategic and International Studies, The Washington Papers. vol. 7. no. 66. Beverly Hills, Calif.: Sage Publications, 1979.

Berger, Raoul. *Executive Privilege.* Cambridge: Harvard University Press, 1974.

Blechman, Barry M., and Kaplan, Stephen S. *Force Without War: U.S. Armed Forces as a Political Instrument.* Washington, D.C.: The Brookings Institution, 1978.

Butler, Charles H. *The Treaty Making Power of the United States.* New York: Banks Law Publishing Co., 1902.

Carroll, Holbert N. *The House of Representatives and Foreign Affairs.* Boston: Little, Brown & Co., 1966.

Cheever, Daniel S., and Haviland, H. Field, Jr. *American Foreign Policy and the Separation of Powers.* Cambridge: Harvard University Press, 1952.

Corwin, Edward S. *The President: Office and Powers, 1787-1957.* New York: New York University Press, 1957.

Crabb, Cecil V., Jr., and Holt, Pat M. *Invitation to Struggle: Congress, the President and Foreign Policy.* Washington, D.C.: CQ Press, 1980.

Crandall, Samuel B. *Treaties: Their Making and Enforcement.* New York: Columbia University Press, 1904.

Cronin, Thomas E., and Tugwell, Rexford G. *The Presidency Reappraised.* 2d ed. New York: Praeger Publishers, 1977.

Dahl, Robert A. *Congress and Foreign Policy.* New York: Harcourt, Brace & Co., 1950.

Dangerfield, Royden J. *In Defense of the Senate.* Norman, Okla.: University of Oklahoma Press, 1933.

Dennison, Eleanor E. *The Senate Foreign Relations Committee.* Stanford: Stanford University Press, 1942.

Destler, I. M. "Executive-Congressional Conflict in Foreign Policy: Explaining It, Coping With It." In *Congress Reconsidered.* 2d ed., edited by Lawrence C. Dodd and Bruce I. Oppenheimer, pp. 296-316. Washington, D.C.: CQ Press, 1981.

———. "Trade Consensus, SALT Stalemate: Congress and Foreign Policy in the 1970s." In *The New Congress,* edited Thomas E. Mann and Norman J. Ornstein, pp. 329-359. Washington, D.C.: American Enterprise Institute for Public Policy Research, 1981.

Eagleton, Thomas J. *War and Presidential Power.* New York: Liveright, 1974.

Farnsworth, David N. *The Senate Committee on Foreign Relations.* Urbana: University of Illinois Press, 1961.

*The Federalist Papers.* Introduction by Clinton Rossiter. New York: Mentor, 1961.

Fisher, Louis. *President and Congress.* New York: The Free Press, 1972.

Fleming, Denna F. *The Treaty Veto of the American Senate.* New York: G. P. Putnam's Sons, 1930.

Franck, Thomas M., ed. *The Tethered Presidency: Congressional Restraints on Executive Power.* New York: New York University Press, 1981.

Franck, Thomas M., and Weisband, Edward. *Foreign Policy by Congress.* New York and Oxford: Oxford University Press, 1979.

Harden, Ralston. *The Senate and Treaties, 1789-1817.* New York: Macmillan Publishing Co., 1920.

Harris, Joseph P. *The Advice and Consent of the Senate.* Westport, Conn.: Greenwood Press, 1968.

Haynes, George H. *The Senate of the United States: Its History and Practice.* 2 vols. Boston: Houghton Mifflin Co., 1938.

Henkin, Louis. *Foreign Affairs and the Constitution.* New York: W. W. Norton & Co., 1972.

Holt, Pat M. *The War Powers Resolution: The Role of Congress in U.S. Armed Intervention.* Washington, D.C.: American Enterprise Institute for Public Policy Research, 1978.

Holt, W. Stull. *Treaties Defeated by the Senate.* Baltimore: Johns Hopkins University Press, 1933.

Kolodziej, Edward A. "Congress and Foreign Policy: The Nixon Years." In *Congress Against the President,* edited by Harvey C. Mansfield Sr. New York: Praeger Publishers, 1975.

Lehman, John. *The Executive, Congress, and Foreign Policy: Studies of the Nixon Administration.* New York: Praeger Publishers, 1976.

Paul, Roland A. *American Military Commitments Abroad.* New Brunswick, N.J.: Rutgers University Press, 1973.

Pritchett, C. Herman. *The American Constitution.* 3rd ed. New York: McGraw-Hill Book Co., 1977.

Robinson, James A. *Congress and Foreign Policy Making.* Homewood, Ill.: Dorsey Press, 1962.

Schlesinger, Arthur M., Jr. *The Imperial Presidency.* Boston: Houghton Mifflin Co., 1973.

Spanier, John, and Nogee, Joseph, eds. *Congress, the Presidency and American Foreign Policy.* New York: Pergamon Press, 1981.

Tugwell, Rexford G. *The Enlargement of the Presidency.* New York: Doubleday & Co., 1960.

Warren, Charles. *The Making of the Constitution.* Boston: Little, Brown & Co., 1928.

Westphal, C. F. *The House Committee on Foreign Affairs.* New York: Columbia University Press, 1942.

Wilcox, Francis O. *Congress, the Executive and Foreign Policy.* New York: Harper & Row, 1971.

**Articles**

Bax, Frans. "The Legislative-Executive Relationship in Foreign Policy: New Partnership or New Competition?" *Orbis,* 1977, pp. 881-904.

Bennet, Douglas J., Jr. "Congress in Foreign Policy: Who Needs It?" *Foreign Affairs,* Fall 1978, pp. 40-50.

Berry, John M. "Foreign Policy Making and the Congress." *Editorial Research Reports,* April 19, 1967, pp. 281-300.

Brewer, F. M. "Advice and Consent of the Senate." *Editorial Research Reports,* June 1, 1943, pp. 341-356.

——. "The Treaty Power." *Editorial Research Reports,* Jan. 18, 1943, pp. 37-54.

"Congress and Foreign Relations." *Annals of the American Academy of Political and Social Science,* September 1953.

"Congress, the President and the Power to Commit Forces to Combat." *Harvard Law Review,* June 1968, pp. 1771-1805.

Cronin, Thomas E. "A Resurgent Congress and the Imperial Presidency." *Political Science Quarterly,* Summer 1980, pp. 209-237.

Darling, W. Stuart, and Mense, D. Craig. "Rethinking the War Powers Act." *Presidential Studies Quarterly,* Spring/Summer 1977, pp. 126-136.

Destler, I. M. "Treaty Troubles: Versailles in Reverse." *Foreign Policy,* Winter 1978-79, pp. 45-65.

Frye, Alton. "Congress and President: The Balance Wheels of American Foreign Policy." *The Yale Review,* October 1979, pp. 1-16.

Fulbright, J. William. "The Legislator As Educator." *Foreign Affairs,* Spring 1979, pp. 719-732.

Gould, James W. "The Origins of the Senate Committee on Foreign Relations, 1789-1816." *Western Political Quarterly,* September 1959, pp. 670-682.

Hamilton, Lee H., and Van Dusen, Michael H. "Making the Separation of Powers Work." *Foreign Affairs,* Fall 1978, pp. 17-39.

Hilsman, Roger. "Congressional-Executive Relations and the Foreign Policy Consensus." *American Political Science Review,* 1978, pp. 725-744.

Johnson, Loch, and McCormick, James M. "The Making of International Agreements: A Reappraisal of Congressional Involvement." *Journal of Politics,* May 1978, pp. 468-478.

Kessler, Frank. "Presidential-Congressional Battles: Toward a Truce on the Foreign Policy Front." *Presidential Studies Quarterly,* Spring 1978, pp. 115-127.

Lanouette, William J. "A New Kind of Bipartisanship for the Foreign Relations Committee." *National Journal,* March 31, 1979, pp. 525-528.

——. "Who's Setting Foreign Policy — Carter or Congress?" *National Journal,* July 15, 1978, pp. 1116-1123.

Lee, Kendrick. "Congress and the Conduct of War." *Editorial Research Reports,* Aug. 24, 1942, pp. 125-140.

Madison, Christopher. "Percy Tests His Bipartisan Style at the Foreign Relations Committee." *National Journal,* June 6, 1981, pp. 1008-1012.

Manley, John F. "The Rise of Congress in Foreign Policy-Making." *Annals of the American Academy of Political and Social Science,* September 1971, pp. 60-70.

Manning, Bayless. "The Congress, the Executive and Intermestic Affairs: Three Proposals." *Foreign Affairs,* January 1977, pp. 306-324.

Patch, Buel W. "American Policy on the League of Nations and the World Court." *Editorial Research Reports,* Jan. 2, 1935, pp. 1-24.

——. "The Power to Declare War." *Editorial Research Reports,* Jan. 6, 1938, pp. 1-18.

——. "Treaties and Domestic Law." *Editorial Research Reports,* March 28, 1952, pp. 239-256.

"Presidential vs. Congressional War-Making Powers." *Boston University Law Review,* Special Issue 1970, pp. 5-116.

Putney, Bryant. "Participation by Congress in Control of Foreign Policy." *Editorial Research Reports,* Nov. 9, 1939, pp. 337-355.

Stevens, Charles J. "The Use and Control of Executive Agreements: Recent Congressional Initiatives." *Orbis,* Winter 1977, pp. 905-931.

Whittle, Richard. "Foreign Relations Committee Searches for Renewed Glory." *Congressional Quarterly Weekly Report,* March 14, 1981, pp. 477-479.

Worsnop, Richard L. "War Powers of the President." *Editorial Research Reports,* March 14, 1966, pp. 181-200.

Zeidenstein, Harvey G. "The Reassertion of Congressional Power: New Curbs on the President." *Political Science Quarterly,* Fall 1978, pp. 393-409.

## Government Publications

U.S. Congress. House. Committee on Foreign Affairs. *Background Information on the Use of United States Armed Forces in Foreign Countries.* 1970 revision by the Foreign Affairs Division, Legislative Reference Service, Library of Congress. 91st Cong., 2d sess., 1970.

——. *Concerning the War Powers of Congress and the President.* H. Rept. 91-1547 to Accompany H.J. Res. 1355. 91st Cong., 2d sess., 1970; H. Rept. 92-1302 to Accompany S. 2956. 92d Cong., 2d sess., 1972.

——. *Selected Executive Session Hearings of the Foreign Affairs Committee, 1943-* . (Historical Series.)

———. *The War Powers Resolution: Relevant Documents, Correspondence, Reports.* Committee print. 97th Cong., 1st sess., June 1981.

U.S. Congress. Senate. Committee on Foreign Relations. *Background Information on the Committee on Foreign Relations, United States Senate.* 3rd rev. ed. 94th Cong., 1st sess., 1975.

———. *Congress, Information and Foreign Affairs.* Foreign Affairs and National Defense Division, Congressional Research Service, Library of Congress. Committee print. 95th Cong., 2d sess., September 1978.

———. *Documents Relating to the War Power of Congress, the President's Authority as Commander-in-Chief and the War in Indochina.* 91st Cong., 2d sess., 1970.

———. *Executive Sessions of the Senate Foreign Relations Committee, 1947- .* (Historical Series.)

———. *Hearings Before the Subcommittee on U.S. Security Agreements and Commitments Abroad.* 91st Cong., 1st and 2d sess., 1969-70.

———. *National Commitments.* S. Rept. 90-797 to Accompany S. Res. 187. 90th Cong., 1st sess., 1967; S. Rept. 91-129 to Accompany S. Res. 85. 91st Cong., 1st sess., 1969.

———. *Termination of Southeast Asia Resolution.* S. Rept. 91-872 to Accompany S. Con. Res. 64. 91st Cong., 2d sess., May 15, 1970.

———. *War Powers.* S. Rept. 92-606 to Accompany S. 2956. 92d Cong., 2d sess., 1972.

U.S. Congress. Senate. Committee on the Judiciary. *Congressional Oversight of Executive Agreements.* S. Rept. to Accompany S. 1472. 93rd Cong., 1st sess., 1973.

## Part III Commerce Power

### Books

Beard, Charles A. *Economic Interpretation of the Constitution of the United States.* New York: Macmillan, 1935.

Benson, Paul R. *Supreme Court and the Commerce Clause, 1937-1970.* Port Washington, N.Y.: Dunellen Publishing Co., 1971.

Beth, Loren P. *The Development of the American Constitution, 1877-1917.* New York: Harper & Row, 1971.

Beveridge, Albert J. *The Life of John Marshall.* 4 vols. Boston: Houghton Mifflin Co., 1919.

Carr, Robert K. *The Supreme Court and Judicial Review.* American Government in Action Series. New York: Farrar & Rinehart, 1942.

Corwin, Edward S. *The Commerce Power versus States Rights.* Princeton, N.J.: Princeton University Press, 1936.

Crosskey, William W. *Politics and the Constitution in the History of the United States.* Chicago: University of Chicago Press, 1953.

Frankfurter, Felix. *The Commerce Clause Under Marshall, Taney and Waite.* Chapel Hill: University of North Carolina Press, 1937.

Gavit, Bernard C. *Commerce Clause of the United States Constitution.* New York: AMS Press, 1970.

Haines, Charles Grover, and Sherwood, Foster H. *The Role of the Supreme Court in American Government and Politics, 1835-1864.* Berkeley: University of California Press, 1957.

Hamilton, Walton H., and Adair, Douglas. *The Power to Govern: The Constitution — Then and Now.* New York: W.W. Norton & Co., 1937.

Kallenback, Joseph E. *Federal Cooperation with the States under the Commerce Clause.* Ann Arbor: University of Michigan Press, 1942.

Kelly, Alfred H., and Harbison, Winfred A. *The American Constitution: Its Origins and Development.* 5th ed. New York: W.W. Norton & Co., 1976.

Liebhafsky, H.H. *American Government and Business:* New York: John Wiley & Sons, 1971.

Morison, Samuel Eliot; Commager, Henry Steele; Leuchtenburg, William E. *The Growth of the American Republic.* 2 vols. 6th ed. New York: Oxford University Press, 1969.

Ogg, Frederic A., and Ray, P. Orman. *Introduction to American Government.* New York: Appleton-Century-Crofts, 1951.

Pritchett, C. Herman. *The American Constitution.* 3rd ed. New York: McGraw-Hill Book Co., 1977.

——. *The Roosevelt Court: A Study in Judicial Politics and Values, 1937-1947.* New York: Macmillan, 1948.

Reynolds, George G. *Distribution of Power to Regulate Interstate Carriers Between the Nation and the States.* New York: AMS Press, 1928.

Swisher, Carl Brent. *American Constitutional Development.* 2d ed. Cambridge: Houghton Mifflin Co., 1954.

Warren, Charles. *The Making of the Constitution.* Boston: Little, Brown & Co., 1928.

———. *The Supreme Court in United States History.* 2 vols. rev. ed. Boston: Little, Brown & Co., 1926.

## Part IV Impeachment

**Books**

The Association of the Bar of the City of New York. *The Law of Presidential Impeachment and Removal,* 1974.

Benedict, Michael L. *The Impeachment and Trial of Andrew Johnson.* New York: W. W. Norton & Co., 1973.

Berger, Raoul. *Impeachment: The Constitutional Problems.* Cambridge: Harvard University Press, 1973.

Black, Charles L. *Impeachment: A Handbook.* New Haven: Yale University Press, 1974.

Brant, Irving. *Impeachment: Trials and Errors.* New York: Knopf, 1972.

Dewitt, David M. *Impeachment and Trial of Andrew Johnson.* New York: Russell & Russell, 1967.

Farrand, Max, ed. *The Records of the Federal Convention of 1787.* 4 vols. New Haven: Yale University Press, 1911.

*The Federalist Papers.* Introduction by Clinton Rossiter. New York: Mentor, 1961.

Haynes, George H. *The Senate of the United States: Its History and Practice.* 2 vols. Boston: Houghton Mifflin Co., 1938.

Riddick, Floyd M. *The United States Congress: Organization and Procedure.* Manassas, Va.: National Capitol Publishers, 1949.

Simpson, Alexander, Jr. *A Treatise of Federal Impeachments.* Philadelphia, 1916; reprint ed., Wilmington, Del.: Scholarly Resources, 1974.

**Articles**

Bates, William. "Vagueness in the Constitution: The Impeachment Power." *Stanford Law Journal,* June 1973, pp. 908-926.

Berger, Raoul. "Executive Privilege vs. Congressional Inquiry." *UCLA Law Review,* 2 (1965): 104.

———. "Impeachment for 'High Crimes and Misdemeanors.' " *Southern California Law Review,* 44 (1971): 395-460.

Bishop, J. W. "The Executive's Right to Privacy: An Unresolved Constitutional Question." *Yale Law Journal* 66 (1957): 477.

Collins, P. R. "Power of Congressional Committees of Investigations to Obtain Information from the Executive Branch." *Georgia Law Journal,* 39 (1951): 563.

Dougherty, J. H. "Inherent Limitations Upon Impeachment." *Yale Law Journal,* 23 (1913): 60-69.

Fenton, Paul S. "The Scope of the Impeachment Power." *Northwestern University Law Review,* November/December 1970, pp. 719-758.

"The Impeachment of Andrew Johnson." *Annals of the American Academy of Political and Social Science,* 10 (1968): 126-133.

"President and Congress: Power of the President to Refuse Congressional Demand for Information." *Stanford Law Review,* 1 (1949): 256.

**Government Publications**

"An Analysis of the Constitutional Standard for Presidential Impeachment." Prepared by the attorneys for the President, The White House, February 1974.

Cannon, Clarence. *Cannon's Precedents of the House of Representatives.* Washington, D.C.: U.S. Government Printing Office, 1935.

Hinds, Asher C. *Hinds' Precedents of the House of Representatives.* Washington, D.C.: U.S. Government Printing Office, 1907.

U.S. Congress. House. Committee on the Judiciary. *Constitutional Grounds for Presidential Impeachment.* 93d Cong., 2d sess., 1974.

——. *Impeachment: Selected Materials.* 93d Cong., 1st sess., 1973.

——. *Impeachment: Selected Materials.* 93d Cong., 2d sess., 1974.

U.S. Congress. Senate. Committee on the Judiciary. *Removal Power of Congress With Respect to the Supreme Court.* 80th Cong., 1st sess., 1947.

U.S. Department of Justice. Office of Legal Counsel. "Legal Aspects of Impeachment: An Overview." February 1974.

## Part V Investigations

**Books**

Barth, Alan. *Government by Investigation.* New York: Viking Press, 1955.

Beck, Carl. *Contempt of Congress: A Study of the Prosecutions Initiated by the Committee on Un-American Activities, 1945-1957.* New Orleans: Hauser Press, 1959.

Bentley, Eric, ed. *Thirty Years of Treason: Excerpts from Hearings before the House Un-American Activities Committee, 1938-1968.* New York: Viking Press, 1971.

Berger, Raoul. *Executive Privilege.* Cambridge: Harvard University Press, 1974.

Carr, Robert K. *The House Committee on Un-American Activities, 1945-1950.* Ithaca: Cornell University Press, 1952.

Chambers, Whittaker. *Witness.* New York: Random House, 1952.

Congressional Quarterly. *Watergate: Chronology of a Crisis.* Washington, D.C.: Congressional Quarterly, 1975.

Dimock, Marshall E. *Congressional Investigating Committees.* Baltimore: Johns Hopkins Press, 1929.

Eberling, Ernest J. *Congressional Investigations: A Study of the Origin and Development of the Power of Congress to Investigate and Punish for Contempt.* New York: Columbia University Press, 1928.

Galloway, George B. *History of the House of Representatives.* New York: Thomas Y. Crowell Co., 1969.

Goldfarb, Ronald L. *The Contempt Power.* New York: Columbia University Press, 1963.

Goodman, Walter. *The Committee: The Extraordinary Career of the House Committee on Un-American Activities.* New York: Farrar, Straus & Giroux, 1968.

Hamilton, James. *The Power to Probe: A Study of Congressional Investigations.* New York: Random House, 1976.

Harris, Joseph P. *Congressional Control of Administration.* Washington, D.C.: The Brookings Institution, 1964.

McGeary, M. Nelson. *The Development of Congressional Investigative Power.* New York: Octagon Books, 1966.

Ogden, August Raymond. *The Dies Committee: A Study of the Special House Committees for Investigation of Un-American Activities, 1938-44.* Washington, D.C.: Catholic University of America Press, 1945.

Pritchett, C. Herman. *The American Constitution.* 3rd. ed. New York: McGraw-Hill Book Co., 1977.

Riddle, Donald H. *The Truman Committee: A Study in Congressional Responsibility.* New Brunswick, N.J.: Rutgers University Press, 1964.

Rieselbach, Leroy N. *Congressional Politics.* New York: McGraw-Hill Book Co., 1973.

Rovere, Richard H. *Senator Joe McCarthy.* Cleveland: World Publishing Co., 1968.

Schlesinger, Arthur M., Jr., and Burns, Roger, eds. *Congress Investigates: A Documentary History, 1792-1974.* 5 vols. New York: Bowker, 1975.

Sundquist, James L. *The Decline and Resurgence of Congress.* Washington, D.C.: The Brookings Institution, 1981.

Taylor, Telford. *Grand Inquest.* New York: Simon & Schuster, 1955.

Wilson, Woodrow. *Congressional Government.* Gloucester, Mass.: Peter Smith, 1885; rev. ed. Cleveland: World Publishing Co., 1967.

Wiltz, John E. *In Search of Peace: The Senate Munitions Inquiry, 1934-1936.* Baton Rouge: Louisiana State University Press, 1963.

**Articles**

"The Application of the Fourth Amendment to Congressional Investigations." *Minnesota Law Review,* January 1968, pp. 665-697.

Cousens, Theodore W. "The Purpose and Scope of Investigation Under Legislative Authority." *Georgetown Law Journal,* 26 (1968): 905.

Dillard, Irving. "Congressional Investigations: The Role of the Press." *University of Chicago Law Review,* 18 (1951): 585-590.

Galloway, George. "Congressional Investigation: Proposed Reforms." *University of Chicago Law Review,* 18 (1951): 478-502.

———. "The Investigative Function of Congress." *American Political Science Review,* February 1927, pp. 47-70.

Kaplan, Lewis A. "The House Un-American Activities Committee and Its Opponents: A Study in Congressional Dissonance." *Journal of Politics,* August 1968, pp. 647-671.

McGeary, M. Nelson. "Congressional Investigations: Historical Development." *University of Chicago Law Review,* 18 (1951): 425-439.

———. "Congressional Power of Investigation." *Nebraska Law Review,* 28 (1949): 516-529.

**Government Publication**

U.S. Congress. Library of Congress. Legislative Research Service. *Congressional Power of Investigation.* Washington, D.C.: U.S. Government Printing Office, 1954.

## Part VI Confirmations

**Books**

Adams, Bruce, and Kavanagh-Barab, Kathryn. *Promise and Performance: Carter Builds a New Administration.* Lexington, Mass: Lexington Books, 1979.

American Assembly, Graduate School of Business. *The Federal Government Service: Its Character, Prestige and Problems.* New York: Columbia University Press, 1954.

Arnold, R. Douglas. *Congress and the Bureaucracy.* New Haven, Conn.: Yale University Press, 1979.

Common Cause. *The Senate Rubberstamp Machine: A Common Cause Study of the U.S. Senate's Confirmation Process.* Washington, D.C.: Common Cause, 1977.

Corson, John J., and Paul, R. Shale. *Men Near the Top: Filling Key Posts in the Federal Service.* Baltimore: Johns Hopkins Press, 1966.

Corwin, Edward S. *The President's Removal Power under the Constitution.* New York: National Municipal League, 1927.

*The Federalist Papers.* Introduction by Clinton Rossiter. New York: Mentor, 1961.

Fenno, Richard F., Jr. *The President's Cabinet: An Analysis of the Period from Wilson to Eisenhower.* Cambridge, Mass.: Harvard University Press, 1959.

Fisher, Louis. *The Politics of Shared Power: Congress and the Electorate.* Washington, D.C.: CQ Press, 1981.

Freidin, Seymour K. *A Sense of the Senate.* New York: Dodd, Mead & Co., 1972.

Harris, Joseph P. *The Advice and Consent of the Senate: A Study of the Confirmation of Appointments by the United States Senate.* Westport, Conn.: Greenwood Press, 1968.

Harris, Richard. *Decision.* New York: E. P. Dutton & Co., 1971.

Haynes, George H. *The Senate of the United States: Its History and Practice.* 2 vols. Boston: Houghton Mifflin Co., 1938.

Horn, Stephen. *The Cabinet and Congress.* New York: Columbia University Press, 1960.

Kilpatrick, Franklin P.; Cummings, Milton C., Jr.; and Jennings, M. Kent. *The Image of the Federal Service.* Washington, D.C.: The Brookings Institution, 1964.

Lasson, Kenneth. *Private Lives of Public Servants.* Bloomington, Ind.: Indiana University Press, 1978.

Mackenzie, G. Calvin. *The Politics of Presidential Appointments.* New York: Free Press, 1981.

Mann, Dean E. *The Assistant Secretaries: Problems and Processes of Appointment.* Washington, D.C.: The Brookings Institution, 1965.

Riddick, Floyd M. *The United States Congress: Organization and Procedure.* Manassas, Va.: National Capitol Publishers, 1949.

Rogers, Lindsay. *The American Senate.* New York: Alfred A. Knopf, 1926.

Rothman, David J. *Politics and Power: The United States Senate, 1869-1901.* New York: Atheneum, 1969.

Stanley, David T.; Mann, Dean E.; and Doig, Jamison W. *Men Who Govern: A Biographical Profile of Federal Political Executives.* Washington, D.C.: The Brookings Institution, 1967.

Tolchin, Martin, and Tolchin, Susan. *To the Victor . . . Political Patronage from the Clubhouse to the White House.* New York: Random House, 1971.

Warren, Charles. *The Supreme Court in United States History.* Boston: Little, Brown & Co., 1926.

**Articles**

"Attacking the Old Boy Network." *Time Magazine,* March 28, 1977.

Babcock, Charles R. "Picking Federal Judges: Merit System vs. Pork Bench." *The Washington Post,* Nov. 7, 1978.

Berlow, Alan. "Carter Gets Patronage Plum of 152 Judges." *Congressional Quarterly Weekly Report,* Oct. 14, 1978, pp. 2961-2963.

——. "Carter Order Raises Doubts Whether Judges Will Be Selected on Merit Basis." *Congressional Quarterly Weekly Report,* Nov. 18, 1978, pp. 3313-3314.

Bickel, Alexander M. "The Making of Supreme Court Justices." *New Leader,* May 25, 1970, pp. 14-18.

Black, Charles L., Jr. "A Note on Senatorial Consideration of Supreme Court Nominees." *Yale Law Journal,* March 1970, pp. 657-664.

Bonafede, Dom. "Nixon's First-Year Appointments Reveal Pattern of His Administration." *National Journal Reports,* Jan. 24, 1970.

Bonafede, Dom, and Glass, Andrew J. "Haig Revamping Staff, Shifts in Patronage Policy Likely." *National Journal Reports,* April 6, 1974.

Broder, David S. "Confirmation Hearings: Playing Charades." *The Washington Post,* Nov. 13, 1977.

Carmen, Ira H. "The President, Politics and the Power of Appointment." *Virginia Law Review,* May 1969, pp. 616-659.

Cook, Rhodes. "FEC Nominee Dispute Shifts from Zagoria to McGarry." *Congressional Quarterly Weekly Report,* Dec. 3, 1977.

Cross, Mercer. "Delay on Top Jobs: Good or Bad?" *Congressional Quarterly Weekly Report,* March 5, 1977.

——. "Interest Group Doubts Rise on Top Jobs." *Congressional Quarterly Weekly Report,* April 30, 1977.

Gellhorm, Ernest, and Freer, Robert E., Jr. "Assuring Competence in Federal Agency Appointments." *American Bar Association Journal,* February 1979, p. 65.

Gimlin, Hoyt. "Challenging of Supreme Court." *Editorial Research Reports,* Oct. 9, 1968, pp. 741-760.

Griffin, Robert P., and Hart, Philip A. "The Fortas Controversy: The Senate's Role of Advice and Consent to Judicial Nominations." *Prospectus,* April 1969, pp. 238-310.

Hager, Barry M. "Confirmation Process: Weaknesses Abound." *Congressional Quarterly Weekly Report,* Feb. 4, 1978.

——. "Bell Questioned Closely at Confirmation Hearings." *Congressional Quarterly Weekly Report,* Jan. 15, 1977.

Hess, Stephen. "Fair and Foul in Senate's Advice." *The Washington Star,* March 20, 1977.

Kaiser, Robert G. "Carter Appointees May Have to Reveal Some Financial Details." *The Washington Post,* Nov. 19, 1976.

——. "The 2,000 Carter Jobs: Who Got Them?" *The Washington Post,* June 6, 1977.

McConnell, A. Mitchell, Jr. "Haynsworth and Carswell: A New Senate Standard of Excellence." *Kentucky Law Journal,* Fall 1970, pp. 7-34.

Mendelsohn, Rona Hirsch. "Senate Confirmation of Supreme Court Appointments: The Nomination and Rejection of John J. Parker." *Howard Law Journal,* Winter 1967, pp. 105-148.

Maro, Anthony. "Despite Carter Vow, Few Aides Disclose Personal Financial Data." *The Washington Star,* Aug. 25, 1978.

Parris, Judith H. "The Senate's Power to Confirm Nominations as a Constraint on Presidential Government." Paper delivered to the American University Conference on the Presidential System of Government, Washington, D.C., April 1976.

Rodell, Fred. "The Complexities of Mr. Justice Fortas." *New York Times Magazine,* July 28, 1968, pp. 67-68.

Slotnick, Elliot E. "The Carter Presidency and the U.S. Circuit Judge Nominating Commission." Paper delivered at the annual meeting of the American Political Science Association, New York, Aug. 31-Sept. 3, 1978.

Steele, John L. "Haynsworth vs. the U.S. Senate (1969)." *Fortune,* March 1970, pp. 90-93.

Swindler, William F. "The Politics of 'Advice and Consent': The Senate's Role in Selection of Supreme Court Justices." *American Bar Association Journal,* June 1970, pp. 533-542.

Tolchin, Martin. "Carter Takes Hands-Off Approach to Patronage, Irking Some in Party." *The New York Times,* May 22, 1977.

Totenberg, Nina. "Will Judges Be Chosen Rationally?" *Judicature* 60 (Aug.-Sept. 1976).

Towell, Pat. "Carter Assurances Secure Victory on Warnke." *Congressional Quarterly Weekly Report,* March 12, 1977.

Wukasch, Barry C. "The Abe Fortas Controversy: A Research Note on the Senate's Role in Judicial Selection." *Western Political Quarterly,* March 1971, pp. 24-27.

**Government Publications**

U.S. Congress. *Congressional Record.* "Disposition of Executive Nominations, Nov. 15, 1978, p. D 1584.

U.S. Congress. House. Committee on Government Operations. *Confirmation of the Director and Deputy Director of the Office of Management and Budget, Hearings, March 5, 9, 1972.* 93rd Cong., 1st sess., 1973.

U.S. Congress. House. Committee on Post Office and Civil Service. *Final Report on Violations and Abuses of Merit Principles in Federal Employment.* Committee Print 94-28. 94th Cong., 2nd sess., Dec. 30, 1976.

——. *Presidential Staffing — A Brief Overview.* 95th Cong., 2nd sess., July 25, 1978.

U.S. Congress. Senate. Committee on Foreign Relations. *The Senate Role in Foreign Affairs Appointments.* Committee Print. 92nd Cong., 1st sess., 1971.

U.S. Congress. Senate. Committee on Governmental Affairs. *Hearings on Nomination of Thomas B. Lance to be Director of the Office of Management and Budget.* 95th Cong., 1st sess., Jan. 18, 1977.

——. *Hearings on Matters Relating to T. Bertram Lance.* 95th Cong., 1st sess., September 1977.

——. *The Regulatory Appointments Process: A Study on Federal Regulation.* 95th Cong., 1st sess., January 1977.

U.S. Congress. Senate. Committee on Intelligence. *Hearings on the Nomination of Theodore C. Sorensen to be Director of Central Intelligence.* 95th Cong., 1st sess., Jan. 17, 1977.

U.S. Congress. Senate. Committee on the Judiciary. *Hearings on the Prospective Nomination of Griffin B. Bell, of Georgia, to be Attorney General.* 95th Cong., 1st sess., Jan. 11, 1977.

——. *Nomination of Clement F. Haynsworth Jr., of South Carolina, to be Associate Justice of the Supreme Court, Hearings, September 16-26, 1969.* 91st Cong., 1st sess., 1969.

———. *Nomination of George Harrold Carswell, of Florida, to be Associate Justice of the Supreme Court, Hearings, January 27-February 3, 1970.* 91st Cong., 2nd sess., 1970.

———. *Nomination of Harry A. Blackmun, of Minnesota, to be Associate Justice of the Supreme Court, Hearings, April 29, 1970.* 91st Cong., 2nd sess., 1970.

## Part VII Amending Power

**Books**

Boorstin, Daniel J. *An American Primer.* Chicago: University of Chicago Press, 1966.

Burns, James MacGregor, and Peltason, Jack Walter, with Cronin, Thomas E. *Government by the People.* 9th ed. Englewood Cliffs, N.J.: Prentice-Hall, 1975.

Crosskey, William W. *Politics and the Constitution in the History of the United States.* 2 vols. Chicago: University of Chicago Press, 1953.

Gillette, William. *Right to Vote: Politics and the Passage of the Fifteenth Amendment.* Baltimore: Johns Hopkins University Press, 1970.

Haynes, George H. *The Senate of the United States: Its History and Practice.* 2 vols. Boston: Houghton Mifflin Co., 1938.

Katz, William L. *Constitutional Amendments.* New York: Franklin Watts, 1974.

Kelly, Alfred H., and Harbison, Winfred A. *The American Constitution: Its Origins and Development.* 5th ed. New York: W.W. Norton & Co., 1976.

Lasson, Nelson B. *History and Development of the Fourth Amendment to the United States Constitution.* New York: Plenum, 1970.

Mathews, John M. *Legislative and Judicial History of the Fifteenth Amendment.* New York: Da Capo Press, 1971.

Mendelson, Wallace. *The Constitution and the Supreme Court.* New York: Dodd, Mead & Co., 1965.

Morgan, Donald G. *Congress and the Constitution: A Study of Responsibility.* Cambridge: Harvard University Press, 1966.

Munro, William B., ed. *Initiative, Referendum and Recall.* New York: D. Appleton, 1912.

Oberholtzer, Ellis P. *Referendum in America.* New York: Da Capo Press, 1971.

Ogg, Frederic A., and Ray, P. Orman. *Introduction to American Government.* New York: Appleton-Century-Crofts, 1951.

Orfield, Lester B. *Amending of the Federal Constitution.* New York: Da Capo Press, 1971.

Pritchett, C. Herman. *The American Constitution.* 3rd ed. New York: McGraw-Hill Book Co., 1977.

Vose, Clement E. *Constitutional Change: Amendment Politics and Supreme Court Litigation Since 1900.* Lexington, Mass.: Lexington Books, 1972.

Warren, Charles. *The Making of the Constitution.* Boston: Little, Brown & Co., 1928.

**Articles**

Feerick, John D. "Amending the Constitution Through a Convention." *American Bar Association Journal,* March 1974, pp. 258-288.

Lacy, Donald P., and Martin, Philip L. "Amending the Constitution: The Bottleneck in the Judiciary Committees." *Harvard Journal on Legislation,* May 1972, pp. 666-693.

Martin, Philip L. "The Application Clause of Article Five." *Political Science Quarterly,* December 1970, pp. 616-628.

Patch, Buel W. "Tax and Debt Limitation." *Editorial Research Reports,* Feb. 13, 1952, pp. 121-140.

"Proposed Legislation on the Convention Method of Amending the United States Constitution." *Harvard Law Review,* June 1972, pp. 1612-1648.

Putney, Bryant. "Revision of the Constitution." *Editorial Research Reports,* April 21, 1937, pp. 285-303.

**Government Publications**

U.S. Congress. House. *The Proposed Amendments to the Constitution of the United States During the First Century of Its History,* by Herman V. Ames. H. Doc. 353, pt. 2. 54th Cong., 2nd sess., 1896.

——. *The Proposed Amendments to the Constitution of the United States, 1889-1928,* by Michael A. Musmanno. H. Doc. 551. 70th Cong., 2nd sess., 1929.

U.S. Congress. Library of Congress. Congressional Research Service. *The Constitution of the United States: Analysis and Interpretation.* Washington, D.C.: U.S. Government Printing Office, 1973.

U.S. Congress. Senate Library. *Proposed Amendments to the Constitution of the United States of America, 1926-1963.* S. Doc. 163. 87th Cong., 2nd sess., 1963.

——. *Proposed Amendments to the Constitution of the United States of America, 1963-1969.* S. Doc. 91-38. 91st Cong., 1st sess., 1969.

## Part VIII Electing the President

**Books**

American Bar Association, *Electing the President: A Report of the Commission on Electoral Reform.* Chicago: 1967.

Association of the Bar of the City of New York. *Report of the Committee on Federal Legislation: Proposed Constitutional Amendment Abolishing the Electoral College and Making Other Changes in the Election of the President and Vice-President.* New York: 1969.

Barker, James David, ed. *Choosing the President.* Englewood Cliffs, N.J.: Prentice Hall, 1974.

Beman, L. T. *Abolishment of the Electoral College.* New York: H. W. Wilson, 1926.

Best, Judith. *The Case Against Direct Election of the President: A Defense of the Electoral College.* Ithaca, N.Y.: Cornell University Press, 1975.

Bickel, Alexander M. *The New Age of Political Reform: The Electoral College, the Convention and the Party System.* New York: Harper & Row, 1968.

——. *Reform and Continuity: The Electoral College, the Convention and the Party System.* New York: Harper & Row, 1971.

Burnham, Walter D. *Presidential Ballots, 1836-1893.* Baltimore: Johns Hopkins Press, 1955.

Congressional Quarterly. *Guide to U.S. Elections.* Washington, D.C.: Congressional Quarterly, 1975.

Daniels, Walter M., ed. *Presidential Election Reforms.* New York: H. W. Wilson, 1953.

David, Paul T., ed. *The Presidential Election and Transition, 1960-1961.* Washington, D.C.: The Brookings Institution, 1961.

Feerick, John D. *From Failing Hands: The Story of Presidential Succession.* Bronx, N.Y.: Fordham University Press, 1965.

——. *The Twenty-Fifth Amendment: Its Complete History and Earliest Applications.* Bronx, N.Y.: Fordham University Press, 1976.

Haworth, Paul L. *The Hayes-Tilden Disputed Presidential Election of 1876.* Cleveland: Burrows Bros., 1906.

Knoles, George H. *The Presidential Campaign and Election of 1892.* Stanford: Stanford University Press, 1942.

League of Women Voters. "Who Should Elect the President?" Washington, D.C.: 1969.

Longley, Lawrence D., and Braun, Alan G. *The Politics of Electoral College Reform.* New Haven: Yale University Press, 1972.

MacBride, Roger L. *The American Electoral College.* Caldwell, Idaho: Caxton Printers, 1953.

O'Neil, Charles A. *The American Electoral System.* New York: Putman, 1887.

Peirce, Neal. *The People's President: The Electoral College and the Emerging Consensus for a Direct Vote.* New York: Simon & Schuster, 1968.

Polsby, Nelson W., and Wildavsky, Aaron. *Presidential Elections: Strategies of American Electoral Politics.* 4th ed. New York: Charles Scribner's & Sons, 1975.

Roseboom, Eugene H. *A History of Presidential Elections.* New York: Macmillan, 1957.

Sayre, Wallace S., and Parris, Judith H.. *Voting for President: The Electoral College and the American Political System.* Washington, D.C.: The Brookings Institution, 1970.

Schlesinger, Arthur M., Jr., ed. *The Coming to Power: Critical Presidential Elections in American History.* New York: McGraw-Hill, 1972.

——. *History of American Presidential Elections.* 4 vols. New York: McGraw-Hill, 1971.

Sindler, Allan P. "Should Direct National Election Replace the Electoral College System?" In *American Politics and Public Policy: Seven Case Studies,* edited by Allan P. Sindler, pp. 3-41. Washington, D.C.: CQ Press, 1982.

Stanwood, Edward. *A History of the Presidency, 1788-1916.* 2 vols. Boston: Houghton Mifflin Co., 1889, 1916.

White, Theodore H. *The Making of the President, 1960.* New York: Atheneum Publishers, 1961.

——. *The Making of the President, 1968.* New York: Atheneum Publishers, 1969.

Wilmerding, Lucius, Jr. *The Electoral College.* New Brunswick, N.J.: Rutgers University Press, 1958.

Zeidenstein, Harvey. *Direct Election of the President.* Lexington, Mass.: D. C. Heath, 1973.

## Articles

Bayh, Birch. "Electing a President: The Case for Direct Popular Election." *Harvard Journal on Legislation,* January 1969, pp. 1-12.

Eshelman, Edwin D. "Congress and Electoral Reform: An Analysis of Proposals for Changing Our Method of Selecting a President." *Christian Century,* Feb. 5, 1969, pp. 178-181.

Feerick, John D. "The Electoral College: Why It Ought to Be Abolished." *Fordham Law Review,* October 1968, p. 43.

Freund, Paul A. "Direct Election of the President: Issues and Answers." *American Bar Association Journal,* August 1970, p. 733.

Gossett, William T. "Direct Popular Election of the President." *American Bar Association Journal,* March 1970, p. 230.

Huddle, F. P. "Electoral College: Historical Review and Proposals for Reforms." *Editorial Research Reports,* Aug. 18, 1944, pp. 99-114.

Lechner, Alfred J. "Direct Election of the President: The Final Step in the Constitutional Evolution of the Right to Vote." *Notre Dame Lawyer,* October 1971, pp. 122-152.

"Proposals to Change the Method of Electing the President: A Pro and Con Discussion on the Various Proposals for Change." *Congressional Digest,* November 1967, pp. 257-288.

Wildavsky, Aaron. "Choosing the Lesser Evils: The Policy-Maker and the Problems of Presidential Disability." *Parliamentary Affairs,* Winter 1959-1960, pp. 25-37.

# INDEX

## D

## E

## F



## G

## K



## L



## M

## N

## Q



## R



## S

## T

## U